Business Analytics

To Aadi and Ayan

Business Analytics

Solving Business Problems With R

Arul Mishra

Eccles School of Business, University of Utah

Himanshu Mishra

Eccles School of Business, University of Utah

Sage

Sage

FOR INFORMATION:

2455 Teller Road
Thousand Oaks, California 91320
Email: order@sagepub.com

1 Oliver's Yard
55 City Road
London, EC1Y 1SP
United Kingdom

Unit No 323-333, Third Floor, F-Block
International Trade Tower
Nehru Place, New Delhi – 110 019
India

18 Cross Street #10-10/11/12
China Square Central
Singapore 048423

Printed in the United Kingdom

Library of Congress Cataloging-in-Publication Data is available for this title.

ISBN: 978-1-0718-1523-6

This book is printed on acid-free paper.

Acquisitions Editor: Leah Fargotstein

Editorial Assistant: Izumi Sunada

Production Editor: Vijayakumar

Copy Editor: Melinda Masson

Typesetter: TNQ Tech Pvt. Ltd.

Indexer: TNQ Tech Pvt. Ltd.

Cover Designer: Candice Harman

Marketing Manager: Jennifer Haldeman

24 25 26 27 28 10 9 8 7 6 5 4 3 2 1

BRIEF CONTENTS

DETAILED CONTENTS

PREFACE

1. MISSION AND PURPOSE

In today's competitive business environment, many organizations are keen to implement artificial intelligence algorithms to enhance their decision-making processes. To accomplish this, they require individuals who not only understand the business landscape but also can apply analytical methods optimally. Business analytics has emerged as a field that equips people with a diverse set of skills in both business and analytics.

Our mission in writing this book is to offer students an accessible and hands-on introduction to analytical methods, such as machine learning, within a business framework. We believe there is a need for a book that not only discusses various business decisions a firm has to make but also recommends analytical methods that can support those decisions. Focusing solely on business theories or analytical methods without considering the synergistic link between them can lead to less beneficial outcomes.

In the real world, businesses typically first encounter problems and then seek out analytical methods to help in decision-making. It's uncommon for firms to have an analytical method in hand and then search for a business problem to which it can be applied. Therefore, our purpose is to discuss common decisions faced by businesses and suggest analytical methods that can best aid in decision-making.

To achieve our objective of bridging the gap between business decisions and analytical methods, each chapter explores diverse business decisions across finance, marketing, human resources, operations, and accounting. Using examples, we present a business scenario and outline decisions that the business might need to make. We then introduce and explain the suitable analytical method for addressing the given business problem. Engaging in a case-study-like discussion, we connect the business problem and analytical method to find a solution. We provide a dataset and details of the R software code used to demonstrate how valuable insights can be derived from applying the analytical method.

2. OUR AUDIENCE

This book has been thoughtfully designed to cater to a diverse audience—including students, professionals, instructors, and managers who aim to harness the power of machine learning in their respective fields. Business majors seeking a deeper understanding of analytical methods and their applications will find this book particularly valuable, as it thoroughly explains these methods and provides application cases with R code for easy execution.

Moreover, students with other majors who are considering pursuing careers in the business sector will appreciate the seamless connection between the business context and analytical methods presented in this book. This comprehensive approach makes it easier for readers to grasp the relevance and applicability of machine learning in various business scenarios.

For professionals and managers interested in self-learning, this book serves as a versatile resource. They can choose to focus on either the detailed explanation of the analytical method or the case study, depending on their needs. By doing so, they can gain a better understanding of how and which analytical methods can be employed to tackle specific business problems effectively.

3. FEATURES AND BENEFITS OF THE BOOK

3.1 A Focus on Business Problems

The idea for this book was born as we began teaching in the business analytics program and searched for suitable textbooks to use in our courses. We realized there was a gap in the available literature when we were unable to find a book that primarily focused on business problems and then leveraged analytical methods to address those problems. Students in any business analytics program must first grasp the business context before attempting to find a solution that leads to the most effective results.

With this goal in mind, we wrote this book to bridge that gap. Each chapter centers on a distinct business context, followed by an appropriate analytical method to help readers tackle the problem at hand. Consequently, every chapter starts with a business context, then delves into the analytical method. Both the context and method are seamlessly combined in the form of an example case, which is implemented using R software. Note that depending on the R version or package version, slightly different values can be obtained in the output. This approach provides readers with the opportunity to gain hands-on experience and develop practical skills throughout their learning journey.

3.2 A Diverse Look at Business Areas

In this book, we have carefully selected a variety of current business contexts that encompass various fields such as finance, marketing, human resources, and supply chain management. Our aim is to provide students with an understanding of the diverse business decisions that an organization may encounter and equip them with a repertoire of analytical solutions. This comprehensive approach can be observed in the different sections of the book, each consisting of three to four chapters.

Part 1: Business Environment Analytics. This section examines various external environments that influence business decisions, encompassing macroeconomic, competitive, and social factors. The analytical methods discussed include linear regression, principal components analysis, and text analysis.

Part 2: Marketing Analytics. Comprising four chapters, Part 2 delves into different aspects of marketing such as segmentation, pricing, advertising, and customer lifetime value. The analytical methods employed in these chapters include clustering, neural nets, and causal experiments.

Part 3: Financial and Accounting Analytics. With a focus on diverse financial and accounting decisions, Part 3 explores the financial health of an organization, loan approval, and forensic accounting using analytical methods such as logistic regression, penalized regression, and outlier detection.

Part 4: Operations and Supply Chain Analytics. This section presents a combination of operations and human resource management topics aimed at understanding a wide array of decisions, including decision-making under uncertainty, backordering, employee satisfaction, and new product testing. The analytical methods used range from random forests and gradient-boosted trees to A/B testing.

Part 5: Business Ethics and Analytics. In addition to assessing the accuracy of business decisions, it is crucial to ensure that they are equitable for everyone involved. Part 5 is dedicated to understanding the sources of bias and exploring ways to measure bias using fairness metrics.

3.3 Accuracy and Equity

In this book, we acknowledge the importance of not only evaluating the performance of analytical methods based on their accuracy but also considering the fairness and equity of the outcomes they produce. With the increasing application of these methods in critical aspects of daily life, such as loan approvals and product recommendations, it is important to ensure that the results are equitable for all groups involved.

To address this concern, we have dedicated an entire chapter to the exploration of fairness and equity in analytical methods. This chapter delves into whether these methods are equitable, the fairness metrics that can be employed for evaluation, the potential sources from which these methods might learn unfairness, and the techniques that can be used to mitigate biases and enhance equity in the results.

3.4 Case Implementation Using R Software

In every chapter that follows the introduction, we demonstrate the implementation of analytic methods using R software. R is a freely available open-source software that makes it easily accessible to everyone. It not only allows for data analysis but also aids in creating graphs and tables for better visualization of the results. Users can download R and follow the code provided in each chapter to perform their own analysis. For those who may not be familiar with R, we've included a dedicated section called "Implementation Using R" in each chapter. This section offers a detailed, step-by-step guide to help you understand and execute the code for each analytic method. The R code for each chapter's main example is also available on R studio cloud and can be accessed from this site: https://edge.sagepub.com/mishra.

4. PEDAGOGICAL AIDS AND HIGH-INTEREST FEATURES

- Case studies drawn from real-world business scenarios, highlighting the practical applications of machine learning across diverse decision-making settings
- Step-by-step tutorials that guide readers through the implementation of analytic methods using R software, helping to develop practical skills and enhance understanding of the techniques discussed

- End-of-chapter questions designed to reinforce learning, stimulate critical thinking, and provide opportunities for self-assessment
- Visual aids, including graphs, charts, and illustrations, that expedite comprehension of complex concepts and ideas
- A clear and concise writing style that facilitates an intuitive understanding of complex topics among readers with varying levels of familiarity with the business domain and/or the analytic methods available

In addition, the book's website, which can be found at sagepub.com or by contacting your sales representative at sagepub.com/findmyrep, offers a wealth of resources to enrich your learning experience, including a test bank, PowerPoint® slides, answers to end-of-chapter questions, datasets, and R code.

It is our hope that this book serves as an essential resource for both business students and professionals, empowering them to leverage analytic methods that result in informed, data-driven business decisions. By presenting a comprehensive and accessible guide, we aim to help shape the future generation of business leaders, equipping them with the essential knowledge and tools needed to excel in the ever-evolving realm of business analytics.

Arul Mishra
Eccles School of Business, University of Utah

Himanshu Mishra
Eccles School of Business, University of Utah

ACKNOWLEDGMENTS

We are deeply grateful to the many individuals who have contributed to the creation of this book. First, our sincere appreciation goes to our editor Leah Fargotstein, who consistently provided constructive insight on the structure and collected reviews to refine the book. We would also like to express our gratitude to Alex Chernev for offering valuable feedback on the book's format. Special thanks go to Joanne Freeman, our remarkable copy editor, and Robert Farrell, whose early-stage insights were crucial in shaping the book proposal. David DeFranza's input on the early drafts and Sanjeev Tiwari's feedback on the code significantly contributed to the book's improvement.

We would also like to thank the following reviewers for their feedback throughout the development of this book:

Moustafa Abuelfadl, University of New England
Jean Azevedo, Marquette University
Martin Bariff, IIT Stuart School of Business
Matthew Drake, Duquesne University
Gurram Gopal, Illinois Institute of Technology
Yue Han, Le Moyne College
Thomas A. Hanson, Butler University
Yavuz Keceli, Alfred University
Joel E. Kincaid, State University of New York at Geneseo
Ansah Kumi, University of Arkansas at Little Rock
Anita Lee-Post, University of Kentucky
Yi Liu, University of the Incarnate Word
Lin Lu, Fairfield University
Brad D. Messner, Seton Hill University
Ravi Narayanaswamy, University of South Carolina Aiken
Yon Shin Park, St. Edward's University
Jeffrey Pullen, Capitol Technology University
Iftikhar Sikder, Cleveland State University
John L. Sparco, Wilmington University
Kenneth L. Thompson, Millsaps College
Kevin S. Walker, Eastern Oregon University
Haibo Wang, Texas A&M International University
Chen Ye, Purdue University Northwest
Aeron Zentner, Coastline College

ABOUT THE AUTHORS

Arul Mishra is the Emma Eccles Jones Presidential Chair Professor of Marketing and Adjunct Professor, School of Computing at the University of Utah. Her research, on a broader level, uses machine learning methods to understand customer decisions and guide firm strategies. Specifically, she derives theoretical and practical insights from data using computational algorithms to understand customer engagement in digital markets, customer preference and choice, financial decisions, online advertising, and creativity. Currently her research involves leveraging language and generative models for business applications. She also examines the ethical consequences of using algorithms. Can algorithms exacerbate or reduce the impact of social biases and inequities? How can algorithms help firms make better decisions?

Methodologically, she uses Natural Language Processing, generative language models, image processing, and field studies to test social phenomena and theories. Arul's research has been published in the *Journal of Marketing Research, Journal of Consumer Research, Journal of Marketing, Marketing Science, Management Science, Journal of Personality and Social Psychology, Organizational Behavior and Human Decision Processes, Psychological Science,* and *American Psychologist*. Popular accounts of her work have appeared in *Scientific American, Los Angeles Times, The Wall Street Journal, Chicago Tribune, MSN Money, The Financial Express,* and *Shape*. Arul teaches or has taught several courses at the Eccles School of Business including Algorithms for Business Decisions for Master students, Consumer Analytics for undergraduate students, and doctoral courses on research theory and methods.

Himanshu Mishra serves as the David Eccles Professor at the Eccles School of Business and as an Adjunct Professor in the Kahlert School of Computing at the University of Utah. He earned his Ph.D. in marketing from the University of Iowa. Himanshu uses machine learning methods to analyze human decisions in social and marketplace settings. He often collaborates with firms to apply the insights he gathers from research. The findings of his research inform consumer decision-making, AI's role in fair decisions, risk assessment strategies, and overall human well-being.

With over 20 years in academia, Himanshu has taught across undergraduate, graduate, and Ph.D. levels. His recent courses involve using machine learning applications to improve business decisions and the importance of algorithmic fairness. His extensive research contributions can be found in top journals and conferences spanning marketing, business, computer science, and psychology—including the *Journal of Marketing Research, IEEE International Conference on Big Data, Psychological Science,* and others. Moreover, media outlets like MSNBC, *The Wall Street Journal,* National Public Radio, and *The New York Times* have featured his work.

GETTING STARTED WITH R AND RSTUDIO

Before you can run the R code provided in this book, you will need to install two key components: R itself and RStudio, a user-friendly interface for R. Both R and RStudio are free open-source software.

DOWNLOADING AND INSTALLING R

- **Step 1: Visit the CRAN Website**
  - To download R, you can go to the Comprehensive R Archive Network (CRAN) at https://cran.r-project.org. CRAN is considered the primary source for R software and documentation.
- **Step 2: Select Your Operating System**
  - CRAN provides R for Windows, macOS, and Linux. Remember to click the link corresponding to your operating system. For example, Windows users would select "Download R for Windows."
- **Step 3: Install R**
  - **For Windows Users:** You can then navigate to the "base" section after selecting the "Download R for Windows" link on the CRAN website.
  - **For macOS Users:** It is important to select the version that matches your Mac's chipset and operating system version.
  - **For Linux Users:** Linux users can find their specific R versions in the "Download R for Linux" section. Remember to select the R version that aligns with your particular Linux distribution.

DOWNLOADING AND INSTALLING RSTUDIO

- **Step 1: Visit the RStudio Website**
  - RStudio can be downloaded from the Posit website at www.posit.co.
- **Step 2: Choose the Right Version**
  - RStudio offers different versions, but for most users, the free, open-source version of RStudio Desktop should suffice. Select "Download RStudio Desktop."
- **Step 3: Install RStudio**
  - Download the installer and follow the prompts to install RStudio on your computer.

INSTALLING R PACKAGES

- **Using R or RStudio Console**
  - Packages in R can be installed using the **install.packages("packageName")** command, where "packageName" is the name of the package you want to install. This can be done in either R's console or RStudio's console. For example, To install the **dplyr** package, simply type **install.packages("dplyr")**
- **Using RStudio's Graphical Interface**
  - Packages can also be installed in RStudio using its graphical interface. Using the 'Packages' tab in RStudio, click 'Install', and enter the name of the package that you want installed.

PART

I

BUSINESS ENVIRONMENT ANALYTICS

1 THE EXTERNAL ENVIRONMENT OF A BUSINESS

CONTENTS

LEARNING OBJECTIVES

1. Understand the importance of internal and external business environments
2. Be aware of the external business environment
3. Learn the macroeconomic, competitive, political, technological, sociocultural business environment
4. Use algorithms to understand the influence of external environment on a business

1.1 WHAT IS A BUSINESS?

What is common to Walmart, Amazon, Godiva, FedEx, and Unilever? They all appear very different, but they are the same on one dimension: They are all businesses. However, if we ask what exactly is a business, what is its main aim, and what are its functions, we may hesitate because a business seems to mean many different things. Since this book is about how analytics affect and improve business decisions, it is important to first know what constitutes a business. Then we can learn the different business decisions and how we can improve them with statistical and machine learning methods. So let's begin by finding out what a business is: A business produces and sells products and services to customers. Products can be goods like toothpaste, chocolate, backpacks, or cars, while services are more intangible such as financial advice, airline transportation, and appliance repair.

The main aim of a business is to create value for its many stakeholders. Value can be thought of in terms of profits for shareholders if the business is a publicly traded company or profits for its owners if it is a simple mom-and-pop business such as a restaurant. Value for employees can take the form of good working conditions and fair remuneration. For consumers, value lies in the quality of products or services that a business offers. If consumers spend money to buy a product, they should be happy—the word commonly used in business is *satisfied*—with the product. We hear the term *value for money* in a business setting because it is used by firms to find out whether its consumers are satisfied with what they have received.

In order to provide value to their stakeholders, businesses separate their functions broadly into five divisions. Marketing handles developing products, setting the right price, finding the right location online or offline to offer the product, and finally persuading consumers to buy. The financial division deals with all financial decisions ranging from forecasting, to controlling, to evaluating the long-term performance of the business. Accounting is closely aligned with finance because it audits the financial decisions made by a business, including keeping track of the day-to-day flow of money, complying with tax laws, and creating periodic financial reports. Human resource management ranges from hiring, motivating, and firing decisions to determining the organizational structure of a business. The supply chain (or operations) is concerned with setting up and maintaining the optimal production and distribution system to get products from the business to consumers.

1.2 INTERNAL AND EXTERNAL ENVIRONMENT OF A BUSINESS

A business has multiple functions, and one can become very involved with factors that are internal to the business. It is easy to focus on designing a new product or introducing a product in a different country in order to create value. However, it is also important for a business to keep a close watch on factors that are external to it. Businesses do not exist in isolation; they are affected by several factors that are not in their control.

Walmart's experience in India highlights how changes in the global marketplace can affect decisions. Walmart enjoyed much success in the Indian market and had an optimistic forecast, given its joint venture with online retailer Flipkart and the growing number of consumers buying online. However, the Indian government imposed regulations that restricted brands from selling exclusively on any specific online site—for example, Flipkart. This created concerns for Walmart because it had in the past negotiated for such exclusive selling rights with certain brands. Hence, political and legal forces can impact the profit potential of a business that operates globally. What Walmart experienced in India is one among myriad factors that make up the external environment of a business firm. These include macroeconomic, competitive, political, technological, and sociocultural factors that can significantly influence business decisions. A firm needs to monitor the external environment to see how it can affect the firm's ability to create value for all its stakeholders. In this section, we will briefly go over some of the important factors that can alter the external environment of a business.

1.2.1 Macroeconomic Environment

Macroeconomic conditions such as levels of employment, minimum wages, interest rates, and inflation rates can all help or hurt the growth of a business. Economic boom times are characterized by increases in business activity, resulting in greater buying and selling, less competition among firms, and consumers with greater disposable income. The stock market does well during boom times, and people have more money to spend, which in turn helps the economy grow. More companies come into existence to cater to growing consumer demands, and an upturn in one business can even fuel upturns in other businesses. For instance, a boom in oil extraction in southeastern New Mexico led to positive effects on the railroad industry starting in 2017. Oil and potash needed to be delivered quickly to oil-extraction areas, and railway cars were the most efficient for this task, resulting in railroad activity nearly tripling in the area. The increased railroad activity in turn resulted in several miles of rails being replaced and maintained, which meant the creation of more jobs.

Conversely, recessions are caused by contracting business activities and greater competition among firms, resulting in businesses becoming less profitable. Recessions also cause shrinking job prospects for people, which translate into higher rates of unemployment. The lack of jobs results in a surplus of skilled employees, which in turn shrinks wages. Many of the macroeconomic factors tend to rely on each other. For instance, the stock market can rise when the monthly job market report indicates a low unemployment rate, showing that the economy is doing well and is able to employ people well.

1.2.2 Competitive Environment

Competition is part and parcel of any business endeavor. If there is enough demand for a product, very soon there will be many firms offering similar products. An important objective of a firm is to compare its performance with that of its competitors. A growth rate of 7% is phenomenal if competitors are on average growing only at 2% but is disappointing if competitors are growing at 15%.

Competitors help provide a firm benchmark on multiple dimensions. They help determine how to price the product—a product with a higher price should offer significant advantages over similar products in the marketplace; where to sell the product—a strong offline competitive presence can help a business establish itself online; and whom to target—recruiting customers who are not loyal will result in low retention.

Consider how the competitive environment is changing for the packaged food industry. We are seeing a current trend of increased sales of packaged foods online. Packaged, as opposed to fresh, food is less perishable and has a longer expiration date, which makes it an attractive buy online. In brick-and-mortar stores, brands from Mondelēz, McCormick, and Smucker's are considered to be leaders. When these brands compete online, their competitive landscape is different because of companies like Amazon. Not only does Amazon have a huge online presence, but it also has its own private-label brands. Of course, Mondelēz and Smucker's are competing offline with private labels such as Costco's Kirkland label and Walmart's Great Value label, but several factors are likely to be different online. Amazon doesn't share the same type of store brand image as Walmart, so the tactics that Mondelēz and Smucker's need to use online must be very different from those they use in Walmart stores; this includes how they target consumers, how they advertise their products, and how they determine what type of promotions to use.

1.2.3 Political Environment

The basic way the political landscape can affect a business is by whether or not there is political stability in a nation. Political instability results in major upheavals that disrupt business functions, consumer spending, taxes, and policies. For instance, a change in the political leadership can result in tax increases for certain industries but lower taxes for others. If we consider the example of governments trying to reduce the level of pollution, we see some nations giving major tax breaks for electric vehicles while other nations seem less motivated to do so. Google and other internet providers face financial, legal, and ethical issues when they operate in countries that may want to have more control over the flow of information among citizens. In such countries, internet providers need to navigate political entities, often in times of change, in order to function successfully without running into trouble.

1.2.4 Technological Environment

The technological environment can influence many business functions because of the introduction of new technology. Some changes in the technological environment can fundamentally alter a business. An interesting example is BlackBerry. It was the pioneer in the smartphone industry and in 2008 was soaring high, with a net worth of $75 billion. However, the iPhone, introduced in 2007 and criticized for not having many safety features, took over the market rapidly—so rapidly that by 2015 BlackBerry's valuation had fallen to less than $7 billion. The reason was that BlackBerry underestimated the user experience that the iPhone provided with its touchscreen, better browser, camera, apps via Apple iTunes, and virtual keyboard. Uber and Airbnb—which revolutionized the transportation and hotel industries, respectively—are classic examples of how new companies can affect markets. In 2010, Uber picked up its first passenger in San Francisco and successfully used smartphone technology to leverage its business. In 2019, it was uncommon not to find an Uber or Lyft (its competitor starting in 2012) app on people's smartphones.

In the automobile industry, we are witnessing a unique example of how technological change can alter an entire industry. While self-driving cars are still some time away from being widely available, there is a heated race going on among automobile companies. Many are acquiring smaller self-driving startups or opening their own research and development facilities in Silicon Valley. The goal is to ride the wave of technological change and not miss it.

1.2.5 Sociocultural Environment

Most of the time, a firm offers its products and services to people. Since people live in a society, their choices reflect the social norms and values that are prominent in their cultures. For instance, what factors should Starbucks consider when entering a tea-drinking market like China? Should McDonald's reconsider its menu options in India, where the majority of the population would never consider beef burgers?

In order to respect the cultural norms of the Indian market, McDonald's separated sections in its kitchen to prepare vegetarian versus meat-based meals. The company even has vegetarian-only restaurants near pilgrimage destinations to cater to people's needs. This is a big change from the way meals have been prepared in previous McDonald's outlets and shows the power of social forces in the marketplace.

Social factors like health consciousness have also changed many product-line decisions in the United States. Why did McDonald's introduce its line of healthy meals? People like fast food because it is tasty. But movies like *Super Size Me* have depicted the harmful effects of eating unhealthy foods, especially fast foods that may have a greater percentage of calories from fats and higher sodium content. The discussion of health effects—such as obesity-causing diabetes, heart problems, and even some forms of cancer—has made healthy eating both a medical issue and a social issue. Healthy eating started affecting people's lifestyles because people realized that the food they were eating and the outlets they were buying from could determine their well-being. McDonald's aims to make its Happy Meals no more than 600 calories, which makes them less calorie rich and more nutritious. The company is reducing the sugar in its chocolate milk and making bottled water, rather than only sodas, one of the featured beverages on its Happy Meal menu list. The introduction of healthy menu options by McDonald's and the popularity of Subway reflect a social factor that has wrought changes in business activity.

1.3 USING ANALYTICS TO UNDERSTAND THE BUSINESS ENVIRONMENT

Analytic methods can help a business better understand the influence of factors that are external to it. For instance, methods can forecast what businesses can do during recession and boom times by having an accurate idea of their cash flows, anticipating how much cash reserve they have and how much they will need, and which business activities they can grow and which they can trim down. For many businesses, taking a look at past data gives them accurate forecasts of what they need to do in the future. They can create what are commonly known as counterfactuals—that is, examining different scenarios by changing macroeconomic variables and looking at the outcomes.

Another area where we see greater use of analytics is on social media platforms such as Facebook, X (previously Twitter), and LinkedIn. These forums have revolutionized how people interact with businesses. Activities such as advertising and publicity that used to be more firm controlled have become more people controlled. Before the advent of the internet, it was said that happy customers tell only three others about their experience or recommend the product, but unhappy customers tell at least ten customers about their bad experience. In a socially connected world, one customer can influence the choices of hundreds of other customers. A *like* endorsement from a friend on Facebook can be a more powerful persuader than firm-sponsored advertisements or promotions. Businesses can leverage the millions of texts produced on social media sites to gather insights into what people are saying about their brand, product, or services and how customers perceive a brand vis-à-vis its competitors.

In the next three chapters, we will discuss how specific analytic methods can help businesses understand the impact of environmental factors that are not in their control.

2 MONITORING THE MACROECONOMIC ENVIRONMENT

CONTENTS

LEARNING OBJECTIVES

1. Understand the influence of the macroeconomic environment on business decisions
2. Define the inputs of a linear regression model
3. Interpret the output of a regression model
4. Predict the impact on business using linear regression

2.1 DEFINING THE MACROECONOMIC ENVIRONMENT

FedEx can make life easier by taking the stress out of getting your packages to remote locations "absolutely, positively on time." One might assume that all FedEx needs to do is to keep its planes and delivery systems well oiled. But there might be other factors, some surprisingly not in FedEx's control, that can affect its business functioning. One set of factors that can affect any business is categorized as economic factors, which can occur at the micro or macro level. Both micro- and macroeconomic factors tend to be outside the control of a particular business but nonetheless can significantly affect its revenue, sales, or demand for its products. Note that consumer demand (or just demand) is defined as the amount of goods that people are willing to buy at a given price.

Microeconomic factors are specific to a particular business and can include market size, distribution channel, suppliers, and competitors. *Macroeconomic factors*, on the other hand, tend to affect the entire economy. They can involve the current unemployment level, interest rates, taxes, gross domestic product (GDP), inflation, consumer confidence, and so on. Therefore, going back to our example of FedEx, it is important for FedEx to evaluate factors not only internal to it, such as price and profit, but also external economic factors such as the current employment rate. If more people are employed, they will have more money to spend on orders from online retailers; hence, FedEx will benefit. However, if unemployment increases, FedEx will need to include this change in its predictions.

2.1.1 Gross Domestic Product

Let's consider an important economic indicator of a country: its GDP. The GDP displays the financial health of a country because it includes the sum total of all goods and services produced in that country during a certain time period (e.g., a month or a quarter or a year). It can be calculated by summing up what everyone earned or what everyone spent. An increasing GDP indicates a growing economy that is likely to boost consumer spending, and businesses are likely to benefit.

2.1.2 Inflation

Similarly, *inflation* can affect many businesses. Inflation occurs in a country if money loses its value (i.e., the same amount of money is able to purchase fewer goods). It results in prices increasing and people being unable to purchase at the level at which they purchased previously. Inflation may be caused either because the supply of products is not able to keep up with the demand or because the cost of products has risen significantly. Inflation increases costs to the business in terms of higher prices for supplies, higher rent, and more being paid for utilities. An extreme case of hyperinflation was witnessed by Zimbabwe in 2008 when the government started transacting in foreign currencies rather than the Zimbabwean dollar, which had been devalued significantly. However, a little bit of inflation is good for the economy since deflation, the opposite of inflation, can be quite harmful too. Deflation occurs when prices start falling. Falling prices motivate people to hold on to their savings because they think that future prices will fall further so their money will get them more. This causes a cycle of people holding on to their money, with the result that the economy—which relies on consumer spending—is thwarted and slows down. A slowing economy can result in a recession or, worst case, a depression. Japan, one of the prominent world economies, entered a period of slowing growth followed by deflation in the early 1990s.

2.1.3 Interest Rate

Another important economic indicator is the *interest rate*; this is the rate the lender levies on the borrower. The federal interest rate influences several other interest rates, such as bank lending rates to individuals, businesses, or other financial institutions. When interest rates are high, consumer spending decreases because there is a greater incentive to save rather than spend. Moreover, people may be less likely to borrow money to buy cars or homes. For businesses, debts can become more expensive because if the businesses borrow from a bank, they have to pay a higher interest rate. This makes them more cautious in borrowing more to grow. However, if interest rates are lower, businesses are motivated to borrow and invest in growth. Therefore, it is common to see central banks like the Federal Reserve increasing the interest rate if the economy seems to be growing too fast, or reducing the interest rate in order to facilitate economic growth. When interest rates are high, luxury product manufacturers are more likely to be affected compared to producers of staple products because the former rely more on people having access to cheap debt. People consider buying luxury products (e.g., handbags, shoes, clothing) when they feel they have disposable income that they don't need to spend on staple products like groceries, rent, and transportation.

2.1.4 Relevant Macroeconomic Environment

Examples abound of industries and companies that failed to consider the larger economic environment and incurred huge losses. In the early '80s, the petroleum industry invested more than $500 billion because it forecast that worldwide demand for oil would increase from 52 to 60 million barrels per day. Prices were expected to rise by 50%, so the investment made sense. But these predictions were based on the rosy outlook of rapid growth in industrialized economies. Reality did not match the optimistic outlook; a slowdown in GDP ensued in the industrialized economies, oil demand fell to 46 million barrels, and the petroleum industry—including drilling, refining, and shipping—was badly hit.

Factors in the economic environment that can affect a business vary. For a farmer, market size, price of fertilizers, or taxes might be more important than consumer confidence. On the other hand, the unemployment rate or interest rate may be more important for financial institutions.

Hence, keeping a close eye on the economic factors that are relevant to one's business is important. To avoid unpleasant shocks or avoid losing out on opportunities, firms must strive to incorporate these macroeconomic factors in their predictions. And it has become easier to do this over the years with the wide availability of different forms of data on economic indicators.

Businesses typically monitor the economic indicators that in the past have had the most impact on demand for their products or services. For Delta Air Lines, oil prices and GDP are likely to inform them whether to expect increased or decreased demand. Hence, changes in the macroeconomic environment can help a business predict future demand.

2.2 IMPACT OF MACROECONOMIC FACTORS ON BUSINESS OUTCOMES

All businesses are interested in improving their performance; they would like to sell more, earn more, and grow more in the next time period compared to the current time period. A time period could be a week, month, quarter, or year. In order to improve, businesses need to know what factors can help them perform better. In other words, they need to get better at predicting. From small manufacturers to large global suppliers, all need to be accurate in terms of predicting, for example, how many units of machinery they will be selling to their buyers in the next time period. Businesses need to understand both (1) how macroeconomic factors influence their sales and (2) how to predict future demand. For instance, if we considered only macroeconomic factors, would we predict that the Federal Reserve's interest rate will impact units ordered? One possibility could be that as the interest rate increases, businesses will be less likely to take out a loan to invest in further production, which could result in no change in the units produced or ordered. A second possibility is that buyers will take a more conservative approach and not order new units. This could result in the orders actually decreasing. Therefore, there is a good possibility that as the interest rate increases, units ordered decrease. Similarly, let's consider what happens when the GDP changes. GDP increases signal that the economy is doing well and that businesses are more likely to invest in growth strategies. This can result in units ordered increasing. Conversely, when GDP decreases, the economy shrinks, and orders may decrease.

Let's consider the influence of one more external variable of inflation. One possibility is that when inflation is very low, near zero, there is not much economic growth. In such a case, units ordered might actually decrease. As inflation increases a bit, orders might increase but might again decrease when inflation increases to a very high value. However, all of these are guesses without much data to back them up. If we had data about units ordered in past time periods, we could see how macroeconomic variables have impacted the number of units ordered. These data could be used to develop a model, which could then be used to make predictions for future time periods.

2.3 REGRESSION FOR PREDICTION

Analytic methods such as regression have commonly been used for prediction. Regression is considered the go-to method in a multitude of data analysis situations. Its popularity lies in the fact that its results are easy to interpret. This means one can find out which input variable has the most, the least, or average influence on the output variable. The results also inform us whether the influence of a variable is positive or negative—for example, does an increasing unemployment rate increase or decrease demand for a product, and by how much? Regression allows decision-makers to clearly see the magnitude and direction of the impact of any input variable.

In the next section, we discuss linear regression as a way to predict the influence of macroeconomic factors on demand for products.

2.3.1 Linear Regression: Error-Based Learning

The simplest method of prediction is linear regression. It not only helps us develop a model that can explain the influence of macroeconomic variables on units ordered but also helps us make predictions about how many units are likely to be ordered in future time periods. We begin by understanding what is needed to run a linear regression.

2.3.2 The Inputs in a Linear Regression

In a regression, there are two types of variables: *predictors* and *outcomes*. Sometimes people refer to them as independent and dependent variables. The predictor (independent) variables are those that influence the outcome (dependent) variable. If a business wants to know the influence of interest rate on units ordered, then interest rate is the predictor variable, and units ordered is the outcome variable. This is because we are assuming that the units ordered depend on the interest rate and not the other way around.

If the values that an outcome variable can take range over a continuum—for example, from 0 to 200 or 1 to 7—then we use a linear regression. Sometimes the outcome variable is not on a continuum. Instead, it appears as a categorical value, such as in predicting whether or not someone will buy a product. In this example, there are only two outcomes possible: yes (will buy) or no (will not buy). We cannot say yes has a higher numerical value than no, or vice versa. Therefore, if the outcome variable takes categorical values such as yes/no, high/low, or red/blue, then we use a logistic regression.

If a linear regression is examining the influence of one predictor on an outcome, it is a *univariate regression*. In our example, a univariate regression would be appropriate if we wanted to know only the influence of interest rate on units ordered. But it is more common to study the influence of several predictors on an outcome. Such a regression is referred to as a *multiple regression*. If we studied the influence of GDP, interest rate, and inflation on units ordered, then we would need to run a multiple regression. We will next discuss how a linear regression works and then use it for prediction.

2.3.3 Visualizing the Data With a Scatterplot

The first step usually is to visualize the data. For a linear regression, we can use a scatterplot to see how the outcome changes for each unit change in the predictor. For instance, we can plot the influence of interest on units ordered. The data could possibly look like the scatterplot in Figure 2.1.

FIGURE 2.1 ■ Visualizing the Data With a Scatterplot

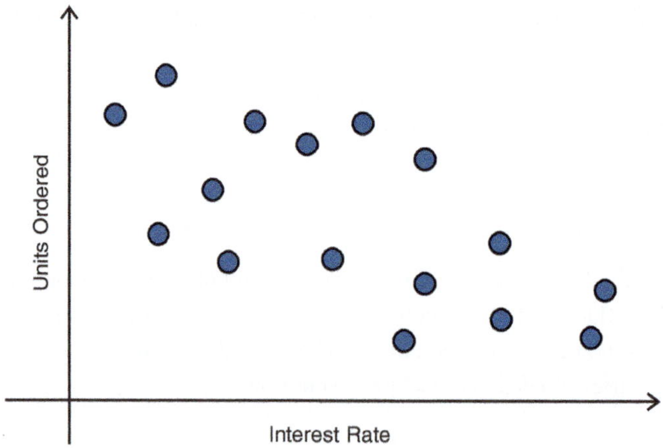

Looking at the scatterplot, what can one infer about the relationship between interest rate and units ordered? Is it positive or negative? Do units ordered increase with increases in the interest rate? From the scatterplot, we can guess that the relationship looks negative: Units ordered decrease as the interest rate increases. But it is still a guess, and we want to be sure. Let's draw a line through the scatterplot. It is easier to interpret the data if they can be represented as a line rather than as several points on the scatterplot. If we can represent the scatterplot in the form of a line, the equation of the line can serve as a model to help us understand the relationship between units ordered and interest rate. For instance, if the line slopes downward, we will infer that units ordered decrease when the interest rate increases, or vice versa. Even more important, we can use the regression model to make future predictions about units ordered based on changes in the interest rate. However, after we proceed to draw a line, we realize that it is possible to draw several lines through the scatterplot (see Figure 2.2).

FIGURE 2.2 ■ Multiple Regression Lines

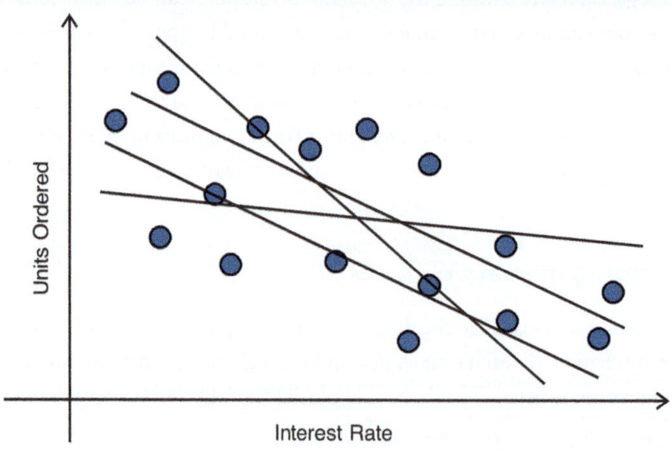

So, which of the many lines that can be drawn through the scatterplot is the one we want? We want the line that captures the predictive capabilities of the scatterplot as closely as possible (i.e., the line that best represents the relationship between the predictor and the outcome). We can use *ordinary least squares* (OLS) to find the line that best fits the data. Let's digress slightly to understand OLS.

2.3.4 Ordinary Least Squares

Regression is called error-based learning because it attempts to ensure that the difference (or error) between the values of the outcome variable predicted by the regression model (the regression line in this case) and the actual values is as low as possible. What do we mean by this? If you look at Figure 2.3, it shows the scatterplot with the best-fitting line. That line predicts how many units will be ordered for each value of interest rate. However, the line does not go through each of the data points and, hence, is not an exact prediction. For some data points the line represents an underestimation of the units ordered, while for other data points it represents an overestimation.

These under- and overestimations of the data points by the regression line are called residuals. If we just add up the residuals to find the total error, then some of the over- and underestimations will cancel each other out. Therefore, to get an accurate estimate, we square the residuals. From the many possible lines, OLS finds the line that has the minimum value of these squared residuals. Hence, OLS is also called least-squares regression.

FIGURE 2.3 ■ OLS Regression Graphical Depiction With Residuals

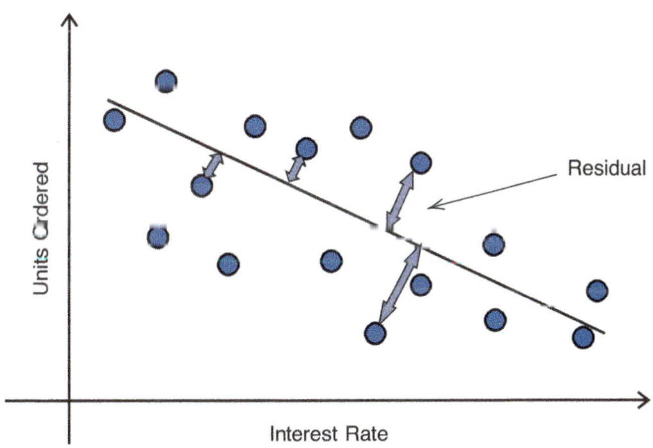

2.3.5 Regression Model

The goal of regression analysis is to find the line that best captures the relationship between the predictor and the outcome variables. When we have just one outcome and one predictor variable, the best-fitting line can be expressed as an equation just like any line. In its simplest form, the equation of a line is $y = mx + b$, where m represents the slope and b represents the intercept.

For a linear regression line, the equation is

$$\text{Outcome} = \hat{\beta}_0 + \hat{\beta}_1 * \text{Predictor}$$

If we are interested in understanding the relationship between changes in the interest rate on units ordered, then the equation of the best-fitting line will be

$$\text{Units Ordered} = \hat{\beta}_0 + \hat{\beta}_1 * \text{Interest Rate}$$

The $\hat{\beta}$s (referred to as beta hats) are called the **coefficient estimates** because the regression equation is estimating the relationship between the predictor and outcome from the sample. While the population is each and every point in the world of the predictor and the outcome, the sample is a subgroup of the population data points that is available to us for regression analysis.

Look at Figure 2.4. It graphically explains different parts of the regression model. The predictor is on the x-axis, and the outcome is on the y-axis; therefore, they are generally represented as *x* and *y* variables, respectively, in the regression model. $\hat{\beta}_0$ is called the intercept and shows what the number of units ordered would be when there is no influence of any predictor variable. $\hat{\beta}_1$ shows the magnitude and direction of the influence of interest rate on units ordered. Magnitude means the degree or scale of influence (i.e., how much of an influence the predictor has on the outcome). It can also be defined as the rate of change in *y* for a unit change in *x*, aptly captured as Δ_y/Δ_x, where Δ is called delta. The nature of influence shows whether the influence is positive (outcome value increases with an increase in predictor values) or negative (outcome value decreases with an increase in predictor values). In the graph, we can see that the nature of influence is negative because as the interest rate increases, the number of units ordered decreases.

FIGURE 2.4 ■ Coefficient of Determination Depiction

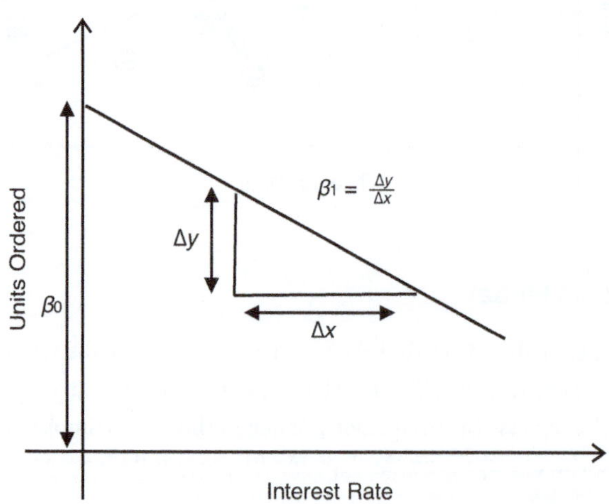

Let's assume we ran a univariate regression and found that, as predicted by our regression model, the estimate of $\hat{\beta}_0$ was 4, and that it was -3 for $\hat{\beta}_1$. The $\hat{\beta}_1$ coefficient informs us that the direction of influence is negative—that is, when the interest rate increases, the number of units ordered decreases. It also informs us about the magnitude of influence: When the interest rate falls by 1 unit, the number of units ordered increases by 3 units. On the other hand, if $\hat{\beta}_1$ had been 3, we would have inferred that the influence of the predictor on the outcome is positive (i.e., when the interest rate increases by 1 unit, the number of units ordered increases by 3 units). Therefore, the beta coefficient indicates the magnitude and direction of influence of the predictor on the outcome. It is important to note that once we have the regression model, we can use it to predict the outcome variable for different possible values of the predictor.

2.3.6 Multiple Regression

If we have several predictor variables that we think would influence the outcome variable, we run a multiple regression. An obvious question that comes to one's mind is why not run several univariate regressions and examine the influence of each predictor on the outcome variable. It is not a good idea to do so because then we are assuming that the predictors have an independent influence on the outcome. In reality many factors have a combined influence on the outcome variable. Therefore, when we have several predictor variables, we run a multiple regression.

For our example, we can run a multiple regression with the number of units ordered as the outcome variable and the interest rate, GDP, and inflation as the predictor variables. The multiple regression equation would be as follows:

$$\text{Units Ordered} = \beta_0 + \beta_1 * \text{Interest Rate} + \beta_2 * \text{GDP} + \beta_3 * \text{Inflation}$$

2.4 APPLICATION OF LINEAR REGRESSION FOR PREDICTION

Now that we understand how a regression works, we can apply it to a dataset and understand how macroeconomic factors can influence a business. Let's work with the example of medical equipment manufacturer MedDiagnostics, which manufactures and sells diagnostic imaging devices like X-ray systems and computed tomography (CT) scanners to hospitals and independent diagnostic centers across 40 different countries. (This example uses hypothetical data.) Therefore, it is in a business-to-business setting where it sells to other businesses rather than individuals. Beyond internal factors specific to the organization, macroeconomic factors can significantly affect units ordered. Therefore, MedDiagnostics wants to determine whether changes in macroeconomic factors such as GDP, interest rate, and inflation in a country will affect units ordered. MedDiagnostics has data from all 40 countries it serves from the last quarter (a three-month time period). The predictor variables are inflation, interest rate, and GDP for each country; the outcome variable is units ordered. Each of the variables is continuous (i.e., none of them is categorical in nature).

Since our aim is to predict the influence of macroeconomic variables on units ordered, we next partition the data into train and test sets.

2.4.1 Partitioning Data Into Train and Test Sets

The main aim of any predictive model is to be able to learn the relationship between the predictor variables and the outcome variable. The model is then used to predict values of the outcome variable for different values of the predictor variables that it has not seen previously, with as little error as possible. Therefore, the data sample from which the model learns the relationship is called the train dataset, and the data sample from which it predicts is called the test (or validation or hold-out) dataset. Such a procedure of testing on new datasets helps assess the predictive ability of the model. If we use all the data available to us to train the model to understand the relationship between the predictor and outcome, then we will not know how well the model will perform on a dataset it has not *seen* before. We might have *overfit* the model to the train set, and it may perform poorly on any new data sample. Such overfitting could occur because of certain characteristics specific to the train set that do not generalize to other sample datasets. Therefore, a common practice is to split the available data into two and use one part to train the model and the other part to test its predictive ability.

Following this procedure to test the model's predictive ability, we partition our data into train and test sets. Since we have the actual value of the outcome variable (i.e., the number of units ordered in a time period), we can easily compare them against the predicted values to understand how similar the linear regression model's predictions are to the observed/actual values. We specify that 70% of the data should be used as train data and 30% as test data; this spilt randomly picks up 70% of the data as train data.

Next, we run a linear multiple regression analysis on the train dataset.

```
## # A tibble: 4 × 5
##   term            estimate std.error statistic     p.value
##   <chr>              <dbl>     <dbl>     <dbl>       <dbl>
## 1 (Intercept)        5.13      0.834     6.15    0.00000235
## 2 inflation          0.102     0.375     0.272   0.788
## 3 interest_rate     -2.37      0.555    -4.27    0.000269
## 4 GDP_growth_rate    1.63      0.392     4.15    0.000358

## # A tibble: 1 × 2
##   r.squared  adj.r.squared
##   <dbl>              <dbl>
## 1 0.537              0.480
```

2.4.2 Interpreting the Regression Output

2.4.2.1 β Coefficient Estimates

When we look at the R output, it gives us information about the coefficient estimates of the intercept and the predictors of GDP, interest rate, and inflation. The first column labeled *term* lists the names of the predictor variables beginning with the intercept. The second column labeled *estimate* provides the coefficient estimate of the predictors. The coefficient estimate value for inflation is 0.1. This is the beta coefficient that informs us of the direction and magnitude of influence of inflation on units ordered. The sign of the coefficient informs us that the direction of influence is positive (i.e., when inflation increases, units ordered increase). It also tells us about the magnitude of influence: When inflation increases by 1 unit, units ordered increase by 0.1 unit. Similarly, we can infer that when the interest rate increases by 1 unit, the number of units ordered decrease by 2.37 units because the beta coefficient is -2.37. The GDP variable captures the rate of change in the GDP. Hence, when the GDP increases by 1 unit, units ordered decrease by 1.63 units because the beta coefficient is 1.63.

The third column provides the **standard error** of the beta coefficient estimates. Intuitively, the standard error captures how precise the estimate of the coefficient is. A smaller value of standard error shows a more precise estimate than a larger value.

2.4.2.2 Significance Testing

The fourth column called the *statistic* reports the t statistic, and the fifth column is the p value. The t statistic is estimated by dividing the coefficient by its standard error. Let's understand the t statistic and p value together because they are related. While the regression provides us with a beta coefficient associated with the predictor, how do we know whether this predictor truly has any effect on the number of units ordered? For this we use the t statistic and p value together to find out whether the predictor has a significant influence on the outcome (i.e., we perform *significance testing*). A p value of less than 0.05 suggests a significant influence, and informs us that the chances of finding the relationship between predictor and outcome in the data when there is no such true relationship in the population is only 5%. Keep in mind that $p < 0.05$ is an arbitrary threshold. One can set a more conservative threshold of 0.01. For the predictor of inflation, we find that the t statistic is 0.27 and the p value is 0.79. Therefore, if we had to interpret the result, we would say the following: Inflation does not have a significant influence on units ordered. However, the results indicate that both the interest rate and GDP have a significant influence on units ordered.

2.4.2.3 Coefficient of Determination

We can find the regression model that best fits the data, but how well it truly explains the relation between predictor and outcome variables is a different question. For this we evaluate the goodness of fit of the regression model using R^2, the *coefficient of determination*. R^2 informs us how much of the variation in the outcome variable can be explained by the predictor variables that we have used. R^2 can vary between 0 and 1. For example, if we get a value of 0.6403, it means that about 64% of the variation in the outcome variable can be explained by the predictors included in our regression model, while 36% is not explained.

Adding more predictor variables increases R^2 but makes the model less generalizable and leads to the problem of overfitting. When we add many predictors so that we can increase the predictive power of our regression model, we may get a model that perfectly fits a specific data sample but would do poorly with other data samples. An overfit model captures not only the relationship we are studying but all other quirks or noise of this specific dataset. Other datasets will have other types of noise, which this regression model will fare poorly in capturing. So a parsimonious model in which we have fewer predictors is better because it is more generalizable. Generalizability indicates how well the regression model will perform on other datasets that are studying the same relationship. In order to adjust for the number of predictors included in the regression model, we can look at adjusted R^2. In our case the following output shows that R^2 is 0.537 and adjusted R^2 is 0.48, which indicates some adjustment because of the three predictor variables that we have included.

```
## # A tibble: 1 × 2
##    r.squared  adj.r.squared
##        <dbl>          <dbl>
## 1      0.537          0.480
```

2.4.3 Performing Prediction With Linear Regression

Once we have interpreted the results of the train data, the next task is to assess how well our regression model predicts units ordered in the test data. This is an important step because in the absence of test data, we will have no way of finding out if we have overfit the model and how well our model will do with new data points.

```
## # A tibble: 1 × 3
##    .metric .estimator  .estimate
##    <chr>   <chr>           <dbl>
## 1  rmse    standard         1.13

## # A tibble: 1 × 3
##    .metric .estimator  .estimate
##    <chr>   <chr>           <dbl>
## 1  rsq     standard        0.773

## # A tibble: 1 × 3
##    .metric .estimator  .estimate
##    <chr>   <chr>           <dbl>
## 1  mae     standard        0.881
```

The output includes `rmse`, `rsq`, and `mae`. Let's understand what each one represents. `rmse` stands for root mean square error and helps capture how close the values estimated by the regression model are to the actual (i.e., observed) values of the outcome variable. Hence, `rmse` is calculated on the test dataset and not the train dataset because we are determining the predictive ability of our regression model. The difference between the actual and estimated values are called residuals. To prevent residual values from canceling each other out, the residuals are squared and added together to find out how close the regression model's estimates are to the actual outcome variable values. The squared residuals are divided by the sample size (i.e., the number of observations) of the test data to obtain the average value of the residuals. `rmse` measures how spread out these residuals are (i.e., `rmse` is the square root of the average value of the residuals). Lower values of `rmse` are considered better and indicate data points close to the regression line (in the univariate case). Higher `rmse` values indicate a poorly fitting regression line with points spread away from the line. A common question concerns what is a good `rmse` value. To determine this, remember that `rmse` values depend on the value of the outcome variable. If the outcome variable values range from 1 to 200, then a `rmse` value of 0.75 is pretty low; however, if the outcome value ranges from 0 to 1, then 0.75 is quite a high `rmse` value. In our case, since units ordered range from 2 to 12, a value of 1.13 is not bad.

`rsq` or *R*-squared is the correlation between actual (i.e., observed) values of orders and the values predicted by the regression model. The value is 0.773.

`mae` denotes mean absolute error and captures the same meaning as `rmse`. One concern with `rmse` is that when large residuals are squared, they can dominate its value (i.e., large residuals get weighed more in `rmse`). Hence, to address this concern, we can calculate the absolute value of the residuals, sum them, and then divide by the sample size to obtain `mae`. The `mae` in our test dataset is 0.881.

2.5 A FEW THINGS TO REMEMBER

Let's go over a few things we need to keep in mind while using linear regression.

- When there is more than one predictor variable, don't run many univariate regressions; always run a multiple regression.
- There is no harm in standardizing the data; it helps in comparing the interpretations across different predictor variables that may be using different scales or units.
- However, standardizing might make interpretations a bit difficult. Keep in mind the parsimony-versus-fit argument when adding or removing predictor variables: Adding predictors can improve R^2 but reduces the generalizability of the regression model.
- There are times when running a linear regression might give inaccurate results. One reason could be the choice of predictor variables that are highly correlated with each other. This results in a problem called multicollinearity. We discuss the use of penalized regression to address multicollinearity in Chapter 10. Similarly, data collected across time may suffer from an issue of dependence called autocorrelation.

Knowing which external variables can impact a business can help a firm formulate strategies and plan for the future. As we saw in our analysis of the impact of macroeconomic factors on units ordered, knowing the magnitude and nature of impact of certain variables allows us to focus on the ones that exert a significant influence and to pay less attention to those that may seem to be important but do not have a significant influence.

In sum, regression is a sound go-to method for conducting several types of analysis such as interpretation and prediction. The code to analyze the MedDiagnostics dataset is available in the next section in R.

2.6 IMPLEMENTATION USING R: PREDICTING UNITS ORDERED FOR MEDDIAGNOSTICS

MedDiagnostics has data from 40 different countries. The data are in a comma-separated values (.csv) file that has columns showing the predictor variables of inflation, interest rate, and GDP and the outcome variable of units ordered. Each of the rows captures a different country. Each of the variables is continuous (i.e., none of them is categorical in nature).

We will perform the linear regression analysis using R software.[1]

After loading the tidymodels package,[2] let's import the dataset.

```
library(tidymodels)
macro <- read.csv(url
("http://data.mishra.us/files/chapter_macroeconomic/macro_environ.csv"))
```

Next, we partition the data into train and test sets in order to avoid *overfitting*. Since we have the actual value of the outcome variables (i.e., the number of units ordered in a time period), we can easily compare them with the predicted values to understand how close our linear regression model's predictions are.

We use the `initial_split` function. This function randomly splits a dataset into train data and test data. However, it requires us to specify what percentage of the total data should be randomly assigned to the train set versus the test set. Using `prop = 0.7`, we specify that 70% of the data should be used as train data and 30% as test data. Since the `initial_split` function randomly splits data, we use R's `set.seed` function to create reproducible results. You may choose to set different `set.seed` values, but given the dataset size coefficient, estimates from your analysis will be slightly different.

```
set.seed(123)
datasplit <- initial_split(macro, prop =0.7,
                                       strata = orders)
trainData <- training(datasplit)
testData  <- testing(datasplit)
```

2.6.1 Multiple Regression on the Train Dataset

Next we run a linear multiple regression analysis on the train dataset. `linear_reg(engine = "lm")` defines an ordinary least-squares regression model. orders~ means variable order is the outcome variable, and `.` means that all variables other than order are predictor variables. It is equivalent to writing `order ~ inflation + interest_rate + GDP_growth_rate`. Using the `tidy()` function, we print the results of the linear regression analysis.

```
lin_model <- linear_reg(engine = "lm")

linear_fit <-
  lin_model %>%
  fit(orders ~ ., data = trainData)

tidy(linear_fit)

## # A tibble: 4 × 5
##   term            estimate  std.error  statistic  p.value
##   <chr>           <dbl>     <dbl>      <dbl>        <dbl>
## 1 (Intercept)      5.13     0.834       6.15      0.00000235
## 2 inflation        0.102    0.375       0.272     0.788
## 3 interest_rate   -2.37     0.555      -4.27      0.000269
## 4 GDP_growth_rate  1.63     0.392       4.15      0.000358
```

The R output gives us information about the coefficient estimates of the intercept and the predictors of GDP, interest rate, and inflation. The β coefficient estimate value for inflation is 0.1 (i.e., when inflation increases by 1 unit, units ordered increase by 0.1 units). Similarly, we can infer that when interest rate increases by 1 unit, units ordered decrease by -2.37 units because the β coefficient is -2.37. The GDP variable captures the rate of change in GDP. Hence, when GDP increases by 1 unit, units ordered decrease by 1.63 units because the beta coefficient is 1.63.

The third column provides the standard error of the beta coefficient estimates. The fourth column is called the *statistic*, and the fifth column is the p value. For the predictor of inflation, we find that the t statistic is 0.27 and the p is 0.79. Therefore, inflation does not have a statistically significant influence on units ordered. However, the results indicate that both interest rate and GDP have a significant influence on units ordered.

Using `glance()`, we can print R^2 and other measures of model performance. For instance, an F test of overall significance (defined with `statistic` and `p value`) shows whether our linear regression model with three predictor variables provides a better fit with the train data than an intercept-only model with no predictor variables.

```
glance(linear_fit)
## # A tibble: 1 × 12
##       r.squared adj.r.squared sigma statistic p.value df    logLik AIC   BIC
##         <dbl>       <dbl>     <dbl> <dbl>     <dbl>    <dbl> <dbl>  <dbl> <dbl>
## 1       0.537       0.480     1.97  9.30      0.000292 3     -56.6  123.  130.
## #...  3 more variables: deviance <dbl>, df.residual <int>, nobs <int>
```

If you want to print traditional linear regression summary tables, you can use the following code. The output of this code is essentially a combined version of what `tidy(linear_fit)` and `glance(linear_fit)` have created.

```
linear_fit %>%
 pluck("fit") %>%
 summary()

##
## Call:
## stats::lm(formula = orders ~ ., data = data)
##
## Residuals:
## Min                          1Q     Median       3Q       Max
## -3.14574               -1.09321  -0.08497  1.11301   3.04204
##
## Coefficients:
##                 Estimate Std. Error t value Pr(>|t|)
## (Intercept)      5.1301     0.8339      6.152     2.35e-06  ***
## inflation        0.1019     0.3745      0.272     0.787806
## interest_rate  -2.3670     0.5549     -4.265     0.000269  ***
## GDP_growth_      1.6283     0.3921      4.153     0.000358  ***
   rate
## ---
## Signif. codes: 0 '***' 0.001 '**' 0.01 '*' 0.05 '.' 0.1 ' ' 1
##
## Residual standard error: 1.972 on 24 degrees of freedom
## Multiple R-squared: 0.5375, Adjusted R-squared: 0.4796
## F-statistic: 9.296 on 3 and 24 DF, p-value: 0.0002924
```

2.6.2 Performing Prediction With Linear Regression

We can assess how well our regression model predicts units ordered in the test data. The `predict()` function helps us predict values of orders based on the variables of `inflation`, `interest_rate`, and `GDP_growth_rate` in the test data. We then combine the prediction made by the regression model (.pred) and the true values of the variable orders. This helps us to estimate key metrics such as `rmse`, `rsq`, and `mae` that inform us about the performance of our model on test data.

```
order_pred <- predict(linear_fit, new_data = testData)

prediction_comparison <- testData %>%
    bind_cols(order_pred)

prediction_comparison %>%
   rmse(truth = orders, estimate = .pred)

## # A tibble: 1 × 3
##   .metric .estimator .estimate
##   <chr>   <chr>          <dbl>
## 1 rmse    standard        1.13

prediction_comparison %>%
    rsq(truth = orders, estimate = .pred)

## # A tibble: 1 × 3
##   .metric .estimator .estimate
##   <chr>   <chr>          <dbl>
## 1 rsq     standard       0.773

prediction_comparison %>%
    mae(truth = orders, estimate = .pred)

## # A tibble: 1 × 3
##   .metric .estimator .estimate
##   <chr>   <chr>          <dbl>
## 1 mae     standard       0.881
```

2.7 UNDERSTANDING THE CHAPTER

Students are encouraged to answer the following questions. They can then review the chapter to check their answers.

1. If a scatterplot is a good visualization tool, why is it difficult to use the scatterplot to infer the relationship between the predictor and outcome variables?

2. The CEO of a company would like to know which factors influence sales. They found that the following multiple regression had the best fit. The model is as follows:

$$Sales = \hat{\beta}_0 + \hat{\beta}_1 Price + \hat{\beta}_2 Spokesperson + \hat{\beta}_3 Advertisement$$

Sales refers to the sales amount, *price* is the price of the product, *spokesperson* refers to whether the products were purchased before or after the current spokesperson was employed, and *advertisement* is the amount spent on the advertisement. The following table summarizes the multiple linear regression model output.

Variable	Estimate	*p* value
Intercept	3.583	0.718
Price	-1.367	0.037
Spokesperson	0.782	0.812
Advertisement	1.306	0.047

a. Using the provided information, would you interpret that price had a significant influence on sales? Was the influence of price on sales direct or inverse?
b. Among all the predictor variables, which variable had the biggest influence on sales? What value from the preceding table would your answer be based on?
c. If the coefficient of determination R^2 was 76.72 when these three predictor variables were used, what would it indicate?
d. Using the model output, can we write the regression equation? If yes, what will it look like?

3. When predictor variables in a multiple linear regression are highly correlated, does it cause autocorrelation or multicollinearity? Why?

ENDNOTES

1. R Core Team. (2021). *R: A language and environment for statistical computing.* R Foundation for Statistical Computing, Vienna, Austria. https://www.R-project.org/.

2. Kuhn, Max, et al., "Tidymodels: A Collection of Packages for Modeling and Machine Learning Using tidyverse Principles" (2020), https://www.tidymodels.org.

3 MONITORING THE COMPETITIVE ENVIRONMENT USING PRINCIPAL COMPONENT ANALYSIS

CONTENTS

LEARNING OBJECTIVES

1. Understand how the competitive environment can influence a business
2. Use data to assess the competitive environment
3. Learn the basics of principal component analysis
4. Visualize and interpret the competitive environment

3.1 THE COMPETITIVE ENVIRONMENT OF A BUSINESS

The goal of any business is to generate revenues by addressing the needs of its customers. The process of serving customer needs would be easy if the business operated alone in the market. However, businesses do not operate in such monopolistic environments. It is common to see many competitors vying for customer attention. Because all competitors share the same set of customers, the success and failure of a business is determined by how well it is able to address the needs of the customers. If competitors are more successful in addressing those needs, then a business has less chance of survival. The noteworthy aspect is that the needs of customers and the capabilities of competitors are not static. Instead, customers' needs keep evolving, and competitors keep coming up with ways to address these needs by acquiring new capabilities.

3.1.1 Examples of How Changes in the Competitive Environment Affect Business

If we consider the example of Blockbuster, we can see very clearly how competition can affect a business. At the turn of the 20th century, Blockbuster was the largest U.S. movie rental company; it operated 10,000 stores and had a market valuation of $5 billion. Blockbuster's customers browsed and rented movies at its retail stores. In 1997, a new competitor called Netflix entered the market. It had no retail locations; rather, it allowed customers to list their preferred movies online, then sent those movies to customers by mail. Netflix was cheaper than Blockbuster but also much slower. A customer who decided to watch a movie that night could go over to a local Blockbuster outlet and pick up the movie but would find Netflix less useful. However, Netflix addressed one weakness of Blockbuster: It had no late fees, an issue that had bothered Blockbuster's customers for some time. In fact, late fees were central to Blockbuster's revenue stream. Netflix kept growing by exploiting this weakness and in 2007 saw an opportunity that Blockbuster completely overlooked. It realized that a growing number of households had a broadband connection, so it started its streaming business. Blockbuster began noticing these changes. It eventually got rid of late fees and started its own streaming service. But it was too late. In 2010, Blockbuster filed for bankruptcy protection, and by 2014 all its retail locations had ceased to exist.[1]

3.1.2 Dynamic Nature of the Competitive Environment

Blockbuster's example highlights the importance of recognizing the dynamic nature of the competitive landscape. Staying abreast of ongoing developments in the market not only helps firms ward off new competitors but also provides an impetus to innovation. Businesses that operate in an intensely competitive environment frequently introduce new products and increase research and development (R&D) spending. Take the example of Amazon. It is currently the market leader in online retail, which is an intensely competitive environment. In 2022 alone, Amazon spent $73 billion on R&D (30% more than what it spent a year earlier) to stay ahead of its competition and prevent new competitors from threatening its future profitability.[2]

It is also important to recognize that firms don't compete with one another on only one dimension—for example, price. They compete on many dimensions. Take the example of a firm that sells commercial heating, ventilation, and air conditioning (HVAC) equipment. It competes on dimensions such as quality, delivery time, price, after-sales technical support, and breadth of selection of its product line. It is imperative for the firm to understand what unique advantages it has over its competitors and in what areas competitors are performing better. This understanding helps in defending and ideally expanding its market share.

Figure 3.1 depicts the dynamic nature of the competitive environment.

FIGURE 3.1 ■ Dynamic Nature of the Competitive Environment

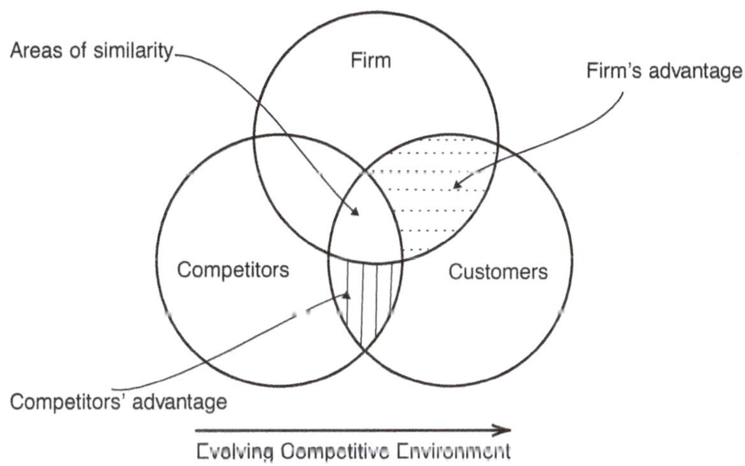

When we look at the intersecting circles, we see that the overlapping areas depict how well the needs of the customers are fulfilled by one firm compared to its competitors. The area labeled *Firm's advantage* shows that it is able to uniquely fulfill the needs of the customers, which its competitors are unable to do. However, the area labeled *Competitors' advantage* indicates the customer needs that its competitors are able to fulfill that this firm cannot. Finally, the area labeled *Areas of similarity* are those needs that are fulfilled both by this firm and by competitors. Therefore, an important decision for a firm is to determine which area it needs to focus on. Should it focus only on the customer needs that it can uniquely fulfill? This could help in the short term, but can it sustain this advantage in the long term if competitors also start fulfilling these needs? Or should the firm improve its offering so that it can fulfill those customer needs that it is currently not catering to? Would it be profitable to do so given the cost of improving its offerings? The arrow shows that the competitive environment is not static; customer needs and competitor capabilities keep evolving (as we saw from the Blockbuster example).

3.1.3 Competitor Analysis

One way for a business to map its advantages and weaknesses vis-à-vis the competition is through competitor analysis. Data that can help in such an analysis come in various forms. For a retailer, the data could be information about its competitors' market share, advertising expenditure, price charged for products, number of new products introduced, and so on. In an online setting, data that can help assess the competitive environment could be competitors' search ranking, social media shares, number of people visiting competitors' sites, number of sites that are linked to or endorse competitors' sites but not the firm's, and so on.

If we visualize the data in the form of rows and columns on an Excel sheet, it is likely to have rows representing each competitor and columns representing their performance on different dimensions as indicated by their buyers. Therefore, this is multidimensional data since it considers the performance of a firm across various dimensions of price, quality, lead time, installation, training, and so on. We can easily compare the performance of each of the firms on one dimension. For instance, by looking at the dataset we can infer which firm offers the best price or is rated the highest on lead time. The problem occurs when the dimensions of comparison start increasing. It becomes challenging to figure out which firms are better or worse *overall* when considering all dimensions. A popular method for handling such multidimensional data is to create a competitive map using **principal component analysis (PCA)**.

3.2 VISUALIZATION USING PRINCIPAL COMPONENT ANALYSIS

PCA is commonly considered a dimensionality reduction algorithm. It transforms data into fewer dimensions, called principal components, while retaining most of its important information.

3.2.1 The Dimensions in a PCA

Let's consider a simple example to understand how PCA works. Imagine we have a dataset with two variables: undergraduate grade point average (GPA) and salary at the first job. It is easy to see that there is some relationship between academic performance and salary. As GPA increases, salary also increases.

The scatterplot in Figure 3.2(a) captures this relationship.

FIGURE 3.2 ■ Two-Dimensional Scatterplot

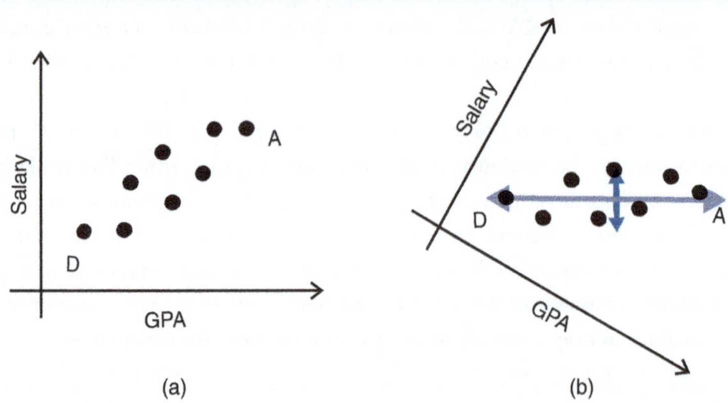

Do you see something very interesting in this scatterplot? If we rotate this plot in a clockwise direction as shown in Figure 3.2(b), we see two dimensions, one of which is bigger (the dotted line dimension) and has more spread-out data points than the other (the solid line dimension). Now, if we project each point to the dotted line as in Figure 3.3(a), we will obtain something like Figure 3.3(b), where each data point can be represented on just one dimension—the dotted line dimension. Intuitively, this is how PCA works. Given any data, PCA creates new dimensions and allows a user to discard dimensions that are small (i.e., have less spread), just as we discarded the solid line dimension. By presenting the data in the form of a few dominant dimensions, PCA helps in visualizing the relative position of data points.

FIGURE 3.3 ■ Projections

3.2.2 Dimensionality Reduction Using PCA

What is the rationale behind discarding dimensions that are less spread out? Let's take an example of individuals with different weights but largely similar heights. If we want to distinguish one individual from the other, the height dimension will not help us. But the weight dimension can help. So we can discard height and keep only weight to distinguish one individual from the other. That's why in data analysis the variables that are more spread out are preferred because they provide more information than variables with little to no spread.

PCA reduces data dimensions by recognizing and using the unique geometric shapes formed by correlated variables in the data. These distinct shapes allow PCA to create new, fewer dimensions that still hold most of the important information from the original data. Let's consider the following figures.

FIGURE 3.4 ■ Relation Between Height and GPA

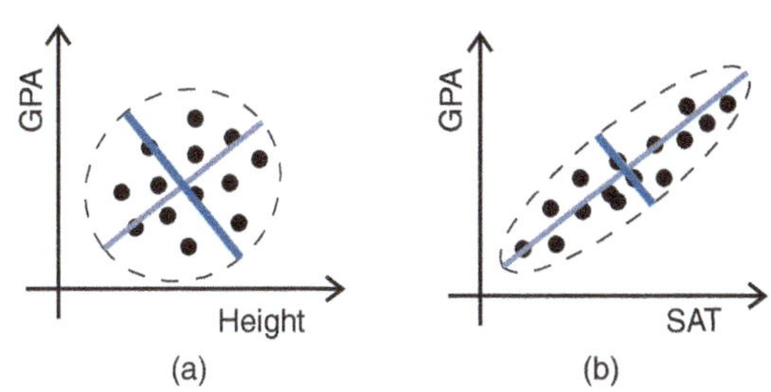

First, let's look at Figure 3.4(a). Since people of all heights are equally likely to perform poorly or well in their studies, there is no association or correlation between height and GPA. Such data look like a circle (e.g., a two-dimensional soccer ball). In this example, both dimensions are equal in size, so they will appear equally important to PCA, and it will not be able to reduce the dimensions of the data.

However, if there is a strong relationship between the two variables, such as in the example between SAT score and undergraduate GPA, the shape of the data looks like a two-dimensional horizontal Frisbee as in Figure 3.4(b). In this case, PCA will choose the more spread-out, larger dimension and will help in reducing the two variables, SAT and GPA, into one dimension.

It is certainly easy to visualize the shape of data and identify larger or smaller principal components when we have two or three variables because we can plot them. But it is challenging to do so if the data have more than three variables, and datasets that have more than three variables are quite common. Therefore, a variance–covariance matrix is used as an input in PCA analysis. The variance–covariance matrix captures essential information about the shape of data summarizing how each variable in the dataset relates to every other variable. Essentially, it provides a high-level view of the data landscape, highlighting the main patterns and relationships without delving into individual data points. By analyzing the variance (how much each variable differs from its mean) and covariance (how two variables change together), PCA can then identify and prioritize the directions (principal components) where the data vary the most. This process efficiently distills the most informative features of the data, allowing for simpler and more insightful analysis of complex, high-dimensional datasets. (The technical details of the PCA are provided in an appendix at the end of this chapter; in that section we discuss the basics of *matrix multiplication, linear transformation, variance and covariance, eigenvalues*, and *eigenvectors*, as well as the *variance–covariance matrix*, which is the input for the PCA.)

It is worth keeping in mind that PCA is an *unsupervised method.* A *supervised method* can analyze data that have a label for the outcome variable. The label can be yes/no as in logistic regression or some numerical value provided as the outcome for each data point as in linear regression. However, when the data do not have a label for the outcome variable, then we use *unsupervised methods.* Such methods cannot be used for prediction, but we can use them to learn important patterns in the data. In essence, PCA does not learn labels like regression, which is a supervised method; however, PCA helps in producing a visual representation of the data.

3.3 APPLICATION OF PCA FOR COMPETITOR ANALYSIS

We will use PCA to examine the competitive environment of Thermaly, a firm that sells commercial HVAC equipment. It competes on dimensions such as quality, delivery time, price, after-sales technical support, breadth of selection of its product line, and so on. It is important for Thermaly to understand what unique advantages it has over its competitors and in what areas competitors are performing better. For Thermaly, the raw data would be its performance relative to its competitors on dimensions such as quality, lead time (i.e., the time interval between placing the order and completion of the production process), delivery time (i.e., time spent in shipping), price, installation and training, after-sales technical support, shipping cost, billing and invoicing, sales staff (i.e., their knowledge, reliability, and friendliness), and breadth of selection in its product line. One source of such raw data could be a survey of HVAC buyers conducted by Thermaly or an independent agent.

We will use PCA to find out which are the closest competitors to Thermaly.

3.3.1 Using Firm Ratings for PCA

Let's assume that the data are obtained from a survey in which buyers rated HVAC manufacturers on various dimensions. (Data for this example are hypothetical.) The dataset has eight HVAC manufacturers: Calvac, Watco, Thermaly, Beamheat, eHeat, Thermexo, ThermaFit, and Nextra. Survey questions asked buyers to rate each manufacturer's performance on scales ranging from 0 (*not satisfactory*) to 100 (*satisfactory*). As an example, a buyer who purchased an HVAC system from eHeat was asked to rate eHeat's performance on installation and training provided on a 0 to 100 scale. A rating of 20 would indicate a very low level of satisfaction while a rating of 86 would indicate a high level of satisfaction. The different dimensions of performance on which the buyers rated the HVAC manufacturers were the following: delivery time, lead time, quality, price, technical support, shipping cost, billing and invoicing, sales staff, and breadth of product selection.

In such multidimensional datasets, the challenge is how to compare one manufacturer with another. Should we choose two or three performance dimensions and create two- or three-dimensional plots for various manufacturers? Which dimensions should we choose, and which dimensions should we discard? All these challenges can be handled by PCA.

We first import the dataset and scale the variables to ensure unit variance before performing the PCA. In this dataset, all the performance measures are in the same units, so one can choose not to scale the data. But if the data are not already scaled, it is advisable to scale the data before performing PCA. What will happen if we don't scale the data? If variables are measured in different units (like age in years and height in inches), variables with larger unit values (200 cm over 2 pounds) will end up exerting more influence in our analysis.

Once we run the PCA, we can use the PCA output and plot the relative position of different manufacturers on two dominant principal components as can be seen in Figure 3.5.

FIGURE 3.5 ■ Principal Component Plot

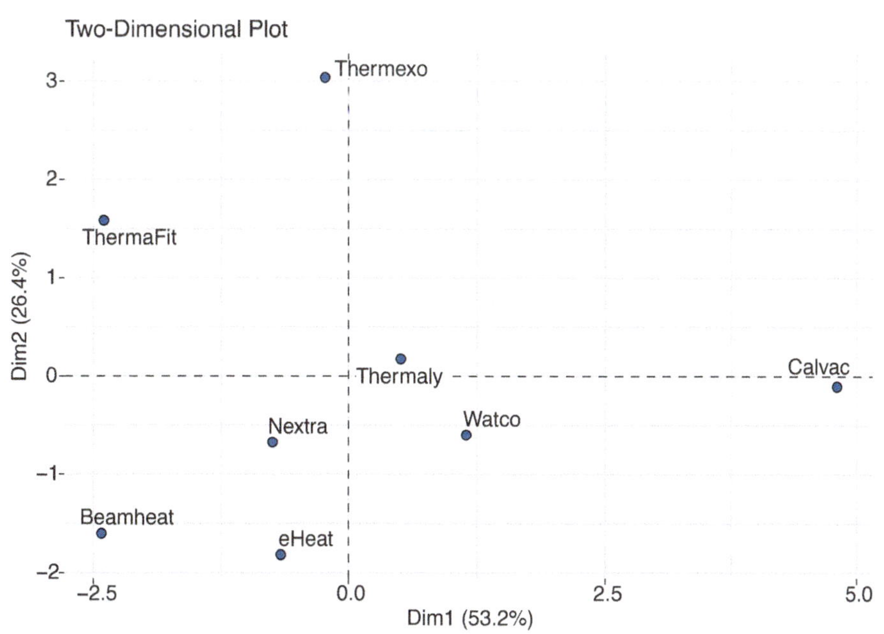

3.3.2 Dimensionality Reduction With PCA

The dimensionality-reduction aspect of PCA can be understood using the plot. Dim1 (53.2%) at the bottom and Dim2 (26.4%) on the left show the amount of spread (variance) or information in these data, explained by the first two principal components, respectively. By adding both of these numbers, we can see that the first two principal components explain more than 79% of the spread in the dataset. This output also helps us visually examine the data and draw some interesting insights. For instance, Thermaly is perceived by users of HVAC as more similar to Nextra and Watco than Calvac.

3.3.3 A Deeper Look With a Biplot

If we want a more granular understanding of how each HVAC manufacturer is rated on various dimensions, we can create a *biplot* that helps us further interpret the PCA output. The biplot (as seen in Figure 3.6) helps us interpret (1) if some dimensions are correlated and, most important, (2) how each manufacturer performs on each of the dimensions.

FIGURE 3.6 ■ PCA Biplot

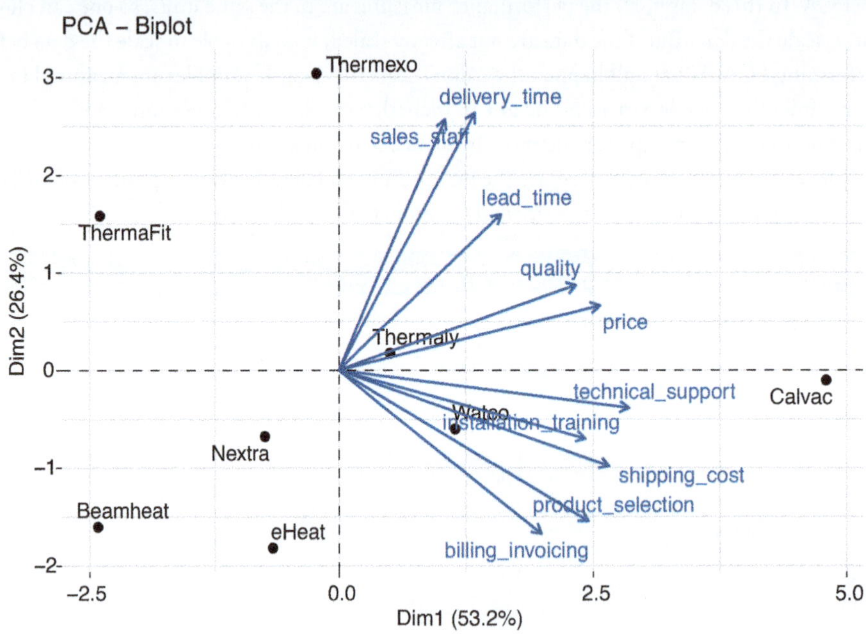

Let's go over the things we need to keep in mind when we look at the biplot. In a biplot, each arrow represents a dimension, and the angle between any two arrows indicates the level of correlation between them. If any two dimensions have a small angle between them, then it shows they are more strongly correlated compared to two dimensions that have a larger angle between them. In our case, we can see that quality and price are more strongly correlated because they have a small angle between them compared to quality and billing_invoicing, which have a larger angle between them. It is also worth keeping in mind that the origin represents the average value for each dimension. Therefore, the manufacturer closer to the origin (Thermaly) has an average value on almost all dimensions.

There is another informative way of looking at the biplot. Notice that each arrow seems to be starting from the origin. Since the origin represents the average value for all the dimensions, the direction of any arrow shows higher values on that dimension. If we extend the arrow opposite to the direction shown on the biplot, it points toward lower values. To illustrate, we extend the "delivery-time" arrow backward into the bottom-left quadrant (see Figure 3.7, which shows the performance of three manufacturers: Thermaly, ThermaFit, and Thermexo). The solid line represents the original direction of the arrow and thus higher-than-average values. The dotted portion is the extension and indicates lower-than-average values.

FIGURE 3.7 ■ Manufacturer Performance

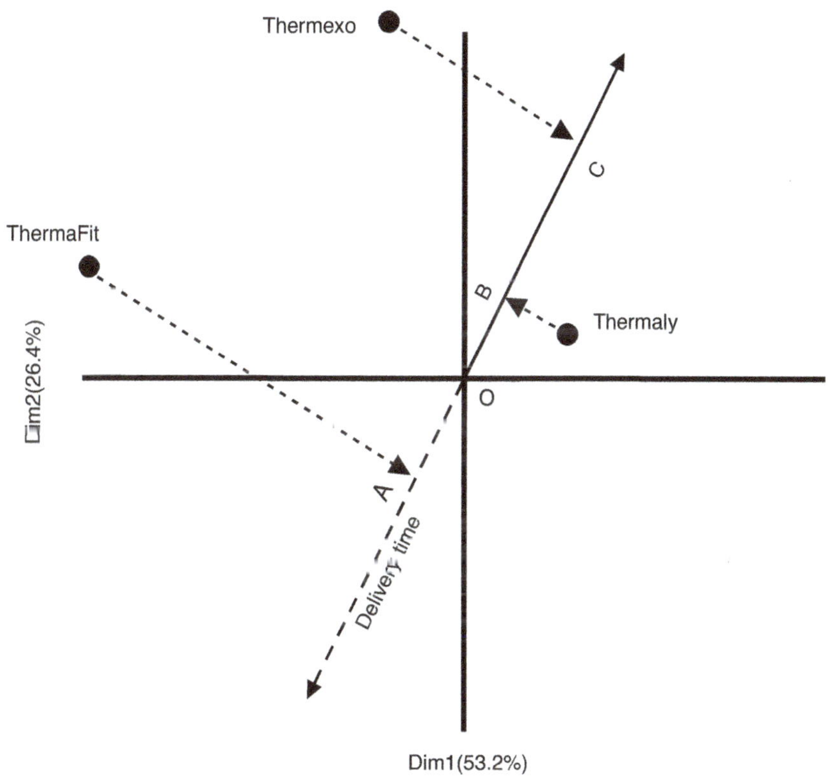

How do each of the three manufacturers perform on the delivery-time dimension? We can determine this by dropping perpendiculars from each of the manufacturers onto the delivery-time arrow. Then we measure the distance from the point of intersection (between the perpendicular from each manufacturer to the delivery-time arrow) and the origin O. The greater the distance on the solid line, the better that manufacturer performs on the delivery-time dimension. For instance, we can see that Thermexo performs better than Thermaly (OC is greater than OB). ThermaFit, on the other hand, performs worse than Thermaly and Thermexo because its perpendicular lands on the lower-than-average side of the arrow (dotted portion).

Following this approach, we can conclude that Calvac performs better than others on each dimension. Thermaly's closest competitors are Watco and Nextra.

3.4 OTHER USES OF PCA

Given its versatility, PCA is used in several applications. PCA is used in image recognition because it helps decompose thousands of pixels into a few important dimensions. PCA has also been used to find the most important financial indicators that should be incorporated in a forecasting model. In marketing it has been used to find out which predictors, among several possible, are most influential in forecasting sales and which are not multicollinear. It can be used for speech recognition, for gene expression, or in any context where high-dimensional data have to be visualized in two or three dimensions. PCA can also help when there are many variables that are actually linear combinations of other variables.

3.5 IMPLEMENTATION USING R: COMPETITOR ANALYSIS

Using the following code, we first import the data and load the required R packages: `factoextra`[3] and `ggplot2`.[4] `row.names=1` in `read.csv()` assigns manufacturers' names as row labels.

```
library(factoextra)
library(ggplot2)
hvac<- read.csv(url("http://data.mishra.us/files/PCA/competitor_data.csv"),
                row.names=1)
```

Next we use the `prcomp` command to run PCA on the dataset. In the code, `center = TRUE` indicates that we want data to be zero centered, and `scale = TRUE` means we want variables to be scaled to have unit variance before performing the principal component analysis.

The next function, `fviz_pca_ind`, uses the PCA output and plots the relative position of different manufacturers on two dominant principal components. Options such as `pointsize`, `pointshape`, `fill`, and `repel` alter the appearance of the plot. The following lines of code help generate the two-dimensional plot in Figure 3.5.

```
hvac.pca <- prcomp(hvac, center = TRUE,scale. = TRUE)
fviz_pca_ind(hvac.pca, pointsize = 2,
             pointshape = 21, fill = "#310FEF",
             repel = TRUE, title = "Two Dimensional Plot")
```

The Figure 3.5 plot shows that the amount of spread (variance) in these data is explained by the first two principal components, respectively. The first two principal components explain more than 75% of the spread in the dataset. This output indicates that Thermaly is perceived by users of HVAC as more similar to Nextra and Watco than Calvac.

To gain a deeper understanding of how each HVAC manufacturer is rated on various dimensions, we can ask for a biplot using the `fviz_pca_biplot` function. The biplot helps us interpret whether some dimensions are correlated and how each of the manufacturers performs on each of the dimensions. The following lines of code help generate the biplot in Figure 3.6

```
fviz_pca_biplot(hvac.pca, pointsize = 2, repel = TRUE)
```

On the biplot, the smaller the angle between the dimensions, the stronger the correlation. Moreover, the manufacturer closer to the origin (Thermaly) has an average value on almost all dimensions. To examine how each of the manufacturers performs on any dimension, we can drop a perpendicular from the manufacturer on to that specific dimension's arrow. For this the arrow can be extended backward if needed.

3.6 APPENDIX: TECHNICAL DETAILS OF PCA

3.6.1 Matrix Multiplication

The process of multiplying two matrices is illustrated as follows. Here A is a $t \times n$ matrix (i.e., it has t rows and n columns), and x has n rows and 1 column.

$$Ax = \begin{bmatrix} a_{11} & a_{12} & \cdots & a_{1n} \\ a_{21} & a_{22} & \cdots & a_{2n} \\ \vdots & \vdots & \ddots & \vdots \\ a_{t1} & a_{t2} & \cdots & a_{tn} \end{bmatrix} \begin{bmatrix} x_1 \\ x_2 \\ \vdots \\ x_n \end{bmatrix} = \begin{bmatrix} a_{11}x_1 + a_{12}x_2 + \cdots + a_{1n}x_n \\ a_{21}x_1 + a_{22}x_2 + \cdots + a_{2n}x_n \\ \vdots \\ a_{t1}x_1 + a_{t2}x_2 + \cdots + a_{tn}x_n \end{bmatrix}.$$

The following is a simple example in which we multiply two matrices, with one being a 3×2 matrix (3 rows and 2 columns) and the second a 2×3 matrix. The resulting matrix is a 3×3 matrix.

$$\begin{bmatrix} 5 & 3 \\ 4 & 2 \\ 1 & 9 \end{bmatrix} \cdot \begin{bmatrix} 1 & 4 & 9 \\ 3 & 6 & 8 \end{bmatrix} = \begin{bmatrix} 5*1+3*3 & 5*4+3*6 & 5*9+3*8 \\ 4*1+2*3 & 4*4+2*6 & 4*9+2*8 \\ 1*1+9*3 & 1*4+6*9 & 1*9+9*8 \end{bmatrix} = \begin{bmatrix} 14 & 38 & 69 \\ 10 & 28 & 52 \\ 28 & 58 & 81 \end{bmatrix}$$

3.6.2 Linear Transformation

One very important concept needed to understand PCA is *linear transformation*. Intuitively it can be understood as a process that changes the shape, size, and orientation of an object like a vector. Linear transformation is closely related to matrix multiplication. When we multiply a vector with a matrix, we get a new vector. In other words, the matrix ends up transforming the vector. A simple example will help us understand this. Figure 3.8(a) depicts a vector $\vec{x} = \begin{bmatrix} 1 \\ 2 \end{bmatrix}$. Now if we multiply this vector by a matrix $A = \begin{bmatrix} 2 & 1 \\ 0 & 2 \end{bmatrix}$ what we get is a new vector $\vec{x'} = A \cdot \vec{x} = \begin{bmatrix} 4 \\ 4 \end{bmatrix}$ as depicted in Figure 3.8(b).

FIGURE 3.8 ■ Linear Transformation

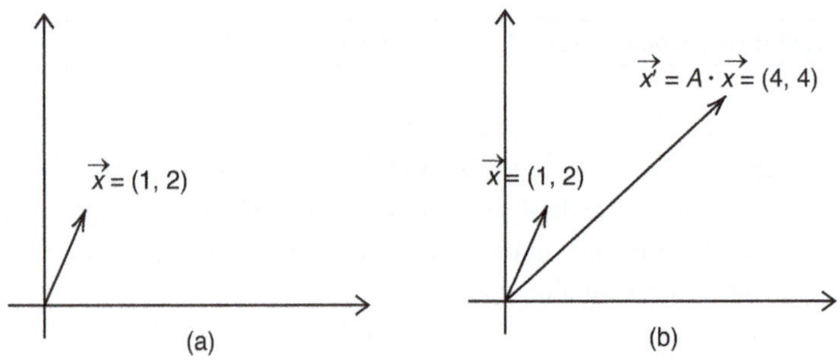

As we can see in Figures 3.8(a) and 3.8(b), a multiplication by matrix A has changed both the direction and magnitude of x. The linear transformation of a vector by a matrix is also referred to as mapping where a matrix A maps a vector $\vec{x}$ onto a new vector $\vec{x'}$.

3.6.3 Variance and Standard Deviation

Standard deviation captures the spread or dispersion of any set of numbers. So if the set of numbers involves the ages of five students in a class, then standard deviation captures whether they are centered on the average age or spread away from the average age. A standard deviation with a small value means that the data points are huddled around the average, and a standard deviation with a high value indicates that the data points are spread away from the average.[5]

The formula to calculate standard deviation is

$$s = \sqrt{\frac{\sum_{i=1}^{K}(x_i - \bar{x})(x_i - \bar{x})}{K-1}}$$

where K is the total number of observations, x_i is a particular value of x, and $\bar{x}$ is the average (mean) of all the values.

Variance is simply s^2; that is,

$$s^2 = \frac{\sum_{i=1}^{K}(x_i - \bar{x})(x_i - \bar{x})}{K-1}$$

3.6.4 Covariance and Correlation

If a dataset has more than one variable, say weight and systolic blood pressure, then covariance captures the relationship between weight and systolic blood pressure. Covariance captures how the two variables move. If they move in the same direction, then we have positive covariance; movement in the opposite direction indicates negative covariance; and if they have no relationship, there is zero covariance. The covariance of a variable with itself is variance. The graph in Figure 3.9 shows that the covariance between weight and systolic blood pressure is positive.

FIGURE 3.9 ■ Covariance Between Weight and Systolic Blood Pressure

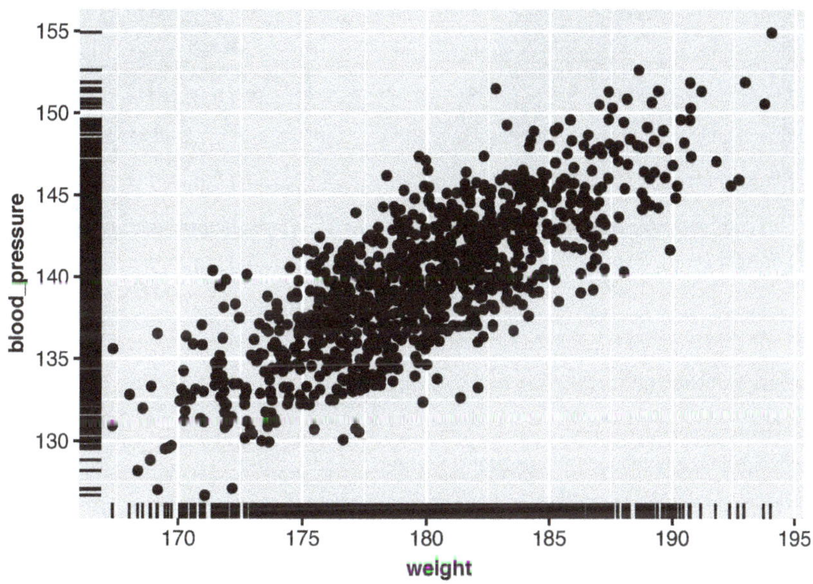

The two graphs in Figure 3.10 depict negative covariance and zero covariance, respectively, between any two variables, X_1 and X_2. For negative covariance, X_1 could be the amount of alcohol consumed and X_2 could be the number of math problems accurately solved. For zero covariance, X_1 could be the amount of alcohol consumed and X_2 could be the number of friends one has.

FIGURE 3.10 ■ Negative and Nearly Zero Covariance

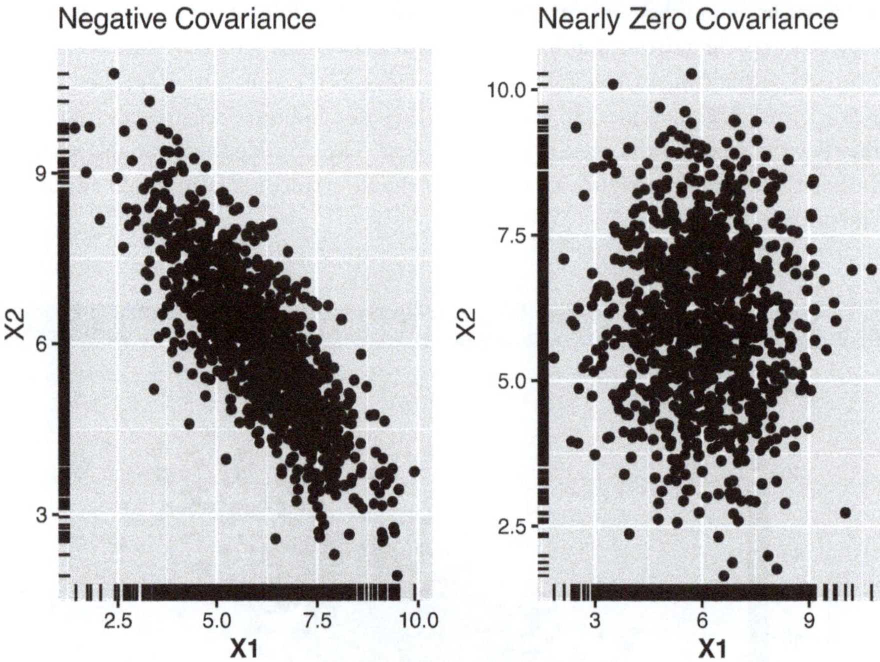

If we have K rows of data with two variables, X and Y, then covariance is

$$Cov(X, Y) = \frac{\sum_{i=1}^{K}(x_i - \overline{x})(y_i - \overline{y})}{K - 1}$$

A variance–covariance matrix shows the variance of each variable and the covariance between each pair of variables. Let's assume we have two variables, which are shown as follows in matrix form. The first column shows the amount of alcoholic drinks consumed, and the second column shows the number of correctly solved math problems.

$$\begin{bmatrix} 5 & 3 \\ 4 & 2 \\ 1 & 9 \end{bmatrix}$$

A variance–covariance matrix will look like this:

$$\begin{bmatrix} 4.33 & -7.33 \\ -7.33 & 14.33 \end{bmatrix}$$

In the preceding matrix, the diagonal values are variance, and the off-diagonal values are covariance. As alcohol consumption leads to less mathematical accuracy, covariance is negative. The following R code can calculate a variance–covariance matrix.

```
X1<-c(5,4,1)
X2<-c(3,2,9)
X<-cbind(X1,X2)
cov(X)
```

If we have three variables (*X*1, *X*2, and *X*3), then our variance–covariance matrix will be a 3×3 matrix.

$$\begin{bmatrix} Cov(X1, X1) & Cov(X1, X2) & Cov(X1, X3) \\ Cov(X2, X1) & Cov(X2, X2) & Cov(X2, X3) \\ Cov(X3, X1) & Cov(X3, X2) & Cov(X3, X3) \end{bmatrix}$$

Since $Cov(X, X) = Var(X)$, the preceding matrix can be written as follows. It is worth remembering that since $Cov(X, Y) = Cov(Y, X)$, the variance–covariance matrix is a symmetric matrix.

$$\begin{bmatrix} Var(X1) & Cov(X1, X2) & Cov(X1, X3) \\ Cov(X2, X1) & Var(X2) & Cov(X2, X3) \\ Cov(X3, X1) & Cov(X3, X2) & Var(X3) \end{bmatrix}$$

It is important to note that covariance is unit dependent, which means that if we measure weight in kilograms or pounds, it will change the value of covariance between weight and blood pressure. If we make covariance unit independent, then we can bypass this problem. One way to do this is to divide covariance by the standard deviation of each variable, which gives us the *correlation*. Correlation (ρ) captures the same relationship as covariance, the main difference is that correlation varies between -1 and 1 and is unit independent.

$$\rho_{(X,Y)} = \frac{Cov(X, Y)}{\sqrt{Var(X)\,Var(Y)}}$$

3.6.5 Geometry of the Covariance Matrix and PCA

Geometrically, the variance–covariance matrix describes the "shape" of the data. Let's use a simple example to understand how it does this.

Imagine we have just two variables: weight and blood pressure. There are *K* patients, so we have a $K \times 2$ matrix (with *K* rows and 2 columns). These data will lead to a simple 2×2 variance–covariance matrix. Consider a situation in which there is no relationship between weight and blood pressure. Let's say the variance–covariance matrix of these data is

$$Covariance\,matrix = \begin{bmatrix} 20.60 & 2.15 \\ 2.15 & 22.9 \end{bmatrix}$$

In that case, the plot of such data will look like Figure 3.11.

FIGURE 3.11 ■ No Relationship Between Weight and Blood Pressure

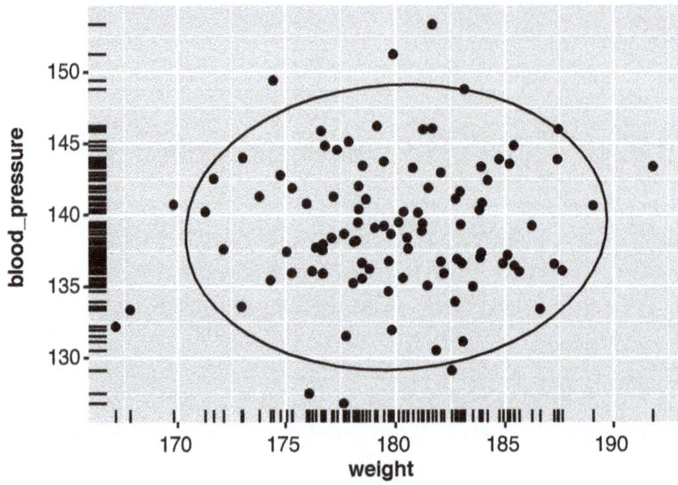

Notice that when weight and blood pressure do not covary a lot (covariance = 2.15), the general shape of these data looks like a circle (two-dimensional soccer ball).

If there is a moderate relationship between weight and blood pressure (i.e., a slightly higher covariance of 11.91), the general shape of the data will change as shown in Figure 3.12. It becomes more like an ellipse (two-dimensional football).

$$\textit{Covariance matrix} = \begin{bmatrix} 21.20 & 11.91 \\ 11.91 & 23.2 \end{bmatrix}$$

FIGURE 3.12 ■ Some Relationship Between Weight and Blood Pressure

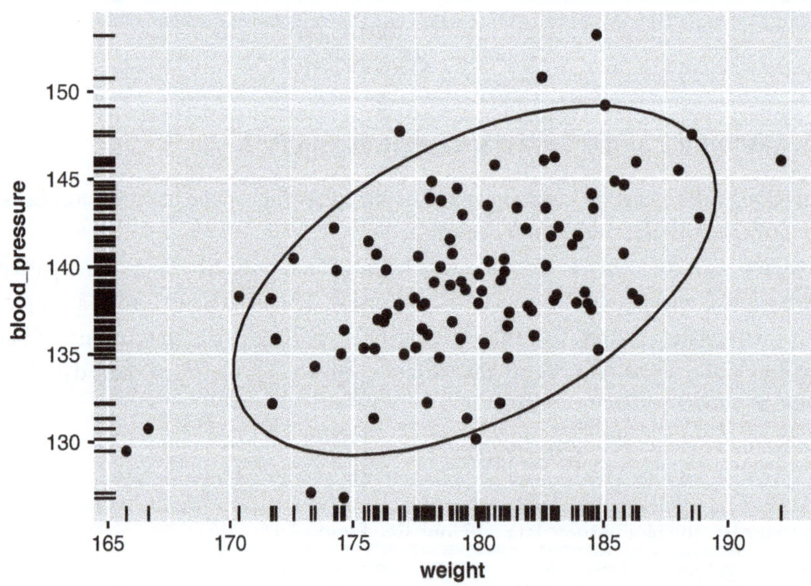

If there is a very strong relationship between weight and blood pressure (i.e., a high covariance of 22.39), the shape of the data looks very different. It looks like a two-dimensional horizontal Frisbee (Figure 3.13).

$$Covariance\,matrix = \begin{bmatrix} 21.52 & 22.33 \\ 22.33 & 22.97 \end{bmatrix}$$

FIGURE 3.13 ■ Strong Relationship Between Weight and Blood Pressure

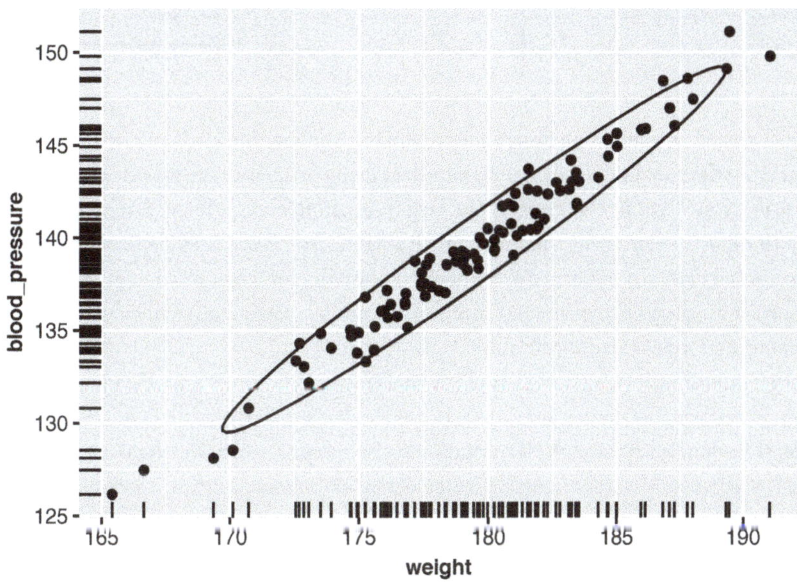

These three examples highlight something very interesting. The variance of weight and blood pressure remained largely unchanged in these examples. The only thing that changed was their covariance. When covariance was low, the data looked like a soccer ball; when covariance was moderate, it looked like a football; but when covariance was high, it looked like a Frisbee.

These examples show how the variance–covariance matrix can capture the geometry of any dataset. This particular quality of the variance–covariance matrix plays a very important role in PCA. Let's consider the third example where the data are shaped like a Frisbee. If we assume the data to be the body, then it is easy to notice that the core skeleton of these data has two bones. As depicted in Figure 3.14(a), one bone (the dotted line) is longer, and the second bone (the solid line) is shorter. Now notice that as the covariance decreases, the size of the shorter bone increases. With moderate covariance (football shape), the solid line bone gets longer, as shown in Figure 3.14(b). And when covariance is very low, this solid line bone becomes quite big, as the soccer-shaped data in Figure 3.14(c) illustrates.

FIGURE 3.14 ■ Variance-Covariance Matrix Captures the Geometry of the Dataset

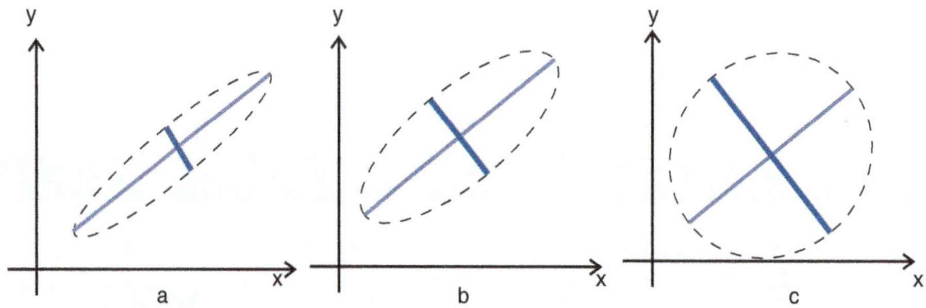

These dotted and solid line bones are principal components of the data. PCA is the process of identifying the core bones (spines) of your data using a variance–covariance matrix and then representing your data in the form of the largest-possible bones. These largest-possible bones capture the most meaning in the most concise form. As Figure 3.14 depicts, the dotted and solid line bones can be represented as a linear combination of x and y variables (similar to linear regression). This shows that principal components are not some entirely new variables; they are linear combinations of existing variables.

Mathematically, the process of identifying the length of the bones and orientation of the bones (i.e., if they are upward or downward sloping or parallel to the x- or the y-axis in our two-dimensional example) is accomplished through eigenvalues and eigenvectors, which we discuss next.

Briefly, eigenvectors represent the orientation of bones, pointing towards the principal directions where the data have most variability. Concurrently, eigenvalues denote the length of these bones, with smaller eigenvalues resembling shorter bones aligned with directions of minimal data variation.

3.6.6 Eigenvalues and Eigenvectors

Eigenvalues and eigenvectors help us see inside a matrix. In German *eigen* means "own" or "self." Eigenvectors are vectors that do not change their orientation when multiplied by a matrix. In other words, the eigenvectors of a matrix do not change their direction when linearly transformed by a matrix. The only thing that happens is that these vectors either shrink or expand due to matrix multiplication. Figure 3.15 shows the eigenvector of a matrix and what happens when this eigenvector is multiplied by the matrix. Here we have a matrix $A = \begin{bmatrix} 2 & 2 \\ 1 & 3 \end{bmatrix}$ and its eigenvector $\vec{x} = \begin{bmatrix} 1 \\ 1 \end{bmatrix}$. Multiplying A and $\vec{x}$ created a new vector $\vec{x'}$, with the result that

$$\vec{x'} = A \cdot x = \begin{bmatrix} 2*1+2*1 \\ 1*1+1*3 \end{bmatrix} = \begin{bmatrix} 4 \\ 4 \end{bmatrix} = 4 \cdot \begin{bmatrix} 1 \\ 1 \end{bmatrix}$$

$\vec{x'}$ has a different magnitude (it has expanded), but its direction is the same as $\vec{x}$. While $\begin{bmatrix} 1 \\ 1 \end{bmatrix}$ is the eigenvector for A, 4 is the eigenvalue (λ).

FIGURE 3.15 ■ Eigenvector of a Matrix

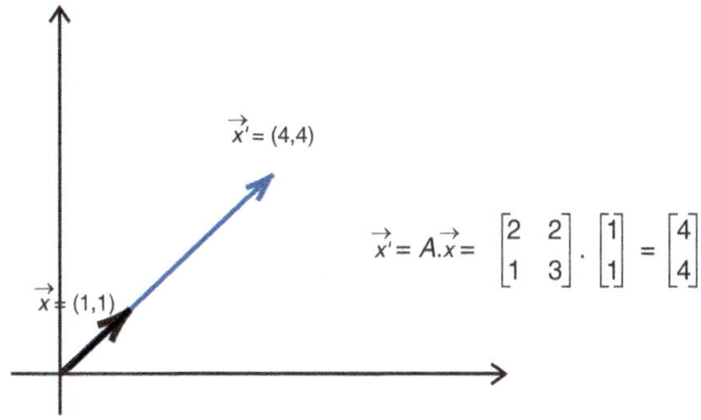

In the context of PCA, if A denotes the variance covariance matrix, then the eigenvector (denoted by $\vec{v}$) when multiplied by A will not change its direction but will be extended or shrunk in the process. Formally,

$$A \cdot \vec{v} = \lambda \vec{v}$$

Here λ is a scaler and represents the magnitude by which the eigenvector is extended or shrunk when multiplied by A; as discussed earlier, it is the eigenvalue of matrix A.

There are a few important aspects of eigenvectors. First, only with a square matrix, which has the same number of rows and columns, is it possible to find eigenvectors. Second, not every square matrix has eigenvectors. Third, each eigenvector of a matrix will be perpendicular (also called orthogonal) to other eigenvectors—a lot like how the x- and y-axes are perpendicular to each other. Fourth, for any $n \times n$ square matrix, there will be n eigenvalues and n eigenvectors. So if the data have 10 variables, the variance–covariance matrix will be 10×10, and there will be 10 eigenvalues and 10 eigenvectors.

Intuitively, eigenvalues capture which bone is longer (and, thus, more important). Smaller eigenvalues are like smaller bones, and larger eigenvalues are like larger bones. Eigenvectors, on the other hand, capture the orientation of each bone. In PCA we try to select large bones and ignore small bones because small bones represent the least variation, so ignoring them will not hurt us as we lose little information. As discussed in the last section, large and small bones are linear combinations of given variables; therefore, principal components identified in PCA are not a subset of original variables but some linear combination of those original variables. In other words, PCA does not discard or select some variables from the original dataset; instead, it creates new variables (principal components) that are linear combinations of the existing variables.

3.7 UNDERSTANDING THE CHAPTER

1. Why is the competitive environment of a business considered dynamic? Can you think of an example where the dynamic environment has changed the competitive landscape (e.g., similar to what happened with Blockbuster versus Netflix)?

2. Why is PCA an unsupervised learning method? How is it different from a supervised method like linear regression?

3. Given the eigenvalues 0.21, 0.374, 0.511, 0.675, 0.791, 0.801, 0.825, and 0.855, approximately how much of the variation is explained by the first three principal components?
   a. ~20%
   b. ~50%
   c. ~80%
   d. ~85%

4. What are the advantages of using a biplot?

5. What role do eigenvalues play in understanding the dimensions of least variation in a dataset? In order to select principal components, should we discard those principal components with the smallest or the largest eigenvalues? (You might need to refer to the technical appendix for details.)

6. Choose the statement that is true about PCA biplots:
   a. Origin represents the average value for each variable.
   b. The angle between two arrows does not represent their level of correlation.
   c. They rarely provide granular understanding.
   d. Origin represents the highest value of each variable.

ENDNOTES

1. Downes, Larry, and Paul Nunes, "Blockbuster Becomes a Casualty of Big Bang Disruption," *Harvard Business Review*, November 7, 2013, https://hbr.org/2013/11/blockbuster-becomes-a-casualty-of-big-bang-disruption; Satell, Greg, "A Look Back at Why Blockbuster Really Failed and Why It Didn't Have To," *Forbes*, September, 5, 2014, https://www.forbes.com/sites/gregsatell/2014/09/05/a-look-back-at-why-blockbuster-really-failed-and-why-it-didnt-have-to/?sh=1cd272f31d64.

2. Macrotrends, "Amazon Research and Development Expenses 2010–2023: AMZN," accessed October 4, 2023, https://www.macrotrends.net/stocks/charts/AMZN/amazon/research-development-expenses.

3. Kassambara, Alboukadel, and Fabian Mundt, "factoextra: Extract and Visualize the Results of Multivariate Data Analyses," R package version 1.0.7, published April 1, 2020, https://CRAN.R-project.org/package=factoextra.

4. Wickham, Hadley, *ggplot2: Elegant Graphics for Data Analysis* (New York: Springer-Verlag, 2016).

5. Average is also referred to as the mean.

4 MONITORING THE SOCIAL ENVIRONMENT USING TEXT ANALYSIS

CONTENTS

LEARNING OBJECTIVES

1. Understand the importance of monitoring a business's social environment
2. Define text data
3. Convert qualitative text data to a quantitative format
4. Summarize text data with a word cloud
5. Mine sentiment from text data
6. Interpret the results of a text analysis for business decisions
7. Identify other text analysis methods

4.1 UNDERSTANDING THE SOCIAL ENVIRONMENT

The social environment encompasses the sum total of a society's norms, beliefs, practices, and behavior. Since people live in a society, their choices reflect the social norms and values that are prominent in their society. Therefore, social forces operating at any given time have the power to influence many business decisions, and scanning the social environment continuously for such changes can determine whether or not a business succeeds.

4.1.1 Examples of How Changes in the Social Environment Affect Business

The food industry is changing its recipes to stay in tune with the social environment. Frito-Lay introduced baked potato chips in 1996. Why did Frito-Lay do this? Shouldn't it just have focused on making its snacks more flavorful since consumers buy snacks for their taste? The reason for this change can be found in the increased health-focused discussions in today's society. People have become more conscious of the ingredients that go into the food they are consuming. They prefer packaged foods that use natural ingredients rather than preservatives or artificial ingredients. Baked foods are preferred over deep-fried foods since the latter have a higher saturated fat content, which research has linked to many illnesses. Frito-Lay and other packaged-food producers realized the influence of health-focused discussions on purchasing behavior.

Similarly, we are witnessing a social trend that sees people moving away from high-sugar carbonated drinks. Since the 1980s, the rate of increase in diabetes has been concerning. A growing literature in the medical field has demonstrated the effects of sugar in causing type 2 diabetes in young children. Much of the uptick in diabetes has been linked to sugar-sweetened beverages,[1] causing the American Heart Association to recommend that people ingest no more than 100 to 150 calories of additional sugar per day. In addition to their link with diabetes, sugar-sweetened beverages have been linked to weight gain and cardiovascular diseases.

These findings and their resultant discussions have changed modern society's sugar consumption. In contrast to a time when people consumed beverages because of their taste or assumed that all beverages are good for hydration, people now are becoming more concerned about how much sugar they may be consuming when they drink a can of soda. It is common to see online searches about how many grams or teaspoons of sugar a carbonated drink contains. These searches indicate people's growing awareness of and concern for what sugar can do to their health. Such concerns fueled by social changes need to be tracked by businesses to determine what type of products should be designed to address these social concerns. The social trend to consume less sugar has forced many carbonated beverage brands to reformulate their drinks or acquire companies that sell drinks like coconut water. Low- or no-sugar versions of soda and several other beverages are an outcome of this social phenomenon.

Another example of a social phenomenon that is causing companies to redesign their products is sustainability. To protect the Earth from future harm, people across the world are demanding products that can be manufactured, used, and disposed of in sustainable ways. From the use of cloth bags in grocery stores and pens that are made from recycled water bottles to reusable coffee cups, fair trade products that use sustainable farming, and demand for electric vehicles, the growing list showcases an important social change that is restructuring many aspects of business—from product design to manufacturing and selling.

Understanding the social environment is especially important for businesses that operate in multicultural regions. For instance, Hyundai needs to be aware of social norms that affect people's travel habits since they sell cars in many different countries that range from the United States and the United Kingdom to India. In different societies, cars may fulfill different social needs—for example, a mode of getting from place A to place B versus signaling prosperity, facilitating family travel versus commuting to the office, carpooling versus a driving experience, style versus comfort, or a means to signal one's environmental consciousness. Amid these many types of needs, businesses must monitor the social environment for changes that could impact them specifically. Hence, we next consider possible ways in which businesses can use social signals as an opportunity to better cater to their customers' desires.

4.1.2 How Can Businesses Monitor the Social Environment?

Traditional methods like consumer surveys may not work in today's rapidly changing, socially connected world where it is important for businesses to gauge consumer reactions on an ongoing basis and respond to them quickly. Surveys tend to be time consuming and have limited sample size (i.e., the number of people who actually complete the survey). Moreover, many of these surveys using rating scales do not have the ability to capture people's true feelings because they ask consumers to convert feelings and thoughts into numeric estimates, which is difficult. Should a business be satisfied with a 6 or 6.2 rating for a product on a 1 to 10 rating scale? If consumers are asked to describe what they think/feel about your products instead of rating them on a scale, they may not have the time, the individuals evaluating these responses might inject their subjectivity, and the number of people businesses can survey (sample size) will be small.

So what can businesses do? In today's fast-paced world, people are continuously producing vast amounts of text in the form of reviews, social media posts, blogs, and tweets (now referred to as posts on the platform X). This people-produced content (commonly referred to as *user-generated content*) captures their feelings, opinions, and ratings on innumerable topics. To provide context, almost 80% of the data available to businesses is in the form of text; hence, it would be useful to analyze and derive insights from it. If businesses have the ability to analyze this textual content, they can find out which social changes people are most concerned about and what exactly their concerns are. By analyzing text, businesses can quickly find out simple things such as whether their brand or a competitor's brand is being mentioned more often. They can also find out whether their product is being discussed positively (e.g., *this is a great brand*) or negatively (e.g., *I am not satisfied with this brand*).

Such positive and negative feelings toward a feature, a brand, a service, a firm, or even an employee are broadly referred to as *sentiment*. Hence, it is common to see text being used for sentiment analysis. This entails the use of text to obtain more complex reactions toward a product, such as whether a food product is considered healthy, harmful, tasty, expensive, or kid friendly. Businesses can use such people-produced text to monitor the changes in the social environment that can affect their decisions. Insights gathered from the social environment can help businesses find out what people want from their products, which, in turn, can help in product redesign. Businesses can use such insights to understand the types of products they should be investing in more heavily by understanding which of their products is garnering more positive sentiment and generating more discussion.

Before we examine how we can keep track of the social environment using user-generated text, let's first understand what types of text can be analyzed and whether these data need to be first cleaned or converted into a more manageable form.

4.2 DEFINING TEXT DATA

The idea of being able to analyze text lies in the larger area of *natural language processing* (NLP). NLP is the process of teaching algorithms how to analyze and understand human language. Two terms are commonly used in text analysis: *corpus* and *document*. *Corpus* (the singular form of *corpora*) is a collection of texts, usually stored electronically. Depending on what we want to find out, a corpus might be a collection of documents such as news articles, emails, blogs, posts, customer reviews, or books on a certain topic. Each *document* is a separate entity or record. Documents can be in different formats such as text, PDF, Microsoft Word, and XML.

When people think of data, the most common image that comes to mind is data arranged in rows and columns, most likely in an Excel sheet. Such data in rows and columns are generally referred to as an *array*. And the data format is most likely to be in the form of numbers such as past sales or historic stock market rates. It is easy to analyze numeric data because we can perform many types of mathematical operations on them, including addition, subtraction, multiplication, and division. When some variables are categorical (e.g., male versus female), we can dummy code them as 0 = Male and 1 = Female and use this in our analysis.

However, text is not in the form of numbers; thus, it is difficult to understand how we can ask an algorithm to perform addition or subtraction using text data. Let's next consider an example that highlights the difference between human and algorithmic processing to understand why and what types of rules algorithms need to process text data.

4.2.1 Human Versus Algorithmic Processing of Text

How can we analyze the following review posted about a product?

> This is the best lamp on the market. I would recommend it to anyone. It gives out a nice soothing light, which still provides a lot of light for reading. I also like that it is not bright white but a more warm white that doesn't appear dull.

These data are not in a numeric form; nor are they in the form of an array. Any person conversant with English can read the review and understand what the writer wanted to convey. But what if we have thousands of such reviews? Then it would become difficult to read through all of them and come up with a holistic assessment of the brand that the business can use to inform its decisions. It would be ideal if we could use algorithms that can understand such text. However, algorithms require a set of rules or procedures to analyze data. They can easily analyze data in numeric form, but there is no universal rule that algorithms can apply to analyze text data. Therefore, we need to convert text data into a form that allows algorithms to apply some rule.

4.3 CONVERTING QUALITATIVE TEXT DATA TO A QUANTIFIABLE FORM

4.3.1 Unstructured Nature of Text Data

In order to convert text data into a quantifiable form, we need to understand that text data are not structured data. Structured data follow a regular pattern (e.g., sales data that fall within a certain range and follow the same pattern for every time period). However, text data don't follow such a pattern because these data capture conversations between people or capture their thoughts on diverse topics. One could argue that text data follow proper grammatical rules and, hence, the text is quite structured. This is very true! Text appears to humans to follow a structure because from a very young age we have been taught this complex framework of grammar, punctuation, and proper use. However, to an algorithm, text appears unstructured because it does not follow a structure that the algorithm is familiar with. Therefore, we first need to put text into a format that appears structured to the algorithm. If text data can be converted into a row–column (i.e., array or matrix) format, then we have taught the algorithm a rule to understand text data.

4.3.2 Preprocessing Text Data

The most common approach to converting text data to a structured form is to break the text data into their most basic unit, which is the word. However, not all words are equally informative to the analysis. For instance, words such as *a* and *the* occur in large numbers in text data. They are called *stop words*. Removing such words not only removes unnecessary and unhelpful information but also reduces the size of the data. Therefore, we first preprocess text data by removing stop words that are uninformative: common words such as *the* and *a*, conjunctions such as *and* and *or*, and proper names (if we are not interested in names). We also remove numbers, punctuation, and white space. Depending on the topic that we are examining, we can specify which words we want to remove from the corpus in the preprocessing step.

4.3.3 Word Count: A Rule to Convert Text to an Array

Remember, our goal is to convert text to a structured form. The easiest and most common way that information can be retrieved from text is to count the number of times a word appears in a document after preprocessing the data and removing stop words. The word count provides numeric information about the text. This is also called the *term frequency* (tf), where each word is called a *term*. For ease of reference, we will call term frequency the *word count*.

We can then create an array in which the columns represent all words included in the text corpora. Each row represents a document, such as one review, one email, or one chapter in a book. The document can be defined as needed by the user. Using this array, the algorithm enters the number of times the words in the columns appear in each of the documents. For instance, if one review stated that "Delta Air Lines staff is very helpful," then beneath the word *helpful* for this row, the algorithm would enter the number 1. Since there could be many possible words used across documents, this matrix tends to be *high dimensional. High dimensional* here refers to the large number of columns compared to rows in an array. An example illustrates why text data are considered high dimensional. Assume we have access to only 100 reviews or 100 emails, with each review or email categorized as a document (represented as rows in the array). However, even after preprocessing, the number of unique words (represented as columns) may number 2,000. This would make our array of text data high dimensional.

Once we have preprocessed the text data, we next create a *word cloud*. A word cloud is a visual representation of text data in which the most important words of the corpus are highlighted via size and/or color. This is also called the bag-of-words method because we look at the informative words in a corpus to make inferences about the topic of discussion.

4.4 ANALYZING TEXT DATA

4.4.1 Visualizing Text Data via Word Clouds

A word cloud is the simplest visualization aid for text data. It helps synthesize millions of documents into a helpful visualization of the most important words—those that appear most frequently. To create a word cloud, we first convert text data into a quantifiable form that the algorithm can understand using word count, as described previously. For example, in order to assess what words are used most frequently when discussing their products, businesses can look at product reviews. Each review related to a product would serve as a document, and the total number of reviews available for analysis would form the text corpus. The business can determine the number of times the word *good* or *excellent* or *dissatisfied* or *bad*—or any other relevant word that remains in each review (represented as a row) after preprocessing—occurs. (This is the word count.) A word cloud is the initial step that provides some idea of which words appear most frequently in the text corpus. These frequent words are most representative of the documents that we are examining. Figure 4.1 is the word cloud from President Lincoln's Gettysburg Address.

FIGURE 4.1 ■ Word Cloud: Gettysburg Address

We can see that the words *nation* and *can* are the most frequently occurring words in the speech; thus, they are displayed as the biggest in the word cloud. We will learn to create a word cloud to monitor the social environment later in the chapter.

Since word clouds are the simplest form of text analysis, they have a few limitations that other complex text analysis methods address. Word clouds tell us which words occur most frequently in the text corpus. However, if we want to find out whether people are expressing positive or negative sentiments about our product or brand, we will need to use sentiment analysis, which we will discuss next. We can guess what the main topic of discussion is in a group of documents using a word cloud to find the five most frequent words. In addition, complex methods such as topic modeling help us determine these topics of discussion. Let's start our discussion of sentiment analysis.

4.4.2 Mining Sentiment From Text Data

Sentiment analysis in a business context is the process of inferring sentiments that people are feeling toward a business or its products. Knowing whether people are feeling positive or negative sentiments is important for the business to take constructive action. If a business can infer the nature of the sentiment and what feature is eliciting that sentiment, it can take a series of actions ranging from simple customer outreach and messaging to offering customized products and engaging in product redesign. Since much of the information from their customers is in the form of text such as emails, opinion pieces, reviews, feedback, blogs, and articles, businesses find it beneficial to extract sentiment from text. For instance, if someone says, "I really like the product, but the packaging is flimsy," they are expressing a conflicting sentiment. In the past, human judges would read through such text to infer whether people were positively or negatively disposed toward a product. However, such a task becomes daunting for human judges if there are millions of lines of text. Sentiment analysis by algorithms allows us to go over large text corpora and extract sentiment from them. Moreover, sentiment analysis cannot be done in real time by humans. Algorithms, on the other hand, can work constantly to find out whether there might be a crisis brewing that a business needs to address immediately or an opportunity that it shouldn't miss out on. We will learn how to perform a sentiment analysis in this chapter.

4.5 CHOICE OF MEAT VERSUS MEATLESS OPTIONS: A REFLECTION OF THE SOCIAL ENVIRONMENT

Consider a restaurant chain that specializes in sandwiches and soups and has locations on the West Coast. Many of its popular menu options are meat based. However, recently it has seen a change in consumer needs and noticed that many of its younger customers have been inquiring about whether some meatless options are available. The chain has learned this information in informal conversations with its customers, the reviews they are writing on Yelp, and news articles that are covering food choices generally. Until recently, the restaurant chain has been offering salad options but feels that additional nonmeat sandwich options would effectively attract new customers and increase the number of items ordered. However, before it adds such meatless options, the restaurant chain wants to make sure that it has researched social trends well and is not following a fad that might fade in a few months. Adding meatless options to its menu would require it to include new suppliers and change its recipes.

The chain could conduct a survey and ask consumers what they thought. But the sample would be limited, the survey could be expensive, and it might not capture hidden trends in the social environment. Therefore, one option that the restaurant chain can explore is to monitor the social trends to determine opinions about meat versus meatless food options. It can gauge emerging social trends by tracking discussions about food. For instance, are people viewing meatless options more positively or negatively? Moreover, social trends could help determine whether the restaurant should invest in one versus the other option. One simple measure that can help answer such questions is to determine the sentiment associated with meat versus meatless options. Inferring sentiment from text is very useful for businesses because sentiment is generally expressed in verbal descriptions. But where can the chain access such text data that can help it infer sentiment? Keep in mind that since the data pertain to discussion about food happenings in society at large, the business cannot gather these data internally.

4.5.1 Mining Text for People's Opinions on Meat Versus Meatless Options

Current tweets[2] could be a good source for such information. Tweets tend to be most timely since people discuss what is on their mind via tweets. Moreover, businesses can gather such tweets on an ongoing basis—every month, every week, or even every day depending on the level of urgency with which they want to keep track of food discussions or trends.

Let's assume that the restaurant chain gathered tweets to infer sentiment regarding meat versus meatless options and collected 60 tweets that used *meat* or *meatless* keywords or hashtags. A tweet is rarely longer than 280 characters. Each tweet forms a document, so the text corpus that will be analyzed contains 60 documents. Based on the hashtags, the tweets are assigned labels of *meat* and *meatless* so that they can be compared by the words that are used when the discussion is about meat-based food options versus meatless food options.

To perform any text analysis, one first needs to preprocess the data. Hence, for the 60 tweets, we will first discuss the preprocessing steps, go over the simplest form of visualizing text data via a word cloud, and then perform sentiment analysis.

4.5.2 Creating a Word Cloud

We will go through the following steps in order to create a word cloud:

- Import the data corpus as a .csv file
- Remove stop words from the corpus
- Calculate the word counts for *meat* and *meatless* labels
- Create a word cloud

We import the data from the 60 tweets. We then ask the algorithm to use the label of *meat* or *meatless* and count how many times a word occurs within these labels. Hence, using the labels of *meat* and *meatless*, the algorithm obtains the word count for each set of tweets. We then ask the algorithm to pick the top 15 most frequent words to create word clouds. Since we want to compare the most frequent words used to describe meat versus meatless options, we create two word clouds.

The tweets are converted into a list of individual words as can be seen here.

```
## # A tibble:  1,212 × 2
##     source     word
##     <chr>      <chr>
##   1 meatless  interest
##   2 meatless  is
##   3 meatless  booming
##   4 meatless  in
##   5 meatless  plant
##   6 meatless  based
##   7 meatless  meat
##   8 meatless  analogues
##   9 meatless  and
##  10 meatless lab
## # ... 1,202  more rows
```

We next remove stop words from the list of words. Remember, stop words are words like *a* and *the* that are less informative to the discussion because they occur very commonly across all text. We also remove numbers, punctuations, and white space.

After removing stop words, we count word frequency, which allows us to create a word cloud of the 15 most frequent words for the tweets with a *meat* label as seen in Figure 4.2.

FIGURE 4.2 ■ Meat Word Cloud

Since this is a smaller dataset, we see fewer than 15 words in the word cloud.

We repeat these steps for tweets labeled *meatless* as seen in Figure 4.3.

FIGURE 4.3 ■ Meatless Word Cloud

In a word cloud, words that are more frequently appear larger than words that appear less frequently. We can change the number of the most frequent words that we want to appear in the word cloud. Here we have specified that the word cloud should contain the most frequent 15 words.

There are many insights we can gather from word clouds. The most frequent word for the meat word cloud is *meat*, while for the meatless word cloud it is *meatless*. This is neither very surprising nor very helpful. Hence, we can look at other words that frequently occur. If we look at the next most frequent words that can be used to inform the discussion for these two food options, we see that meat options are described using words such as *beef, animals, planet*, and *killing*, while meatless-option discussions include words such as *meat, delicious, vegetarian*, and *meal*.

By looking at the word cloud, businesses can get the gist of the conversation surrounding a specific topic, or they can compare the words defining two topics. After seeing the word cloud, the restaurant chain may decide to revamp its menu to attract consumers who value meatless food options. The chain also now can use specific words to advertise its meat and meatless menu options differently.

However, what if the restaurant chain wants to obtain a deeper understanding of the meatless trend from the text data? One simple method that can benefit most businesses is conducting a sentiment analysis.

4.5.3 Mining Sentiment

In order to perform sentiment analysis, we can use sentiment lexicons. Sentiment lexicons contain a compilation of words with their associated sentiments for a particular language. These lexicons are very similar to a dictionary, but instead of giving meanings they categorize words as positive or negative or rate the words on a plus–minus sentiment scale. For instance, in a sentiment lexicon, the word *cancer* will not include its meaning but is most likely to have a negative sentiment associated with it. Thus, these lexicons allow the algorithm to check whether a certain word occurring in the text data is associated with positive or negative sentiments. Note: One limitation is that if the sentiment lexicon does not contain a word, then the algorithm will not be able to process that word's sentiment.

In order to perform a sentiment analysis, we first use a lexicon that assigns a positive or negative sentiment label to each word. Once words have sentiments assigned to them, we count these sentiments by the source, which is the *meat* or *meatless* label.

```
## # A tibble: 4 x 3
##   source    sentiment       n
##   <chr>     <chr>       <int>
## 1 meat      negative       27
## 2 meat      positive       14
## 3 meatless  negative        6
## 4 meatless  positive       35
```

When we look at the output, we can compare how many words in the meat versus the meatless tweets are labeled as expressing a positive or negative sentiment. We find that in the meat-related tweets, 14 words are said to express positive sentiment while 27 words are said to express negative sentiment. For the meatless-related tweets, we find a slightly different pattern, which shows that 35 words express positive sentiment and 6 words express negative sentiment.

We repeat this process with another lexicon that assigns a numerical positive or negative sentiment score to each word on a scale of −5 to +5. Hence, we sum sentiments (instead of counting as we did earlier) across the *meat* and *meatless* labels.

```
## # A tibble: 2 × 2
##   source     sum
##   <chr>      <dbl>
## 1 meat         -30
## 2 meatless      56
```

The analysis indicates that meat-related tweets received an overall rating score of −30, while the meatless tweets received a score of 56. Overall, the pattern of findings stays the same across the two lexicons. From our sentiment analysis using the 60 tweets, the restaurant chain could conclude that more positive sentiment is associated with the discussion of meatless options and that sentiment is more negative in tweets discussing meat options.

What can the restaurant chain learn from such sentiment analysis? While it can infer which words are more frequently associated with meat versus meatless options (from the word cloud), it now has learned from the sentiment analysis whether the frequently used words convey positive or negative sentiment. Having this information is a good first step in the chain's decision of whether to include more meatless options on its menu based on the discussion happening in society at large.

4.5.4 Possible Business Strategies Using Text Analysis

In terms of developing business strategies, the restaurant chain wanted to determine whether it should include more meatless options and whether such an addition would lead to positive or negative sentiment. Given the text analysis, the restaurant chain can choose from the following options: consider offering one or two more meatless options and keep its meat options the same, add several meatless options and remove some meat options, or try a more extreme option of opening a subsidiary focused just on meatless menu options. Moreover, in terms of communication with its customers, the restaurant chain can pick positive associations with meat and meatless options and inform its customers how it is different from other restaurant chains and how it matches with current customer needs. This could include mentioning how it is procuring its supplies from environmentally friendly suppliers, how it is using sustainable ways of preparing food, and so on.

We confined our data to 60 tweets that we scraped to help gain insights from text using a simple dataset. However, businesses can consider larger text corpora such as Facebook posts, several thousand tweets, Yelp reviews, or news articles to monitor the words most representative of their brand. Businesses can also keep track of consumer conversations over time to see how the discussion regarding their brand versus competing brands might be changing. Hence, text analysis provides a very dynamic way of monitoring people's perceptions of a specific topic, brand, or policy. Instead of conducting expensive surveys and asking people to indicate how they feel about products, text analysis allows businesses to continuously monitor the social environment and infer people's sentiment about their products in a very cost-effective manner.

Businesses can use such sentiment analysis to infer the sentiment surrounding the discussion, as well as monitor words used in the discussion that are indicative of sentiment.

4.6 OTHER TEXT ANALYSIS METHODS

There are other text analysis methods that one can use beyond word cloud and sentiment analysis. Imagine that we wanted to find the main topic of discussion about a brand like Boeing during the past week. In this case, we need to know not just the sentiment but other topics such as quality, loyalty, or customer care. For such text analysis, *topic modeling* can be used. Topic modeling helps to find hidden topics from text documents. For instance, it would be difficult to look at chapters of different books or a bunch of news articles and then determine what main topics occurred in them. Do the book chapters focus on comedy or tragedy, or are they based on historical data? Using words that occur most frequently, topic models help to determine which topics occur prominently in which documents. Topic models use the principle of probabilistic modeling.

A common topic model is the Latent Dirichlet Allocation (LDA). This model uses words in text corpora for clustering documents with similar words together. Therefore, a topic is essentially a cluster of the most representative words. These words facilitate inference about the topic being discussed—for example, whether consumers are discussing the safety, price, or fuel efficiency of an automobile brand. Topic modeling is valuable not only for clustering similar documents but also for identifying various topics within a specific document. A single document may encompass several topics, and topic modeling helps determine the proportion of each topic within that document. Overall, topic modeling is instrumental in clustering large volumes of documents and extracting salient topics from them. This technique is widely used in various applications; businesses employ topic models to categorize customer reviews and to recommend products, while news sites utilize topic modeling to suggest articles to readers based on their historical reading interests.

Many text analysis methods depend on counting the frequency of specific words for conducting analysis. For example, if both *good* and *bad* occur 50 times in a corpus, conventional count-based methods would assign equal importance to these words without considering their meanings or the sentiments they convey. Thus, for analyses requiring understanding of word meanings, more sophisticated methods are essential.

Consider a traveler planning a vacation in Amsterdam, who has previously visited Paris, enjoyed the Louvre, and wished to find a similar museum in Amsterdam. Simple count-based text analysis would fall short in this scenario. In contrast, text analysis algorithms capable of inferring word meanings from context, known as **word-embedding algorithms**, would be more effective. These algorithms translate words into vectors in a way that capture their meanings, facilitating analysis that goes beyond mere word counts. Word-embedding methods, like word2vec and GloVe, can effectively address queries, such as identifying the Amsterdam equivalent to the Louvre (likely the Rijksmuseum), or disambiguating the term *cancer* to distinguish between references to the disease or the astrological sign.

Furthermore, since sentiment analysis often considers words as the primary unit of analysis, it might struggle to differentiate sentiments in phrases like "this product is not bad" versus "this product is bad," as both contain the word *bad*. Word-embedding algorithms mitigate this issue by considering the context in which words appear, offering a more nuanced understanding of sentiment in text.

Similarly, models like GPT-4, or ChatGPT, utilize a form of word embeddings as part of their architecture to understand and generate text effectively. GPT-4 employs a variant called transformer embeddings, which not only captures the meaning of individual words but also considers the relationship and context between words in a sentence. This contextual understanding allows GPT-4 to generate coherent and contextually relevant responses, making it a powerful tool for various natural language processing tasks, including sentiment analysis, text completion, and conversational agents.

Since text forms a big chunk of information available to businesses, they are constantly looking for ways to extract this valuable information. Moreover, much of the available text has been voluntarily produced by people and can be easily available to the business compared to other sources of information such as surveys, focus groups, or interviews. In this chapter, we learned how to convert text into a form that can be understood by the algorithm, and we performed two types of analysis: creating a word cloud and mining sentiment to monitor the social environment. Depending on the questions that the business wants answered using text, it can consider using a simple visualization such as the word cloud, engaging in a deeper analysis using sentiment analysis or topic modeling, or deriving semantic associations in text using word-embedding algorithms. Text analysis opens a largely untapped source of business insights.

4.7 IMPLEMENTATION USING R: CHOICE OF MEAT VERSUS MEATLESS OPTIONS

In order to find out whether it would be profitable to include meatless options on its menu, a restaurant chain has decided to use tweets to find out people's sentiments toward such options. Let's assume that the restaurant chain collected 60 tweets that contained *meat* or *meatless* keywords or hashtags. Each tweet forms a document; thus, the text corpus that will be analyzed contains 60 documents. Based on the hashtags, the tweets are assigned labels of *meat* and *meatless*.

4.7.1 Creating a Word Cloud

We import data from 60 tweets and preprocess it using R's `tidyverse`[3] and `tidytext`[4] package. We first load the three packages of `tidyverse`, `tidytext`, and `wordcloud`.[5] These three packages are sufficient to preprocess the text data and create a word cloud. After reading in the data, we ask the algorithm to use the label of *meat* or *meatless* and count how many times a word occurs within these labels. Using these labels, the algorithm obtains the word count for each set of tweets. We then ask the algorithm to pick the top 15 most frequent words to create two word clouds, which allow us to compare the most frequent words used to describe meat versus meatless options.

```
library("tidyverse")
library("wordcloud")
library("tidytext")
```

```
tweets<- read.csv(url("http://data.mishra.us/files/tweets_sentiment.txt"))

t_word<- tweets%>%
  unnest_tokens(word,text)
```

After importing tweets using `read-csv()`, the first step is creating a new object or list, `t_word`, using the code `tweets%>% unnest_tokens(word,text)`.

Let's understand what this code is accomplishing. The function `%>%` works as a pipe that passes on `tweets` to the function `unnest_tokens`, which performs the task of *tokenization*. Thus, tokenization takes the tweets and converts them into a list of individual words. If we see inside `t_word`, we will see the following:

```
t_word

## # A tibble: 1,212 × 2
##    source   word
##    <chr>    <chr>
##  1 meatless interest
##  2 meatless is
##  3 meatless booming
##  4 meatless in
##  5 meatless plant
##  6 meatless based
##  7 meatless meat
##  8 meatless analogues
##  9 meatless and
## 10 meatless lab
## # ... 1,202 more rows
```

The first column, source, shows the label, *meat* versus *meatless*, assigned to a tweet. The second column shows the words that form a tweet. Next, using the following lines of code, we can create a word cloud with tweets under the meat label, as seen in Figure 4.2.

```
t_word %>%
  filter(source == "meat") %>%
  anti_join(stop_words) %>%
  count(word,sort="TRUE") %>%
  with(wordcloud(word,n, max.words = 15))
```

As explained earlier, we pipe (`%>%`) the list of words, `t_word`, into a filter function, `filter(source = "meat")`, where we only consider words of tweets with the *meat* label. Once filtered, these words are piped to the next function, `anti_join(stop_words)`. This function removes stop words from the list of words. Remember, stop words are words like *a* and *the* that are less informative to the analysis because they occur very commonly across all text. We also remove numbers, punctuation, and white space.

After removing stop words, we count word frequency using count(word). And using this frequency, we create a word cloud of the 15 words that appear most often.

Since this is a small dataset, we see less than 15 words in the word cloud. Using `max.words`, we can change the number of most frequently used words that appear in the word cloud.

We repeat these steps for tweets labeled *meatless* to get the word cloud in Figure 4.3.

```
t_word %>%
  filter(source == "meatless") %>%
  anti_join(stop_words) %>%
  count(word,sort="TRUE") %>%
  with(wordcloud(word,n, max.words = 15))
```

We can now compare the word clouds for the meat versus meatless options.

4.7.2 Mining Sentiment

In order to perform sentiment analysis in R, we can use sentiment lexicons that are already built into R's "tidytext" package. We will use the `afinn` and `bing` lexicons. The `bing` lexicon categorizes words as positive or negative. The `afinn` lexicon rates the words on a -5 to 5 scale, with -5 indicating a negative sentiment and +5 indicating a positive sentiment. Therefore, if we used an `afinn` lexicon, we would receive a sentiment rating.

We begin by using the `bing` lexicon to create a list in which each word is assigned a sentiment tag or label. This list is called a `t_sentiment`, as can be seen in the following code:

```
## BING LEXICON
t_sentiment<- t_word %>%
  anti_join(stop_words)%>%
  inner_join(get_sentiments("bing"),by = "word")
```

The words that `t_word` created earlier are piped to the function `anti_join(stop_words)`, which removes common stop words. Then we use `inner_join` to find the sentiment of each word in `t_word` by using the bing lexicon. The `inner_join` step does this by matching the word in `t_word` with the same word and its sentiment in the bing lexicon.

Once words in `t_word` have sentiments assigned to them, we count these sentiments by the source, which is the *meat* or *meatless* label.

```
t_sentiment%>%
  dplyr::count(source,sentiment)
```

```
## # A tibble: 4 × 3
##   source    sentiment     n
##   <chr>     <chr>     <int>
## 1 meat      negative     27
## 2 meat      positive     14
## 3 meatless  negative      6
## 4 meatless  positive     35
```

When we look at the output using the "bing" lexicon, we can compare how many words in the meat versus the meatless tweets are labeled as expressing positive or negative sentiment.

We repeat this process with the afinn lexicon. If prompted to download `afinn`, then we select `Yes`. Recall the afinn lexicon assigns a numerical positive or negative sentiment score to each word on a scale of -5 to +5. Therefore, we sum these sentiments (instead of counting as we did with the bing lexicon) across the meat and meatless labels.

```
t_sentiment<- t_word %>%
   anti_join(stop_words)%>%
   inner_join(get_sentiments("afinn"),by = "word")
```

```
t_sentiment%>%
  group_by(source) %>%
  dplyr::summarise(score = sum(value))
```

```
## # A tibble: 2 × 2
##   source    score
##   <chr>     <dbl>
## 1 meat        -30
## 2 meatless     56
```

The analysis indicates that meat-related tweets received an overall rating score of -30 while the meatless tweets received a score of 56.

4.8 UNDERSTANDING THE CHAPTER

Students are encouraged to answer the following questions. They can then review the chapter to check their answers.

1. Why does the social environment affect businesses? Come up with one example of a social belief that can affect the clothing industry.

2. Would text be defined as qualitative or quantitative data? What is the simplest way to convert text data to a numeric form?

3. In text data, how is a document different from a corpus? Can you think of any examples?

4. A word cloud relies on (a) document count, (b) word count, (c) sentiment count, or (d) corpus count. Choose the correct option.

5. Which of the following statements is *false* regrading preprocessing (cleaning) text data before analysis?
   a. Preprocessing data can reduce the size of the data.
   b. Removing stop words is one kind of preprocessing.
   c. Removing white space is one kind of preprocessing.
   d. Converting all words to lowercase is one kind of preprocessing.
   e. Articles like *a* and *the* should never be removed during preprocessing.

6. A word cloud is used to do which of the following?
   a. Show which words appear most frequently in a corpus via visualization
   b. Display word frequency via a matrix
   c. Show rare words in the corpus
   d. Display words with opposite meanings in the corpus

7. Is it possible to perform text analysis without relying on word count? If yes, then which method can do so?
   a. Word cloud
   b. Latent Dirichlet Allocation
   c. Word embedding

ENDNOTES

1. Malik, V. S., B. M. Popkin, G. A. Bray, J.-P. Després, W. C. Willett, and F. B. Hu, "Sugar-Sweetened Beverages and Risk of Metabolic Syndrome and Type 2 Diabetes: A Meta-Analysis," *Diabetes Care* 33, no. 11 (2010): 2477–2483.

2. For the purposes of this chapter, we refer to these posts on X (previously Twitter) as tweets since the terminology in use at the time of data collection for this chapter was tweets.

3. Wickham, H., M. Averick, J. Bryan, W. Chang, L. D'Agostino McGowan, R. François, G. Grolemund, A. Hayes, L. Henry, J. Hester, M. Kuhn, T. L. Pedersen, E. Miller, S. M. Bache, K. Müller, J. Ooms, D. Robinson, D. P. Seidel, V. Spinu, K. Takahashi, D. Vaughan, C. Wilke, K. Woo, and H. Yutani, "Welcome to the Tidyverse," *Journal of Open Source Software* 4, no. 43 (2019), 1686, https://doi.org/10.21105/joss.01686.

4. Silge, Julia, and David Robinson, "tidytext: Text Mining and Analysis Using Tidy Data Principles in R," *Journal of Open Source Software* 1, no. 3 (2016), https://doi.org/10.21105/joss.00037.

5. Fellows, Ian, "wordcloud: Word Clouds," R package version 2.6, August 24, 2018, https://CRAN.R-project.org/package=wordcloud.

PART II

MARKETING ANALYTICS

5 MARKET SEGMENTATION USING CLUSTERING ALGORITHMS

CONTENTS

LEARNING OBJECTIVES

1. Understand the STPs of marketing
2. Decide how to segment customers
3. Learn the different bases of segmentation
4. Cluster to segment customers with *k*-means and *k*-medoid
5. Use *k*-means for finding customer segments to target
6. Interpret the output of clustering analysis

5.1 SEGMENTING CUSTOMERS

Vegan-Always is a new restaurant opening in Phoenix. It wants to send out coupons to customers who enjoy vegan food. Should it send these coupons to all residents of Phoenix? While this can be done, not only would such extensive coupon distribution become very expensive, but not everyone would be interested in the restaurant's offerings. Since not all customers are alike or share the same tastes, sending the same marketing message to everyone is not efficient or profitable. The best strategy for Vegan-Always is to divide the entire population of Phoenix in such a way that it can send the coupons only to those who are likely to visit the restaurant. One way the restaurant can do this is by using psychographics or lifestyle factors. People who are more environmentally conscious have turned to veganism and might be more interested in such a restaurant.

Similarly, demographics can be another way to find groups of customers who would be relevant for the restaurant. Such a process of dividing the market into groups of customers with similar characteristics and selecting the most appropriate group(s) for the business to target is called market segmentation. One way to think of segmentation is as a comprise between mass marketing (which assumes that all customers are the same) and individual-level customization (which assumes that all customers are unique). Instead of targeting each customer, segmentation allows a business to target groups of customers who are similar in the way they respond to the product. In today's data-driven markets, it is now possible to segment at a deeper level; hence, microsegmenting is becoming popular. For example, based on past buying behavior and similarity to other customers, Amazon has the ability to create microsegments and recommend very specific products to each of its customers.

The first step in market segmentation is to know why customers are buying a product. What benefits is the product offering that a customer may be interested in? The business needs to identify all customer needs that a product or service can fulfill. For instance, an automobile can be purchased to satisfy transportation needs or status needs. Knowing exactly which need is being satisfied for which group of customers can help in more accurate messaging and targeting. Identifying product-related needs can run the gamut from using traditional methods such as focus groups and surveys to the recent natural language processing (NLP) methods that can be used to mine customer opinions and reviews. Customer needs may not be restricted to just product features but may also include the company reputation. In the 1990s, Nike lost sales because of news that it was using child labor in its manufacturing units. The company had to change its working conditions because customers also wanted Nike to use the right practices. Once customers' needs are identified, customers can be categorized into groups with similar needs that form the different *segments* for that business. Developing a market with an imaginary buyer whose characteristics are inaccurate is a recipe for failure. Many products have failed not because they were bad but because they were marketed to the wrong set of customers.

After businesses have grouped customers with similar characteristics in terms of how they respond to product benefits, they can then decide which of these customer groups are most profitable to target. The process of determining which of the segments offer good market opportunities is called *targeting*. Finally, when businesses have segmented customers and decided which of these segments to target, they need to determine how they want to position their products in the minds of their customers. *Positioning* can be described as instilling a meaning in customers' minds that is unique to that product. We will first understand segmentation in detail before moving on to targeting and positioning. Segmentation, targeting, and positioning are generally known as the *STPs of marketing* since these three steps tend to be conducted together.

An initial step in segmentation is to group customers by similarities in their characteristics. Customers may seek similar benefits from a product because they live in the same region. For instance, customers who share geographic similarity may face the same weather conditions; people living in colder climes may need heavier jackets that can provide warmth compared to those living in warmer places where such jackets may not be necessary.

We next discuss the different basis on which customers could be grouped together in terms of similar characteristics.

5.5.1 Basis of Segmentation

Geographic. Customers can be segmented based on where they live. For instance, an insurance company might offer different types of insurance based on whether customers are located in regions prone to tornadoes, floods, or earthquakes.

Demographic. A very common way to segment customers is by demographic features such as age, education, gender, income, and occupation. For example, businesses may target millennials differently from baby boomers. Baby boomers account for a large share of the market currently because they control a major portion of the disposable income in the United States, which makes them a very attractive segment of the market. Hence, it is important that a business planning to target baby boomers understand the features of this segment. Are they health conscious? Are they tech savvy? Would they be willing to buy online? Are they philanthropic compared to other segments? Businesses also need to keep in mind that features defining a group change with time. Women now purchase repair tools as often as men.

Psychological. Customers can be segmented based on their different psychological factors, such as motivation, personality, and perceptions. Customers can purchase a brand to satisfy a prestige motive or for a functional motive. Rolex and Timex both manufacture watches, but people might be buying them for different motives. Personality can also be used to segment customers. Companies could consider the Big 5 personality traits[1] such as whether an individual is extroverted, disinhibited, neurotic, conscientious, or open to experience. Or a business could focus on personality traits that have been shown to affect marketplace decisions, such as impulsivity, loyalty, frugality, innovativeness, variety seeking, and risk aversion. Despite psychological factors being very informative of how customers may behave in the marketplace, it is difficult to obtain this information. Until recently, one way has been through the use of surveys, but this cannot be done for all customers and may be inconvenient and expensive. Some work has demonstrated that digital footprints of customers can be used to predict their personality. Digital footprints can be in the form of text, messages in online forums, number of likes, size of the networks frequented, and so on. Knowing the personality of customers allows for deeper customization of messages and recommendations targeting these individuals.

Sociocultural. This could include stages in the life cycle, such as whether one is single, married, or an empty nester, or social class, such as whether one belongs to the upper, lower, middle, or working class. It also could include cultural values, a very personal way that individuals define their core beliefs. Since cultural segmentation maps onto core beliefs and values, it can help the business or brand connect with a customer at a more meaningful level. In this age of globalization, with products marketed across the world, being able to connect to unique cultures is a challenge and yet a big asset if it can be done successfully.

Psychographic. The psychographic basis of segmentation includes activities, interests, and opinions of customers. Customers who like to vacation in Yellowstone are likely to share similar interests and require different messaging tactics than those who prefer a Disneyland vacation. Customers with different political opinions (e.g., conservative versus liberal) may respond to different marketing strategies. Those who are risk averse may not be open to buying a product that is positioned as adventurous.

Benefit Sought. What kind of benefits are people likely to look for when buying a product? Let's take the example of running shoes. They could provide more than one benefit, such as durability, comfort, speed, and appearance. They could even be used for some form of social signaling to inform others that one is a runner. Multivitamins are another example of a product that could convey different benefits for different segments of customers—such as strength, prevention of illness, and boosting of immunity.

Usage Volume. Customers can be segmented based on how often they buy a product and how often they use it (i.e., whether they are heavy, medium, or light users). It is possible that heavy users form a smaller percentage of the total users of a product but may actually buy a substantial share of the product. Hence, they are an important segment to focus on.

Product Attitude. Having information about the type of attitude customers hold about a brand can help determine how they will react to a new or modified offering by the brand. Some customers may have extremely favorable or extremely unfavorable brand attitudes. For example, some PC users would not think of using a Mac, and vice versa. Such potentially nonconvertible customer segments may not be worth targeting.

5.2 TARGETING POTENTIAL CUSTOMERS

Segmentation reveals specific market opportunities. Once customers have been segmented based on how they respond to product features, the business needs to evaluate the customer segments and decide which to target. It rarely happens that a product has mass appeal. Therefore, finding the segments that are likely to purchase the product is important. We can understand the process of selecting viable segments to target through the following questions that a business needs to ask.

- Are there enough segments in the market worth targeting? Having a product that is liked by a very small group of customers indicates that the business may have a niche product, which may not be profitable on a broader level.
- Is the segment stable, and will it remain stable for some time? It's not ideal if the target segments are comprised of people who are interested in fads. Growing and stable segments are more attractive and more likely to be profitable in the long term.

- Are the segments accessible? For instance, a large segment of customers may be interested in the product but may be in a place where it cannot be accessed easily.
- How well does this product compare with the competition in the chosen target segments? If the product is not the innovator or the first entrant in the market, chances are there are one or more businesses already catering to the segments that the business finds attractive. The business needs to find out how their product compares to existing products. If the business already has very strong competitors catering to a segment and the segment is also very brand loyal, it may be very hard to break into such a market.

5.3 POSITIONING THE PRODUCT IN CUSTOMERS' MINDS

Positioning is defined as an effort by a business to identify a unique selling proposition that allows its product to occupy a clear, distinctive, and attractive position in the minds of target customers relative to competing products in the market. Successful positioning includes communicating the benefits of the product as well as communicating a unique selling proposition.

Many examples exist of businesses and their brands occupying a unique position in the minds of their customers. Some are so successful that the brands have become synonymous with the product category. For instance, one says Kleenex to mean facial tissue, FedEx to mean shipping, or Xerox to mean photocopying. Oral-B realized that if it wanted customers to change their toothbrushes rather than keep using worn-out ones, the company needed to communicate this to the customer. The company introduced a patented dye on the brush head that fades with usage and indicates that it is time to get a new toothbrush. Lay's tries to position itself on taste through its slogan of *Betcha can't eat just one*, and Volkswagen positions itself by focusing on driving pleasure with its tagline *Drivers wanted.*

A brand can position itself based on a specific product attribute, or it can position itself in comparison to a competitor's offering. Some automobile brands position their vehicles using product attributes; for example, Honda and Toyota focus on durability, reliability, and functional benefits while Volvo focuses on safety and Volkswagen focuses on drivability. Other automobile brands position themselves versus other brands, such as Hyundai against Toyota, to show that they offer the same or greater benefits.

We next discuss how segmentation has changed in a data-rich marketplace.

5.4 DATA-DRIVEN SEGMENTATION

As mentioned earlier, the higher volume of data available to businesses makes the following types of segmentation feasible: segmentation based on behavioral data, dynamic segmentation, and microsegmentation.

5.4.1 Behavioral Segmentation

In the world of Big Data, an abundance of information, including click-through and search data, is available about people's behavior: which products they are buying, where they are buying these products, how much they are paying, whether a product is more likely to sell in specific packaging, and so on. Behavioral data can be used to extrapolate demographic and psychographic information. Many times it is difficult to find out the specific personality traits of consumers that result in their purchasing a brand (e.g., is a customer more or less frugal?). However, behavioral data, even from social media, can be used to predict the general personality of customers. Moreover, with the proliferation of online retailers, it has become easy to conduct ongoing studies to figure out customer preferences. Instead of trying to determine the segment of customers that is most likely to purchase a brand by a study based on attitudes (e.g., how much do customers like this brand?), a product can be introduced via small samples, and actual purchase behavior can be monitored. Also, based on sales data, products can be modified in real time based on which features customers most prefer. Hence, data-driven markets allow a feedback loop by which businesses can observe actual customer purchases and fine-tune market segments.

5.4.2 Dynamic Segmentation

Another outcome of rich data about customers allows a business to keep updating its customer segments. Rather than segmenting all customers once and assuming that their tastes are not going to change, dynamic segmentation assumes that tastes will change and keeps updating what offering would be best preferred by a specific customer segment. Many aspects in an individual's life can change. For example, a chocolate manufacturer cannot assume that just because a customer has purchased dark chocolate in the past they will continue to do so. Their personal, family, or health needs could change, causing them to move to buying sugar-free or nut-free chocolates. Dynamic segmentation takes into account the possibility that customer tastes change and, hence, that the segment they belong to is not static. Again, it is important that businesses hone their ability to sift through the wealth of information available to them and use the most recent information, whether behavioral or otherwise, to segment customers.

5.4.3 Microsegments

As mentioned earlier, it has now become possible to cater to very small segments of customers by understanding their preferences in depth and customizing products accordingly. This also leads to hyperpersonalization, where each offering uniquely targets a specific customer based on both demographic and behavioral data gathered about that customer. For instance, insurance companies can augment existing data such as age, gender, and current product portfolio with online behavior such as time spent on their website to better segment customers and offer the customer a very customized product.

As important as data are for segmentation, the algorithm chosen to perform the segmentation is equally important. Many times we just have different types of data about customers without information about a business outcome such as sales or whether or not such a customer is loyal. That is, the data tend to be unlabeled. Because we do not have any outcome labels, we do not have the ability to compare model performances. The most common task of unsupervised learning is exploratory analysis, which uses visualization methods (the simplest being clustering) to examine the data and gather insights.

Let's go over what algorithms are commonly used for segmentation.

5.5 CLUSTERING ALGORITHMS FOR SEGMENTATION

Clustering is frequently used to segment customers into groups with similar need sets. For instance, if we want to find out which of our customers are most likely to recommend our product or our business, we can cluster them by similarity of attributes and try to gather insights from the clusters formed. Clustering is the process of grouping together data points that share some similarity, such that data points within a cluster are more similar to one another as well as more dissimilar to data points in a different cluster. Hence, clustering does exploratory data analysis and is considered an unsupervised algorithm because it explores data patterns rather than confirms a specific relationship. Clustering algorithms are used when the data lacks labels.

Several clustering algorithms exist, such as *k*-means, *k*-nearest neighbors, hierarchical and Gaussian mixture models, and so on; there are several types and subtypes of clustering algorithms as depicted in Figure 5.1. Clustering mainly occurs either by partitioning a large set of observations into smaller sets or by creating a treelike structure to depict the relationship between observations. In clustering, the process of dividing is called partition clustering, and *k*-means, *k*-nearest neighbors, and mixture models fall into this category. Clustering by creating a treelike structure, also called a dendrogram, involves relating each observation to another observation. Such hierarchical clustering can build up from one observation, find the nearest next observation, and so on to create a tree structure (agglomerative clustering), or it can begin by considering all observations to be in one cluster and then break down the cluster using the distance metric (divisive clustering).

FIGURE 5.1 ■ Clustering Methods

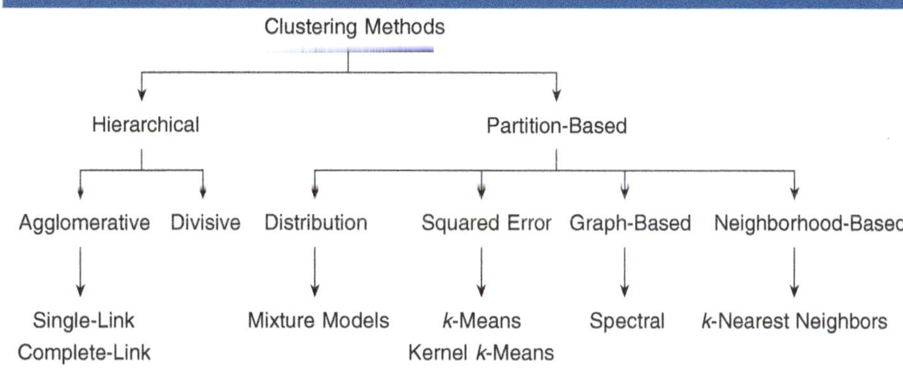

We will use *k*-means, as well as a slight improvement—*k*-medoid—as clustering methods for segmentation.

5.5.1 The Relationship Between Distance and Similarity

The *k*-means algorithm is based on the intuitive notion that similar observations are likely to be clustered together. The distance between observations is a way to measure similarity: Less distance between observations implies that the observations are likely to be similar, and more distance indicates dissimilar observations. Thus, if the distance between two observations is less, it implies that the observations are similar and can be clustered together within the same cluster. If the distance between two observations is large, it implies that they are dissimilar and probably cannot be clustered together.

We next discuss how distance is used as the metric to measure similarity of the observations.

Let's understand how distance is calculated between two observations. Assume that the two observations are from two customers and that we have information about two variables— age and income. We can use these two variables to assess the level of similarity between these two customers. If we call the two customers A and B, then the two variables can be depicted as follows for customer A:

$$x_{A1} = \text{age}, x_{A2} = \text{income}$$

And for customer B:

$$x_{B1} = \text{age}, x_{B2} = \text{income}$$

The distance between two customers ($A \rightarrow B$) is calculated using the following formula, which is also called the Euclidean distance formula.

$$distance_{A\rightarrow B} = \sqrt{(x_{A1} - x_{B1})^2 + (x_{A2} - x_{B2})^2}$$

We use the two different attributes x_1 and x_2 for both A and B to find the distance between A and B. If we had information on a third customer, let's say C, then we could determine distance measures between customers A and B, B and C, and A and C. Using this distance, we could state whether A was more similar to B or to C since less distance indicates more similarity. Clustering algorithms utilize distance as a way to group observations together. Observations that are more similar are clustered together but separately from observations that are less similar. We next discuss the most commonly used clustering algorithm, *k*-means.

5.5.2 The *k*-Means Algorithm

For any clustering algorithm, the goal is to find groups of similar observations among all the observations in the given dataset. To accomplish this goal, the *k*-means algorithm uses Euclidean distance to find out which observations are more versus less similar. But this would become a very inefficient task if we needed to find distance estimates between each observation and every other observation. Therefore, the first step in a *k*-means algorithm is to decide how many clusters we, the user, want the algorithm to output. This is an issue with many clustering algorithms, where the number of clusters has to be provided by the user, and the algorithm accordingly clusters observations into the specified number of groups. For instance, if we ask the algorithm to cluster 100 observations into 5 groups, it will go ahead and do so, and if we ask it to cluster the same 100 observations into 20 groups, it will do that also. We will discuss the issue of choosing the appropriate number of clusters later.

We illustrate the steps of the *k*-means algorithm as follows:

1. Randomly select *k* points as initial centroids
2. **repeat**
3. Assign data points to the closest centroid
4. Recalculate the centroid of each cluster
5. **until** *Centroids do not change*

Now let's visually understand these steps using a figure. Figure 5.2(a) shows observations, with each point representing a customer's age (*x*-axis) and income (*y*-axis). We set $k = 3$, which means we want the algorithm to assign observations to one of the three clusters. Once we provide the number of clusters, the *k*-means algorithm randomly selects *k* locations as center points or *centroids*. Figure 5.2(b) shows these randomly selected centroids. The distance from each observation to each of the *k* centroids is measured, and then each observation is assigned to the centroid closest to it. At the end of the first iteration, each observation has been assigned to one of the *k* clusters. The color of the points in Figure 5.2(b) indicates their cluster membership.

FIGURE 5.2 ■ *k*-Means

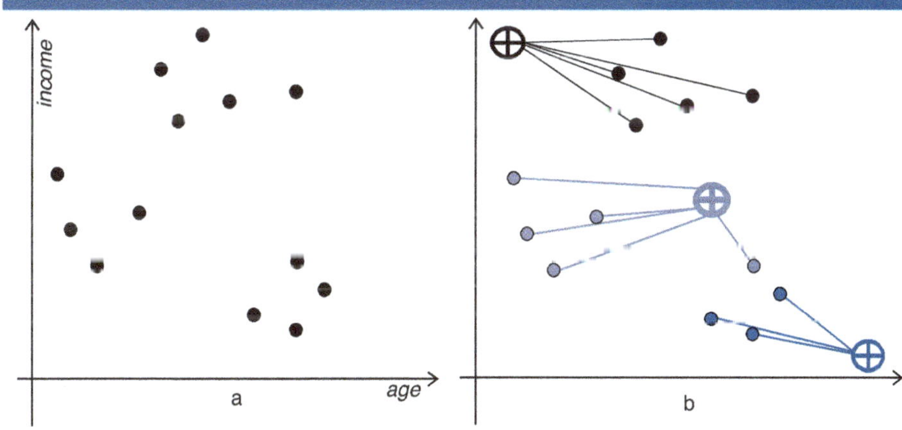

The *k*-means algorithm next finds the new centroids of the newly formed *k* clusters. Recall that a centroid is nothing but the central point of a cluster. Since the initial centroids were randomly chosen, we can see that the location of the new centroid changes (see Figure 5.3(a)). Again, the distance of each observation to these new *k* centroids is calculated, and the observations are reassigned to the centroid closest to it.

FIGURE 5.3 ■ *k*-Means After Iteration

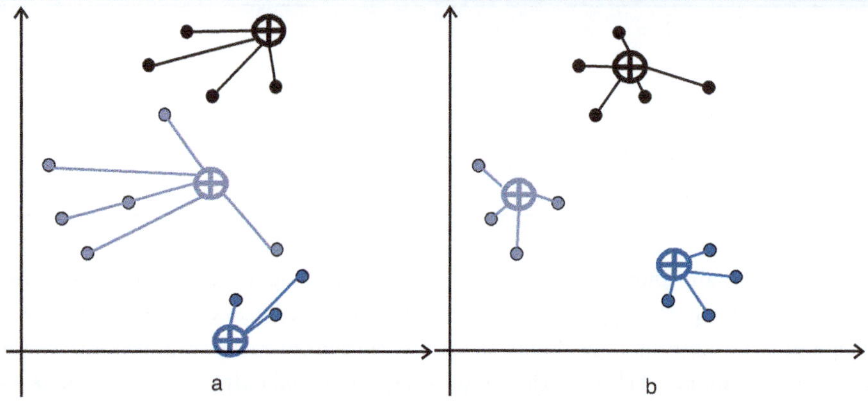

In this next iteration, *k* clusters are again formed. In the subsequent iteration, centroids are calculated for these *k* clusters, and the process is repeated till the centroids do not change (see Figure 5.3(b)). The stability of the centroids indicates that this is the optimal allocation of observations to *k* clusters. If we ask for a different number of clusters, then the *k*-means algorithm will go through the same process until it finds the optimal allocation of observations to the number of clusters that we have specified.

5.5.3 The *k*-Medoid Algorithm

One of the issues with *k*-means is that outliers can influence the clusters that are generated. An improvement over the *k*-means algorithm is *k*-medoid, which modifies *k*-means to take care of this issue. While *k*-means randomly chooses centroids of various clusters, *k*-medoid first chooses data points as centers of clusters. Then instead of using Euclidean distance, it uses Manhattan distance to find the closest cluster center to a point. Manhattan distance is calculated by measuring the absolute distance between any two points and uses the following formula:

$$d_{manhattan} = \sum_{i=1}^{n} |x_i - y_i|$$

By using Manhattan distance to calculate the proximity of a point to a cluster center, *k*-medoid is less influenced by outliers and noise in the data.

An example of using *k*-means and *k*-medoid to segment customers will help us understand how the algorithm can be used for segmentation.

5.5.4 Using *k*-Means to Segment Customers

We pick an example with just two variables because it is easy to visualize, although *k*-means can be used for a large number of variables. (The data for this example are hypothetical.) A common query of most retail stores is whether they should target customers who spend more or customers who have been their patrons for longer (i.e., is amount of money spent or duration more important?). Therefore, we have two input variables: *amount spent* and *duration of patronage*. We first scale the data by subtracting the means and dividing by the standard deviation (details of scaling and standardization are provided in the Technical Appendix). Scaling the data prevents data distortions that would occur in clustering if the input variables are on different scales; the variable with a bigger unit would be overrepresented.

Then we tell the *k*-means algorithm how many clusters we want it to output. This is an important consideration for most clustering algorithms, which require that the user specify the number of clusters into which the observations need to be segmented. Here we ask it to output three clusters. Figure 5.4 illustrates the three clusters.

FIGURE 5.4 ■ *k*-Means Segmentation Plot

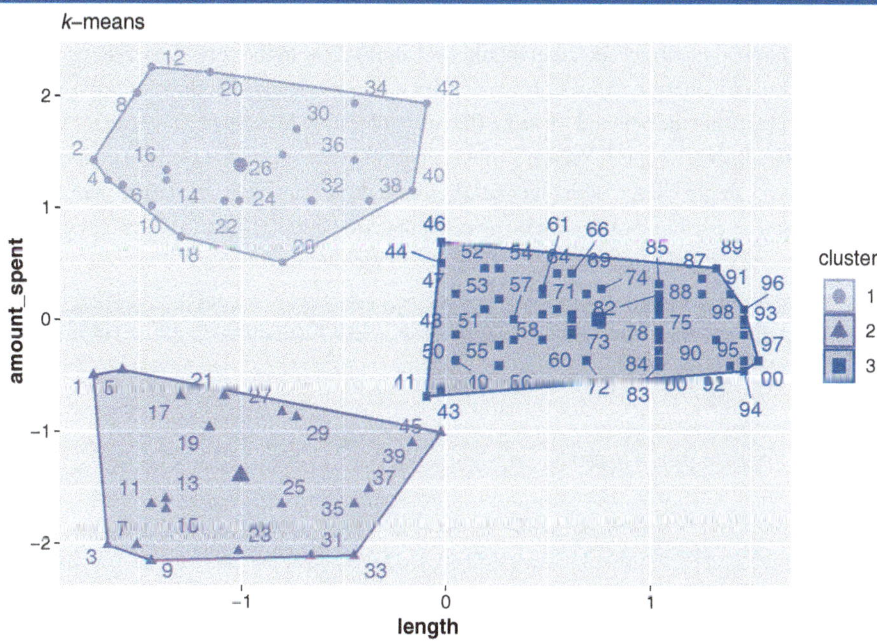

Along with the cluster, we can also instruct the algorithm to output the value of the cluster center. This information is useful for interpreting the output because it provides the average characteristics of a customer in that cluster or segment.

```
##        length  amount_spent
## 1  -1.0092435    1.38324959
## 2  -1.0058705   -1.39737047
## 3   0.7424104    0.00520243
```

We can then interpret that members of cluster 1 have an average patronage duration of -1.009 months and have spent \$1.383,[2] whereas members of cluster 2 have a similar patronage length to those in cluster 1 (-1.006 months) but have spent substantially more (-\$1.397). One insight that the business can derive from these two segments is that customers in cluster 2 seem to spend more and might be more profitable for the business to target. It would also be important for the business to find out what features of customers in cluster 1 make them stay for the same duration but not spend as much. Would some form of incentive such as coupons for loyal customers motivate them to spend more?

An important question (some even call it a challenge) in any clustering analysis is knowing the best number of clusters to choose. Since we must specify the number of clusters for the algorithm, how do we know whether three or seven will be the best number of clusters? Many times it depends on the question we are trying to answer. Or we can use past information that shows the number of clusters obtained when we used similar data. A *silhouette* helps us answer the question of choosing the optimal number of clusters. A silhouette analysis is based on the simple intuition that if an observation is in a cluster, then that observation should be closer to those in the same cluster than to those in other clusters. A silhouette coefficient for each observation is calculated and varies between -1 and +1, with +1 indicating the best and -1 being the worst allocation to a cluster. The average silhouette coefficient for all observations is known as the average *silhouette width*. An average silhouette width near 1 indicates a tight cluster, with observations in the cluster close together rather than spread all over. For instance, if a four-cluster solution gives a silhouette value of 0.7, and a seven-cluster solution gives a silhouette value of 0.3, it means that the four-cluster solution is better.

FIGURE 5.5 ■ Silhouette Width: *k*-Means

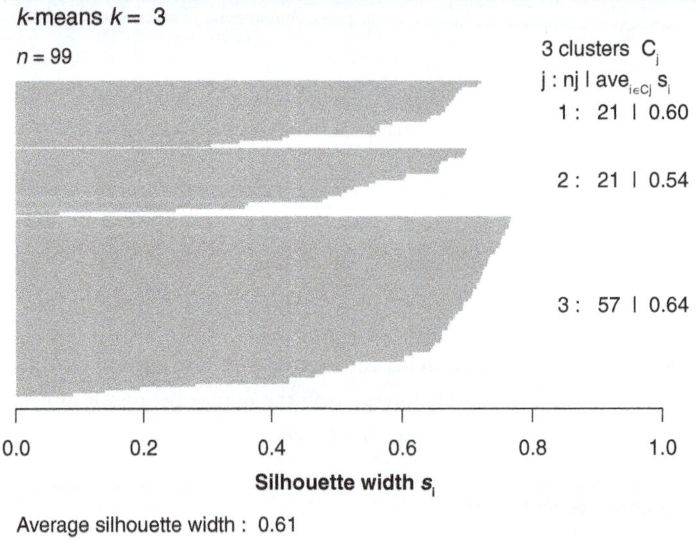

In our case, we find that with a three-cluster solution the average silhouette width is 0.61, as shown in Figure 5.5. We can try different values of *k* and see how the average silhouette width changes. We can next run the same analysis using *k*-medoid and instruct the algorithm to output three clusters (see Figure 5.6).

FIGURE 5.6 ■ *k*-Medoid Segmentation Plot

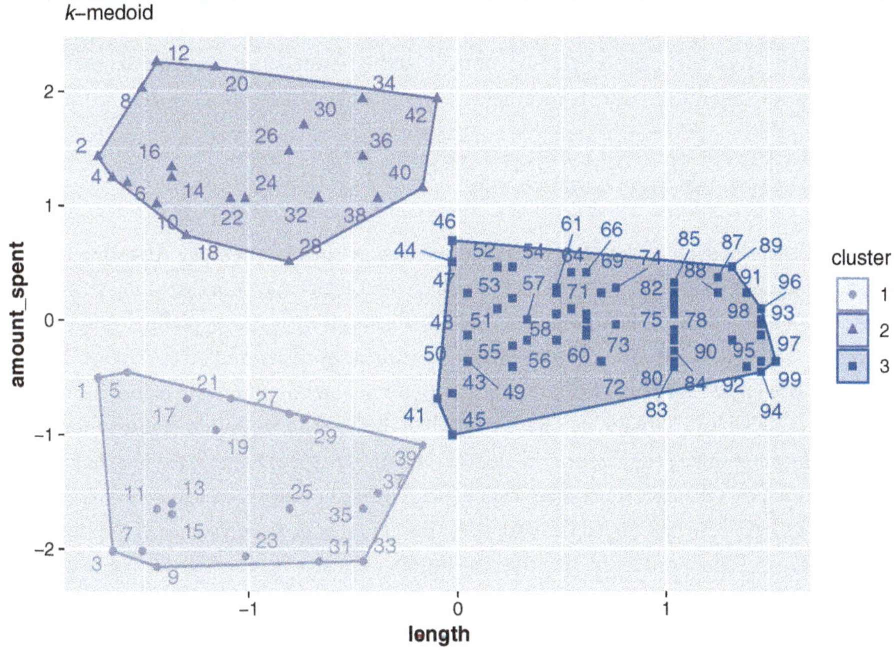

FIGURE 5.7 ■ Silhouette Width: *k*-Medoid

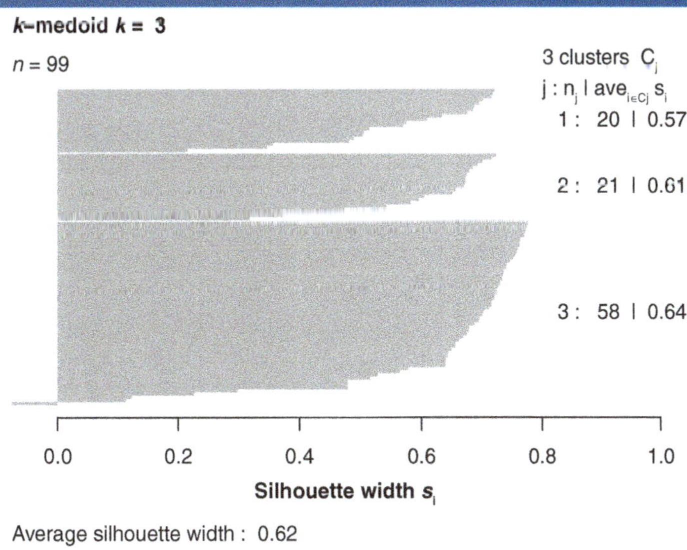

In this case we see that the average silhouette width using *k*-medoid is 0.62 (see Figure 5.7) and not much different from a *k*-means solution. This could be because there are not many outliers in the data. If the number of outliers increased, the *k*-medoid would output a better solution.

Therefore, we can conclude our clustering analysis with the following insights. When we want to perform segmentation, we can use a clustering algorithm such *k*-means or *k*-medoid.

We use clustering because our data are unlabeled (i.e., they do not have an outcome label). In the example, we find that when amount spent and patronage duration are used and we ask for three clusters, we can obtain the average characteristics of customers in the three clusters. The differences between these customers inform us how the business can present effective product offerings to customers in these three segments.

5.6 IMPLEMENTATION USING R: SEGMENTATION USING k-MEANS AND k-MEDOID

To analyze and plot data, we will use two packages: `cluster`[3] and `factoextra`.[4] After importing the data, we center and scale it using the `scale()` function with `center = TRUE` and `scale = TRUE` options; `center = TRUE` subtracts the column means of a variable from their corresponding column values, and `scale = TRUE` divides the (centered) columns of a variable by their standard deviations. This process converts values of each variable into their *z* scores. This is an important step before cluster analysis since each variable of a dataset can be measured on different scales. In our dataset, for example, duration of store patronage is measured in months, but amount spent is measured in dollars. Scaling the data ensures that there are no distortions due to difference in scales used across variables.

Once we have read and scaled the data (`df`), the actual code to run *k*-means is quite simple. In the `kmeans()` function, centers specifies the number of clusters (*k*), then `nstart = 25` sets 25 initial random centroids and selects the best one. A higher value of `nstart` gives more stable solutions, but for larger datasets this may end up taking more computing time.

```
library(cluster)
library(factoextra)

set.seed(12345) #Set seed for reproducibility

df <- read.csv(url(
"http://data.mishra.us/files/chapter_segmentation/segmentation_kmeans.csv"))

df <- scale(df,center = TRUE, scale = TRUE)

k_means <- kmeans(df, centers = 3, nstart = 25)
```

The following code helps produce Figure 5.4 using `fviz_cluster()` function. `repel = TRUE` prevents datapoints from lumping together and makes them readable.

```
fviz_cluster(k_means, data = df,
             repel = TRUE,
             main = "k-means segmentation plot"
)
```

We can also print cluster centers for each of the three clusters, as we saw in Figure 5.4. This is very helpful when our data have more than two variables and it becomes harder to plot clusters. By using cluster centers, we can assess the average characteristics of each cluster. Consistent with the plot, here our output shows that members of cluster 1 have an average patronage duration of –1.009 months and have spent $1.383, whereas members of cluster 2 have a patronage length of –1.006 months and have spent –$1.397. Due to centering and scaling, amount spent and length have negative values. Cluster numbers might change in different runs of the `R` code (e.g., cluster 1 may be labeled as cluster 2).

```
print(k_means$centers)

##         length amount_spent
## 1   -1.0092435   1.38324959
## 2   -1.0058705  -1.39737047
## 3    0.7424104   0.00520243
```

Silhouette, a tool to detect the quality of clusters, can help in estimating the right value of *k*. The silhouette coefficient varies between –1 and +1. An average value (also known as average silhouette width) near 1 shows a tight cluster, with observations within a cluster close together compared to observations between clusters. As the value moves away from +1 to –1, it indicates reduced within-cluster cohesion.

The following code calculates distance and generates silhouette plots, as we saw in Figure 5.5. The `dist()` function calculates the Euclidean distance between points (`method="euclidean"`).

```
dis=dist(df, method="euclidean")
sil = silhouette (k_means$cluster, dis)
plot(sil,main=paste("K-Mean k = ", 3))
```

The silhouette plot shows that the average silhouette width is 0.58. We can try different values of *k* (or `centers` in the *k*-means calculation) to see how the average silhouette width changes.

The following code performs *k*-medoid clustering on the same data. There are only two differences in this code compared to the one that produces *k*-means. First, instead of the `k-means()` function, we use `pam()`, which stands for "partitioning around medoids." Second, for cluster analysis and calculation of silhouette width, we use Manhattan distance. This produces the cluster plot and silhouette width we saw in Figures 5.6 and 5.7.

```
k_medoid <- pam (scale(df), k = 3, metric = "manhattan")

fviz_cluster(k_medoid, data = df,
             repel = TRUE,
             main = "k-means segmentation plot"
)
```

```
dis=dist(df, method="manhattan")
sil = silhouette (k_medoid$clustering, dis) # for silhouette plots
plot(sil, main=paste("K-Medoid k = ",3))
```

Since there are not many outliers, the results of *k*-means and *k*-medoid are very similar.

5.7 UNDERSTANDING THE CHAPTER

Students are encouraged to answer the following questions. They can then review the chapter to check their answers.

1. If a car manufacturer customizes features of the car based on the terrain, which type of segmentation is the manufacturer using?
2. Which of the following characteristics is *true* about segmentation?
   a. Having a unique selling proposition
   b. Positioning the product in the minds of the customers
   c. Grouping together customers based on similar need sets
   d. Grouping together customers based on opposite need sets
   e. Communicating the benefits of the product through coupons
3. Can a business having global operations ignore sociocultural aspects while advertising the product in different world regions?
4. Would it be advisable for a business to target a segment of consumers that many of its competitors are also targeting because that set of customers has the maximum likelihood of purchasing the product? Discuss pros and cons of such a strategy.
5. How can a business determine the optimal number of segments in which to group customers if it is using a *k*-means algorithm?
6. How does a *k*-medoid algorithm improve clustering over the *k*-means algorithm?

ENDNOTES

1. Costa, P. T., and R. R. McCrae, "The Revised Neo Personality Inventory (NEO-PI-R)," *The SAGE Handbook of Personality Theory and Assessment* 2, no. 2 (2008): 179–198.
2. Due to centering and scaling, amount spent and length have negative values.
3. Maechler, M., P. Rousseeuw, A. Struyf, M. Hubert, and K. Hornik, "cluster: Cluster Analysis Basics and Extensions," R package version 2.1.2 (2021).
4. Kassambara, A., and F. Mundt, "factoextra: Extract and Visualize the Results of Multivariate Data Analyses," R package version 1.0.7, April 1, 2020, https://CRAN.R-project.org/package=factoextra.

6 PREDICTING PRICES WITH NEURAL NETS

CONTENTS

LEARNING OBJECTIVES

1. Understand the influence of product price on customer choice
2. Recognize the impact of perceived value on determining the right price
3. Understand neural networks, both shallow and deep
4. Interpret the output of neural networks
5. Use neural networks for price prediction

6.1 UNDERSTANDING PRODUCT PRICING

Managers across businesses consider product pricing the single most important decision that they make because price can influence whether a customer decides to purchase a product or not. Such a buy/no-buy decision is said to determine whether a business succeeds or fails. Take the example of MoviePass, a movie theater subscription service. It was hailed as a savior that would revive people's interest in watching movies in theaters in the age of online streaming services. Introduced in the summer of 2017, MoviePass initially offered a subscription of $10 per month, permitting unlimited movie access for which a member could watch one movie per day—an amazing offer! MoviePass quickly increased its subscription base and grew to include about 3 million members.

But if one takes a moment to think about the pricing for MoviePass, it appears unsustainable. Consider a member who watches even three movies a month. They would pay just $10 for the three movies, but MoviePass would have to pay much more than $10 to the theaters. How is such a pricing model sustainable? It turned out that it is not. The more members utilized the service, the more MoviePass had to pay to theaters, creating a financially detrimental loop. By 2018, MoviePass was facing troubled waters. It increased its subscription fee and also limited access to movies during the first week of their release. With further troubles such as its glitchy app, as well as concerns about security, the stock of MoviePass's parent company plummeted, and the service was discontinued in 2019. MoviePass became a case study of pricing mistakes that businesses should not commit. It offered too low a price when customers might have paid more for the service. Its initial price was unsustainable since it was well below the actual cost of the service. Hence, how could it, or any business, expect to make any profit in this scenario? It introduced a service (watching movies in a movie theater) that did not have many takers in the first place given the popularity of streaming services. More important, MoviePass did not realize that its competition, the streaming services, offered a lot more for a lot less.

6.2 THE POWER OF PRICING

Price directly and significantly affects profit margins. It is considered one of the most important levers that a business can adjust in order to increase profitability. Pricing can help a business increase its profit to a greater extent than can changes in other business variables such as advertising, cost, and supply chain. In practice as well as in theory, it has been shown that increasing price by even 1% can significantly increase profits.

Price is also considered a signal of value and quality. When customers evaluate a product's quality, they have to use other proxy variables that can be compared and quantified to decide whether the quality of the product is high or low. Quality by itself is an intangible variable since it cannot be directly measured. Therefore, price becomes the common metric used to evaluate the quality of a product. In fact, customers commonly use the heuristic of "high quality, high price" when making their product purchase decisions.

However, many businesses are uncertain of how to increase or decrease prices because they are hugely concerned about how their customers may react to such a price change. For instance, a hotel chain can consider increasing its room prices by just 1% because it has added a service. However, the hotel chain knows that when customers make hotel reservations they will be using a travel search engine like Kayak to decide which hotel to stay in. Such engines predominantly use price as the variable of comparison, and even a difference of $5 or $10 can sway a customer's choice. On the other hand, businesses are wary of decreasing prices because a price reduction can cause the product to be considered less of a premium product since customers hold the belief that premium products do not need to offer discounts to sell. In addition, once a product's price is reduced, this becomes the reference price in the minds of consumers, which makes it difficult for the business to subsequently increase price.

Multiple articles and even television shows have debated the question of whether the price is right. Many times new entrants in an established industry (e.g., paint) might just use competitor prices as a benchmark and price their products lower (if they offer the same benefits and want to gain market share) or price at parity (if they offer more benefits than their competitors). But what if the new entrant is offering paint that uses sustainable practices that make its manufacturing cost higher? Or what if the industry is not well established and customers do not have clear reference prices? In such cases calculating the *perceived value* of a product or brand helps the business determine the optimal price. We will discuss that next.

6.2.1 Perceived Value

Determining the right price for a product is affected by multiple factors. First, managers are uncertain whether customers will be willing to pay this price or whether they will perceive it as too high or too low. If the product is priced too high, customers won't buy it. If it's priced too low, customers might question whether there is something wrong with the product. Another important consideration is that the business is leaving money on the table if customers would be willing to pay more for the product. So how can managers determine the optimal price? They can learn what the *perceived value* is for a product in the minds of their customers. Perceived value can be defined as the maximum price that customers are willing to pay for a product.

When businesses offer their brands in the marketplace, it is unlikely that they are the only ones to do so; many competing brands are also being offered. For instance, in the toothpaste category a customer can choose from Colgate, Crest, Sensodyne, Close-up, Pepsodent, Arm & Hammer, and many others. They offer very similar benefits, so how can Colgate stand out and become the brand chosen by the customers? Merely listing product features may not be sufficient; the brand needs to describe how the features translate into benefits for the customer. That is, the brand must help the customer see beyond features to actual benefits (fluoride helps fight tooth decay; calcium prevents plaque). This process of converting features to benefits is essential for increasing the perceived value of a brand. Higher perceived value results in greater willingness to pay because customers can see clearly why they are paying more for this brand. The most important outcome of higher perceived value is that it helps a brand stand out from its competition. The price of the product can be used to influence perceived value: Lower pricing such as that of Trader Joe's and Walmart can be used to convey a good deal, and premium pricing can be used by companies like Apple to convey exclusivity.

6.2.2 Price Wars

A second factor affecting what customers perceive to be the right price for a product is the presence of competing brands and the price they are asking for a comparable set of product features. If a competing brand sets a lower price for a product with a similar set of features, then that poses a threat to other brands, which would either have to lower their prices or offer more benefits for the same price. If a competitor offers a lower price than the other brands in a specific product category, it may spark a price war. Price wars occur when a firm in an industry (e.g., one airline) drops prices in an attempt to attract more customers to increase its market share. Price wars tend to have detrimental consequences for many businesses, especially those that are relatively small players in the field. In fact, price wars are often initiated by businesses that hold a larger market share and can sustain price cuts (which translate into lower profits) for longer. This causes many smaller entities to go out of business or sell out to the larger business, resulting in monopolistic environments. The 1992 airline pricing war is considered to have been detrimental for the airline industry[1]. It began in May 1992 with a Northwest Airlines promotion that allowed children traveling with an adult to fly free of charge. American Airlines responded to the challenge and cut fares by 50% on all its flights on all routes for the next few months. Every other airline responded by offering similar deep discounts. This resulted in big bargains for customers, who made so many reservations that they clogged phone lines! However, it did not go well for the airlines. American Airlines is said to have lost more than $1 billion while the industry as a whole lost around $13 billion. Similarly, in the mid-2010s, a streaming price war unfolded, involving major platforms like Netflix, Hulu, and Amazon Prime Video, each offering extensive content at competitive prices. New pricing models emerged, with AT&T TV Now and CBS All Access introducing plans from just $5.99 per month. While consumers enjoyed access to diverse content, streaming companies faced challenges in maintaining profitability due to need for more content and technological costs. The arrival of new competitors like Disney+ and Apple TV+ heightened competition, necessitating ongoing content creation and strategic pricing to attract and retain subscribers, thereby affecting financial sustainability.

6.2.3 Pricing Cues

A third factor affecting value perception includes several marketing activities that can nudge customers' reference prices. For instance, businesses have used messaging to inform customers that they are paying the right price. Product bundling such as "Buy one, get one free" is used to signal customers that they are getting a good deal or value for their money since they are getting two products for the price of one. Similarly, many price cues in the retail environment can make customers feel comfortable with the price they are paying. These cues include discount signs (25% or 50% off), prices ending in a 9 or .99, and price-match guarantees. Changing prices of signpost products has also been used by businesses to signal store pricing. Signpost products are products like milk or soda for which customers have a clear reference price; a higher-than-usual price for signpost products signals a premium store, and a lower price signals a discount store.

6.3 ROLE OF ANALYTICS IN PRICE PREDICTION

Therefore, finding the right price is an important decision for businesses because it influences profit margins, market share, and future growth potential. Businesses use different analytic methods to determine the optimal price given the information available in terms of input or predictor variables. For instance, if businesses are using competitors' prices or their own historical prices to estimate the price for a product, then methods such as linear regression or support vector regression can be used. If businesses want to estimate perceived value from customers, they can conduct surveys in the marketplace to figure out how high or low to price a product about which there is little past information (e.g., a new product for which there is no historical price information). Surge (or dynamic) pricing is also used by rideshare firms because they are unsure about demand and supply. Surge pricing allows demand to dictate pricing. For instance, Uber and Lyft increase ride prices if there is a lot of demand (e.g., if the pickup location is a crowded sports stadium post-match). They are equally likely to reduce prices if there is a lack of demand. Several online retailers use dynamic pricing to figure out the right price. If demand is high, then prices can be increased; but if demand for a product is low, then lowering prices to increase sales is a common strategy. The important factor for such businesses is to have the ability to monitor demand so that they can adjust prices in real time. Thus, they commonly use monitoring algorithms to set prices because they can provide not just quick but efficient price predictions. The algorithms monitor changes in demand/supply in real time and set prices accordingly. Since price is dependent on product features as well as competitor pricing, algorithms use these as inputs in their prediction.

We next consider how we can use algorithms for price prediction. The example we will be using in this chapter is that of estimating house prices by a large real estate firm. House prices are dependent on many internal and external factors. Current and anticipated levels of economic development in a city, location of the city as a tourist destination, and inflow versus outflow of population might be some of the external factors. Internal features of the house include number of bedrooms or bathrooms, views, and proximity to schools and shops. For the purposes of this chapter, we will use neural nets and see how they can be used for predicting house prices. Neural nets is a recent machine-learning method being used by businesses to improve their predictions. It is the basis of *deep learning* methods that we are hearing so much about! We will first gain a basic understanding of neural nets and then move on to using them for price prediction.

6.4 THE ARCHITECTURE OF NEURAL NETWORKS

The most intuitive way to describe a neural net is as an algorithm that mimics how neurons transfer information in the brain. To recap, an algorithm is a set of instructions put together in the form of a code that can perform a specific task. Our brain helps us process vast quantities of information such as understanding the meaning of text, doing complex calculations, deciphering what an image means, and, most important, creating new things such as a new painting, poem, or product. The basic aim of a neural net is to have the ability to process like the human brain. And just as our brain has many "deep" layers of processing, neural nets with many layers are called deep learning algorithms. To stay consistent with the terminology we will refer to predictors as features or input variables and to outcome variables as outputs.

Let's begin with a very simple example of trying to convert a weight from kilograms to pounds. If we know the conversion formula, then we are good. However, what if we did not know the formula? In that case we would have to guess and try different conversion values to see which one would give us the most accurate conversion. Let's also assume that we have been given one example that we can use to check our answer: 10 kilograms = 22.046 pounds. This is sometimes referred to as the *ground truth*. Armed with this information, let's try our first guess. It seems that the same weight would be expressed as a lower value if in kilograms but as a higher value if in pounds. Hence, the conversion from pounds to kilograms should be more than 1. Let's try 3.

Visually we can understand this as follows: The input circle shows the weight in kilograms, the processing part contains our conversion formula, and we receive an output. Each of these circles is also referred to as a *node* or *neuron*. The conversion value we are using is called a *weight* parameter. The output circle represents our *prediction*. Figure 6.1 represents the simplest-possible neural network.

FIGURE 6.1 ■ Simple Neural Net Logic

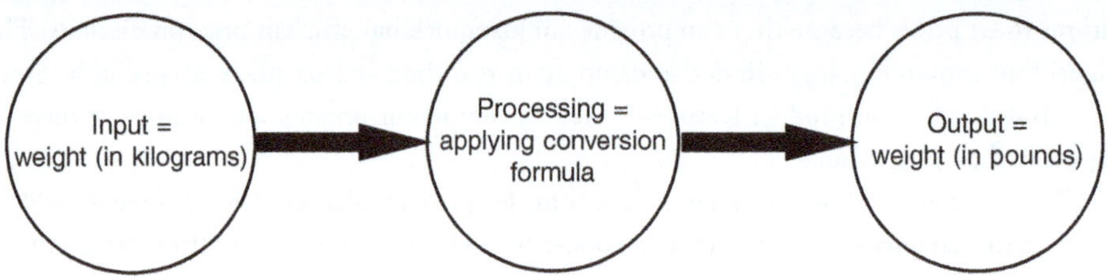

With our first guess (i.e., a weight of 3 pounds for an input of 10 kilograms), the processing stage multiplies 10 by 3 for an output answer of 30 pounds. How would we know whether this is correct or not? We can compare it with the example we have: 10 kilograms = 22.046 pounds. However, our calculations show that 10 kilograms = 30 pounds! So our answer is off by 7.954. This is the error in our prediction that we need to minimize as much as possible to make our predictions more accurate. Looking at the output, we can infer that if we reduced our weight a bit, we should be able to reduce the error. Let's try 2.5 as our updated weight; this gives an output of 25 pounds when 10 kilograms is the input. With this updated weight of 2.5, we get an error of 2.954 when compared with the ground truth. By updating the weight, we have moved closer to the actual value. If we further updated the weight to 2.0, we would receive an output of 20 pounds. This would give an error of -2.046. The negative value indicates that we have overshot the ground truth because we have moved from getting a positive error to a negative error. So we probably need to adjust the weight value to something between 2.5 and 2.0. This process of adjustment is called *tuning* the weight parameter. Eventually we will arrive at a value for the weight as 2.2046. Here, we used the error to adjust our weight values, so in essence we were *learning* from the error.

One question that we should ask is that if a regression can be used to predict the output from the inputs, why do we need neural networks? In our kilogram-to-pound example, the conversion formula for a linear regression would be in the form of a beta coefficient. If we had a series of kilogram values and their corresponding pound values, we could use a linear regression to estimate the beta coefficient. That is, the conversion formula in a neural net would be in the form of weights while for a linear regression it would be in the form of a beta coefficient. Moreover, in a regression framework, we can look at the beta coefficients and exactly state the direction and magnitude of influence of the input (predictor variable) on the output (outcome variable). Thus, while the beta coefficient gives us the ability to interpret the relationship between input and output, using a neural net for such an estimation task would not allow us to obtain information about the exact value of the weight that the neural net was learning and updating. The neural net learns the weight value from the available data and then uses it to predict the output value from provided input values. However, the neural net does not output the weight value it used in its prediction. That is the reason neural nets are called *black box methods*: They do not give us the ability to make such interpretations about the relationship between input and output variables. Why then do we use neural nets?

They are used for the following reasons. First, there may be several variables that can serve as inputs to the algorithm, and we do not have a good idea about which of these variables are most influential in predicting the outcome variable. In such an instance, an algorithm that can determine the most informative predictors is very helpful. The process of selecting informative predictors, algorithmically is called *feature selection*. Neural nets can determine the best input variables on their own; in a linear regression, we, as users, need to determine which variables should serve as inputs. Second, linear regression, as the name suggests, assumes that the relation between input and output is *linear*. If it is not, then we would have to specify other forms of nonlinear regression. The predictions of neural nets are not limited by the nature of the relationship, linear or nonlinear, between the input and output. Third, neural nets can handle unstructured data such as text, images, audio, and video. Moreover, they work well even if the number of observations is less than the number of input variables or predictors. Regression models would not converge in such instances. Fourth, as we will see when we explore the architecture of neural nets, they are built from layers, each containing several nodes connected by weights. While a single node might operate like a simple model, such as linear regression, the strength of a neural network comes from stacking many layers and creating connections between nodes across those layers. This structure helps neural networks understand complex or nonlinear patterns in data to make better predictions. The concept is similar to using simple LEGO blocks to build a complex and interesting structure.

6.5 A DEEP DIVE INTO NEURAL NETS

Let's enhance our understanding of neural nets by building a simple neural net to predict house prices. Our neural net has only two inputs: location of the house and the year built. The values have been standardized so that they vary between 0 and 1. Our neural net will have the following parts as depicted in Figure 6.2: the input layer, one hidden layer, and an output. Let's examine each of them in detail.

FIGURE 6.2 ■ Layers of a Simple Neural Net

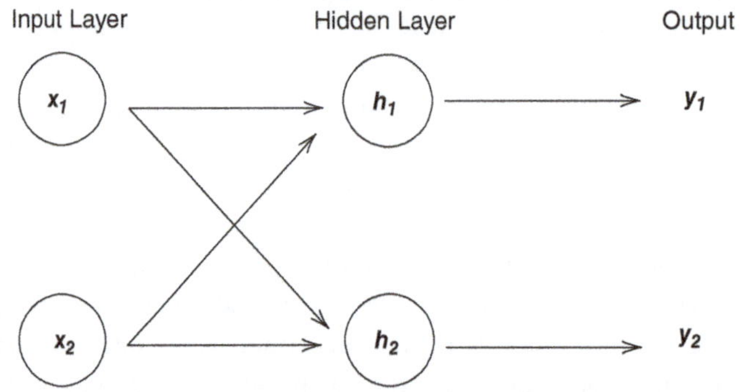

The input layer nodes (or neurons) are determined by the number of inputs we provide to the neural net. Since we are providing two inputs, location and year, in our example the input layer has two nodes; let's call them x_1 and x_2. If we had 100 input variables, the neural net would have 100 nodes in the input layer. The first level of processing occurs in the hidden layer. In our neural net we are using two nodes in the hidden layer, h_1 and h_2. We can have many more. Since the number of nodes in the hidden layer as well as the number of hidden layers can be specified by the user, they are called *hyperparameters*. Hyperparameters are specified by the user and are different from *parameters*, which are computed by the algorithm (please see the Technical Appendix for a detailed description). The inputs from both x_1 and x_2 are fed into each of the hidden layer nodes (i.e., h_1 receives an input from x_1 as well as from x_2). The important thing to keep in mind is that the inputs to the hidden layer nodes are weighted. Therefore, we need to multiply the input values with a weight. The path from x_1 to h_1 has a weight of w_{11} while the path from x_1 to h_2 has a weight of w_{12}. The initial value of these weights can be chosen randomly, and the neural net will keep updating it to improve the predicted value. Figure 6.3 shows the neural net with weights added.

FIGURE 6.3 ■ Neural Net With Weights Added

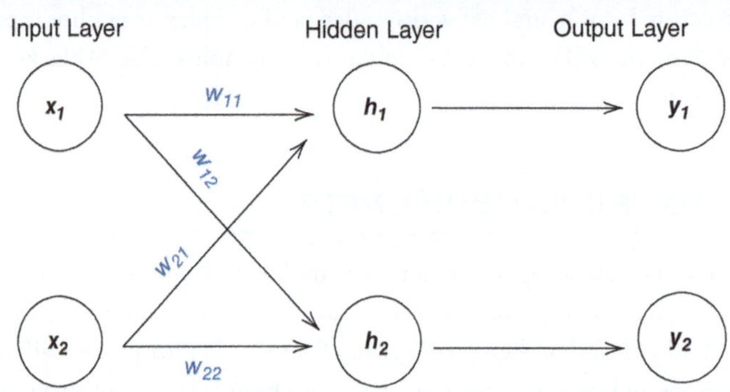

The input to h_1 is:

$$x_1 * w_{11} + x_2 * w_{21}$$

The input to h_2 is:

$$x_1 * w_{12} + x_2 * w_{22}$$

The hidden layer processes the input to provide the output. Just as neurons in the brain determine whether the information they have received requires the firing of a subsequent step, so does a neural net. This decision of whether to fire or not is governed by an *activation function*, which determines whether and to what extent a node should activate based on the input it receives. Different types of activation functions can be chosen based on the input data and the nature of the output. If the output variable is a numeric or continuous value estimate, such as the price of a house, we commonly have one node in the output layer with a linear activation function, directly outputting the calculated value. In our case, both the hidden layer nodes would inform the output of house price. For a numeric output, the common activation functions are linear or rectified linear unit (ReLU) activations. A linear output would simply be an average of the outputs y_1 and y_2.

$$\hat{y} = (y_1 + y_2)/2$$

If we have data specifying the actual house prices, then we can compare the value predicted by the neural net with the actual prices. Mean square error (MSE), commonly used for such comparisons, would be the average squared difference between the predicted and actual house prices.

Imagine a situation in which we have many inputs and multiple hidden layers, with each hidden layer having several nodes. In this case, performing such calculations would become computationally challenging. Matrix multiplication helps out significantly because it efficiently handles the transfer and transformation of inputs through the hidden layers of a neural network. In fact, much of the computation in deep learning is based on some form of matrix multiplication. The input to each of the hidden layers can easily be transformed into matrices that are then multiplied. The following matrix multiplication succinctly captures the inputs to our hidden layer.

$$\begin{bmatrix} w_{11} & w_{21} \\ w_{12} & w_{22} \end{bmatrix} \cdot \begin{bmatrix} x_1 \\ x_2 \end{bmatrix} = \begin{bmatrix} w_{11} * x_1 + w_{21} * x_2 \\ w_{12} * x_1 + w_{22} * x_2 \end{bmatrix}$$

The neural net algorithm will complete its first iteration (also called a *run* or *loop*) and will give a prediction. This is compared to the actual value, or ground truth, and the prediction error is then calculated. The error will inform us how each of the weights needs to be updated (i.e., increased or decreased in value). If there are several inputs and several hidden layers, then managing the process of weight updating can become difficult. The main aim of updating the weights is to make the prediction error as low as possible. Hence, a method called *gradient descent* is used to update weights. This is a process that helps the algorithm find the minimum value of error. It is also referred to as *back propagation* because the prediction error is propagated backwards to update the weights. Details of gradient descent are provided in the Technical Appendix. The rationale behind gradient descent is very similar to the optimization procedure used in ordinary least squares (OLS) regression; however, gradient descent uses an iterative process to adjust model parameters and minimize error incrementally. With these updated weights, the neural net performs its next iteration and again gives out an output, which should have a smaller error.

We next discuss how neural nets can be applied to the specific instance of predicting house prices.

6.6 PREDICTING HOUSE PRICES USING NEURAL NETS

The main aim of any predictive modeling is to generate predictions that are as accurate as possible. In the realm of price prediction, we will use a neural net to do so. As a benchmark, we will also compare the prediction generated by the neural net with that of a linear regression. The data we will use for house price prediction are from the Boston house pricing dataset originally provided by Harrison and Rubinfeld (1979)[2] and subsequently included into the R package `mlbench` by Leisch and Dimitriadou (2021),[3] which has information on several houses sold in Boston in the 1970s. In this example, house features are used as inputs, and the outcome is house prices. Some of the features are the per capita crime rate, proximity to the Charles River, rooms per home, nearness to highways, pupil–teacher ratio in schools, property tax rate, and whether the house was owner-occupied or not. The goal is to develop a model that will predict the price of a house based on its features.

To predict house prices, we will use a neural net with one hidden layer. Hence, it is a *shallow neural net*.

1. We first split the data into train and test sets so that the neural net can learn on the train set and test its predictions on the test set, just as we saw in chapter 2 when we used microeconomic factors to predict oil demand. Here the output variable is house prices in thousands of dollars. For the house-pricing dataset, we split the data to randomly give 80% of the data to the train set and 20% to the test set.

2. We next implement a *cross-validation* procedure. Cross-validation is performed to avoid overfitting because overfitting results in choosing a model that performs well on train data but poorly on test data. A common cross-validation procedure used is to partition/divide the train data into *k*-parts such that in any one iteration *k*-1 sets are used for training, and the performance of the model is tested on the *k*th set. For the house-price prediction task, we use a five-fold cross-validation: We divide the train data randomly into five parts and use four parts for training and one part for testing. We perform the process of splitting data into train and test sets five times, creating different random parts each time. A detailed description of cross-validation is available in the Technical Appendix.

3. Subsequently, we specify the number of nodes in our hidden layer of the neural net. Recall that we are able to specify different numbers of nodes in the hidden layer as well as specify how many hidden layers we want our neural net to have as hyperparameters. A neural net with more than one layer would be considered a deep neural net. In our case we use only one hidden layer with nodes varying from 15 to 25. We allow the algorithm to try a different number of nodes between 15 and 25 to find the one with the least prediction error.

4. In order to check how well the neural net performs in predicting house prices, we use *root mean square error* (RMSE). RMSE is the average squared error of the predicted price from the true or actual house price. For different parameter values specified in the model, we can obtain different RMSE values. The plot in Figure 6.4 captures the accuracy of the predictions, using RMSE for different values of the parameter—different hidden nodes and decay that are discussed in more detail in the Implementation Using R section.

FIGURE 6.4 ■ RMSE Cross-Validation

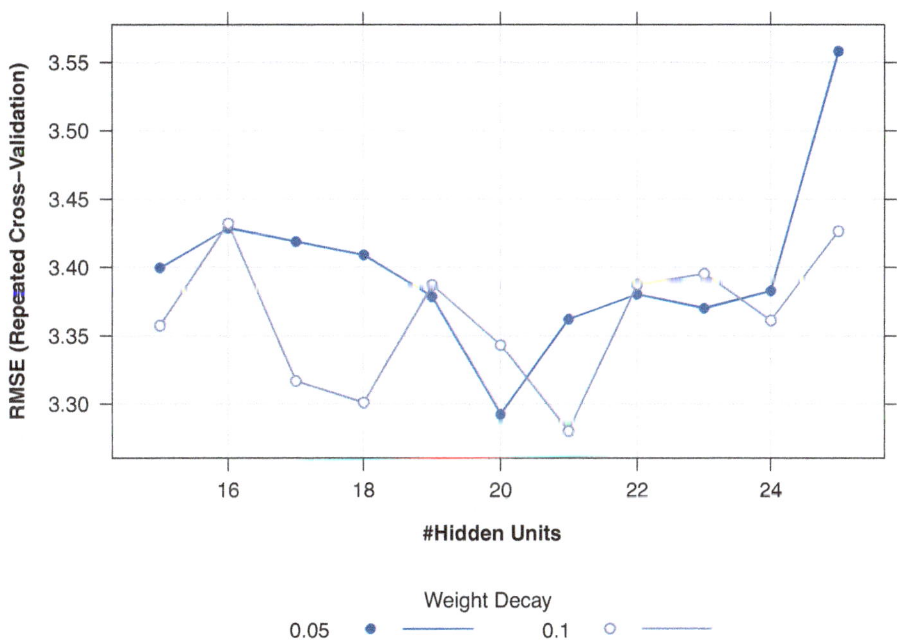

5. The selected neural net model is the one with smallest RMSE. This model now can be applied to the test data, using predictor variables of the test data to estimate house prices. We can then compare these estimates with the true house price (remember our test data have the information on true house prices). Again, we can estimate the RMSE to see how our selected model performs on test data. Since our output variable is continuous in nature, we can also obtain R^2—the *coefficient of determination* of the neural net model. It

helps us find out what percentage of the variation in the output can be explained by the input variables used in the model. R^2 is the square of the correlation between the actual home prices and predicted home prices. The analysis also outputs MAE, which is the *mean absolute error*, another metric for measuring the accuracy of the model.

```
##      RMSE  Rsquared       MAE
## 2.6467193 0.9361146 1.9453898
```

6. Finally, we can compare the predictions of the neural net model with those of a linear regression on test data.

```
##      RMSE  Rsquared       MAE
## 4.4226051 0.8330442 3.3215093
```

If we compare the R^2 values, we see that we obtain a higher, and hence better, R^2 of 0.93 with neural nets than with a linear regression of 0.83. Similarly, the RMSE values are lower with a neural net than linear regression, indicating that the prediction error is less with neural nets.

6.6.1 Business Insights From Neural Nets

In sum, using a neural net we are able to predict house prices with less error than when using a linear regression. Moreover, by using thirteen input variables, the neural net model is able to explain 86% of the variation in house prices. Therefore, utilizing neural nets allows us to efficiently predict house prices. Even if the number of predictor variables increases, neural nets have better ability to handle them compared to traditional methods like regression since neural nets can perform feature selection by themselves and do not need the user to specify which predictors to include in the model. Moreover, neural nets can predict well even if the relationship between the predictor and the outcome is not linear, an important assumption that limits methods like linear regression. However, neural nets are opaque methods that do not provide insights into the exact functional form of the input variables being used in the model to predict the outcome; this limits their ability to be used as an explanatory method.

6.7 IMPLEMENTATION USING R: PREDICTING HOUSE PRICES

First, we load three packages: `caret`,[4] `mlbench`, and `doParallel`.[5] The function `registerDoParallel(cores=4)` helps in parallelizing by speeding up calculations. You can change `cores = 4` to some other number depending upon the number of cores your computer's processor has.

```
library(caret)
library(mlbench)
library(doParallel)
registerDoParallel(cores = 4)
```

We then load the housing data available in the package `mlbench`[3] and *set seed*. Setting seed ensures that when you run this code on your machine, you get results that are similar to the ones reported in this book. For your own analysis, you can set any seed, and the results will deviate slightly from the results reported in this book. It will happen because a different seed will assign a different set of observations to the test and train datasets.

```
data(BostonHousing)
set.seed(12345)
```

The following lines of code split the data into train and test datasets. The `createDataPartition` function randomly samples 80% of row numbers from the dataset (that is what `p = .8` specifies). We then split `BostonHousing` data into two sets. By using `BostonHousing[inTrain]`, we are selecting the rows from `BostonHousing` data that correspond to the numbers that are saved in `inTrain`. For the test set, we select rows from `BostonHousing` that are not in `inTrain`. This way the train set has randomly chosen 80% observations, and the test set has 20% observations.

```
inTrain <- createDataPartition(BostonHousing$medv, p = .8,list=FALSE)
train <- BostonHousing[inTrain,]
test <- BostonHousing[-inTrain,]
```

Since the goal of this analysis is to build a neural net model that can predict house price, we use the 14th variable `medv`, which represents the median value of homes in thousands of dollars, as our output variable. All other variables are input (i.e., predictor) variables. We separate output and input variables in both test and train datasets.

```
train_predictor <- train[,-14]
train_outcome <- train [,14]

test_predictor <- test[,-14]
test_outcome <- test [,14]
```

We next specify the cross-validation procedure. We use five-fold cross-validation and repeat this cross-validation process five times.

```
ctrl <- trainControl(method = "repeatedcv", # cross-validation
                     number = 5, # 5 folds
                     repeats = 5)
```

We next specify values for the two parameters `decay` and `size`. `decay` specifies the regularization parameter to avoid overfitting, and `size` specifies the number of nodes in the hidden layer (note that our implementation here uses only one hidden layer). Since values of `decay` and `size` change the predictive power of our model and it is impossible to know optimum values a priori, we try various values and let the best combination of decay and size emerge from their performance in the train dataset. We can then test how well these parameters perform on test data. bag = FALSE means we are not using bagging.

```
avnnetGrid <- expand.grid(decay = c(.05,.1),
                          size = c(15:25),
                          bag = FALSE)
```

size = c(15:25) indicates that we want to estimate a neural network with 15 to 25 nodes in the hidden layer, and decay = c(0.05,.1) shows that we want to try the two decay values of 0.05 and 0.1. Since there are 11 different values of size and 2 values of decay, the analysis will generate the performance of 22 different models, each one representing a combination of decay and size.

Now we are ready to train the different models and see how well they perform. But we need to be aware of an important issue with neural nets. When using neural nets, there is always a possibility that a model does not reach globally optimal estimates. This could happen due to the set of random weights assigned at the beginning of model estimation. Since, each neural net starts with randomly initialized weights that get updated in the subsequent back propagation, sometimes different seeds lead to different optimal weights. This issue results in a situation in which the selected model might not be the best model and may lead to overfitting. One way to counter this issue is to test the performance of the same model with the same dataset but with different random seeds. The model averaged neural network (avNNet) fits several neural networks via the nnet package using different seeds on the same data, then averages the predictions of the networks. method = "avNNet" in the subsequent lines of code implements this approach.

tuneGrid = avnnetGrid informs the model about decay and size parameter combinations; trControl = ctrl provides cross-validation details to the training process; preProc = c("center", "scale") centers and scales the data, an essential step in fitting any neural net model; linout = TRUE suggests that the prediction involves a continuous variable. If the outcome variable had been binary, then linout would have been FALSE. Finally, allowParallel=TRUE enables use of parallel processing, and maxit = 100 tells the model to perform 100 iterations or weight updates for each model.

```
avnnet_fit <- train(train_predictor, train_outcome,
                    method = "avNNet",
                    tuneGrid = avnnetGrid,
                    trControl = ctrl, linout = TRUE,
                    preProc = c("center", "scale"),
                    trace = FALSE,
                    allowParallel=TRUE,
                    maxit = 100)
```

Depending upon the computer, the preceding code could take 30 seconds to a few minutes to perform all estimations. When completed, we can use `plot(avnnet_fit)` to request the `decay` and `size` combination that performed the best, as seen in Figure 6.4.

```
plot(avnnet_fit)
```

We see that the model with `weight = 0.1` and `size = 25` has the lowest RMSE. If we type `avnnet_fit` in the R console, we will see that a long output, ending with `RMSE`, was used to select the optimal model using the smallest value. The final values used for the model were `size = 25, decay = 0.1,` and `bag = FALSE`. This is consistent with what we can see in the previous plot.

We can now assess how well this model performs on our test data. The `predict` function predicts the output from using the input variables in the test dataset, and `postResample` compares the obtained predictions of house prices (`predicted_price`) with their true value (`test_outcome`) and provides performance measures such as *RMSE* and R^2.

```
predicted_price <- predict(avnnet_fit, test_predictor)
postResample(pred = predicted_price, obs = test_outcome)

##      RMSE  Rsquared       MAE
## 2.6467193 0.9361146 1.9453898
```

The output of sample (test data) performance of the chosen model is comparable to its performance with train data. This indicates less likelihood of overfitting.

We next check how the neural net model compares with linear regression. The following code runs a linear regression with the test dataset.

```
linear_fit <- train(medv ~ .,
               data = train,
               method = "lm")
linear_pred <- predict(linear_fit, test)

postResample(pred = linear_pred, obs = test$medv)
##      RMSE  Rsquared       MAE
## 4.4226051 0.8330442 3.3215093
```

When we compare the RMSE and *R*-squared of the two models, we see that the neural net model performs better than linear regression with the test data. Note, these predicted values can vary depending on hyperparameter values, cross-validation process and initial weights.

6.7.1. Tidymodels Implementation

The tidymodels[6] framework offers another way to implement neural nets in R. It is a collection of packages that work together and offer a convenient way to implement complex machine-learning workflows.

After loading the required packages, we split the data into train (70%) and test (30%) sets using `prop = 0.7` in the `initial_split()` function.

```
library(tidymodels)
library(mlbench)
library(doParallel)

set.seed(12345)
data(BostonHousing)
datasplit <- initial_split(BostonHousing, prop = 0.7,
                           strata = medv)
trainData <- training(datasplit)
testData <- testing(datasplit)
```

In `recipe()` we first define the outcome and predictor variables. `medv ~ .` specifies that the outcome variable, median house value, is predicted by all other variables. `step_normalize(all_numeric_predictors())` normalizes all numeric variables to have a mean of zero and standard deviation of 1.

```
rec_nn <- recipe(medv ~ ., data = trainData) %>%
step_normalize(all_numeric_predictors())
```

Next we specify the model. `mlp()` describes a single-layer feed-forward neural net model. `set_engine()` defines the model engine. Here we choose `nnet` as the model engine. `set_mode("regression")` specifies that the outcome variable is continuous and not categorical. Here we are adopting a different approach compared to the code in the last section. We are not specifying the range for the number of nodes in the hidden layer, as we did earlier. Instead, we are using `hidden_units = tune()`, which suggests that the appropriate number of nodes should be determined through fine-tuning. Similarly, we specify the appropriate regularization parameter `penalty` to avoid overfitting, and the maximum number of iterations or weight updates for each model, `epochs`, is determined through fine-tuning. `translate()` helps in understanding model arguments such as `hidden_units`, `penalty`, and `epochs` with respect to our model engine `nnet`. Compared to our code in the previous section, `hidden_units` is `size`, `penalty` is `decay`, and `epochs` is `maxit`.

```
neural_net_model <-
 mlp(hidden_units = tune(),
    penalty = tune(),
    epochs = tune()) %>%
 set_engine("nnet") %>%
 set_mode("regression")%>%translate()
neural_net_model
## Single Layer Neural Network Specification (regression)
##
## Main Arguments:
##   hidden_units = tune()
##   penalty = tune()
##   epochs = tune()
##
## Computational engine: nnet
##
## Model fit template:
## nnet::nnet(formula = missing_arg(), data = missing_arg(), size = tune(),
##     decay = tune(), maxit = tune(), trace = FALSE, linout = TRUE)
```

`grid_regular()` creates a grid of three tuning parameters: `hidden_units`, `penalty`, and `epochs`. The `levels` argument specifies the number of levels that need to be created for each tuning parameter. For `levels = 5`, five levels of each tuning parameter will be created. Since we have three tuning parameters, there will be $5^3 = 125$ combinations of tuning parameters, and 125 different models will be fit.

```
neural_grid <- grid_regular(
  hidden_units(),
  penalty(),
  epochs(),
  levels = 5)
```

In order to find the best (the least susceptible to overfitting) among the 125 models, `vfold_cv()` specifies V-fold (also known as K-fold) cross-validation, where the training data is split into approximately equal-sized parts. Here `v = 10` specifies 10 partitions of the data. To reduce execution time, we can use more than one core available on a computer. With `registerDoParallel(cores = 5)`, we will be using five cores to parallelize the grid search process. If you have more cores available, then you can change the value of `cores`.

```
nn_folds <- vfold_cv(trainData, v = 10)
doParallel::registerDoParallel(cores = 5)
```

Next we define a workflow using `workflow()`. It specifies the model (`neural_net_model`) and adds the recipe `rec_nn` defined in an earlier step.

```
nn_wf <- workflow() %>%
     add_recipe(rec_nn)%>%
     add_model(neural_net_model)
```

Now we can start the grid search process using `tune_grid()`. It will compute performance metrics (e.g., RMSE and R-squared) for each of the 125 parameter combinations stored in the data frame `neural_grid`. `resamples = nn_folds` will use the tenfold cross-validation specified in `nn_fold`. In `control_grid()`, `save_pred = TRUE` means that predictions made by each of the 125 models will be saved. `parallel_over = "everything"` parallalizes the grid search process to reduce the execution time.

```
nn_res <- tune_grid(
   nn_wf,
   grid = neural_grid,
   resamples = nn_folds,
   control = control_grid(save_pred = TRUE,
   parallel_over = "everything")
)
```

Once the fine-tuning process is complete, we can identify the top-performing models. `show_best` displays the top five models and their performance estimates. We can then select the top-performing model using `select_best`. Note, we are using RMSE to choose the best model, but we can also choose the best model by using *R*-squared as the metric `select_best(nn_res, "rsq")`. We will then see different best models if we use RMSE vs. *R*-squared. We can finalize the workflow using the best model.

```
show_best(nn_res, "rmse")

## # A tibble: 5 × 9
##   hidden_units penalty epochs .metric.estimator mean     n  std_err .config
##          <int>   <dbl>  <int>   <chr> <chr>    <dbl> <int>   <dbl> <chr>
## 1            7       1    505   rmse standard  3.75    10   0.214 Preprocess~
## 2            5       1    752   rmse standard  3.79    10   0.264 Preprocess~
## 3            3       1    752   rmse standard  3.85    10   0.212 Preprocess~
## 4           10       1    257   rmse standard  3.88    10   0.198 Preprocess~
## 5            7       1   1000   rmse standard  3.90    10   0.205 Preprocess~
```

```
best_rmse <- select_best(nn_res, "rmse")
final_nn <- finalize_workflow(
      nn_wf,
      best_rmse)
```

The final steps involve predicting the performance of this model on our test data. `last_fit()` helps us accomplish this. Using `collect_metrics()` we can see the RMSE and *R*-squared estimates of the chosen model. Note, the rmse and rsq values are different when we use the `tidymodels` package versus the `caret` package to build the neural net. The differences can be attributed to underlying differences in how these packages handle aspects like model training, prediction, and evaluation, even when settings are consistent across them.

```
final_res <- last_fit(final_nn, datasplit)
collect_metrics(final_res)

## # A tibble: 2 × 4
##   .metric  .estimator  .estimate .config
##   <chr>    <chr>           <dbl> <chr>
## 1 rmse     standard        3.46  Preprocessor1_Model1
## 2 rsq      standard        0.857 Preprocessor1_Model1
```

6.8 UNDERSTANDING THE CHAPTER

1. Why is product price a signal of product quality?
2. What is a neural network with one hidden layer called, and what is one with multiple hidden layers called?
3. What is a "black box algorithm"? If neural net is a black box algorithm, justify why businesses should keep using such algorithms.
4. Data are split into train and test sets (choose the statement that is *false*)
   - **a.** To avoid model overfitting
   - **b.** By using *k*-fold cross validation
   - **c.** By using gradient descent
   - **d.** To increase model generalizability
5. In the context of training neural network models, which of the following statements accurately describes the typical usage of train and test data?
   - **a.** Train data are used to evaluate the model's final performance, and test data are used to train the model.
   - **b.** Both train and test data are used to train the model.

c. Train data are used to train the model, and test data are used to evaluate its generalization performance.
d. Test data are used to set the model hyperparameters, and train data are used to evaluate the model's performance.

6. If you see the following input equation and are told that this is the input to node h_2 in the hidden layer from the three input nodes x_1, x_2, and x_3:

$$x_1 * w_{12} + x_2 * w_{22} + x_3 * w_{32},$$

which of the following statements is *true*?
a. w_{12} is the weight from the input x_1 to hidden layer node h_2.
b. w_{22} is the weight from the input x_1 to x_2.
c. w_{32} is the weight from the input h_3 to h_2.
d. w_{12} can be ignored because its value is always less than 6.
e. Gradient descent works only for linear regression.

7. How are hyperparameters different from parameters? Pick the correct option from the following.
a. Both perform the same function and are the same.
b. Hyperparameters are learned from the data during the training process.
c. Parameters are set before the training begin and are defined by the user.
d. Hyperparameters are provided by the user.

ENDNOTES

1. McDowell, Edwin, "Airlines Tally the Damage From Summer's Fare War," *The New York Times*, September 12, 1992, https://www.nytimes.com/1992/09/12/business/airlines-tally-the-damage-from-summer-s-fare-war.html.

2. Harrison, David, Jr., and Daniel L. Rubinfeld, "Hedonic Prices and the Demand for Clean Air," *Journal of Environmental Economics and Management* 5 (1978): 81–102.

3. Leisch, Friedrich, and Evgenia Dimitriadou, "mlbench: Machine Learning Benchmark Problems," R package version 2.1-3 (2021).

4. Kuhn, Max, "caret: Classification and Regression Training," R package version 6.0-94 (March21, 2023), https://CRAN.R-project.org/package=caret.

5. Microsoft Corporation and Steve Weston, "doParallel: Foreach Parallel Adaptor for the 'parallel' Package," R package version 1.0.17 (2022), https://CRAN.R-project.org/package=doParallel.

6. Kuhn, Max, et al., "Tidymodels: A Collection of Packages for Modeling and Machine Learning Using tidyverse Principles" (2020), https://www.tidymodels.org.

7 ADVERTISING AND BRANDING WITH A/B TESTING

CONTENTS

LEARNING OBJECTIVES

1. Understand the importance of advertising
2. Conduct causal testing and collecting primary data
3. Understand A/B testing
4. Evaluate the different steps in A/B testing

5. Interpret the results of A/B testing
6. Understand the new versions of online causal testing

7.1 ADVERTISING: SPREADING THE MESSAGE

The earliest example of advertising *predates* the modern capitalist system. The walls of Pompeii exhibit examples of early advertising—such as merchant promotions for different wares, announcements for gladiatorial games, and information sought about a lost animal. In the last two centuries, advertising has evolved from a tool to sell unbranded commodities to a communication tool that accomplishes many objectives, from creating awareness of a new brand and selling more products to conveying the unique brand image of an offering. Advertisements for BMW or Coca-Cola are not merely attempts to persuade us to buy their products; they are also efforts to imprint a unique image of the brand in consumers' minds.

Regardless of the objective of their advertisements, businesses have for many decades confronted a unique challenge: Since there are a multitude of ways to create an advertisement, how can the business decide which advertisement will be the most effective? Let's take the example of a toothpaste manufacturer who, after much internal deliberation, wants to test whether a new version of its advertisement would be more effective than the current version it has been using. In order to persuade consumers to buy its toothpaste, the manufacturer can advertise its toothpaste as "promoting healthy teeth" (the new version) or "preventing cavities" (the previous version). The "preventing cavities" message focuses on preventing a negative outcome while the "healthy teeth" message focuses on achieving a positive outcome. It would be more efficient to run only the advertisement that is most effective in increasing sales. The manufacturer is unsure about which message to use and is very interested in determining the advertisement that would be the most effective. (Note: In some cases, many new versions of the same advertisement can be tested using the method that is detailed later in this chapter.)

In the pre-internet era, the effectiveness of advertising was tested using the split-cable scanner method in which a test market (e.g., a city) was selected. Each of several thousand households enrolled in the test received an ID card, which was scanned every time a household member purchased goods at retail stores. This helped keep track of what products were purchased by the household. The household televisions were connected to a cable network, and different versions of the advertisement were shown to different households. For instance, in the case of the toothpaste manufacturer, some households might see the advertisement "promoting healthy teeth," and some might see the "preventing cavities" advertisement. Subsequent to airing the advertisements, the purchase of that toothpaste in retail stores would be monitored to find out which advertisement resulted in the most sales (i.e., which was the most effective in persuading consumers to buy).

Split cable has now been replaced with online advertising tests that are less expensive and quicker to run. Therefore, the internet-era version of the advertisement that generates more clicks will inform the retailer, causally, which version is more effective in generating interest in the product. That is, the retailer can find out which version of the advertisement *caused* more clicks. Before we begin discussing the nuances of causal testing, let's examine the difference between causation and correlation. The difference highlights why many businesses still think that insights derived from causal testing are more informative than those derived through correlational observations.

7.2 CAUSAL VS. CORRELATIONAL

Let's use the toothpaste manufacturer's example to understand the difference between causal and correlational testing. Consider that the manufacturer is interested in determining how advertising expenditure affects sales of toothpaste. It looks at historical data and sees a pattern. When it spends more on advertising, it sells more toothpaste. Does this mean that an increase in advertising causes an increase in sales? The answer is no. The relationship between advertising expenditure and sales is an example of correlation. It merely shows that both are related but says nothing about advertising causing sales. There are many factors that can influence sales and advertising expenditure; for instance, it is possible that the manufacturer increased its advertising budget when it had more revenue and reduced its advertising budget when it had less revenue. When using historical data, regression analysis often helps us estimate an association between any two variables without there being any causal link between them. On the other hand, causal testing clearly establishes X-causes-Y relationships such as "increasing price reduces demand" or "an advertisement promoting a positive outcome leads to more sales than one that promotes the prevention of a negative outcome." Such a method of causally testing for a relationship is called *experimentation* or *A/B testing* or *randomized controlled trials (RCTs).*

7.3 A/B TESTING FOR ADVERTISING EFFECTIVENESS

A/B testing's long history of usage evolved from medical research in which patients were given different treatments to find out which treatment helped most to save people's lives. Ronald Fisher, over 100 years ago, formalized experimental design by introducing the procedure of randomly assigning people to different groups or treatments to find out the efficacy of each treatment. Fisher applied this method in agriculture, conducting experiments to determine the optimal quantity of fertilizer for soil. He did this by varying the amounts of fertilizer in different soil patches and measuring the resulting plant yields. By the 1950s, we started seeing a lot more experiments, referred to as clinical trials in medicine, in which researchers tested the efficacy of medicines and treatments by keeping all factors constant and varying only the treatment factor. This meticulous approach, where only one factor or variable is altered while others are kept constant, is known as a *controlled* trial. Such trials allow experimenters to accurately assess the impact and effectiveness of the treatment factor on the outcome. A/B testing is still considered the gold standard of causal testing because it allows us to single out the influence of one factor on the outcome while controlling for all other factors by keeping everything but that one factor constant.

A/B testing is used quite a bit in marketing. It is used to maximize traffic to web pages, create the most persuasive version of an advertisement, develop optimal promotions, find the optimal price for a product, design a new product, and determine the right strategy to retain customers.

7.4 STEPS IN A/B TESTING

The process of A/B testing an advertisement proceeds in a stepwise manner. We will discuss each of the steps and focus more deeply on the analytical aspects of A/B testing that will help us run effective A/B tests and validate the findings.

7.4.1 Primary Source of Data

It is worth keeping in mind that A/B testing is one of the few data analysis methods that is inherently a data collection method. Unlike analysis methods such as regression or any deep learning method that uses existing data (also called *secondary data*), A/B testing starts with collecting primary data from a sample of the population. Therefore, A/B testing often becomes the chosen method of analysis since it helps the business gather *primary data* that are pertinent to the question it wants answered (e.g., which advertisement, what prices, which segment of customers); moreover, the fact that it provides a way of causally obtaining results makes it easier to understand cause and effect. Going back to our toothpaste example, the manufacturer does not have any existing data that they can rely on to find out which advertisement, "promoting healthy teeth" or "preventing cavities," would be more effective in persuading consumers. Hence, they need to collect primary data to help answer their questions.

7.4.2 Selection of Target Market

As we discussed in Chapter 5, the process of selecting the appropriate target market in the case of A/B testing entails finding which customers would be most interested in buying the toothpaste. Within this target group of consumers, the manufacturer can then test which version of the advertisement would generate the most interest as captured via click-throughs.

7.4.3 Creation of Advertisements

Advertisement creation, at one time an elaborate and time-consuming endeavor, has become simpler and quicker in the internet era. Many small businesses can quickly design and run online advertisements using simple design tools. For any A/B testing, we first create the different versions of the advertisement we want tested. The number of versions will determine how many *groups* or *cells* we have in our experiment. In our case, we just have two versions—the "preventing cavities" version and the "promoting healthy teeth" version. Therefore, we have a two-cell experimental design.

We next discuss the process of drawing samples to run the A/B test and the statistical tests that will inform us which of the versions is more effective in generating a greater number of click-throughs.

7.4.4 Estimating Effect Size

One critical question needs to be addressed before conducting an A/B test: What magnitude of improvement in performance is considered meaningful when introducing a new advertisement compared to an existing one? If an existing advertisement has a 10% click rate, what percentage improvement are we aiming for with a new advertisement? Is a 5% improvement our goal? The answer varies, as there is no universal benchmark, and it is subjective to each company's unique circumstances and objectives. Consider the case of a large e-commerce company attracting 10 million daily visitors. A 0.5% enhancement in click rate could translate into a substantial improvement. Conversely, for a smaller e-commerce entity receiving 1,000 daily unique visitors, a 5% improvement might not be as consequential or indicative of significant progress. The meaningful influence of a new intervention (e.g., new advertisement) over an existing one is referred to as *effect size* or *minimum preferred causal effect*. Estimating effect size before running an A/B test helps in estimating sample size (discussed in the next section) and also in assessing the results of an A/B test.

7.4.5 Estimating Sample Size

Since it is impossible to include everyone in the target market in an A/B test, firms use a smaller subgroup of the target market also known as the sample. Samples are subsets of the population (i.e., everyone in the target market) and serve as practical microcosms of the larger population. While samples are drawn from the population, what we see in samples may not reflect what is happening in the entire population. Why? Samples don't always capture the true nature of the population because of *sampling error*. Whenever we draw a subset of the population, we run the risk of introducing sampling error. One way to think about sampling error is to understand it as the uncertainty in the conclusion we are drawing from the sample. The size of the sample used in A/B testing affects sampling error. Larger samples tend to reduce the magnitude of the sampling error. In order to understand how to calculate the most appropriate sample size, we need to understand the concepts of Type I and Type II errors.

Consider that we ran an A/B test and found that the "promoting healthy teeth" advertisement led to more click-throughs (i.e., consumers found it to be more persuasive) than the "preventing cavities" advertisement. Therefore, two possible conclusions about our A/B test can be drawn:

> **Conclusion 1:** The percentage of people in the population who found the "promoting healthy teeth" advertisement more persuasive than the "preventing cavities" advertisement is *actually the same* as the percentage who found the "preventing cavities" advertisement more persuasive. Sampling error is responsible for the difference observed in the A/B test.
>
> **Conclusion 2:** The percentage of people who found the "promoting healthy teeth" advertisement more persuasive than the "preventing cavities" advertisement is *actually larger in the population*. Sampling error is *not* responsible for the difference observed in the A/B test.

Conclusion 1 is commonly referred to as the null hypothesis (H_0) and Conclusion 2 as the alternate hypothesis.

Now let's consider two possible realities at the population level. These realities exist regardless of what the results are from our sample.

> **Reality 1:** The persuasiveness of the "promoting healthy teeth" and the "preventing cavities" advertisements is *the same*.

Reality 2: The persuasiveness of the "promoting healthy teeth" advertisement is *actually greater than* that of the "preventing cavities" advertisement.

So what happens when our conclusions don't match with the reality? The simple answer is Type I and Type II errors 🙂. Let's understand why this happens.

	Reality 1 (no difference)	*Reality 2 (yes difference)*
Conclusion 1 (no difference)	🙂 $1 - \alpha$	☹ Type II error, $p = \beta$
Conclusion 2 (yes difference)	☹ Type I error, α	🙂 *power* $= 1 - \beta$

In this table, α (alpha) is the probability of rejecting the null hypothesis when it is true. We want to keep α as small as possible because if α is small, the probability of committing a Type I error (*false positive*) is small. One way to understand this is to say that we want to minimize the chance of concluding that the "promoting healthy teeth" advertisement is more persuasive than the "preventing cavities" advertisement (Conclusion 2) when in reality there is no difference between them (Reality 1).

This table says the following: If Reality 1 matches with Conclusion 1, then we are happy 🙂.

A Type II error is drawing Conclusion 1 (no difference) when a difference actually exists (Reality 2). Just as α plays an important role in assessing the chance of committing a Type I error, β plays an important role in assessing the chance of committing a Type II error (*false negative*). Thus, β tells us what the chances are we would conclude that no difference exists between the "promoting healthy teeth" and "preventing cavities" advertisements when in reality there is a difference between them.

Power of an A/B test is the probability that if there truly is a difference in the population, the test will successfully detect it. Power is simply $1 - \beta$. As you can guess, we ideally want to keep β low so that the power of our test is high. A more formal way to define power is the following: *It is the probability of rejecting the null hypothesis (Conclusion 2) when the null is actually false (Reality 2).* In our case, we are comparing a "promoting healthy teeth" advertisement with a "preventing cavities" advertisement. If our A/B test has high power, and if the "promoting healthy teeth" ad is actually better, our test is likely to show that clearly. With lower power, we would not detect a real difference in effectiveness between the two advertisements, even if one exists, leading to a potential Type II error.

Sample size estimation relies on the following three important metrics that we have understood: α, power (i.e., $1 - \beta$), and effect size. Determining the correct sample size is important to ensure the validity of the test results. It is generally advised to keep alpha at $\alpha = 0.05$ and power at around 0.80. Lowering α or increasing power will increase the required sample size. Figure 7.1 depicts the relationship among power, α, and sample size. In this case, we have held the effect size constant at 10%.

We see that as sample size increases, power also increases. However, the gain in power due to sample size flattens out at around 0.80 (i.e., 80% power). In other words, an increasingly large sample size is needed for small increases in power. We can also see that the same sample size has different effects on power depending on the value of α. If α is 0.05, we need a smaller sample size to attain the same power than if α is 0.01.

FIGURE 7.1 ■ Alpha, Power, and Sample Size

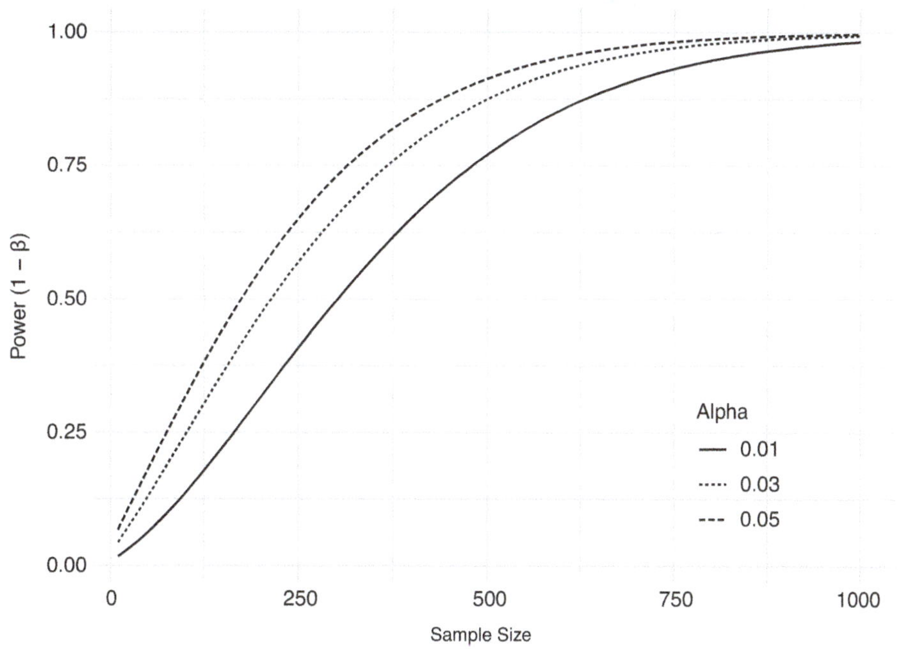

For the toothpaste advertisements, the click-through rate for the existing "preventing cavities" advertisement is 10%, and let's say we expect the new advertisement to generate at least a 15% click rate. If we set α to 0.05 and power to 0.80, the minimum sample size to attain 80% power is approximately 686 people in each group.

```
##
##      Two-sample comparison of proportions power calculation
##
##                n = 685.5969
##               p1 = 0.1
##               p2 = 0.15
##        sig.level = 0.05
##            power = 0.8
##      alternative = two.sided
##
## NOTE: n is number in *each* group
```

7.5 EXPERIMENTAL DESIGN TO TEST FOR EFFECTIVE ADVERTISEMENT

Consider that the toothpaste manufacturer is now ready to run the A/B test to find the version of the advertisement that results in a higher click rate using the sample size estimated in the prior section. (The data for this example are hypothetical.) The following points need to be kept in mind while running any A/B test.

1. The participants in the A/B test should be selected *randomly* from the population of all the relevant customers. Note: People recruited to take part in an A/B test are generally referred to as *participants.*
2. The participants are randomly assigned to view one of the two advertisements. This means that participants do not self-select to see a specific version of the advertisement and that we are not assigning them to one group or the other using a rule. We are doing so without using any criteria (i.e., any participant has an equal chance of being assigned to any group). Random assignment is crucial for the integrity of A/B testing. It ensures that individual characteristics like age, gender, income, or personality traits don't influence which advertisement a participant sees. Hence, the influence of the main variable (i.e., X) we are testing on the outcome variable (i.e., Y) is not impacted by these participant characteristics. When we observe differences in how effective each advertisement is, we can be confident that these differences are due to the advertisements themselves, and not because of the specific characteristics of the participants in each group..
3. No participant should see any advertisement more than once. That is, each participant should provide their response only once.
4. Each participant should see only one version of the advertisement. If a participant is randomly assigned to see the "preventing cavities" version, then they should not see the "promoting healthy teeth" version. Such a design that limits a participant to only one version is called a *between-participants design*. A different design that allows participants to see both versions of the advertisement and provide their ratings is called a *within-participant design*. However, we are using a between-participants design in this A/B test.

Following these steps, the "preventing cavities" version of the advertisement was shown to 700 randomly chosen participants, and the "promoting healthy teeth" version was shown to a different set of 700 participants in our between-participants design. On viewing the advertisement, either participants clicked on the advertisement they viewed, or they did not. The click rate served as the dependent variable that we used to compare the effectiveness of the two versions. The click rate data are depicted in the following table:

	Preventing cavities	Promoting healthy teeth
Clicked	77	119
Didn't click	623	581

7.5.1 Statistical Test

The preceding table shows that while 11% of participants who were shown the "preventing cavities" version clicked on it, 17% of participants shown the "promoting healthy teeth" version clicked on it. The difference in the percentage of participants' click rate indicates that the "promoting healthy teeth" version of the advertisement is more persuasive. But we are arriving at this conclusion merely by comparing the 11% and the 17% click rates and stating that the latter is greater than the former. We have to keep in mind that this conclusion is based on a sample of potential customers drawn from a population, and it is possible that this pattern does not exist in the entire population. Stated differently, one could argue that the pattern of data has emerged by chance. In order to address the issue of whether the result emerged just by chance, we perform statistical testing. We compare the click rate for the two versions to determine whether the difference actually exists in the population or whether the difference could have emerged merely by chance.

The task now is to assess if there is a causal relationship between the differing click rates (the interest generated) of the two versions of the advertisement. The null hypothesis (H_0) is that there is no relationship. In other words, the persuasiveness of both versions is the same, and there is no difference in participants' click rate when shown either version. The alternate hypothesis (H_1) is that there is a relationship between the type of advertisement and the click rate, suggesting a difference in the advertisements' level of persuasiveness. A statistical test will help us assess if the null hypothesis should be accepted or rejected.

An appropriate statistical test in this context is Pearson's chi-squared test. Applying it to our data, we get the following results:

```
##
##  Pearson's Chi-squared test
##
## data: click_rate
## X-squared = 10.465, df = 1, p-value = 0.001216
```

These results show that the obtained chi-squared (χ^2) value is too large to have arisen just by chance. A p value of 0.001216 denotes the probability of incurring a Type I error—that is, rejecting the null hypothesis when it is correct. Given that the p value is less than the alpha value (0.05) we set in our sample size estimation, we can reject the null hypothesis and conclude that there is a statistically significant relationship between the type of advertisement and the click rate.

7.5.2 Insights From A/B Testing

Therefore, using the results of the A/B test, we can conclude that the "promoting healthy teeth" version of the advertisement is more effective in generating a click rate compared to the "preventing cavities" version. This tells us that the "promoting healthy teeth" version is more persuasive in generating interest in this brand of toothpaste, and there is greater likelihood that using this version will result in increasing sales. It is important to note that our conclusion is based on a *causal* examination that lets us know that the version of the advertisement shown caused the difference in click rate. The relationship of the advertisement to the click rate is causal because we kept every other factor in the A/B test constant and changed only the version of the advertisement in order to examine the impact of this change on the click rate. Moreover, we were able to collect primary data by recruiting participants in the A/B test.

A/B testing is commonly used on several online platforms like Google, Facebook, and Instagram. The usual metrics that are tested determine which ad features result in greater click rates or which visual elements of the product web page result in greater engagement, more browsing behavior, positive word-of-mouth, and, of course, purchase. Several different promotions are tested at the same time to find out which is most effective at attracting consumers' attention. It is commonly believed that social proof such as the number of existing consumers, number of likes and followers, or satisfaction ratings featured prominently on a website can increase confidence that new customers will have an incentive to enroll. However, A/B testing can inform which of the social platforms have the most impact on increasing enrollment for a specific product or service. Not everything works for all products, and this can result in merely cluttering the website with too much information. The biggest advantage of A/B testing is that the design helps to isolate the influence of one specific factor by keeping everything else constant.

The online platforms have several tutorials on how to run these A/B tests, along with analytics to evaluate not just the results of the A/B test but also how the behavior of consumers has changed on the product's website. For instance, the Google Analytics site mentions that when McDonald's Hong Kong wanted to increase mobile orders, use of predictive models built into Google Analytics enabled it to boost app orders severalfold, which added to its profitability. A good example of A/B testing comes from the digital media company Upworthy. It conducted several A/B tests to determine which headlines for the same news article would generate the most clicks. The findings of the thousands of A/B tests that the company has conducted have been made publicly available through the Upworthy Research Archive.[1]

The process for A/B testing that we have delineated is the core of any type of A/B test. However, it is worth discussing the possibilities made available by the utilization of machine-learning models for A/B tests.

7.6 MACHINE-LEARNING-BASED A/B TESTING FOR FINDING EFFECTIVE ADVERTISEMENTS

Advertising is another key area that has been transformed by machine learning. It has been used by advertisers to enhance the relevancy of their ads and increase the return on investment of their advertising campaigns. Consider the following scenarios in which businesses are seeking answers:

1. A business has 15 different variants of its display advertisement and wants to show customers only the advertisement that will generate the most clicks.
2. A newspaper wants to select the most engaging headline from multiple options for a news article to captivate readers' interest.
3. Researchers conducting a drug trial want to determine whether their new drug is more (or less) effective than the existing treatment while minimizing the number of people who are exposed to a less effective treatment.

There is clearly no existing data that can help the businesses find the answers they are looking for. Hence, the only way available to gather data in such conditions is to run some form of A/B testing to gather primary data by assigning people to multiple groups to find the most effective display ad, headline, or drug. However, running A/B tests that require testing several different conditions with sufficient sample sizes would be both time and resource consuming. One big issue in all these cases is that businesses don't want to waste precious resources on testing each option to find the optimal one. For instance, testing which of the 15 advertisements is the most effective would require that an equal number of participants be assigned to each of 15 groups, which in essence means that a large number of participants would actually be assigned to 14 suboptimal groups. Ideally, businesses would want to identify the most effective display advertisement and assign more participants to it rather than waste resources on testing less effective versions. *Reinforcement-learning algorithms* (specifically, multi-armed-bandit-based algorithms) attempt to achieve precisely that outcome. They are used in diverse areas ranging from online advertising to clinical oncology.

Reinforcement-learning algorithms operate similarly to how animals learn. These algorithms try out different strategies and learn from the outcome. If the outcome is rewarding, those strategies are given more weight than if no reward was obtained. In the context of display advertising, a reinforcement-learning algorithm will try different variants of an ad and learn which ad variant leads to more reward (i.e., clicks) than the others. Note that the algorithm will find the most effective advertisement, but it will not learn what makes an advertisement effective and provides no information to the advertiser on how to improve an ad.

Therefore, reinforcement learning occupies a somewhat intermediate position between supervised and unsupervised learning. Unlike supervised learning, where models are trained with labeled data containing correct answers, reinforcement learning operates in an environment where correct answers or labels are not available. Conversely, unlike unsupervised learning, similarities in data cannot be exploited (e.g., clustered). Multi-armed-bandit-based algorithms are such reinforcement learners. This algorithm metaphorically relates to slot machines (or "one-armed bandits"), emphasizing exploration and exploitation to find the most rewarding outcomes. However, the only way to find out which slot machine is "better" is to play. And each play requires inserting a coin, which could result in a loss, making the process of learning expensive. The multi-armed-bandit-based algorithm uses a Bayesian updating process called Thompson sampling to find the optimal option. The approach allows for optimizing decisions over time, ensuring that strategies leading to higher rewards are prioritized.

7.7 IMPLEMENTATION USING R: A/B TESTING FOR ADVERTISING EFFECTIVENESS

The R code for A/B testing tends to be relatively simple. Hence, we will provide the code with the annotation that will help explain whether that line of code is useful in estimating sample size or performing power analysis.

7.7.1 Sample Size Estimation

R implementation of A/B testing starts with sample size estimation. The `power.prop.test()` function helps in estimating sample size. We need to provide four values: `power = 0.8` indicates that we are setting the power of our A/B test to be 0.80; `p1 = 0.10` and `p2 = 0.15` indicate that we expect 10% of the participants in the first group (those shown the "preventing cavities" version of the advertisement) and 15% of the participants in the second group (those shown the "promoting healthy teeth" version) to click on the advertisement; `sig.level = 0.05` is the value of α.

```
power.prop.test(power = 0.8, p1 = 0.10, p2 = 0.15, sig.level = 0.05)
##
##      Two-sample comparison of proportions power calculation
##
##               n = 685.5969
##              p1 = 0.1
##              p2 = 0.15
##       sig.level = 0.05
##           power = 0.8
##     alternative = two.sided
##
## NOTE: n is number in *each* group
```

7.7.2 Statistical Test

The `chisq.test` function implements Pearson's chi-squared test. In order to apply this test, we first need to enter the data in a table (the data are the same as included in the table earlier in the chapter). The `correct = FALSE` in the `chisq.test` function implies that since our sample size is large, we are not using any continuity correction. If the sample size is small (fewer than 30 participants per cell), then it is advisable to use `correct = TRUE`.

```
click <- c(77,119)
no_click <- c(623,581)
click_rate <- cbind(click,no_click)
chisq.test(click_rate,correct = FALSE)
##
##  Pearson's Chi-squared test
##
## data: click_rate
## X-squared = 10.465, df = 1, p-value = 0.001216
```

7.8 UNDERSTANDING THE CHAPTER

Students are encouraged to answer the following questions. They can then review the chapter to check their answers.

1. If a business wants to test different versions of an advertisement for its brand, should it rely on primary or secondary data? How can it generate primary data?

2. What is the difference between a Type I and a Type II error in the context of A/B testing?

3. What does the power of an A/B test signify in a study comparing the effectiveness of two different advertisements?
   a. The power indicates the likelihood of correctly detecting no difference between the two advertisements when there isn't any actual difference.
   b. The power represents the probability that the test will successfully identify a true difference in the effectiveness of the two advertisements in the population.
   c. The power of an A/B test signifies the chance of making a Type II error, which means not detecting a real difference between the two advertisements.
   d. The power is utilized to ensure that the null hypothesis is never rejected, maintaining the integrity of the study's results.

4. Why do we need to estimate the right sample size for an A/B test?
   a. To make the A/B test easier to conduct
   b. To get the most accurate results in the A/B test
   c. To use as little information as possible in the A/B test
   d. To make sure everyone can be part of the A/B test

5. What is the most recent method of conducting A/B testing online?

6. Which of the following statements is true about the random assignment of participants in experiments?
   a. It determines in which order participants see the A/B test stimuli.
   b. Experiments cannot be run if participants are randomly assigned.
   c. Random assignment means participants are assigned to the experiment groups using no criteria.
   d. Random assignment means participants are randomly assigned only to the control group.
   e. Random assignment means participants can self-select which group they want to be in.

7. What makes reinforcement learning different from supervised and unsupervised learning?
   a. Reinforcement learning requires labeled data with correct answers.
   b. Reinforcement learning focuses on exploration and exploitation to find the most rewarding outcomes without having labeled data.
   c. Reinforcement learning only exploits similarities in data.
   d. Reinforcement learning uses the Bayesian updating process to directly find correct answers or labels.

ENDNOTE

1. Matias, J. Nathan, Kevin Munger, Marianne Aubin Le Quere, and Charles Ebersole, "The Upworthy Research Archive," accessed September 25, 2023, https://upworthy.natematias.com.

8 USING NEURAL NETS FOR CUSTOMER ANALYTICS

CONTENTS

LEARNING OBJECTIVES

1. Understand the importance of retaining a customer
2. Note the impact of a firm's actions on consumer retention
3. Learn how neural networks work
4. Interpret the output of a neural network
5. Use neural networks to predict customer churn

8.1 RETAINING EXISTING CUSTOMERS

- To increase repeat purchase, the cosmetics retail chain Sephora builds a beauty profile for its loyal customers. This profile is used to generate specific recommendations for different products depending on each customer's hair and skin type or skin concerns.[1]
- TD Bank created a special ATM (Automated Thanking Machine) that surprised clients with personalized thank-you gifts ranging from Disneyland tickets for a single mom, to roses for older clients, to airline tickets for a mother who wanted to visit her sick daughter.[2]
- Mastercard sent spontaneous gifts to its existing customers that ranged from small gifts like cupcakes from Magnolia Bakery to more extravagant ones like concert tickets and VIP celebrity meetings. The campaign involved thousands of cardholders, spanning 25 countries.[3]

These examples represent a defensive strategy used by businesses to retain their customers. Defensive strategies are different than offensive strategies, which often require investing in advertising and offering deep discounts to recruit as many new customers as possible for the business. A defensive strategy involves finding innovative ways to retain existing customers. In this chapter, we will use neural nets for measuring a business's ability to retain customers.

8.2 RATIONALE FOR A DEFENSIVE STRATEGY

The rationale for retaining customers is that the cost of attracting a new customer could be 5 to 25 times more than keeping an existing one.[4] This higher cost motivates every business to be customer-centric or customer focused, which shows that the customer is the focal point of company actions. Recall the "we try harder because we are number 2" slogan from Avis, indicating that the only way to win against Hertz is by making their customers happy. In marketing, the term for customer happiness is *customer satisfaction*. A satisfied customer is the most important aim of any business. For instance, customer-centric businesses like Hilton empower employees to act in putting customers first. Employees have discretionary powers that allow them to redress any customer grievances before they escalate. Similarly, Trader Joe's employees are encouraged to be as customer-centric as possible, including providing speedy responses to complaints and queries and even opening products and offering samples to customers.

Satisfied customers also become loyal customers who stick with a business and are less likely to get lured away by competing brands. Businesses continuously are devising strategies to keep their customers loyal. For instance, loyalty programs—ranging from frequent flier airline miles to membership programs—are designed for exactly this reason. Such loyalty programs at enterprises that include airlines, hotels, and retail outlets provide deep discounts and special rewards to encourage the continued patronage of customers who sign up.

Along with being a reliable source of revenue for a firm, a satisfied customer helps attract new customers. Satisfied customers are happy to refer a product or service to others and, hence, perform a critical job of recruiting new customers on the firm's behalf. One way customers show their satisfaction is through spreading positive word-of-mouth (WOM). The extensive use of social media has made the spread of WOM faster by reaching a wider audience. Kleenex capitalized on this when it sent kits filled with Kleenex brand get-well items to people who posted on Facebook that they were ill or fighting a cold. When 100% of the recipients posted about their Kleenex surprises, the buzz surrounding this led to over 650,000 impressions and 1,800 interactions between the brand and social media users.[5]

Why should businesses care about WOM? Customers rely far more on information provided by other customers than they do on business-provided information. For instance, customers rely on product reviews by other customers. Similarly, referrals by other customers carry more weight than business-provided messages via advertisements. Moreover, acquisition of these new customers is not only inexpensive for a business; research also indicates that customers who have been referred by other customers are more profitable than those acquired through a firm's promotional methods.[6]

While benefits accruing from satisfied customers are numerous, the harm that can result from dissatisfied customers who leave a business can also be significant. Dissatisfied customers are more likely to spread negative WOM than satisfied customers are to spread positive WOM. It has been found that 23% of customers who had a positive experience with a business told 10 or more people about it, whereas 48% of customers who had a negative experience told 10 or more people.[7] Social media also facilitates the spread of negative WOM. It has become a common forum for dissatisfied customers to share their views of a business. Social media posts from dissatisfied customers start a chain of communication with other customers posting similar bad experiences that can soon devolve into a publicity nightmare for the business. It has been found that negative WOM gathers more attention and spreads faster than positive WOM. Negative WOM also results in greater loss of sales compared with gains from positive WOM. Customers often use social media to lodge complaints against airlines like Delta, United, or American about overbooked or delayed flights. For instance, United Airlines' baggage handling came under scrutiny when a musician found that the way the baggage was transferred could result in broken musical instruments. The musician created a video called United Breaks Guitars[8] that went viral and provided a forum for other customers to share similar negative experiences.

8.3 MONITORING SATISFACTION

Considering the enormous role satisfied customers play, it is important for businesses to continuously monitor customer satisfaction levels because most customers do not inform the firm that they are planning to leave. Silent churn (attrition or defection) occurs when the customer has decided to no longer be a customer but the business is unaware of this. Quantifying past customer retention is easy since it involves looking back to determine when a customer stopped transacting with the business. However, looking forward and predicting if the customer will continue to patronize a business is difficult because it requires estimating many unknowns about the customer: the need for the product, the fit of *this* product with the need, other offerings in the market, changes in situation, and so on.

One approach businesses use to assess satisfaction is to ask customers directly how satisfied they are. This can be accomplished by using a survey. Businesses commonly survey customers to find out their level of satisfaction with a product or service encounter. However, surveys can be lengthy, and customers may not be inclined to complete them. In addition, surveys capture overall satisfaction but provide no information about the likelihood of a specific customer to churn. The biggest challenge of using aggregate satisfaction measures is that the relationship between customer satisfaction and customer spending behavior is very weak.[9]

A second way of determining customer satisfaction levels that is similar to surveys is the *Net Promoter Score*, which involves the use of just one question to find out how satisfied customers are. The Net Promoter Score relies on a single scale that asks customers how likely it is that they will recommend a particular product or service. One version of the scale records responses on a 0 to 10 scale. However, such survey tools are backward-looking because although they can explain whether a customer has stopped patronizing a firm for a certain period of time, they do not help much in predicting whether the customer will continue to do business with the firm in the future.

8.4 PAST BEHAVIOR AS A PREDICTOR OF CHURN

To address some of the limitations of directly asking customers to indicate their level of satisfaction, businesses use the behavior of customers to predict their likelihood of churn. The main aim of such prediction models is to use past data such as characteristics of customers who have either stayed or left to determine their future behavior. For instance, if a retailer is considering the potential drop-off rate for an annual time period, it would first determine how many customers it had during the previous year (let's say it had 1,000 customers) and how many of those customers are still doing business with it in the current year (of the 1,000 only 800 are still making purchases, indicating a 20% drop-off). An important element in predicting future behavior could be the actions of customers right before they dropped off—that is, whether they reduced the frequency of their purchases or the amount spent or modified their actions in any other way that could be relevant in determining drop-off. These prediction models can help businesses identify which of their customers are likely to drop off and interventions that can be used to prevent losing these customers.

We next consider how we can use analytics for predicting customer drop-off. The example we will be using in this chapter is that of predicting whether individual customers will continue with their membership or will drop off during a specific time period. For instance, when consumers purchase products from Costco, the firm knows when the customer became a member and when they dropped off. There are several possible prediction models, such as probabilistic models, that make several assumptions to neural nets. In this chapter, we will again use neural nets to predict drop-off. Since we have already described and used neural nets in Chapter 6, we will next provide a brief overview (you are encouraged to reread Chapter 6 to gather more details about neural nets).

8.5 PREDICTING CUSTOMER DROP-OFF USING NEURAL NETS

We will be using a neural net to predict customer drop-off. The data used for this example are a subset of churn data from R package `modeldata`. The MLC++ software package also has an extended version of the dataset. Let's assume that we have three inputs—x_1, x_2, and x_3—which could be account length (i.e., the length of time the customer has been doing business with the firm), calls per day (i.e., the number of calls the customer makes in a day), and the number of times customer service was contacted regarding an issue. Using these three inputs, the neural net would then learn to tag the customer as "yes, will drop off" or "no, will not drop off." The neural net would have an input layer (with three nodes if we have three input variables), hidden layer(s), and the output layer (with two nodes if we have two outputs of "yes" and "no"). We can specify different numbers of nodes in the hidden layer. Assume that we have three nodes. The inputs from x_1, x_2, and x_3 are fed into each of the hidden layer nodes. That is, h_1 receives an input from x_1 and x_2 as well as from x_3. As in any neural net formulation, the inputs to the hidden layer nodes are weighted. Therefore, we multiply the input values with a weight. The path from x_1 to h_1 has a weight of w_{11}, while the path from x_1 to h_2 has a weight of w_{12}. The initial value of these weights can be chosen randomly, and the neural net will keep updating it to improve the predicted value. Figure 8.1 shows the neural net with the different layers and weights.

FIGURE 8.1 ■ Neural Net With Different Layers and Weights

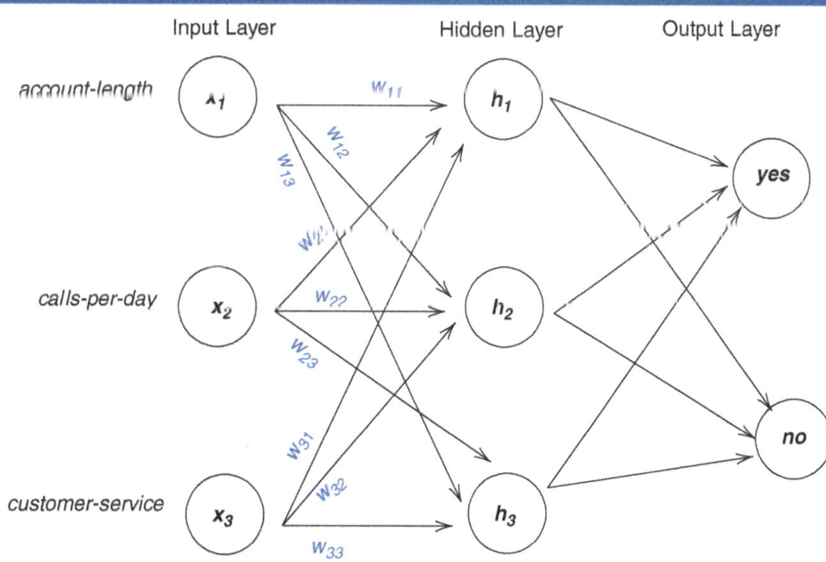

The input to h_1 is as follows:

$$x_1 * w_{11} + x_2 * w_{21} + x_3 * w_{31}$$

The input to h_2 is as follows:

$$x_1 * w_{12} + x_2 * w_{22} + x_3 * w_{32}$$

The input to h_3 is as follows:

$$x_1 * w_{13} + x_2 * w_{23} + x_3 * w_{33}$$

The hidden layer processes the input to provide the output. Just as neurons in the brain determine whether the information they have received requires firing of a subsequent step, so does a neural net. This decision of whether to fire or not is called *activation* in neural nets. Several different types of activation functions are possible and are dependent on what type of output we need. In our case, since we want an output of "yes" or "no," we use SoftMax in the output layer, which provides a label of whether the customer will drop off or not. SoftMax is commonly used as an activation when the output is categorical because the output probabilities nicely add up to 1. It also works well to normalize the data and can handle positive and negative input values. A SoftMax activation allows us to receive two outputs: y_1 and y_2. Each output is associated with one label and provides the probability of that label, ranging from 0 to 1. In our case, the output with SoftMax activation would be the following:

$$SoftMax(\hat{y}) = \frac{e^{y_1}}{e^{y_1+y_2}}$$

The neural net algorithm will complete its first iteration (also called a *run* or *loop*) and will give a prediction. If the data we are using to train the neural net have labels of which customers dropped off and which did not, then the neural net can compare its predictions with the true labels (the *ground truth*). The difference between the labels predicted by the neural net and the ground truth will be the error. Since the error is categorical, two types of errors are possible in our case: when the neural net incorrectly labels a customer as "yes, will drop off" although the customer will not drop off (also called a *false positive* error) or when the neural net labels a customer as "no, will not drop off" although the customer actually will drop off (a *false negative* error).

A confusion matrix is typically used to tabulate such errors, and we will create one when we discuss the customer-drop-off prediction model for membership renewal. It is important for businesses to know the false positive and false negative rate because it affects their cost. A business loses money both by not being able to identify customers who will drop off (false positives) and by identifying customers who will not drop off as those who will (false negatives). Finally, the error is *back propagated*, and the weights are updated before the next iteration of the neural net. The error informs us how each of the weights needs to be updated (i.e., increased or decreased in value). The main aim of updating the weights is to make the prediction error as low as possible. If there are several inputs and several hidden layers, then managing the process of weight updating can become difficult. Hence, a method called *gradient descent*, which is a process of optimization, is used to update weights. After the weights are updated, the next iteration of the neural net is run; this process continues till the error is minimized.

We next discuss how neural nets can be applied to the specific instance of predicting customer drop-off.

The data we will use for predicting customer drop-off are from a telecommunication company. These data have 19 inputs such as the state of residence, the duration of relationship, calls per day, and whether there is a voicemail plan, international plan, and night minutes. The data also have labels of whether the customer dropped off or not. This forms the ground truth against which we will compare the predictions of the neural net. Hence, we are using *supervised learning* because we have the ground truth.

To predict customer drop-off, we will use a neural net with one hidden layer. Hence, it is a *shallow neural net*.

8.5.1 Train/Test Split and Cross-Validation

We first split the data into train and test sets so that the neural net can learn on the train set and test its predictions on the test set. Here the output variable is the label of "yes" or "no." We split the data to randomly give 80% of the data to the train set and 20% to the test set.

We next implement a *cross-validation* procedure. Cross-validation is performed to avoid overfitting, which happens if we choose a model that performs well on train data but poorly on test data. A common cross-validation procedure is to partition/divide the train data into k parts, such that in any one iteration $k - 1$ sets are used for training while the accuracy of a model is tested on the kth set. For the customer-drop-off prediction task, we use a five-fold cross- validation (i.e., we divide the train data randomly into five parts and use four parts for training and one part for testing). We perform the process of splitting data into train and test sets five times, creating different random parts each time. A detailed description of cross-validation is available in the Technical Appendix.

8.5.2 Hyperparameters

Subsequently, we specify the number of nodes in our hidden layer of the neural net. In our case, we use only one hidden layer, with nodes varying from 25 to 35. Since we, as users, specify the number of hidden layers and the number of nodes in the hidden layers, these are hyperparameters (see the Technical Appendix for a detailed description). We allow the algorithm to try a different number of nodes between 15 and 25 to find the one with the least prediction error. We can specify a different range (e.g., from 1 to 50 or 100) and then hone this down to a smaller range providing an optimal outcome (see Figure 8.2). Note that using a larger range will take computationally longer than when we specify a smaller range.

FIGURE 8.2 ■ Cross-Validation to Find Optimal Nodes in the Hidden Layer

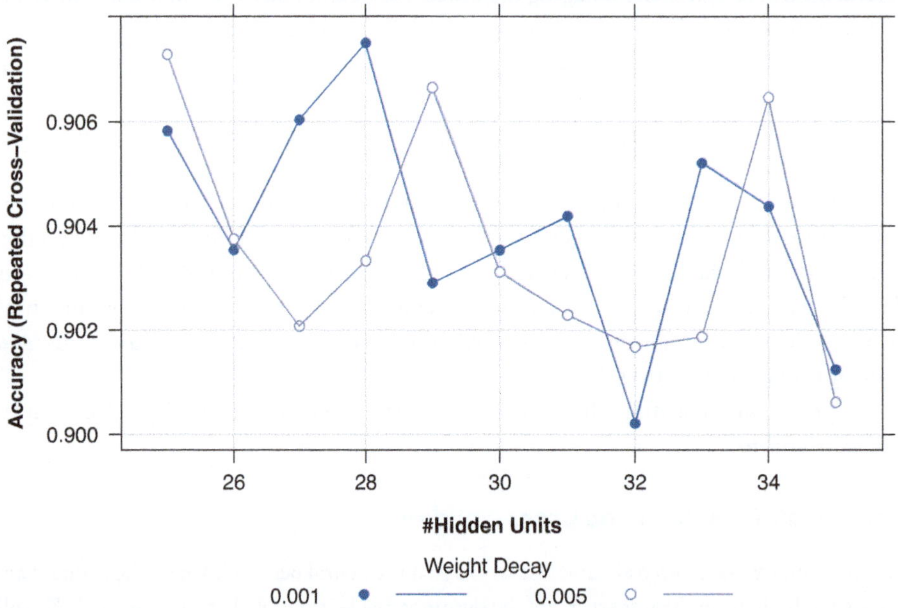

8.5.3 Testing the Performance of the Neural Net Model

We first consider how well the neural net model performs on the test data. For this, we check model predictions against the ground truth.

```
##  Accuracy   Kappa
## 0.8916667 0.5438596
##           Reference
## Prediction  no yes
##         no  194  16
##         yes  10  20
```

We see that the out-of-sample (test data) accuracy of the chosen model (accuracy = 0.8916667) is comparable to its performance with train data. This indicates less likelihood of overfitting.

In order to check how well the neural net performs in predicting customer drop-off, we use the confusion matrix, which describes the two types of error used for categorical outputs: false positives and false negatives. The confusion matrix plots the false positive and false negative errors as well as the accuracy of the neural net. A confusion matrix represents results in a 2 × 2 matrix. As Figure 8.3 shows, the columns represent the ground truth: how many customers are not going to drop off (*no*) and how many are going to drop off (*yes*). Each of the four cells represents the number of times the predictions matched or mismatched the ground truth. For instance, True Positive represents the number of times the ground truth (*no*) and the prediction (*no'*) matched. On the other hand, False Positive shows the number of times the ground truth was *yes* but the prediction was *no'*. Based on ground truth, *P* is the total number of customers who will not drop off, and *N* is the total number of customers who will drop off.

FIGURE 8.3 ■ Confusion Matrix Table

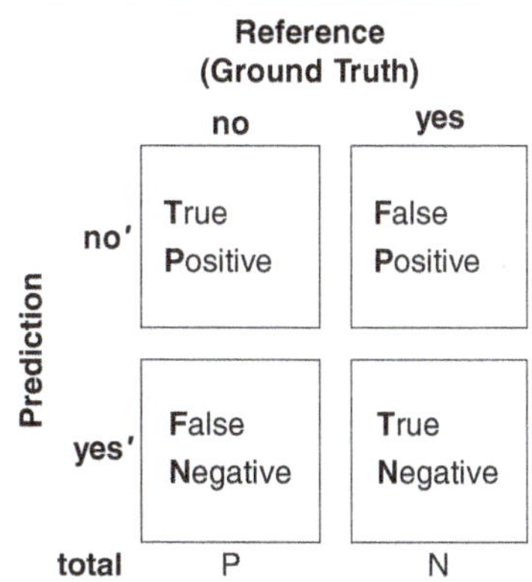

The confusion matrix helps us calculate many metrics.

$$\text{Accuracy} = \frac{TP + TN}{P + N}$$

$$\text{False Positive Rate} = \frac{FP}{N}$$

$$\text{False Negative Rate} = \frac{FN}{P}$$

For the customer-drop-off prediction model, the confusion matrix is the following.

```
##  Reference
##     Prediction   no  yes
##             no  194   16
##            yes   10   20
```

In this table, *reference* is ground truth, and *prediction* is the prediction of the chosen neural net model. The table shows that there are 10 customers who did not drop off but our model predicted would drop off (i.e., they were false negatives). And there were 16 customers who actually dropped off but our model predicted would not drop off (i.e., they were false positives). Since there are 194 + 10 = 204 customers who are not going to drop off based on the ground truth, *P* is 204. But there are 16 + 20 = 36 customers who dropped off, so *N* is 36.

Using this information, we can calculate that the false negative rate is 10 / 204 = 0.05 and the false positive rate is 16 / 36 = 0.44. Therefore, for these parameters of the neural net, the false negative rate is 5%, and the false positive rate is 44%. That is, if the firm were to act on these recommendations, then it would not be able to identify approximately 16 customers who might drop off. However, there was only a 2% error in misidentifying those who would not drop off as those who would. Note that variations in predictions across different model runs can occur due to chosen hyperparameter values, cross-validation, and randomness in weight initialization; nonetheless, the insights derived from the model typically remain consistent.

8.5.4 Business Insights

Therefore, utilizing neural nets allows us to efficiently predict whether a business will be able to retain a customer or whether the customer will drop off in the next time period. Even if the number of predictor variables increases, neural nets have better ability to handle them compared to traditional methods like regression. Such prediction models allow businesses to know not just which of their customers have dropped off in the past but also those who might drop off in the future. Knowing the drop-off rate allows firms to investigate what they may be doing right (if drop-off is low) or doing wrong (if drop-off is high). They then can develop strategies to ensure that dissatisfied customers' concerns are addressed so they do not leave. Moreover, knowing which customers are likely to drop off versus those who have stayed loyal allows a firm to come up with customized strategies for these two differing groups of customers.

8.6 IMPLEMENTATION USING R: PREDICTING CUSTOMER CHURN

This dataset uses customer information from a telecommunication company to predict if a customer is going to drop off or not. A subset of the churn data is used from the R package `modeldata`.[10]

The input variables in this dataset are the following:

state: state customer resides in (categorical)

account_length: how long a customer has been with the firm

area_code: area code of customer location

international_plan: whether customer subscribed to international plan (categorical yes/no)

voice_mail_plan: whether customer subscribed to voicemail plan (categorical yes/no)

number_vmail_messages: number of voicemail messages customer received

total_day_minutes: number of day minutes used

total_day_calls: number of day calls made

total_day_charge: total amount charged for day calls

total_eve_minutes: number of evening minutes used

total_eve_calls: total number of evening calls

total_eve_charge: total amount charged for evening calls

total_night_minutes: number of night minutes used

total_night_calls: number of night calls

total_night_charge: total amount charged for night calls

total_intl_minutes: number of international minutes used

total_intl_calls: total number of international calls

total_intl_charge: total amount charged for international calls

number_customer_service_calls: how many times customer service was contacted

The outcome variable is churn, which has a value of 0 (i.e., customer remained with the firm) or 1 (i.e., customer dropped off).

First, we load three packages: `caret`,[11] `mlbench`,[12] and `doParallel`.[13] The function `registerDoParallel(cores = 4)` helps in parallelizing and speeding up calculations. We can change `cores = 4` to some other number depending upon the number of cores the computer's processor has.

```
library(caret)
library(mlbench)
library(doParallel)
registerDoParallel(cores = 4)
```

We then load the data and *set seed*. Setting seed ensures that when you run this code on your machine, you get results that are similar to the ones reported in this book. For your own analysis, you can set any seed, and the results will deviate slightly from the results reported in the book. This occurs because a different seed will assign a different set of observations to the test and train datasets. After setting seed, we remove the first two variables, state and area_code, as they will not be used in this analysis.

```
churn <-
read.csv(url("http://data.mishra.us/files/churn_chapter/customer_churn.csv"))
set.seed(123456)
churn <- churn[,-c(1,2)]
```

The following lines of code split the data into train and test datasets. The `createDataPartition` function randomly samples 80% of row numbers from the dataset (that is what `p = .8` specifies). We then split churn data into two sets. By using `churn[inTrain,]`, we are selecting the rows from churn data that correspond to the numbers that are saved in `inTrain`. For the test set, we select rows from churn that are not in `inTrain`. This way, the train set has 80% observations, and the test set has 20% of the randomly chosen observations.

```
inTrain <- createDataPartition(churn$churn, p = .8, list=FALSE)
train <- churn[c(inTrain),]
test <- churn[-inTrain,]
```

Since the goal of this analysis is to build a neural net model that can predict whether a customer is going to drop off or not, we use the 18th variable `churn` as our output variable. All other variables are input (i.e., predictor) variables. We separate output and input variables in both the test and train datasets. We then convert the outcome variable from 1 to "yes" and 0 to "no" using the `ifelse` function.

```
train_predictor <- train[,-18]
train_outcome <- train [,18]
train_outcome <- ifelse(train_outcome == 0, "no", "yes")

test_predictor <- test[,-18]
test_outcome <- test [,18]
test_outcome <- ifelse(test_outcome == 0, "no", "yes")
```

We next specify the cross-validation procedure. We use five-fold cross-validation and repeat this cross-validation process five times.

```
ctrl <- trainControl(method = "repeatedcv", # cross-validation
                     number = 5, # 5 folds
                     repeats = 5,
                     classProbs = TRUE # report class probability
                     )
```

We next specify values for the two parameters `decay` and `size`: `decay` specifies the regularization parameter to avoid overfitting, and `size` specifies the number of nodes in the hidden layer (note that our implementation here is using only one hidden layer). Since the values of `decay` and `size` change the predictive power of our model and we don't know the optimum values a priori, we try various values and let the best combination of `decay` and `size` emerge from their performance in the train dataset. We can then test how well these parameters perform on test data; `bag = FALSE` means we are not using bagging.

```
avnnetGrid <- expand.grid(decay = c(.001,.005),
                          size = c(25:35),
                          bag = FALSE)
```

Using `size = c(25:35)` indicates that we want to estimate a neural network with 25 to 35 nodes in the hidden layer, and `decay = c(0.001, .005)` shows that we want to try the two decay values of 0.001 and 0.005. Since there are 11 different values of size and 2 values of decay, the analysis will generate the performance of 22 different models, each one representing a combination of decay and size.

When using neural nets, there is always a possibility that a model does not reach globally optimal estimates because of the random weights assigned at the beginning of model estimation. Since each neural net starts with randomly initialized weights that get updated in the subsequent back propagation, sometimes different seeds lead to different optimal weights. These issues result in a situation where the chosen model might not be the best model and may lead to overfitting. One way to counter this issue is to test the performance of the same model with the same dataset but with different random seeds. A model-averaged neural network (`avNNet`) fits several neural networks via the `nnet` package using different seeds on the same data, then averages the predictions of the networks; `method = "avNNet"` implements this approach.

The use of `tuneGrid = avnnetGrid` informs the model about `decay` and `size` parameter combinations; `trControl = ctrl` provides cross-validation details to the training process; `preProc = c("center", "scale")` centers and scales the data, an essential step in fitting any neural net model; and `softmax = TRUE` fits classification networks with the outcome variable as a factor variable. Note that since a customer could either drop off (*yes*) or not (*no*), our outcome variable is a factor variable. The addition of `allowParallel = TRUE` enables use of parallel processing, and `maxit = 50` tells the model to perform 50 iterations or weight updates for each model.

```
avnnet_fit <- train(train_predictor, train_outcome,
                    method = "avNNet",
                    tuneGrid = avnnetGrid,
                    trControl = ctrl,
                    softmax = TRUE,
                    preProc = c("center", "scale"),
                    trace = FALSE,
                    metric = "Accuracy",
                    allowParallel = TRUE,
                    maxit = 50)
```

Depending upon the computer, the preceding code could take a few to several minutes to perform all estimations. If it is taking a long time on your computer, reduce the `maxit` to a lower number. When completed, we can use `plot(avnnet_fit)` to request the decay and size combination that performed the best. This will produce Figure 8.4.

```
plot(avnnet_fit)
```

FIGURE 8.4 ■ Cross-Validation to Find Optimal Nodes in the Hidden Layer

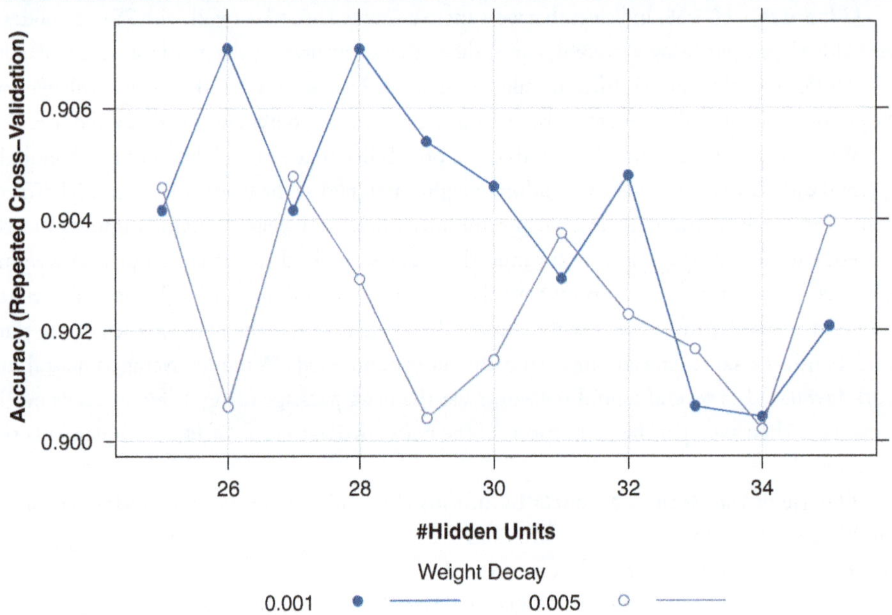

We see that the model with `decay = 0.001` and `size = 26` has the highest accuracy. If we type `avnnet_fit` in the R console, we notice that a long output ending with `Accuracy was used to select the optimal model using the largest value. The final values used for the model were size = . . .` This is consistent with what we can see in the preceding plot.

We can now assess how well this model performs on our test data. The `predict` function predicts the output using the input variables in the test dataset. `postResample` compares the obtained predictions of churn (`predicted_outcome`) with their true value (`test_outcome`) and provides performance measures such as *accuracy* and *kappa*.[14]

```
predicted_outcome <- predict(avnnet_fit, test_predictor)

postResample(pred = factor(predicted_outcome), obs = factor(test_outcome))
## Accuracy     Kappa
## 0.8916667 0. 5438596
```

We see that the out-of-sample (test data) accuracy of the chosen model (`accuracy = 0.8916667`) is comparable to its performance with train data. This indicates less likelihood of overfitting.

While accuracy gives us a global metric to measure our model's performance, it says nothing about how good this model is at predicting each of the two possible outcomes: "yes" versus "no." For a firm concerned about churn, a positive outcome is that a customer will not drop off, and a negative outcome is that a customer will drop off. It is likely that a model is very good at predicting people who will not drop off but not so good at predicting those who will drop off. The accuracy metric does not reveal this information. Ideally, we should be able to assess the false positive and false negative rates. The confusion matrix helps us estimate accuracy as well as false positive and false negative rates.

Now, let's generate the confusion matrix.

```
confusionMatrix(data = factor(predicted_outcome),
                reference = factor(test_outcome))$table
##  Reference
##   Prediction   no  yes
##          no   194   16
##          yes   10   20
```

In this table, *reference* is ground truth, and *prediction* is the prediction of the chosen neural net mode. It shows that ten customers did not drop off although our model predicted that they would drop off (i.e., they were false negatives). Sixteen customers actually dropped off, but our model predicted that they would not drop off (i.e., they were false positives). Since there are 194 + 10 = 204 customers who are not going to drop off based on ground truth, *P* is 204. But there are 16 + 20 = 36 customers who dropped off, so *N* is 36. Again, note these predicted values can vary depending on hyperparameter values, cross validation process and initial weights.

Using this information, we can calculate that the false negative rate is 10 / 204 = 0.05 and the false positive rate is 16 / 36 = 0.44.

8.6.1 Tidymodels Implementation

The `tidymodels`[10] framework offers another way to implement neural nets in R. It is a collection of packages that work together and offer a convenient way to implement complex machine learning workflows.

After importing the dataset, we remove the first two variables state and area_code as they will not be used in this analysis. Since the outcome variable churn is a numeric variable, we need to convert it to a factor variable so it is consistent with the categorical nature of the outcome variable (e.g., churn: *yes* (1) vs. *no* (0)). We then split the data into train (80%) and test (20%) sets using `prop = 0.8` in the `initial_split()` function.

```
library(tidymodels)
library(mlbench)
library(doParallel)

set.seed(123456)
churn_data <- read.csv(
  url("http://data.mishra.us/files/churn_chapter/customer_churn.csv"))
churn_data <- churn_data[,-c(1,2)]

churn_data$churn <- as.factor(churn_data$churn)
datasplit <- initial_split(churn_data, prop = 0.8,
                           strata = churn)
trainData <- training(datasplit)
testData <- testing(datasplit)
```

In `recipe()`, we first define the outcome and predictor variables. `churn ~ .` specifies that the outcome variable `churn` is predicted by all other variables. `step_normalize(all_numeric_predictors())` normalizes all numeric variables to have a mean of zero and standard deviation of 1.

```
rec_nn <- recipe(churn ~ ., data = trainData) %>%
  step_normalize(all_numeric_predictors())
```

`mlp()` specified the model, which is a single-layer, feed-forward neural net model. `set_engine()` defines the model engine, and we choose nnet as the model engine. `set_mode("classification")` specifies that the outcome variable, churn, is categorical. Unlike in the earlier code, in which we specified a range from which the number of hidden layers could be chosen, here we let the algorithm pick the optimal number of nodes. `hidden_units = tune()` is used to determine the optimal number of nodes through fine-tuning. The regularization parameter, `penalty`, is included to avoid overfitting, and the maximum number of iterations or weight updates for each model, `epochs`, is determined through fine-tuning. `translate()` helps in understanding model arguments such as `hidden_units`, `penalty`, and `epochs` with respect to our model engine, `nnet`. To understand how to compare the terms with the previous set of codes, `hidden_units` is `size`, `penalty` is `decay`, and `epochs` is `maxit`.

```
neural_net_model <-
  mlp(hidden_units = tune(),
      penalty = tune(),
      epochs = tune()) %>%
  set_engine("nnet") %>%
  set_mode("classification")%>% translate()
```

```
neural_net_model <-
  mlp(hidden_units = tune(),
      penalty = tune(),
      epochs = tune()) %>%
  set_engine("nnet") %>%
  set_mode("classification")%>% translate()

neural_net_model
## Single Layer Neural Network Specification (classification)
##
## Main Arguments:
##    hidden_units = tune()
##    penalty = tune()
##    epochs = tune()
##
## Computational engine: nnet
##
## Model fit template:
## nnet::nnet(formula = missing_arg(), data = missing_arg(), weights =
missing_arg(),
##    size = tune(), decay = tune(), maxit = tune(), trace = FALSE,
##    linout = FALSE)
```

`grid_regular()` creates a grid of three tuning parameters: `hidden_units`, `penalty`, and `epochs`. The `levels` argument specifies the number of levels that need to be created for each tuning parameter. For `levels = 5`, five levels of each tuning parameter will be created. Since we have three tuning parameters, there will be $5^3 = 125$ combinations of tuning parameters, and 125 different models will be fit.

```
neural_grid <- grid_regular(
   hidden_units(),
   penalty(),
   epochs(),
   levels = 5)
```

Using *k*-fold cross-validation, the best model among the 125 possible models is chosen to avoid overfitting, and `v = 10` specifies that the data are partitioned into 10 parts. Using more than one core available on a computer can reduce computation time. With `registerDoParallel(cores = 5)`, we will be using five cores to parallelize the grid search process.

```
nn_folds <- vfold_cv(trainData, v = 10)
doParallel::registerDoParallel(cores = 5)
```

Next we define a workflow using `workflow()`. It specifies the model (`neural_net_model`) and adds the `recipe` `rec_nn` defined in an earlier step.

```
nn_wf <- workflow() %>%
    add_recipe(rec_nn)%>%
    add_model(neural_net_model)
```

Now we can start the grid search process using `tune_grid()`. It will compute performance metrics (e.g., root mean square error [RMSE] and *R*-squared) for each of the 125 parameter combinations stored in the data frame `neural_grid`. `resamples = nn_folds` will use tenfold cross-validation specified in `nn_fold`. In `control_grid()`, `save_pred = TRUE` means that predictions made by each of the 125 models will be saved. `parallel_over = "everything"` parallalizes the grid search process to reduce the execution time.

```
nn_res <- tune_grid(
   nn_wf,
   grid = neural_grid,
   resamples = nn_folds,
   control = control_grid(save_pred = TRUE,
   parallel_over = "everything")
)
```

After the tuning process is completed, the top five models are identified and their performance estimates outputted using `show_best`. We can then select the top-performing model using `select_best` and finalize the workflow. Note that we are using accuracy to choose the best model, but we can also choose the best model by using `roc_auc` (Receiver Operating Characteristic Area Under Curve).

```
show_best(nn_res, "accuracy")
```

```
## # A tibble: 5 × 9
##    hidden_units penalty epochs .metric .estimator  mean     n std_err    .config
##           <int>   <dbl>  <int>   <chr>      <chr> <dbl> <int>   <dbl>      <chr>
## 1            10       1    505 accuracy    binary 0.904    10 0.00617 Preproces~
## 2             7       1    505 accuracy    binary 0.903    10 0.00412 Preproces~
## 3            10       1    257 accuracy    binary 0.902    10 0.00517 Preproces~
## 4            10       1    752 accuracy    binary 0.901    10 0.00714 Preproces~
## 5            10       1   1000 accuracy    binary 0.900    10 0.00563 Preproces~
```

```
best_accuracy <- select_best(nn_res, "accuracy")
final_nn <- finalize_workflow(
  nn_wf,
  best_accuracy
)
```

Final steps involve predicting the performance of this model on our test data. `last_fit()` helps us accomplish this. Using `collect_metrics()`, we can find the `accuracy` and `auc_roc` estimates of the chosen model.

```
final_res <- last_fit(final_nn, datasplit)
collect_metrics(final_res)

## # A tibble: 2 × 4
##   .metric   .estimator .estimate  .config
##   <chr>     <chr>          <dbl>  <chr>
## 1 accuracy  binary         0.905  Preprocessor1_Model1
## 2 roc_auc   binary         0.939  Preprocessor1_Model1
```

To produce a confusion matrix, we will use `collect_predictions()`, which stores actual churn (ground truth) and the prediction made by the model on test data in a data frame, `confusion_data`. `conf_mat()` produces a confusion matrix. Note the values in the confusion matrix are different when we use the `tidymodels` package versus the `caret` package to build the neural net. This is not surprising because different tools can yield slightly different results even when performing similar analyses. The differences can be attributed to underlying differences in how these packages handle aspects like model training, prediction, and evaluation, even when settings are consistent across them.

```
confusion_data <- collect_predictions(final_res)
conf_mat(confusion_data, churn, .pred_class)
```

```
##             Truth
##   Prediction   0   1
##            0 206  22
##            1   1  12
```

8.7 UNDERSTANDING THE CHAPTER

1. Is it more expensive to retain existing customers than recruit new customers?
2. How does cross-validation improve the predictions of the neural net?

3. Interpret the impact of decay and size values used in the following R code on the number of models that will be tested:

```
avnnetGrid <- expand.grid(decay = c(.001,.005),
                  size = c(15:35), bag = FALSE
```

4. Data are split into train and test sets ______. (Choose the statement that is *false.*)
   a. To avoid model overfitting
   b. By using *k*-fold cross-validation
   c. By using gradient descent
   d. To increase model generalizability

5. Choose the statement that is *false* regarding the back-propagation process for neural nets:
   a. Errors are back propagated.
   b. Weights are updated through back propagation.
   c. Neural nets do not use back propagation.
   d. Back propagation is used to minimize errors.

6. The Net Promoter Score considers those who received the following score(s) on a scale of 0 to 10 as passively satisfied:
   a. 7 and 8
   b. 0 to 6
   c. 9 and 10
   d. 2 to 8
   e. 13 to 17

7. What is the primary purpose of utilizing cross-validation in the training process of neural networks? Pick the option that is *incorrect.*
   a. Increase model accuracy
   b. Reduce overfitting
   c. Adjust hyperparameters
   d. Increase overfitting
   e. Decrease training time

ENDNOTES

1. Nastasoiu, Alina, and Mark Vandenbosch, "Competing With Loyalty: How to Design Successful Customer Loyalty Reward Programs," *Business Horizons* 62, no. 2 (2019): 207–214.
2. St. Louis, Molly, "9 Companies That Nailed the Whole 'Surprise and Delight' Thing," *Inc.*, August 28, 2017, https://www.inc.com/molly-reynolds/9-companies-that-nailed-the-whole-surprise-and-del.html.
3. Ibid.
4. Reichheld, Frederick F., & W. Earl Sasser, "Zero Defections: Quality Comes to Services," *Harvard Business Review* 68, no. 5 (1990): 105–111.

5. Ismail, Kaya, "5 Successful Surprise and Delight Marketing Campaigns," March 29, 2019, https://www.cmswire.com/digital-marketing/5-successful-surprise-and-delight-marketing-campaigns/.

6. Villanueva, J., S. Yoo, and D. M. Hanssens, "The Impact of Marketing-Induced Versus Word-of-Mouth Customer Acquisition on Customer Equity Growth," *Journal of Marketing Research* 45, no. 1 (2008): 48–59.

7. Dixon, M., K. Freeman, and N. Toman, "Stop Trying to Delight Your Customers," *Harvard Business Review* 88, no. 7/8 (2010): 116–122.

8. Andres, Tommy, "A Broken Guitar, a YouTube Video and a New Era of Customer Service," July 5, 2019, https://www.marketplace.org/2019/07/05/a-broken-guitar-a-youtube-video-and-a-new-era-of-customer-service/.

9. Keiningham, T., S. Gupta, L. Aksoy, and A. Buoye, "The High Price of Customer Satisfaction," *MIT Sloan Management Review* 55, no. 3 (2014): 37.

10. Kuhn, Max, et al., "Tidymodels: A Collection of Packages for Modeling and Machine Learning Using tidyverse Principles" (2020), https://www.tidymodels.org.

11. Kuhn, Max, "caret: Classification and Regression Training," R package version 6.0-94 (March 21, 2023), https://CRAN.R-project.org/package=caret.

12. Leisch, Friedrich, and Evgenia Dimitriadou, "mlbench: Machine Learning Benchmark Problems," R package version 2.1-3 (2021).

13. Microsoft Corporation and Steve Weston, "doParallel: Foreach Parallel Adaptor for the 'parallel' Package," R package version 1.0.17 (2022), https://CRAN.R-project.org/package=doParallel.

14. This metric compares observed accuracy with expected accuracy (obtained from random chance). It varies between 0 and 1 with 1 indicating perfect predictions.

PART III

FINANCIAL AND ACCOUNTING ANALYTICS

9 LOAN CHARGE-OFF PREDICTION USING AN EXPLAINABLE MODEL

CONTENTS

LEARNING OBJECTIVES

1. Manage long- and short-term risk assessment
2. Mitigate risk with credit underwriting and loan charge-off model
3. Comprehend the use of human versus model loan charge-off prediction
4. Master the explainable prediction model
5. Use logistic regression for model transparency
6. Understand the odds ratio and confusion matrix

9.1 USING ANALYTICS FOR FINANCIAL DECISIONS

An area of business that is seeing a rapid increase in the use of analytics is the financial sector. It is important for financial institutions as well as finance departments within organizations to leverage information in novel ways to stay profitable and grow their business. Information transparency is also important to satisfy different stakeholders such as customers, investors, and regulators. Historically, analytic models have been commonly used in finance since finance relies heavily on different econometric and statistical models for its predictions. When we think of forecasting models in finance, the first case that comes to mind is stock market predictions. However, we are seeing an influx of machine-learning models in finance for myriad uses such as improving lending or generating viable leads for achieving growth objectives.

- Financial institutions are using analytic models such as data robots to improve accuracy in their *underwriting decisions* to predict which customers have a higher likelihood of default.
- Models that provide reasons for their predictions are being used in financial decision-making so that businesses can explain their decisions to their stakeholders.
- Artificial intelligence (AI) solutions are helping banks and credit lenders improve underwriting decisions that can enhance the inclusion of a large section of borrowers—for example, millennials. Such improvements in the AI system not only increase fair outcomes for the borrowers but also allow the financial institutions to increase their customer base of younger-generation clients.
- AI systems are also converting complex jargon used in financial decisions to explanations in simple English using natural language processing (NLP). This helps answer many customer financial questions in an easy-to-understand manner, increasing trust in the institution.
- Robo-advisors are now commonly used for financial planning.

9.2 RISK ASSESSMENT: EXTERNAL VERSUS INTERNAL FACTORS

An important aspect of forecasting is determining the different types of risk a business faces, which can positively or negatively affect its financial health. Some of these risks could involve factors external to the business over which it has relatively less control while other risks could involve internal factors.

As we discussed in Chapter 1, external risks include macroeconomic factors like interest rates, economic recessions, new regulations, and sociocultural changes. For instance, variations in interest rates or economic downturns can have distinct impacts on various businesses. The type of risk that the fashion industry might experience because of macroeconomic factors would be different from what an engineering firm would experience. Businesses also need to be aware that many of these factors could be correlated; for example, changes in oil prices are likely to affect inflation and interest rates, impacting industries by altering consumer spending and credit risks.

Internal risk can be operational, stemming from potential breakdowns in daily activities, or financial, due to investment strategies, funding, or poor financial estimations. If we take the example of banks, an important financial estimation they have to perform is to determine how many of their borrowers—firms or individuals—are likely to pay back their loans on time and how many of them are going to default. The uncertainty regarding borrowers' ability to repay loans is fundamentally an external risk; however, the decision to lend and the correct estimation of default are internal mechanisms. If these borrowers are likely to default, banks need to know if some preemptive measures can be taken to prevent default.

Analytics methods are now being used routinely to predict whether a business has enough liquidity to meet its future payment, growth, or investment requirements. Consider the example of a bank that is trying to predict the proportion of loan losses it could incur in a given year that is likely to negatively impact its year-end financials. Such predictions are important to help the bank prevent such loan losses or, at worst, know how much cash reserves it needs to maintain to sustain such losses. Loan losses are also called loan charge-offs. A charged-off loan is the amount of the loan that the bank (or any creditor) declares cannot be collected because of the situation of the borrower. A charge-off (or write-off) is mainly an accounting procedure in which a business acknowledges that the loan is uncollectible, but it is not loan forgiveness. The uncollectible amount is entered into accounting as a charge against business earnings. It is generally calculated as *loan charge-off = loan amount − amount recovered*.

9.2.1 Loan Charge-Off Models

Analytic models that are used for such prediction are called *loan charge-off models*. In these predictions, the algorithm's prediction error can have a significant influence on the bank's forecasting abilities. Accurate prediction is very important, and under- versus over-predicting the charge-off error can lead to different estimates. For instance, underpredicting how much of the loan will need to be charged off is a more expensive prediction error because the bank is likely to be short of funds. Overpredicting a charge-off may be less harmful because the bank will be overprepared for a loss that does not occur. Of course, in this case the bank could use the money gainfully elsewhere.

The ability of banks to handle such charge-offs is considered by regulators as an important factor in evaluating the credit rating of the bank, as well as threats to its financial health such as bankruptcy risks. Charge-off provisions are considered an important outcome variable in assessing the level of distress faced by banks because of changes in both internal and external factors. When banks that suffered large losses (because of many different reasons) were analyzed, it was found that only those that had the ability to bear the brunt of charge-offs with enough capitalization (i.e., enough money to cover debt obligations and operating costs) were able to recover more quickly. Undercapitalized banks took more than a year to recover. Therefore, an important way banks or any lenders try to assess and safeguard against risk due to internal factors is through a process of credit underwriting.

9.3 CREDIT UNDERWRITING: PROTECTING AGAINST RISK

The goal of credit underwriting is to reduce loan charge-offs. For millions of individuals and multiple businesses, many transactions are debt-based—that is, individuals and businesses buy goods or services with money that has been borrowed from an entity that provides credit. For instance, if someone wants to buy a car costing $20,000 but doesn't have that much cash with them, they can borrow the amount and agree to pay an interest of, say, 3% on the amount borrowed. They will also be allowed to pay back the amount over, say, 10 years. But before one can borrow the amount, the lender will first need to approve their loan application—that is, determine whether they can be lent that amount and at what rate of interest. This process of loan application evaluation is known as credit underwriting. The term *underwriting* emerged because personnel from lender organizations used to write their names *under* the loan amount that they determined appropriate for the risk the lender was taking. The risk is the likelihood that the loan does not get repaid or gets only partially repaid. Hence, the underwriter evaluates the financial standing of the loan applicant to determine not just the loan amount but also the interest rate; a higher risk (of not repaying) would result in a higher interest rate.

9.3.1 Human Underwriters and Prediction Models

Traditionally, credit underwriting has been conducted by human underwriters because they need to keep in mind the various rules that might apply as well as synthesize the unique features of every loan application. The ability to pull information from various sources to determine loan approval makes human experts best suited for such decisions. Underwriters tend to rely on experience, market knowledge, a set of rules, and decisions made in the past. But this can make the underwriting process time consuming and expensive because it can take experts time to reach a decision. Several organizations have started using analytic models in credit underwriting for reasons of efficiency (a lot of data can be assimilated and synthesized by models) and cost (models can reach decisions faster).

9.3.2 Explainable Prediction Models

Different types of models have been used for credit underwriting. These models include logistic regression, decision trees, time series, panel data models (if a time component is added to the outcome), and complex structural models (in which sensitivity to specific influences can be disentangled using if–then possibilities). However, there are some important aspects that most lenders worry about when using models for underwriting: that the model's decision is transparent and explainable to the applicant whose loan was denied and that the model does not discriminate on demographic features of the applicant such as race, gender, or age. One solution is to combine the expertise of underwriters and prediction models. For cases that are not complicated, analytic models can be used to provide a decision. But for complex cases or those on the boundary, human expertise can be leveraged to reach a final decision. This saves time and allows organizations to use human underwriters' time efficiently.

Moreover, there are several glass box or transparent models that show which predictors were used in the model and how they affected the outcome variable. The simplest case would be a linear or logistic regression that allows interpretation of the influence (magnitude and direction) of the predictors on the outcome. There are several other models that inherently exhibit explainability and interpretability, such as decision trees, generalized linear models (GLMs), and naïve Bayes classifiers.[1] For the purposes of this chapter, we will use logistic regression as an explainable model.

9.4 LOGISTIC REGRESSION

Let's examine logistic regression in the context of loan charge-off. As we discussed earlier, lenders would like to utilize relevant predictors of the borrowers to determine whether or not to lend. Let's assume that a bank—let's call it Carta Bank—wants to build an explainable model using some important predictors for approving loans to individual borrowers. These predictors can be used to train a model to learn which of Carta Bank's borrowers will repay the loan or default. The training data will consist of existing/past borrowers of the bank about whom the bank has information on the predictor variables (e.g., individual characteristics such as income or credit score) as well as whether they repaid the loan (i.e., information about the outcome variable). Once the model has been trained, it can be used to predict whether a new borrower will repay the loan or default.

We can include these predictors in our logistic regression model. The *outcome variable* Y (in this case loan-status) associated with each row of predictors/features indicates whether the borrower paid back the loan with no delay or whether the loan had to be charged off. Since the outcome is categorical in nature rather than continuous, we use logistic regression, which is best suited to handle categorical outcome variables.

9.4.1 Using Categorical Variables as Outcome

As explained earlier, the aim is to find a function f such that we have a model $Y = f(X) + \varepsilon$. In other words, our model helps explain how changes in X (the predictor variable) will influence Y (whether a borrower will repay the loan). This will help the bank not only to determine whether to lend but also to prepare for any future charge-offs.

A simple option is to estimate probability of repayment as a function of X, similar to a linear regression. That is, $p(Y) = a + b^* X_1 + c^* X_2 + d^* X_3 + \varepsilon$. However, since probability always ranges between 0 and 1, a linear-regression-like estimation will provide values of probability that will not be bounded by 0 and 1. There will be some negative probability values that make interpretation much harder.

Our outcome variable is whether the borrower repaid or the loan had to be charged off. This is a categorical variable, which means there is no ordering between repaying and not repaying.[2] Therefore, repaying is not numerically more or less than not repaying. Using a linear-regression-like approach assumes that the outcome variable is measured on an interval scale.

Considering these limitations, one option is to regard the log odds of repaying as a linear function of X. Let's understand what the odds are and how they are related to probability.

9.4.2 Odds

Odds denote the ratio of the number of times an event will occur to the number of times the event will not occur. The odds of 1 to 9 for a horse winning a race denote that out of 10 races the horse will win once and lose 9 times—that is, a 10% probability of winning ($p = 0.1$) is represented as odds of 1 to 9. Formally, odds are represented as follows:

$$Odds = \frac{\text{Probability of event occurring}(p)}{\text{Probability of event not occurring}(1-p)}$$

We could ask why we use odds instead of probability. Odds are preferred because they offer the following advantages. Let's understand through this example: If I am twice as likely to vote in an election than you and your probability of voting is 0.3, then my probability is 0.6. However, if your probability is 0.6 and I am twice as likely to vote, we will come up with a number that is absurd: 1.2. A probability of 1.2 is absurd because, as you may recall, probability is constrained to the range between 0 and 1; hence, 1.2 doesn't make sense as a probability value. But this is not a problem with odds. A 0.6 probability is 0.6/0.4 = 1.5 odds. If I am twice as likely to vote, then my odds are 3, which is the probability of $p/1 - p = 3 => p = 3 - 3p = p = 3/4 = 0.75$. Therefore, odds are better *scaled* than probability.

In addition, if we take the logarithm of odds (log odds), then they are not bounded by 0 and 1 and can take any value between $-\infty$ and $+\infty$, as Figure 9.1 explains.

FIGURE 9.1 ■ Log Odds

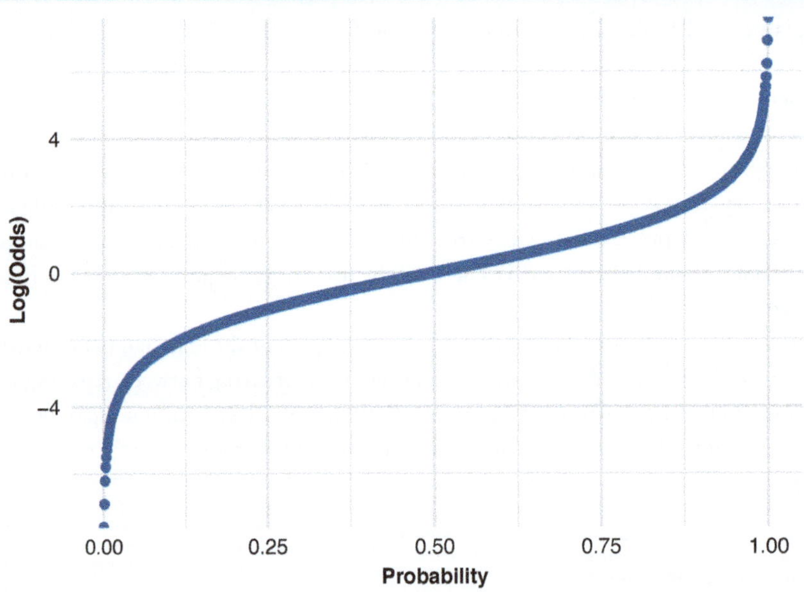

Therefore, considering log odds to be a linear function of X will protect us from generating meaningless results like negative probabilities, which we would have done had we considered loan repayment to be a linear function of X. Formally, log odds of repaying as a linear function of X can be written as follows:

$$In\left[\frac{p}{1-p}\right] = a + b^* X_1 + c^* X_2 + d^* X_3 + \varepsilon$$

Solving gives us the probability that a borrower would repay (p) as follows:

$$p = \frac{1}{1+e^{-a-b^*X_1-c^*X_2-d^*X_3-\varepsilon}}$$

This equation represents logistic function, also known as sigmoid function. It has the desired property that the values of p will always fall between 0 and 1 for any value of a, b, c, d, or X, as Figure 9.2 indicates.

FIGURE 9.2 ■ Logistic Function (Also Known as Sigmoid Function)

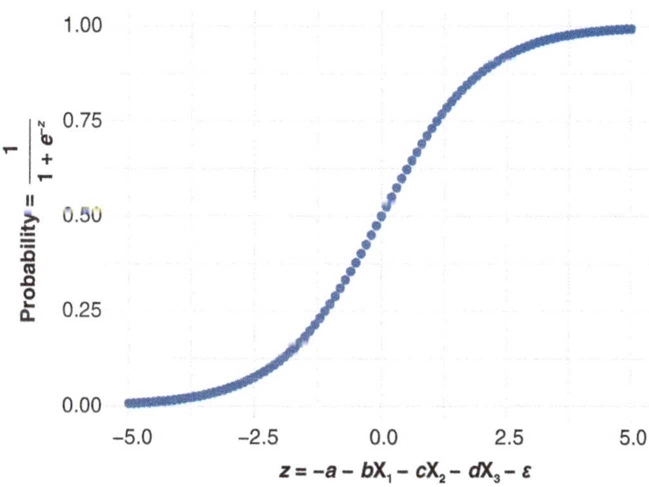

The goal of logistic regression is to obtain values of a, b, c, and d. It is commonly accomplished through maximum likelihood estimation (MLE).

9.5 USING LOGISTIC REGRESSION FOR CHARGE-OFF PREDICTION

Continuing to work with the Carta Bank example, we will next turn to logistic regression to predict whether a loan will be repaid or have to be charged off, using borrower characteristics as predictors. (In this chapter, we use hypothetical data.) The outcome variable of `loan_status` helps the bank determine whether a borrower has paid off the loan or been unsuccessful in paying off the loan, which resulted in the loan having to be charged off. For ease of explanation, we will refer to the classes of the outcome variable as *yes, loan was paid off* versus *no, loan was not paid off*. In the past, the bank's underwriters have used the following predictors:

- employment_length: how long a person is continuously employed
- annual_income: gross income earned in a year
- delinquency: number of delinquencies in the last 2 years
- inquiries: number of credit inquiries in the last 12 months
- credit_length: length of credit history (in years)

Hence, we will use the same predictors to train the logistic regression model.

We first randomly divide the data into two parts: train and test; this is because we want to first train our logistic regression model to learn how the predictors in the dataset affect the final outcome of whether or not a loan is paid back. Using this learning, the model's predictions can then be tested using the test dataset.

```
##                          Estimate     Std. Error   z value    Pr(>|z|)
## (Intercept)               5.54020e-01  8.38418e-01  0.660792  5.08746e-01
##employment_length          1.43724e+00  1.90484e-01  7.545182  4.51656e-14
##annual_income             -2.44222e-06  3.39063e-06 -0.720285  4.71350e-01
##delinquency_2years        -1.22530e+00  2.11356e-01 -5.797327  6.73801e-09
##inquiries_last_12months   -8.29770e-02  9.26845e-02 -0.895262  3.70647e-01
##credit_length             -3.40727e-02  2.08330e-02 -1.635515  1.01941e-01
```

9.5.1 Logistic Regression: Model Output Interpretation

From the model output, we see a few terms such as *estimate, standard error*, z *value*, and p *values*. Let's understand what these terms signify.

Estimate (or coefficient estimate) captures the relationship of a predictor variable with the outcome variable. Let's look at the coefficient estimate of the predictor `employment_length`. It is 1.437. Since logistic regression uses *log odds*, 1.437 indicates that every unit increase in the years a person is employed increases the log odds of being current on loan payments (vs. the loan having to be charged off) by 1.437. To make this interpretation easier, we can convert these log odds into simple odds by exponentiating 1.437 (i.e., calculating $e^{1.437}$). Since $e^{1.437} = 4.209$, this indicates that the odds of the loan payment being current increases by a factor of 4.209 for every year increase in employment length.

However, when we consider the number of delinquencies in the last 2 years as the predictor (`delinquency_2years`), the interpretation is different. The analysis indicates a coefficient estimate of –1.225; this shows that the log odds of being current on loan payments decreases by 1.225 for every extra delinquency in the last 2 years. In terms of simple odds, it indicates that the odds of being current on loan payments drop by a factor of 0.294 (since $e^{-1.225} = 0.294$).

Standard error is the standard deviation of a particular coefficient estimate.

Standard error and estimate influence the z value since z = estimate / standard error. If we consider the z value of `employment_length`, it is *estimate* (1.437) / *standard error* (0.19) ≈ 7.6. The z value helps us estimate the p value. If we look at the standard normal curve in Figure 9.3, a z value of 1.96 or −1.96 gives a p value of 0.05.

FIGURE 9.3 ■ Standard Normal Curve

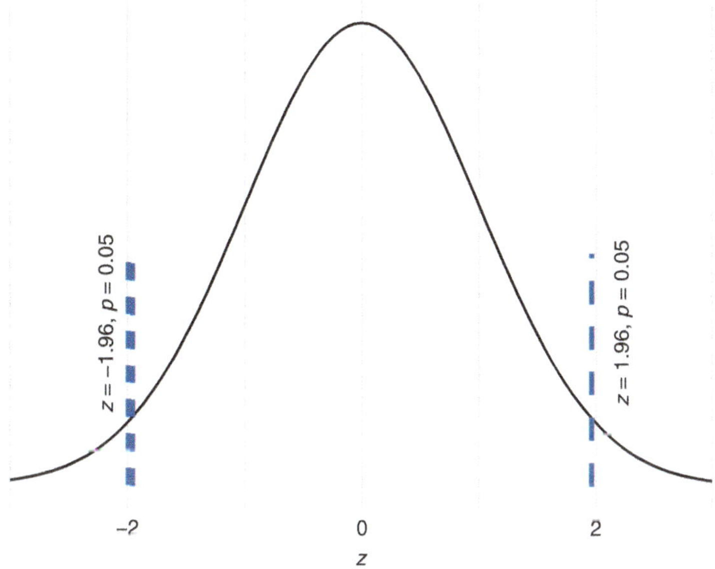

If the p value is less than 0.05, an estimate is considered statistically significant. The p value states that the chances of finding a nonzero coefficient in the sample when the coefficient is actually zero in the population is only 5%. A $p < 0.05$ criterion is based on statistical significance testing convention.

Next, we examine how good our model is at predicting the outcome variable in the test (also called hold-out) dataset. Remember that in our test data we have information about the true outcome, which is referred to as the *ground truth*. In other words, we know whether a loan is in good standing (i.e., it will be paid off) or whether it needs to be charged off. What we want to assess is how accurate our model is at predicting the correct outcome. Once the model provides its predictions about the outcome, we can compare these predictions against the ground truth.

The logistic regression model will first output as its outcome predicted probabilities of whether or not a loan will be paid off. In order to make the outcome easier to understand and implement, we convert the predicted probabilities into a binary response of *yes, loan was paid off* versus *no, loan was not paid off.* To convert probabilities into a binary class, we set a threshold of 50% probability. If the probability predicted by our model is 50% or less, we classify that prediction as *no, loan was not paid off.* Probabilities above 50% predicted by our model are classified as *yes, loan was paid off.*

Accuracy is a common metric used to assess how well the logistic regression model is able to predict outcomes. While accuracy gives us a global metric to measure our model's performance, it says nothing about how good this model is at predicting each class (*yes, loan was paid off* and *no, loan was not paid off* are the two classes of predictions in our case). It is likely a model is very good at predicting loans that will need to be charged off (i.e., the borrower will default on payments) but not so good at predicting loans that will remain current (i.e., the borrower will keep making loan payments). Accuracy does not reveal this information. Ideally, we should be able to assess (a) false positive rate, which captures the percentage of loans that the model incorrectly predicted as "current" when they were actually "charged off" (which can be verified using the ground truth data, since we have the true information of whether a loan was charged off or not in our test dataset), and (b) false negative rate, which captures the percentage of loans the model again incorrectly predicted as "charged off" when they were actually "current." It is important to know false positive and false negative rates because of *cost considerations*. A firm loses money both by not being able to identify potential loans that will stay current and by incorrectly identifying a set of loans as likely to be charged off. In some businesses, the cost for *false positive* predictions is higher than for *false negative* predictions. In our case of loan charge-offs, lenders do not want to miss out in identifying potential charge-offs (*false positives*). If they can correctly identify charge-offs before the borrower defaults, they can take some proactive measures to prevent defaults and maintain the loan on a "current" status. A very important tool that helps us calculate accuracy, false positives, and false negatives (among many other relevant metrics) is the *confusion matrix*.

9.5.2 Confusion Matrix

The confusion matrix, as the name suggests, represents a 2 × 2 matrix. As Figure 9.4 shows, the two outcomes in the ground truth of the test data set can be *yes, loan was paid off* (or stayed current), which is referred to as *p*; and *no, loan was not paid off*—that is, it needed to be charged off—which is referred to as *n*. Similarly, the columns represent the logistic regression model's predictions of whether a loan was current (*p'*) or charged off (*n'*).

True positive (TP) represents the number of times the ground truth (*p*) and model prediction (*p'*) matched. *False positive* (FP) shows the number of times the ground truth determination was *n* but the model prediction decision was (*p'*), which is a mismatch. Similarly, *false negative* (FN) shows a mismatch when the ground truth was *p* but the model prediction was (*n'*). *True negative* (TN) again indicates a match between the ground truth (*n*) and model prediction (*n'*).

FIGURE 9.4 ■ Confusion Matrix

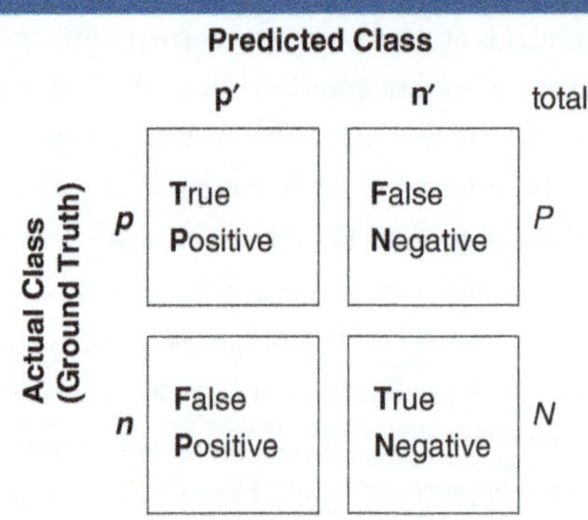

The confusion matrix helps calculate many metrics.

$$\text{Accuracy} = \frac{TP + TN}{P + N}$$
$$\text{False Positive Rate} = \frac{FP}{N}$$
$$\text{True Positive Rate} = \frac{TP}{P}$$

We can also calculate precision and recall. *Precision* is the fraction of true positives to the total number of people classified by the model as positive (i.e., the sum of TP and FP).

$$\text{Precision} = \frac{TP}{TP + FP}$$

Recall (also known as sensitivity) is the fraction of true positives identified by the model to the total number of actual positives in the data (where P is the sum of TP and FN predictions of the model).

$$\text{Recall} = \frac{TP}{P}$$

We next output the precision and recall values.

```
##          Sensitivity         Specificity  Pos Pred Value
##             0.875000            0.815789        0.933333
##       Neg Pred Value           Precision          Recall
##             0.688889            0.933333        0.875000
##                   F1          Prevalence  Detection Rate
##             0.903226            0.746667        0.653333
## Detection Prevalence   Balanced Accuracy
##             0.700000            0.845395
```

9.5.3 Setting a Threshold for Classification

Many classifiers produce only a class label. In the context of the loan charge-off data, when classifiers are asked to predict a class based on predictor variables, they will produce results in the form of "current" and "charged off." These are called discrete classifiers. A decision tree is one such classifier. Other classifiers can produce the probability of an observation being in a specific class. Hence, they would produce the probability of a particular borrower being able to pay back the loan (or not). In logistic regression, predictions are made in the form of probability. Let's consider a few predicted probabilities for the test data.

```
##        1         3         6         8         9        12
## 0.398904  0.993232  0.999999  0.996948  0.988442  0.142816
```

As we can see, these probabilities on their own do not classify any loan as "current" or "charged off." As we did earlier, we need to set a threshold to classify people into one or the other group. So if we set the threshold at 50% probability, then all probability values above 50% can be classified as *yes, loan will be paid off.*

Fixing a specific threshold value depends on our tolerance for a *false positive rate* and *true positive rate.* If we set a very high threshold, say at 90% probability, we will end up with a very low false positive rate, but we will also have a very low true positive rate because many borrowers who will pay back the loan will be classified as *no, loan will not be paid off.* On the other hand, if we keep the threshold very low, say at 10% probability, we will have a very high true positive rate as we will identify all the borrowers who will pay back the loan; however, we will also have a very high false positive rate because many borrowers who won't pay back their loan will be identified as those who will. By changing the threshold, we make a trade-off between the true positive rate and false positive rate. Hence, it is important to ask how we can find out the overall performance of our classifier that provides a continuous output (e.g., probability). The receiver operating characteristic (ROC) curve provides an overall assessment of a classifier.

Let's look at Figure 9.5, which plots the true positive rate on the y-axis and the false positive rate on the x-axis for different threshold values. The triangle shows that when the threshold is 90%, both true and false positive rates are very low. This shows that while we can have a zero false positive rate for very high threshold values, we also can get a zero true positive rate. On the other hand, the square shows that when the threshold is set at 10%, we get high true and false positive rates. The diagonal line shows how a random classifier would perform.[3] As we increase the threshold value, a random classifier is likely to identify observations as relevant *yes, loan will be paid off* from both those who will pay off their loans and those who won't.

FIGURE 9.5 ■ True Positive and True Negative for a 90% and 10% Threshold

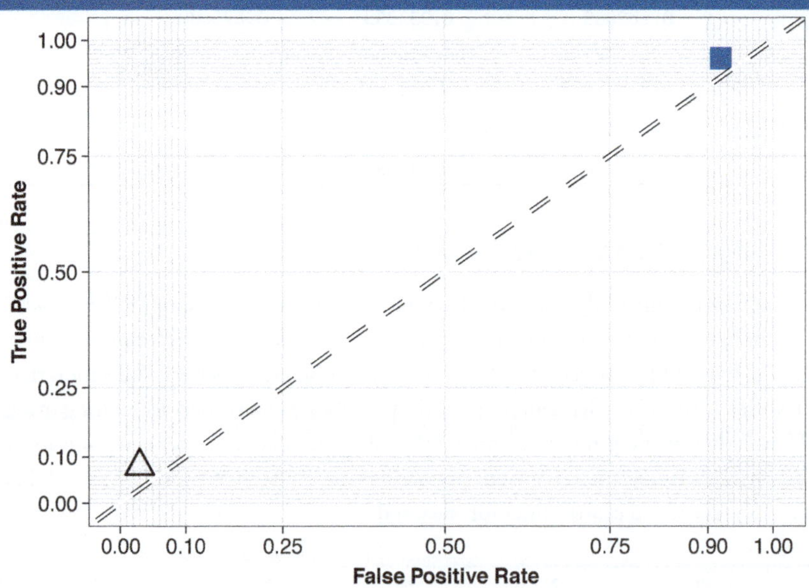

A perfect classifier (something that doesn't exist) will reach a 100% true positive rate as soon as we lower the threshold to just below 100%. It will not classify any irrelevant observation as relevant and, thus, will have a zero false positive rate. Figure 9.6 depicts such a classifier's ROC curve.

FIGURE 9.6 ■ A Perfect Classifier

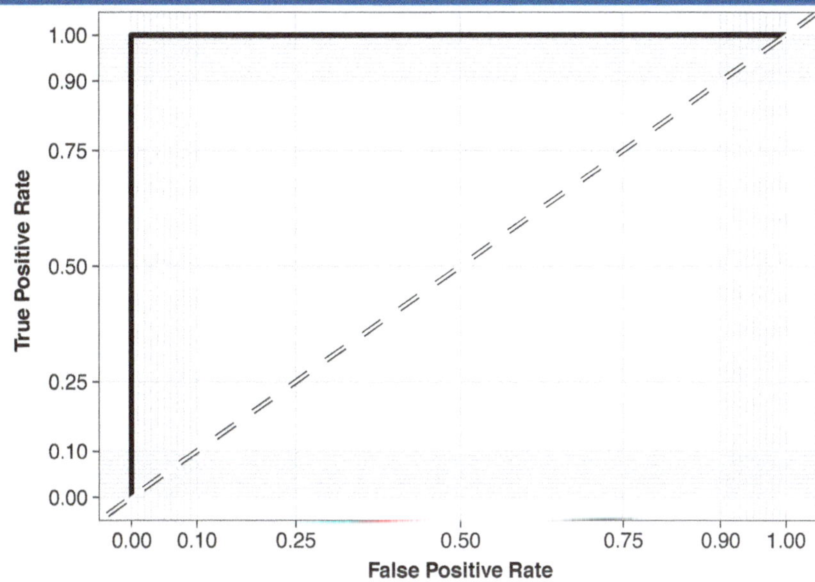

Figure 9.7 is the ROC curve for the charge-off logistic model we fit earlier. It shows how the model performs with the test data at various levels of probability threshold. As we can see, when the probability threshold is set at infinity, both the true positive rate and false positive rate are zero. At 90% probability threshold, the true positive rate is approximately 75%, and the false positive rate is 3%. At a 50% probability threshold, the true positive rate is 90% and the false positive rate

FIGURE 9.7 ■ A ROC Curve for the Charge-Off Logistic Model

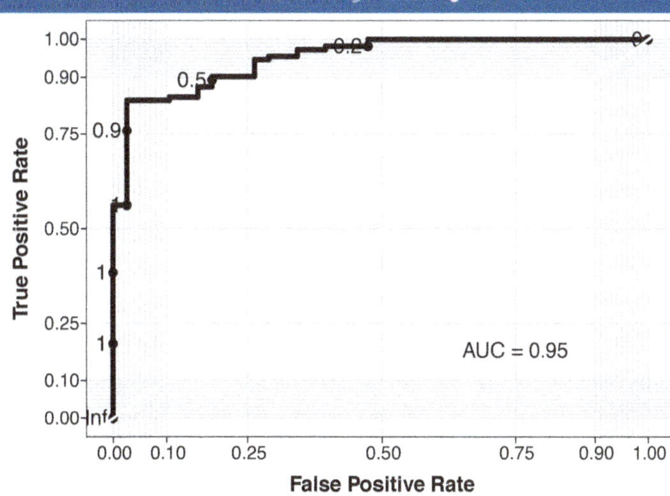

is around 17%. The area under the ROC curve is known as AUC, and its value in this case is 0.95. AUC values can range between 0 and 1. A prediction model that makes 100% wrong predictions has an AUC of 0.0; a model that makes 100% correct predictions has an AUC of 1.0. AUC should be more than 0.50, and a higher value of AUC denotes a good prediction model.

9.5.4 Business Insights and Conclusion

Using Carta Bank's example, in this chapter we saw that lenders can use logistic regression to find out which of their borrowers are likely to pay off their loan versus those who are likely to default. A higher likelihood of default means the loan will need to be charged off, increasing the risk to the bank. We discussed how different metrics such as accuracy, precision, and recall can be used to determine the quality of predictions made by the logistic regression model. Moreover, the AUC ROC curve helps examine whether the model predictions are higher for false positive versus false negative rates. Hence, these predictions help lenders take preemptive action to prevent defaults. Logistic regression is an explainable or transparent model because the model allows us to see which of the predictors influence the outcome. Such a transparent model allows lenders to explain to loan applicants why their loans have been approved versus denied. Hence, these transparent models are preferred in the domain of loan approvals, unlike neural nets that are opaque models. Logistic regression has other applications in the financial sector such as in predicting stock price movement by using historical factors as predictors of trading volume, financial ratios, and relevant economic indicators in order to maximize returns. Similarly, logistic regression can be used as a prediction model for finding out whether an IPO will succeed or fail on introduction. It can also be used by insurance companies to find out whether a policy holder is likely to file a claim in the next period by using factors such as similarity of the policy holder to others who have filed or not in the past, policy type, and coverage amount. In a similar manner, the transparent logistic regression model can be used to determine the creditworthiness of a borrower. Finally, logistic regression is the go-to method when dealing with categorical variables.

9.6 IMPLEMENTATION USING R: LOAN APPROVAL

To implement logistic regression in R, we first import the data and the libraries `ggplot2`,[4] `caret`,[5] and `plotROC`.[6]

```
library(ggplot2)
library(caret)
library(plotROC)
```

```
df <-
read.csv(url("http://data.mishra.us/files/chapter_chargeoff/chargeoff.csv"))
```

We then check the data to verify if R is reading the data in the correct format—for example, whether it is reading a categorical variable as categorical and a continuous variable as continuous. We check by sampling the first few rows of the data.

```
head(df)
##    employment_length  annual_income  delinquency_2years inquiries_last_12months
## 1                  3         132811                   3                       1
## 2                  4         162044                   3                       7
## 3                  6         155457                   2                       2
## 4                 10         156609                   5                       4
## 5                  2         114947                   1                       1
## 6                 10         223357                   0                       3
##    credit_length    loan_status
## 1             35              1
## 2             39              0
## 3             35              1
## 4             19              1
## 5              9              1
## 6              5              1
```

Is R considering `loan_status`, our outcome variable, as a categorical variable and the five predictor variables as continuous variables?

```
lapply(df, class)
## $employment_length
## [1] "integer"
##
## $annual_income
## [1] "integer"
##
## $delinquency_2years
## [1] "integer"
##
## $inquiries_last_12months
## [1] "integer"
##
## $credit_length
## [1] "integer"
##
## $loan_status
## [1] "integer"
```

As we can see from the output, R is erroneously considering `loan_status` to be a continuous variable. To correct this, we first have to direct R to change the class of the outcome variable to be read in as categorical (i.e., factors). This is accomplished through the following code.

```
df$loan_status <- as.factor(df$loan_status)
```

After making the change, we again check the class of all the variables.

```
lapply(df, class)
## $employment_length
## [1] "integer"
##
## $annual_income
## [1] "integer"
##
## $delinquency_2years
## [1] "integer"
##
## $inquiries_last_12months
## [1] "integer"
##
## $credit_length
## [1] "integer"
##
## $loan_status
## [1] "factor"
```

R is now assigning the correct class to all the variables. Hence, we can next randomly divide these data into two parts: train and test; `split = 0.7` sets 70% of the data as train data and 30% as test data. Also, setting seed ensures that the data are always split the same way. It helps in replicating results.

```
set.seed(123)
split = 0.7
train_index <- sample(1:nrow(df), split * nrow(df))
test_index <- setdiff(1:nrow(df), train_index)
train_data <- df[train_index,]
test_data <- df[test_index,]
```

Logistic regression can help in learning how these predictor variables influence a borrower's `loan_status`. The `loan_status ~ .` specifies the outcome variable as a function of all the predictor variables. The `family = binomial(link='logit')` ensures that logistic regression is run.

```
predictionModel<-glm(loan_status~ .,data=train_data,
     family=binomial(link='logit'))

summary(predictionModel)$coefficients
##                            Estimate   Std. Error  zvalue    Pr(>|z|)
## (Intercept)               5.54020e-01 8.38418e-01 0.660792 5.08746e-01
## employment_length         1.43724e+00 1.90484e-01 7.545182 4.51656e-14
## annual_income            -2.44222e-06 3.39063e-06 -0.720285 4.71350e-01
## delinquency_2years       -1.22530e+00 2.11356e-01 -5.797327 6.73801e-09
## inquiries_last_12months -8.29770e-02 9.26845e-02 -0.895262 3.70647e-01
## credit_length            -3.40727e-02 2.08330e-02 -1.635515 1.01941e-01
```

The logistic regression model outputs values such as estimate, standard error, *z* value, and *p* values. Please refer to the earlier sections of the chapter to refresh your understanding of what these terms signify.

If the *p* value is less than 0.05, an estimate is considered statistically significant.

Next we check how good our model is at predicting the outcome variable in the test dataset. Once the model provides its predictions about the outcome, we compare these predictions against the ground truth.

```
test_data$prediction <- predict(predictionModel,
                        newdata = test_data, type ="response")
```

In the preceding code chunk, `type = "response"` produces predicted probabilities for each row of the predictor variables in the test data. We need to first convert it into a binary response of *yes, loan was paid off* versus *no, loan was not paid off.* To convert probabilities into binary class, we set a threshold of 50% probability. If the probability predicted by our model is 50% or less, we classify that prediction as *no, loan was not paid off.* Probabilities above 50% predicted by our model are classified as *yes, loan was paid off.* The following code converts probabilities into a binary yes/no response.

```
test_data$binary_prediction<-ifelse(test_data$prediction > 0.5,1,0)

test_data$binary_prediction<-as.factor(test_data$binary_prediction)
```

We use the *confusion matrix* to calculate accuracy and false positive/false negative rates.

```
library(caret)

t(confusionMatrix(test_data$binary_prediction,test_data$loan_status,
                                        positive = "1")$table)
```

```
##  Prediction
##   Reference  0   1
##           0 31   7
##           1 14  98
```

Precision and recall values can be produced along with many other metrics by using the following code:

```
confusionMatrix(test_data$binary_prediction,test_data$loan_status,
            positive = "1")$byClass
##            Sensitivity         Specificity  Pos Pred Value
##               0.875000            0.815789        0.933333
##         Neg Pred Value           Precision          Recall
##               0.688889            0.933333        0.875000
##                     F1          Prevalence  Detection Rate
##               0.903226            0.746667        0.653333
##   Detection Prevalence   Balanced Accuracy
##               0.700000            0.845395
```

In logistic regression, predictions are made in the form of probability. We can check this easily with the following R code. Here, we are printing the predicted probabilities for the test_data.

```
head(predict(predictionModel, newdata = test_data, type ="response"))
##          1          3          6          8          9         12
##   0.398904   0.993232   0.999999   0.996948   0.988442   0.142816
```

If we set the threshold at 50% probability, then all probability values above 50% can be classified as *yes, loan was paid off.*

As explained earlier, by changing the threshold, we make a trade-off between true positive rate and false positive rate. Therefore, to obtain a continuous output (e.g., probability), we examine the overall performance of our classifier with the ROC curve. The triangle in Figure 9.5 shows that when the threshold is 90%, both true and false positive rates are very low. This shows that at very high threshold values, while we can have a zero false positive rate, we also get a zero true positive rate. On the other hand, the square shows that when the threshold is set at 10%, we get high true and false positive rates. The diagonal line signifies a random classifier; as we increase the threshold, it is likely to identify observations as relevant from both truly relevant and truly irrelevant observations.

A perfect classifier (something that doesn't exist) will reach a 100% true positive rate as soon as we lower the threshold to just below 100%. It will not classify any irrelevant observation as relevant and thus will have a zero false positive rate. Figure 9.6 depicts such a classifier's ROC curve.

Now we will create an ROC curve for the charge-off logistic model. First, we create data frame `roc_data` with prediction and `loan_status` columns from `test_data`. Here `loan_status` is the *ground truth*. We then create a basic ROC plot using the `ggplot2` and `geom_roc` functions from the `plotROC` package. Finally, using the `calc_auc` function we calculate the AUC value.

```
library(plotROC)
library(ggplot2)

roc_data <- as.data.frame(cbind(test_data$prediction,
                                test_data$loan_status))

basicplot <- ggplot(roc_data, aes(d = V2, m = V1)) +
  geom_roc(n.cuts = 8, labelsize = 4)

styplot <- basicplot + style_roc(xlab = "False Positive Rate",
                                ylab ="True Positive Rate")

auc <- round(calc_auc(basicplot)$AUC, 2)

styplot <- styplot + annotate("text", x = .75, y = .18,
                                label = paste("AUC =", auc))

styplot
```

The ROC curve in Figure 9.7 for the charge-off logistic model shows how the model performs with the test data at various probability threshold levels. When the probability threshold is set at infinity, both the true positive rate and false positive rate are zero. At a 90% probability threshold, the true positive rate is approximately 75%, and the false positive rate is 3%. At a 50% probability threshold, the true positive rate is 90%, and the false positive rate is approximately 17%. The area under the ROC, AUC's value, can range between 0 and 1. A prediction model that makes 100% wrong predictions has an AUC of 0.0; a model that makes 100% correct predictions has an AUC of 1.0. In our case, AUC is 0.95.

9.10 UNDERSTANDING THE CHAPTER

1. How are explainable or transparent models different from opaque models? What are the advantages of using an explainable model for financial decisions?
2. Why is charging off loans a problem for a financial institution?

3. What are the advantages of odds over probability?
   a. Odds are normalized between 0 and 1.
   b. The log of odds is bounded by 0 and 1.
   c. Odds provide a measure of the fraction of times an event is expected to occur in many trials.
   d. Odds are independent of probability.
   e. Odds scale better than probabilities.

4. Logistic regression is most appropriate when data are which of the following?
   a. Unlabeled and continuous
   b. Labeled and continuous
   c. Unlabeled and categorical
   d. Labeled and categorical

5. Assume that a logistic regression performed on standardized data produced $B = 1.579$. If the associated variable is increased one standard deviation, what is the impact on the outcome variable?
   a. The outcome variable increases by 1.6.
   b. The outcome variable increases by 1.6%.
   c. The likelihood of the outcome increases by 1.6%.
   d. The outcome variable increases by 4.9.
   e. The odds of the outcome increase by 4.9.

6. If an event has a 25% probability of occurring, what are its odds?
   a. The odds are 0.5 or 50/50.
   b. The odds are 0.039 or 25 to 1.
   c. The odds are 0.25 or 1 in 4.
   d. The odds are 0.4 or 40/50.

7. Which of the following is a way to interpret the results of a logistic regression model?
   a. Look at the coefficient estimates
   b. Look at the predicted probabilities
   c. Look at the confusion matrix
   d. All of the above

8. When should you consider using logistic regression?
   a. For multiclass classification problems
   b. For regression problems with continuous output
   c. For binary classification problems
   d. For unsupervised learning tasks

9. How does logistic regression differ from linear regression in terms of its output?
   a. Logistic regression produces continuous output, while linear regression produces discrete output.
   b. Logistic regression produces probabilities, while linear regression produces continuous values.

c. Logistic regression produces class labels, while linear regression produces probabilities.

d. Logistic regression and linear regression have the same output.

ENDNOTES

1. Logistic regression, decision trees, generalized linear models (GLMs), and naïve Bayes classifiers are often utilized in contexts where interpretability is crucial due to their straightforward and transparent structures. While these models align with the principles of explainable AI (XAI) due to their interpretability, XAI more broadly encompasses a range of methods and techniques aimed at enhancing the explainability of various AI models, including more complex and less transparent ones like neural networks. One such method is a partial dependence plot (PDP) that we discuss in Chapter 13.

2. *Categorical variables* (also called *nominal variables*) are variables that represent some categories with no ordering among those categories. Consider three outcome variables: *red, blue,* and *green*; we would have no reason to assume that green is more than red or red is more than blue. We can only categorize them into bins; we cannot give them a cardinal order. *Male* or *female* gender is another example of categorical variables. *Ordinal variables* are a lot like categorical variables except they are ordered from less to more or from low to high. Take the example of income levels: lower middle class, middle class, and upper middle class. You can order them from less to more or low to high, but there is no uniform difference between lower middle and middle versus middle and upper middle. *Interval variables* (also called *continuous variables*), on the other hand, can also be ordered, but there is a fixed difference between them. An example is income in dollars. If we consider income, we might find that four different people make $100, $200, $300, and $400 per week. In this case, these values can be ordered, and the scale that is used to measure them is equally spaced—that is, the distance between 100 and 200 is 100, and the distance between 300 and 400 is also 100.

3. A coin flip is a good example of a random classifier.

4. Wickham, H., *ggplot2: Elegant Graphics for Data Analysis* (New York: Springer-Verlag, 2016).

5. Kuhn, Max, "caret: Classification and Regression Training," R package version 6.0-94 (March 21, 2023), https://CRAN.R-project.org/package=caret

6. Sachs, M. C., "plotROC: A Tool for Plotting ROC Curves," *Journal of Statistical Software: Code Snippets* 79, no. 2 (2017): 1–19, https://doi.org/10.18637/jss.v079.c02.

10 FORECASTING THE FINANCIAL HEALTH OF A BUSINESS USING PENALIZED REGRESSION

CONTENTS

LEARNING OBJECTIVES

1. Gauge the financial health of a business
2. Understand the importance of bankruptcy forecasting for investors, lenders, and businesses
3. Use penalized regression for forecasting financial health
4. Determine multicollinearity and feature selection with LASSO

10.1 FINANCIAL HEALTH OF A BUSINESS

In any firm, the finance department serves the important functions of control, planning, decision-making, and ensuring regulatory compliance. The department provides a backward look at how the business performed by examining many financial reports, including balance sheets, income statements, and cash flow statements that indicate to the business where its strengths and weaknesses lie. It also provides an important forward look in the form of many forecasts, including cash flow forecasts, scenario planning, and sensitivity analysis. Forecasting (or prediction) models are very commonly used in finance to inform lenders, the business itself, and several different types of investors where they need to invest their resources in the coming time periods. These forecasts also consider credit ratings, market conditions, and the broader economic outlook. Where should a business invest? Should it increase prices or offer promotions? Can it provide employee raises, or is it time to cut costs? Can it invest in a new location or a new product? Financial management provides an overall look at the financial health of a firm, helping in strategic decision-making across various departments. Therefore, financial forecasting helps provide business leadership with an overall picture to develop strategies that avoid decision-making silos. Such forecasting also helps lenders determine whether to offer a loan and helps business borrowers determine how much they should borrow.

10.2 IMPORTANCE OF FORECASTING FINANCIAL HEALTH OF THE BUSINESS

Different entities in the firm need to determine the financial health of the business since it is a critical input in their decisions. Owners and management need to know how the business is performing its main functions to determine which areas need further investment versus which areas might need to be divested. Incorrect forecasts or erroneously ambitious ventures can result in resources running out and ventures having to be terminated midstream at great financial, organizational, and human cost. General Electric started more than 100 years ago as an electric and electronic product manufacturing company but was able to grow into many different areas—including GE Capital, a financial services branch. However, after the financial crisis of 2008, regulatory pressures, and the unprofitable acquisition of French transportation company Alstom's power business in 2015, GE had to divest its financial division after management determined that further investment in this division would be problematic for GE's other divisions.

Employees also need to be aware of their organization's financial health for a variety of reasons. Knowledge of the company's financial standing helps in assessing job security and in making informed career planning decisions. Awareness of organizational finances also fosters motivation and can align individual objectives with the organization's goals. Transparent communication about financial health also nurtures an environment of trust, facilitating better understanding of management decisions, including those concerning incentives, compensation, and organizational changes.

10.2.1 The Influence of Borrowing on Financial Health

Determining financial health is important for a business so that it can understand whether it needs to borrow money, how much to borrow, and at what interest rate; it also needs to identify which areas are growth areas that merit further investment. Many businesses cannot operate without borrowing. Borrowing helps grow the business, but it also adds costs in terms of interest payments. The interest payable on debt provides a tax shield on the taxable amount. For instance, if the tax rate is 30% and the interest expense is $1,000, then a business receives a tax shield of $300 (interest expense × tax rate). In fact, *trade-off theory* in finance suggests that there is a trade-off between the tax shield provided by debt and the financial distress of not being able to repay the debt. If we avoid the extremes, trade-off theory will predict that risky businesses focused on intangible assets, such as technology startups, will have less debt compared to businesses that own tangible assets such as hotels. Companies want to maintain an optimal debt ratio to ensure that lenders and investors don't lose faith in them. Therefore, one way to assess the value of a business is to consider its market value as dependent on its equity and debt.

```
Market value = Equity + tax shield from debt - cost of financial distress
```

The trade-off theory can be illustrated as shown in Figure 10.1.

FIGURE 10.1 ■ Tax Shield Provided by Debt Versus the Financial Distress

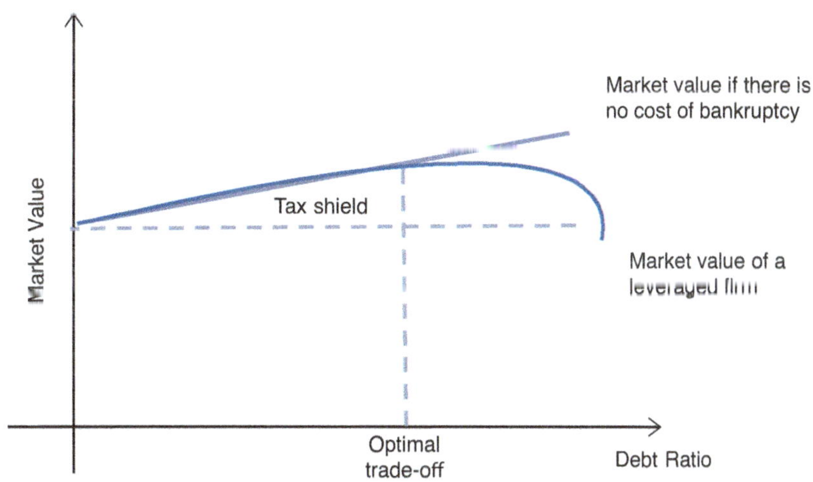

10.2.2 Debt Ratio and Borrowing Ability

As can be seen from Figure 10.1, a business that operates just on equity and is not dependent on debt is not influenced either by the tax shield or by the chance of financial distress because of debt. It can face distress for other reasons but not because of its inability to pay back debt. Let's look at the curve and the straight line. The curve shows a leveraged business—that is, one that has taken a loan and owes a debt to its lenders. We can see that initially, when the debt amount is low, the business gets a tax shield for the debt. Given the low debt, the business may not be facing a huge amount of debt servicing (i.e., paying back the principal and interest for each period of the loan). Please refer to Section 10.9: Glossary of Financial Terms for definitions. If the business goes to the market to borrow, the lenders will use the debt ratio of the business to evaluate its financial health. A low debt ratio can help the business borrow at a lower rate of interest. This reduced interest can help it grow and do well, which in turn can increase its market value. The business can also borrow more. The more its debt increases, the more its tax shield will grow initially. Everything is fine as long as the tax shield is able to offset the probability of financial distress because of the firm's debt servicing costs. However, the probability of financial distress becomes quite high when the debt servicing crosses a threshold where the tax shield is not able to match the level of borrowing. Borrowing beyond this point results in greater likelihood not only of financial distress but also of bankruptcy.

Consider Sears, which declared bankruptcy after being in business for 125 years and having at one time enjoyed the title of the largest retailer in the United States. Over the years, Sears accumulated significant debt, which, coupled with operational inefficiencies and strategic missteps, led to financial distress. While debt can sometimes offer leverage and tax shields, in Sears's case, it became a burden, reducing its financial health. Sears tried to raise cash by closing hundreds of its stores as a cost-cutting measure. This laid off thousands of workers and caused distress to its employees. The inability to keep up with the technological changes resulted in Sears slowly falling behind. Several post hoc theories have been suggested for its demise, including lack of investment to modernize offline stores and not investing in a strong online presence. The demise of this previously formidable retailer shows that knowing the financial health of a business and strategically basing its borrowing on its ability to pay off the debt in a timely manner is important for all company stakeholders.

10.3 IMPORTANCE OF KNOWING FINANCIAL HEALTH FOR LENDERS

Lenders can be banks or any financial institution that lends money to businesses for different activities. Lenders need to evaluate the financial health of a business before they determine whether to lend to a business, ensuring that the business will remain solvent and pay off its debt. Lenders need to continuously evaluate the creditworthiness of the borrower over the period of the loan. Usually, a lender evaluates the total assets of a business against its total liabilities, as stated in the balance sheet, to determine its financial health. As we discuss in detail later, several financial and operating ratios are used for this purpose. Businesses with good financial health are considered more creditworthy and are likely to qualify for a loan, while businesses with poor financial health may be denied a loan or may obtain it only at a significantly higher interest rate. A good credit rating—for example, a triple-A rating—allows a business to borrow from lenders at a lower rate. Conversely, a higher interest rate indicates that the lender does not consider the business to be particularly creditworthy and is charging the higher rate as insurance against the possibility that the business will default on its loan payment. In extreme cases, as we discuss in Section 10.4.1 on private equity, a business in financial distress can borrow only at very high interest rates.

It is not surprising that lenders take these precautions because businesses can start experiencing financial difficulties through factors unfolding in their macroenvironment (e.g., the financial crisis of 2008) or because of their own past decisions (e.g., GE deciding to buy Alstom or Toys "R" Us having accumulated significant debt while facing increased competition from online retailers and changing consumer preferences). When a business continues to experience financial difficulties, bankruptcy looms as a possibility.

10.3.1 Poor Financial Health: Bankruptcy

If the business continues to experience financial difficulties, such as those we can see in Figure 10.1, it will start to default on its loan payments, resulting in increased financial distress. Such distress is a cause of concern for lenders, who have to decide whether additional investment is warranted in an attempt to reverse the distress or to allow further defaults by the business. In such cases, businesses can declare bankruptcy. Bankruptcy is the legal acknowledgment by the business that it is unable to pay off its debts. Businesses file for either Chapter 7 or Chapter 11. In a Chapter 11 filing, a business can be restructured in such a way that it gets another chance. If it subsequently does well, it can pay off its debts and work its way out of bankruptcy. For instance, Toys "R" Us filed for Chapter 11 in 2017, hoping that it would be able to restructure the company and pay off its debts. However, it was not able to do so and had to file for Chapter 7 in 2018. Chapter 7 filing does not allow the business to continue to operate; in such cases the business will cease to exist. One form of Chapter 7 bankruptcy occurs when all assets of the business are liquidated so that some of its debts can be paid off. In situations where the business owners cannot pay back their debts, then the lenders step in and take over whatever is left of the business.

There are numerous examples of companies that were successful at one time later experiencing financial distress. For example, David's Bridal, a large wedding dress retailer with a presence in several states, found that changing tastes and focus on nontraditional dresses by millennials resulted in lowered profits and an inability to pay their debt. Mattress Firm filed for Chapter 11, shutting down approximately 900 stores in 2018. It struggled with adapting to changes introduced in mattress manufacture and competition from startups such as Tuft & Needle, Casper, and Purple. Online mattress purchases have seen a huge spike, even though mattresses were touted as a product that consumers need to physically feel and experience prior to purchase. This resulted in Mattress Firm needing to reconsider how it offers its product to consumers who no longer feel the need to try out a mattress before purchasing it.

All lenders do not face the same decision of whether to let a business file for bankruptcy. It depends on the type of business. For example, consider lenders to two businesses: a restaurant versus a biotech startup. Initially, both need the same level of investment from the lenders. If a few years later both companies file for bankruptcy, the situation from the point of view of the lender will differ. In the case of the restaurant, the entire setup is still functional, and an easy option for the lender is to get someone else to run the restaurant. However, in the case of the biotech startup, the space or the setting is unimportant; the investment is in human capital and what it can produce—the ideas and innovations that are generated by the employees. If the biotech does not do well, then what can the lender salvage? Unfortunately, not much.

10.4 IMPORTANCE OF KNOWING A BUSINESS'S FINANCIAL HEALTH FOR INVESTORS

A business can have different types of investors. For instance, it might have venture capitalists investing in it during the initial stage of development. In later stages, several financial institutions, including private equity firms, may invest or buy stakes in the business. This allows them to have a say in the working of the business—for example, which divisions to identify for growth versus divestment. Finally, if the company is traded on the stock market, individual investors also are interested in knowing the financial health of a business to determine whether and how much to invest in it. Depending on the level of investment—for example, a financial institution investing millions versus an individual investor purchasing one share of stock for a few dollars—investors can utilize different means to understand whether and how much to invest. Again, the financial health of a business, assessed by using different types of financial ratios, becomes the means to determine the level of investment. In certain circumstances, when investors might assess that a business has potential but is not performing optimally, they might buy a major stake to have a greater say in operations. Private equity is one such type of investor. Private equity firms tend to invest in businesses that have unrealized potential but are struggling financially, possibly because of high debt; make them grow rapidly; and—if (as predicted) the business does have unrealized potential—reap the benefits.

Hence, it is important for the business, lenders, and investors to accurately identify whether a business does have the potential to grow or whether the trajectory of financial distress is likely to continue. An entire area in finance is devoted to understanding and predicting what variables can be used to predict whether a business is going to experience financial distress or, in extreme cases, go bankrupt.

10.5 FORECASTING FINANCIAL HEALTH

Several predictors have been considered that can help predict creditworthiness. Let's understand this using an example from the perspective of a lender such as a bank. When a business approaches a bank asking for a loan, the bank is likely to utilize several criteria to first determine the financial health of the business and then decide whether or not to give a loan. Let's assume that a bank wants to determine variables that can help it assess the financial health of the business. Let's also assume that the bank is being conservative in its estimate and defines creditworthiness in terms of future financial distress or possibility of bankruptcy. It can focus on financial as well as nonfinancial predictors, but many times lenders prefer to look at financial predictors to understand the financial health of a business.

10.5.1 Financial Ratios

Businesses report several financial ratios that help lenders evaluate their financial health, such as debt–equity ratio, current ratio, earnings ratio, and operating ratio. These ratios are commonly available on the balance sheet of a business's financial statements. Please see the detailed definitions of these ratios in the glossary provided in Section 10.9 of this chapter.

For any type of forecasting, businesses tend to use a process of *variable selection* to sort the relevant from the irrelevant variables. If a business knows which variables are relevant, it can use only those variables in its forecasting models. Another reason for variable selection is to improve the accuracy of predictions; better predictions result in less costly mistakes. Similarly, when predicting financial health, it is important to perform variable selection to find the relevant predictors to use in prediction models. Moreover, many financial predictors tend to be correlated, some of them quite highly; this causes some predictors to appear significant when they are not—that is, the presence of collinear predictors results in incorrect predictions. Let's understand what multicollinearity is.

10.6 MULTICOLLINEARITY

Collinearity occurs when two predictor variables are highly correlated. Multicollinearity occurs when several such variables are present in the dataset. Multicollinearity can occur for a variety of reasons in business data, such as when predictors are dependent on the same underlying cause or when data collection is observational. In our case, since financial ratios are based on financial indicators, the likelihood of multicollinearity is high. Multicollinearity causes the following issues. First, when multicollinearity exists in a regression model, it may not be appropriate to use ordinary least squares (OLS) regression. This is because OLS assumes that the predictor variables are independent—that is, uncorrelated (in fact, predictor variables are called *independent variables* for this reason). The presence of multicollinearity makes it difficult to interpret the coefficient estimates of individual predictors. Recall from Chapter 2 in which we discussed linear regression that we used beta coefficients to determine whether a predictor variable had a significant influence on the outcome variable. If several of the predictors are highly correlated, the influence of a specific predictor on the outcome (e.g., significance level) will change depending on which predictors are included in the regression model, resulting in incorrect assessments from the analysis. Second, one of the assumptions of OLS is that we examine the change in the outcome variable for a unit change in the predictor, holding all other predictors constant. However, if two predictors are highly correlated, such an assumption would not be fulfilled. Moreover, if our aim is to find which predictors are the most versus least influential, multicollinearity will make the task difficult. Third, as the correlation among predictors increases, standard errors also increase because it becomes difficult to determine whether the variation in the outcome is caused because of predictor 1 or predictor 2. Therefore, the standard error of both predictors increases. High incidents of standard error make it difficult to reject the null hypothesis even though the null may be false. Therefore, the likelihood of Type I error increases (i.e., the inability to reject a false null hypothesis). Finally, multicollinearity can result in an overfitted model because of the inclusion of two predictors that are very similar in the way they relate to the output. An overfit model would be quite inaccurate and poorly generalizable while making predictions on a new dataset. This occurs because the model has learned spurious relations given the multicollinearity present in the original dataset that may not be present in the new dataset on which the model is asked to predict. A bit needs to said about the bias–variance trade-off to understand the problem caused by overfit models (please refer to the Technical Appendix for a detailed discussion of the bias–variance trade-off). When we have an overfit model, the bias of the model is low because it fits the training data really well; however, the variance of the model is high because it doesn't predict well on the new data.

10.6.1 Testing for Multicollinearity

Given the possibility of multicollinearity occurring when using financial variables to determine the financial health of a business, we need a method that can address multicollinearity as well as help in the selection of variables. The first step is to have a method to detect whether a dataset has multicollinear predictors. The simplest way to test for multicollinearity is by looking at the scatterplot between different predictor variables. A linear relationship between any two predictors indicates a high degree of correlation between them. Similarly, a correlation matrix between all the predictors would quantify the level of correlation among the predictors. Large changes in beta coefficient estimate values depending on when one or the other predictor is or is not included in the regression could be another indication of multicollinearity. For instance, if earnings ratio had a high coefficient estimate value when current ratio was not included but the coefficient value was reduced significantly in magnitude when current ratio was included in the regression, this would indicate a high correlation between earnings ratio and current ratio.

Finally, the *variance inflation factor (VIF)* is used to quantify the level of multicollinearity. VIF is a metric that helps in determining inflated variance of the beta coefficient for a specific predictor variable because of multicollinearity with other predictor variables. Stated differently, VIF tells us how much the variance (the spread of predictor values) is inflated due to these correlations. Since VIFs capture the relationship among predictor variables, the VIF is calculated by regressing each predictor against every other predictor. Such a regression will provide an R^2 value, which is then put into the following equation for the ith predictor:

$$1/(1 - R_i^2)$$

As you may recall, R^2 is the coefficient of determination in an OLS regression model that informs us how well the predictor(s) is(are) able to predict the outcome variable. In this case, R^2 indicates how well other predictors are able to predict the ith predictor.

Hence, we can calculate the value of VIF for each predictor variable. There are some cut-offs that help us evaluate whether the correlation between the predictors is very high. For instance, a VIF of 1.7 for a predictor indicates that the variance of that predictor's estimate is 1.7 times what it would have been in the absence of multicollinearity. A VIF of 3.5 indicates 3.5 times more variation. A simple rule of thumb is that VIF values of more than 5 indicate high multicollinearity.

One way to address multicollinearity is through the use of stepwise regression. However, this can get computationally inefficient. Hence, in this chapter we discuss the use of penalized regression, which provides an efficient way to handle multicollinearity through variable selection.

10.7 USING PENALIZED REGRESSION FOR EVALUATING FINANCIAL HEALTH

One type of regression that can address issues of multicollinearity is called penalized regression. It introduces a penalty that penalizes the model for having too many predictor variables. Either the predictors may be less relevant, or they may be correlated. Penalized models shrink the beta-coefficient estimates of the less relevant predictors so that they can either be removed or have very little impact in predicting the outcome variable.

The functional/mathematical formulation of penalized regression allows it to work differently than OLS regression. For example, we use a set of predictor variables in the OLS model to predict an outcome. We then compare the predicted value to the actual value (ground truth) to examine the quality of the OLS model's predictions. If the difference is high, the quality is poor; if the difference is low, the quality is good. Therefore, we try to minimize the difference between the actual and predicted values. As explained earlier, one issue with multicollinearity is that it results in a model that is overfit; it explains the training data well, but its predictions on test (i.e., new) data are quite poor.

Penalized regression addresses this situation by adding a shrinkage penalty to the beta-coefficient estimates of the predictors. The shrinkage penalty fits a new prediction model that introduces a small amount of bias but greatly reduces the variance. With the addition of the shrinkage, the output intuitively becomes less sensitive to changes in the value of the predictor; hence, there is less variance when the model is used to make predictions on a new dataset. For the purposes of this chapter, we will focus on a specific type of penalized regression—LASSO (Least Absolute Shrinkage and Selection Operator)[1]—which not only helps to address multicollinearity but also allows for variable selection. The other form of penalized regression is ridge regression, which does not help in variable selection. Specifically, the penalty term used in the LASSO helps shrink the coefficient estimates of the less important predictors to zero. When the beta coefficients of some predictor variables have been shrunk to zero, they are no longer included in the prediction model. Hence, this process serves as a variable selection method for LASSO.

Let's assume that we have $i = 1$ to n observations and $j = 1$ to p predictors and their corresponding beta coefficients.

Linear regression minimizes the difference between the observed outcome values and predicted outcome values as captured in the following equation:

$$\sum_{i=1}^{n}\left(y_i - \sum_{j=1}^{p}\beta_j x_{ij}\right)^2$$

In LASSO, we add the penalty term

$$\lambda|\beta_j|$$

to the minimization equation of the linear regression. Hence, in LASSO we minimize:

$$\sum_{i=1}^{n}\left(y_i - \sum_{j=1}^{p}\beta_j x_{ij}\right)^2 + \lambda\sum_{j=1}^{p}|\beta_j|$$

When $\lambda = 0$, LASSO converts to OLS. As the value of λ increases, the penalty increases, and the value of the coefficient estimates shrinks to zero. That is, λ controls the value of the penalty that is applied to the regression. The value of λ can vary from 0 to positive infinity.

Another intuitive way to think about the shrinkage penalty is to think of $c(\beta)$ as the cost applied by penalized regression on the size of the β coefficients. β coefficients determine how much the estimated outcome values deviate from the observed values (i.e., the deviance between the data and the model). Adding a penalty on the size of the β coefficients and forcing them to be near zero improves prediction.

LASSO is especially useful when a model includes several predictor variables and the business is not able to decide which of these are relevant and which are not. Consider a grocery store with outlets across several geographic regions. There are many predictors that can affect the sale of fresh baked goods, including the presence of local bakeries, the cost of eggs (which could change by region), the cost of milk, the cost of transportation, the nearness of farms, population density around a specific store, income level, regionally popular flavors—and the list can keep going. Which of these are the most important predictors of sales for a specific store? By using LASSO for variable selection, the grocery store can determine which sales predictors are important and can focus its resources on these relevant predictors. LASSO can also solve the problem of one form of Big Data—when there are more predictors than observations. In such an instance, OLS regression will not converge because it needs at least as many observations as predictors. If the data have two predictors, then the OLS needs at least two observations or data points to converge (provide a solution). In instances when firms are not sure about which predictors are most relevant, they may include tens of predictors and would need at least as many observations for the OLS to work.

Let's use a specific example to understand how LASSO can help in predicting the financial health of businesses from the perspective of a lender.

10.7.1 Predicting Financial Health Using LASSO

Let's consider the example of Altra Bank, a made-up example for the purposes of this chapter that lends to several businesses and, hence, needs to know the financial health of each so that it can determine whether the business will be able to pay back the debt amount or whether it is likely to default on its payments. Having information about the financial health of a business allows Altra Bank to decide whether to give a loan and how much interest to charge. During its more than 50 years in this business, Altra Bank has determined that the financial health of a business rarely changes overnight and that any changes for the worse can be detected through certain predictors. Moreover, Altra Bank has observed that the financial ratios of a business, as calculated from the balance sheet, are good predictors of financial health.

In the past, Altra Bank has used these financial ratios to find out which businesses it has lent to need to be monitored more closely. However, recently it has learned that ratios including operating variables such as sales are also worth considering when forecasting the financial health of a business. Therefore, it obtained data containing 16 different ratios for 665 businesses that have good versus poor financial health. The metric in the data for assessing financial health is whether a business has or has not gone bankrupt. The data contain information on several financial ratios such as debt–equity ratio, current ratio, and operating ratio for businesses that did or did not go bankrupt. Similar to other lenders, Altra Bank also uses data on these ratios to build a model that can help it make predictions about the financial health of the businesses it is determining whether to lend to or not. Altra Bank also wants to determine whether some ratios are better predictors than others; hence, having data with labels of whether a business went bankrupt is very useful in building the model. (The data used in this example are hypothetical.)

The data have the following 16 financial ratios, some of which are operational ratios, marketing ratios, or accounting ratios.

current_ratio_1 = current assets / short-term liabilities

earning_ratio_1 = EBIT (earnings before interest and taxes) / total assets

debt_equity_ratio_1 = book value of equity / total liabilities

accounting_ratio_1 = total assets / total liabilities

operating_ratio_1 = (inventory * 365) / sales

marketing_ratio_1 = net profit / sales

operating_ratio_2 = profit on operating activities / financial expenses

marketing_ratio_2 = (total liabilities – cash) / sales

current_ratio_2 = (current assets – inventories) / long-term liabilities

current_ratio_3 = (current assets – inventory – receivables) / short-term liabilities

operating_ratio_3 = profit on operating activities / sales

current_ratio_4 = (current assets – inventory) / short-term liabilities

earning_ratio_2 = EBITDA (earnings before interest, taxes, depreciation, and amortization—i.e., [profit on operating activities – depreciation] / total assets)

current_ratio_5 = current assets / total liabilities

debt_equity_ratio_2 = long-term liabilities / equity

operating_ratio_4 = total costs / total sales

Using the data, we can begin to do several tests and then build the model. The first test we will conduct is to examine whether the data include collinear predictors (i.e., whether a high correlation, either positive or negative, exists among some of the 16 predictors). We obtain a correlation plot as shown in Figure 10.2. As expected of financial ratios, the plot shows that quite a few ratios are correlated more than 0.5 with one another. For example, marketing_ratio_1 and earnings_ratio_2 are correlated −0.97 with each other.

FIGURE 10.2 ■ Correlation Plot

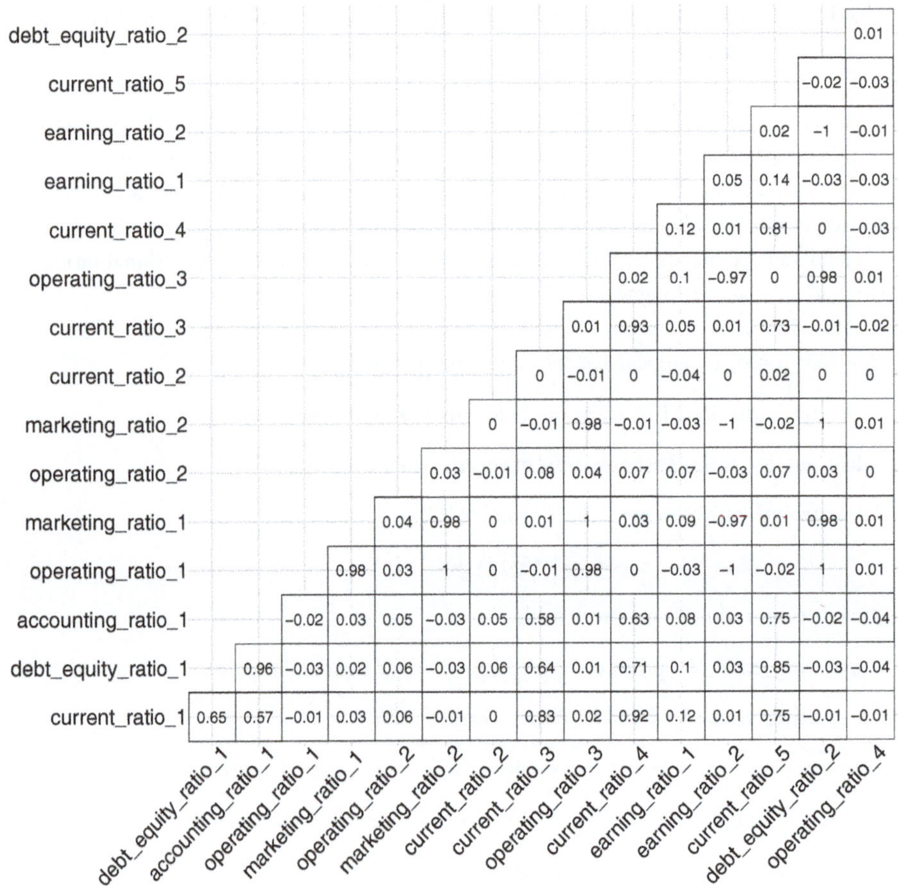

Next we can check for multicollinearity using the VIF for each of the predictors.

```
##     current_ratio_1 debt_equity_ratio_1 accounting_ratio_1 operating_ratio_1
##            4.565160          614.931070         624.345293          1.969324
##  marketing_ratio_1    operating_ratio_2  marketing_ratio_2   current_ratio_2
##           11.756341            1.083820           2.825103          1.338527
##     current_ratio_3    operating_ratio_3    current_ratio_4   earning_ratio_1
##            2.346815           27.912590           3.912966          2.240309
##     earning_ratio_2     current_ratio_5 debt_equity_ratio_2 operating_ratio_4
##           24.330196            3.678511           2.641648          1.019840
```

The VIF of some of the financial ratios is very high (e.g., debt_equity_ratio_1 = 614.93 and accounting_ratio_1 = 624.34).

Now that we have established that some of the financial ratio predictors that we plan to use in our model are highly correlated, we can use penalized regression. We use LASSO to first perform a variable selection as to which are the best predictors of financial health.

We next define the outcome variable: *yes, a business will go bankrupt* versus *no, a business will not go bankrupt*. We use *penalized logistic regression* because the dependent variable is binary in nature (yes/no).

Since the outcome is binary, we will use the AUC ROC (area under the curve receiver operating characteristics) curve to examine the quality of predictions of the LASSO model. AUC is the ratio between a false positive (firms that did not go bankrupt but are identified by the model as having gone bankrupt) and a true positive (firms that went bankrupt and are identified by the model as having gone bankrupt). Higher values of AUC are better because they indicate whether the model is able to distinguish between the *yes* and *no* outcomes. AUC = 1 indicates that the model is able to correctly classify *yes* as *yes* and *no* as *no*. AUC = 0.8 means that 80% of the time the model will classify *yes* and *no* correctly. AUC = 0.5 means that the model cannot distinguish between *yes* and *no* and is considered random in its predictions. AUC = 0 means that the model is reversing its predictions completely and classifying *yes* as *no* and *no* as *yes*.

In the training dataset, we can also plot the AUC values for different values of log(λ). In Figure 10.3, we can see that the best values of AUC are those of log(λ) between −8 and about −9. The values on top of the graph indicate the number of dummy-coded predictors being used.

FIGURE 10.3 ■ AUC Values for Different Values of Log(λ)

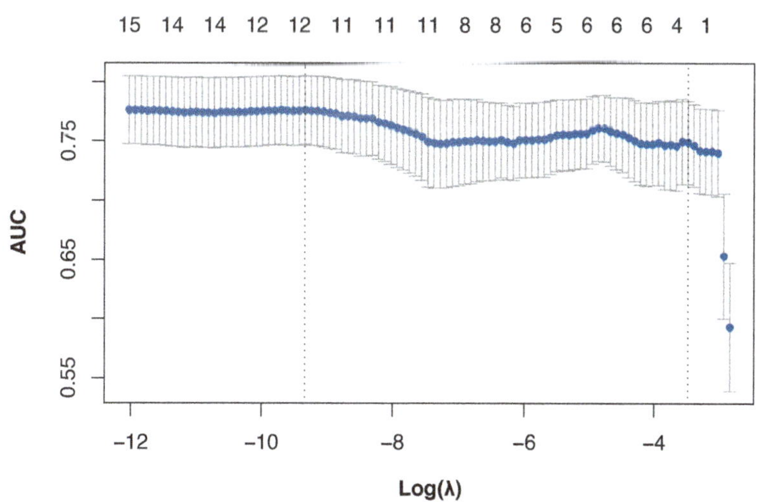

In order to run a penalized regression prediction model, we split the data into train and test sets. We then run a LASSO on the train set to perform variable selection. We also standardize the data to ensure that they are easy to interpret. It is important to note that if we don't standardize values, LASSO can result in extreme values and difficulty in comparing predictors that may be measured on different units. We then run LASSO, which outputs beta coefficient values for all 16 predictors but shrinks the beta coefficients of predictors it considers less relevant to zero.

From the output, we can see that the LASSO model we ran using 16 predictors has shrunk the beta-coefficient values of 4 predictors to zero. In other words, it has *selected* 12 predictors as being relevant for predicting the outcome variable: financial health.

```
## [1] 8.837698e-05
## 17 x 1 sparse Matrix of class "dgCMatrix"
##                                  s1
## (Intercept)            1.346913e+01
## current_ratio_1        9.231917e-02
## debt_equity_ratio_1    1.297786e+01
## accounting_ratio_1    -1.416379e+01
## operating_ratio_1      .
## marketing_ratio_1      3.031253e+00
## operating_ratio_2      3.493792e-03
## marketing_ratio_2      .
## current_ratio_2       -1.985339e-05
## current_ratio_3        2.416489e+00
## operating_ratio_3     -4.810050e+00
## current_ratio_4       -2.503380e+00
## earning_ratio_1        4.965877e-01
## earning_ratio_2        .
## current_ratio_5        7.127187e-01
## debt_equity_ratio_2    .
## operating_ratio_4      9.021487e-03
```

We have trained our penalized regression model. But the important part is seeing how useful it is for prediction. We next use the model and examine how well it performs on data in a separate test.

To evaluate the quality of the LASSO model's predictions and because the outcome is binary, we consider the AUC ROC curve (Figure 10.4). The AUC ROC curve is calculated (and plotted) as the ratio between false positives (firms that did not go bankrupt but are identified as having gone bankrupt) on the x-axis and true positives (firms that went bankrupt and are identified as having gone bankrupt) on the y-axis. If the model predicts poorly, then the value of AUC will be low since AUC increases as the predictive ability of the model improves. That is, higher values indicate better prediction.

FIGURE 10.4 ■ AUC ROC Curve

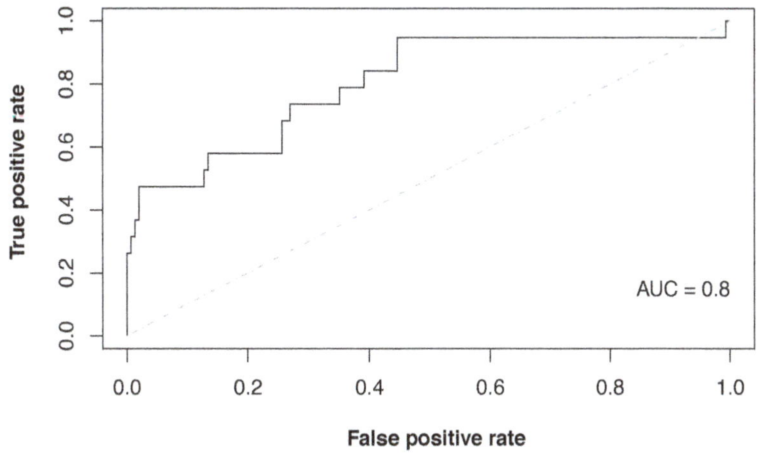

Now that we have developed a model with the most relevant predictor variables (i.e., ratios), let's see how Altra Bank can use this model to determine the financial health of a business that has requested a loan. If the financial ratio values for the business are as shown in the following table, Altra Bank can use the predictive LASSO model to determine whether the business is likely to go bankrupt. Note, since the model was trained using a yes/no outcome, it will predict in a similar manner: Given these ratios, it will predict that *yes, the business will go bankrupt* or *no, the business will not go bankrupt.*

```
## lambda.min
## [1,] "0"
current_ratio_1    debt_equity_ratio_1 accounting_ratio_1  operating_ratio_1
1.65               0.85                1.79                17.31
marketing_ratio_1  operating_ratio_2   marketing_ratio_2   current_ratio_2
0.084              22.81               0.269               0.517
current_ratio_3    operating_ratio_3   current_ratio_4     earning_ratio_1
0.179              0.205               1.75                0.198
earning_ratio_2    current_ratio_5     debt_equity_ratio_2 operating_ratio_4
0.09               1.27                0.75                0.075
```

We provide the trained LASSO model with the financial ratios of the new firm and ask the model to generate a prediction. The prediction value of `0` means that our model is predicting that this business will go bankrupt. Given this prediction, Altra Bank can now decide whether to go ahead with a loan.

10.7.2 Business Insights and Other Applications

Therefore, using a penalized regression model, we can build predictive models even if the data are collinear—a common problem when using financial ratios as predictors. Note that linear and logistic regression's estimates are affected by the presence of multicollinearity—resulting, for example, in the model's inability to reject a false null hypothesis. However, penalized regression can provide estimates even in the presence of multicollinearity. It handles correlation among predictors through the inclusion of the shrinkage penalty that helps find the model of best fit even in the presence of multicollinearity. In terms of business insights, using LASSO, in this chapter we developed a penalized regression model that can help lenders allocate loans and businesses determine their financial health.

In addition to selecting which variables are the most important to determine the financial health of an organization, LASSO can be used in other areas of finance such as assets optimization by selecting the critical assets that can result in an optimal asset portfolio. It can also be used for fraud detection in financial transactions—by finding the variables that help financial organizations identify which transactions do not appear regular and could, hence, be fraudulent. Moving beyond the financial sector, LASSO can be used to identify the most important variables to predict employee satisfaction or for optimal inventory management or effective campaigns that maximize customer engagement.

10.8 IMPLEMENTATION USING R: EVALUATING THE HEALTH OF A BUSINESS

The data contain 16 financial ratios, some of which are marketing related and some accounting related as mentioned earlier. First we read in the data on the 16 predictor variables and the libraries: `ROCR`,[2] `glmnet`,[3] `psycho`,[4] `tidyverse`,[5] `ggplot2`,[6] and `car`.[7]

```
library(ROCR)
library(glmnet)

trainData <-
   read.csv(url("http://data.mishra.us/files/train_bankruptcy.csv"))
testData <-
   read.csv(url("http://data.mishra.us/files/test_bankruptcy.csv"))

predictors <- trainData[,c(1:16)]
bankruptcy <- trainData$class
```

We then check for the correlation among the 16 predictor variables. R provides the correlation plot as shown in Figure 10.2. As we can see from the plot, there are quite a few ratios that are correlated more than 0.5 with one another.

```
library(psycho)
library(tidyverse)
library(ggcorrplot)

correl <- cor(predictors)
ggcorrplot(correl,hc.order=FALSE,
```

```
        type="lower",lab=TRUE,lab_size = 5,
        outline.color = "black",tl.cex = 17,
        colors = c("white", "white"))+
        theme(legend.position = "none")
```

Next we can check for multicollinearity using VIF for each of the predictors.

```
library(ggplot2)
library(car)
predictionModel <- glm(as.factor(trainData$class) ~ .,
                              data = trainData,family=binomial(link='logit'))
vif(predictionModel)
##    current_ratio_1 debt_equity_ratio_1 accounting_ratio_1  operating_ratio_1
##           4.565160          614.931070          624.345293           1.969324
## marketing_ratio_1   operating_ratio_2   marketing_ratio_2    current_ratio_2
##          11.756341            1.083820            2.825103           1.338527
##    current_ratio_3   operating_ratio_3     current_ratio_4     earning_ratio_1
##           2.346815           27.912590            3.912966           2.240309
##    earning_ratio_2     current_ratio_5 debt_equity_ratio_2  operating_ratio_4
##          24.330196            3.678511            2.641648           1.019840
```

The VIF of some of the financial ratios is very high (e.g., debt_equity_ratio_1 = 614.93 and accounting_ratio_1 = 624.34). Because some financial ratios are highly correlated and we are dealing with a binary outcome (*yes, a business will go bankrupt* versus no, *a business will not go bankrupt*), we use penalized logistic regression.

The `model.matrix` function helps to dummy code the categorical (yes/no) variable so that the `glmnet` function can use the values. The function also helps create a matrix of the predictor variables.

To examine the quality of predictions of the LASSO model, we look at the AUC ROC curve. AUC is the ratio between false positive and true positive. Higher values of AUC are better because in our case they indicate whether the model is able to distinguish between the *yes* and *no* outcomes. In the training dataset, we can also plot the AUC values for different values of $\log(\lambda)$. From the plot in Figure 10.3, we can see that the best values of AUC are those of $\log(\lambda)$ between −12 and about −9. The values on top of the graph indicate the number of dummy-coded predictors used.

```
predictors <-data.matrix(predictors)
set.seed(1287994)

cv.binomial <- cv.glmnet(x = predictors, y = as.factor(bankruptcy),
                         alpha=1, family="binomial",
                         nfolds=4, standardize = TRUE, type.measure = "auc")
plot(cv.binomial)
```

We then use the `glmnet` function to run the penalized regression. Since we are running a penalized logistic regression, we specify that it is binomial. The term `alpha` helps us specify whether we want to run a LASSO or ridge regression: *alpha* = 1 will execute a LASSO while *alpha* = 0 will run a ridge regression. Since in this case we are interested in variable selection, we will run a LASSO. Remember that although we do shrink predictor coefficient estimates to near zero with ridge, it still uses all predictors, which makes it difficult to choose variables with ridge regression.

Recall that the shrinkage parameter λ can vary between zero and infinity. To find the optimal value of λ, we use cross-validation. Here we conducted a four-fold cross-validation. We also standardize the data to ensure that they are easy to interpret; more important, the developers of LASSO suggest that not standardizing can result in extreme values and difficulty in comparing predictors that may be measured on different units. Finally, we also ask R to output the optimal value of λ, which is called `lambda.min`.

We can then find out which predictors LASSO shrunk to 0 using the `lambda.min` parameter. We see that it has shrunk the β parameters of 4 of the predictors to zero and, hence, selected 12 from the initial 16 predictors.

```
(best.lambda <- cv.binomial$lambda.min)
## [1] 8.837698e-05
y4<- coef(cv.binomial, s="lambda.min", exact=FALSE)
print(y4)
```

```
## 17 x 1 sparse Matrix of class "dgCMatrix"
##                                    s1
## (Intercept)               1.346913e+01
## current_ratio_1           9.231917e-02
## debt_equity_ratio_1       1.297786e+01
## accounting_ratio_1       -1.416379e+01
## operating_ratio_1         .
## marketing.ratio_1         3.031253e+00
## operating_ratio_2         3.493792e-03
## marketing_ratio_2         .
## current_ratio_2          -1.985339e-05
## current_ratio_3           2.416489e+00
## operating_ratio_3        -4.810050e+00
## current_ratio_4          -2.503380e+00
## earning_ratio_1           4.965877e-01
## earning_ratio_2           .
## current_ratio_5           7.127187e-01
## debt_equity_ratio_2       .
## operating_ratio_4         9.021487e-03
```

We have trained our penalized regression model. But the important part is seeing how well it can be used in prediction. We now use the trained model with the optimal value of λ and evaluate how it performs on a separate test dataset.

```
test_predictors <- testData[,c(1:16)]
test_predictors <- data.matrix(test_predictors)
pred = predict(cv.binomial, newx = test_predictors,
               type = "response",s ="lambda.min")
pred <- prediction(pred, testData$class)

perf <- performance(pred,"tpr","fpr")
auc_ROCR<- performance(pred,measure ="auc")
```

We again use the AUC ROC curve to examine the prediction of the LASSO model on the test dataset. This is calculated (and plotted) as the ratio between false positives on the x-axis and true positives on the y-axis. Higher AUC values indicate better model prediction. Figure 10.4 plots this curve.

```
plot(perf,colorize=FALSE, col="black") # plot ROC curve
lines(c(0,1),c(0,1),col = "gray", lty = 4 )
text(1,0.15,labels=paste("AUC = ", round(auc_ROCR@y.values[[1]],
                                   digits=2), sep=""),adj=1)
```

Using the trained model, we can now use it to predict whether a business will go bankrupt. If we provide the values of the 16 financial ratios of a new business to the model, it will provide a prediction of 0 (*will go bankrupt*) or 1 (*will not go bankrupt*).

current_ratio_1	debt_equity_ratio_1	accounting_ratio_1	operating_ratio_1
1.65	0.85	1.79	17.31
marketing_ratio_1	operating_ratio_2	marketing_ratio_2	current_ratio_2
0.084	22.81	0.269	0.517
current_ratio_3	operating_ratio_3	current_ratio_4	earning_ratio_1
0.179	0.205	1.75	0.198
earning_ratio_2	current_ratio_5	debt_equity_ratio_2	operating_ratio_4
0.09	1.27	0.75	0.075

We enter these data as `new_data`. Since for `glmnet` the data have to be in the form of a matrix, we convert it to a matrix with one row (`nrow = 1`) and 16 columns (`ncol = 16`). For the `predict` function, we use `type = class` so that the output is in the form of a class (`will face bankruptcy = 0` versus `will not facebankruptcy=1`) with the highest predicted probability.

```
new_data=c(1.65,0.85, 1.79,
17.31,0.084,22.81,0.269,.517,0.179,0.205,
              1.75,0.198,0.09,1.27,0.75,0.075)

new_data<-matrix(new_data, nrow=1, ncol=16, byrow=TRUE)

pred=predict(cv.binomial, newx=new_data,
              type="class",s="lambda.min")

pred
##   lambda.min
## [1,] "0"
```

The value `0` means that our model predicts that this business will eventually go bankrupt. Altra Bank can use the model's predictions to determine whether to offer the business a loan.

10.9 APPENDIX: GLOSSARY OF FINANCIAL TERMS

Balance Sheets: Financial statements that provide an overview of a company's assets, liabilities, and shareholders' equity at a certain point in time.

Bankruptcy: A legal process in which a person or business declares the inability to repay outstanding debts. It can offer some protection from creditors and provide a way to reorganize or liquidate assets.

Borrow Money: To obtain funds from a lender with the promise of repaying it in the future, usually with interest. The person borrowing money is also called a debtor.

Chapter 7: A type of bankruptcy under U.S. Bankruptcy Code that involves the liquidation or selling of a debtor's nonexempt assets to pay off creditors.

Chapter 11: A type of bankruptcy under U.S. Bankruptcy Code that allows businesses to continue operating while they restructure their debt obligations and business affairs and plan for the future under the guidance of the bankruptcy court.

Credit Ratings: A rating given to a business or individual that indicates their creditworthiness or ability to repay borrowed funds. One credit rating agency is Standard and Poor's (S&P).

Current Ratio: This ratio considers the relationship between current assets (the assets that can be easily converted into cash, such as inventory) and current liabilities (e.g., short-term debts, dividend payments, and taxes). It is a measure of the *liquidity* of a business (defined as the ease with which an asset can be converted into cash without affecting its market value). Current ratio helps lenders determine how equipped the business is in terms of repaying its debts, especially its short-term debt payments. A higher current ratio (current assets to current liabilities) indicates higher liquidity. A current ratio of 2 is said to indicate sound financial health, while anything less than 1 can constitute a warning sign.

Debt–Equity Ratio: This ratio evaluates the relationship between liabilities of the business (what it owes; specifically long-term debts, which appear on the right side of the balance sheet) and shareholder equity (total assets minus total liabilities). It is one of the most common ratios used to evaluate the health of a business. What is considered a good debt–equity ratio depends on the industry—values nearer 1 are generally considered better. As the value of the debt–equity ratio increases beyond 1, it indicates that the business is more dependent on debt financing than on its own equity. Problems arise when the reliance on debt keeps increasing, meaning the likelihood of financial distress increases.

Debt Ratio: A financial metric that compares a company's total debt to its total assets, used to evaluate financial risk.

Debt Servicing: The process of making principal and interest payments on borrowed funds over time.

Default: Failure to fulfill the repayment of a loan, including interest or principal, at the agreed-upon terms and time.

Earnings ratio: This ratio is the current earnings of a firm and captures the financial performance of a business before taking into account taxes and other liabilities. It allows investors to look at how the business is performing every year because of the operating decisions made for that year; it does not take into account financial decisions that carry over from previous years such as interest and taxes. Thus, it provides a good picture of a business's net income or profit in a given year.

Economic Outlook: An analysis or opinion regarding the future state of the economy or economic conditions.

Equity: The value of ownership interest in a business, calculated by deducting liabilities from assets.

Financial Distress: A condition in which a company faces difficulties in meeting its financial obligations, such as paying off debt.

Financial Health: The overall economic status of a business, including its income, expenses, debts, and long-term sustainability.

Financial and Operating Ratios: Metrics used to evaluate a business's financial health and operational efficiency.

Growth Areas: Parts or aspects of a business showing potential for expansion or development.

Intangible Assets: Nonphysical assets like patents, copyrights, and brand reputation or image that add value to a business.

Interest Payments: Money paid to a lender by a borrower as compensation for the use of borrowed funds, usually calculated as a percentage of the principal amount.

Interest Rate: The percentage charged by a lender to a borrower for using their money. The borrower pays this in addition to repaying the borrowed amount (the principal).

Lenders: Individuals or institutions that give a temporary loan or credit to borrowers with the expectation it will be paid back with interest.

Leveraged Business: A company that has used borrowed capital (debt) to increase the potential return on equity.

Leveraged Buyout (LBO): A financial transaction where a company is purchased using a combination of equity and significant amounts of borrowed money, often using the company's assets as collateral.

Market Value: The estimated amount for which a business or asset could be sold by a willing buyer to a willing seller.

Operating Costs: Expenses related to the business's primary operations, such as the costs of materials, labor, and overhead. These costs are deducted from a company's revenue to calculate its operating profit.

Operating Efficiency: The performance of a business in terms of its use of resources to produce goods and services. A high operating efficiency means that a business utilizes its resources wisely, resulting in higher profits.

Operating Ratio: This indicates the operating efficiency of a business by considering the relationship between operating costs (the costs incurred in the day-to-day operations of the business) and sales (the amount earned by selling products and services). In other words, it examines whether the business has been able to keep costs low compared to how much it is selling. A lower operating ratio is considered better and indicates greater efficiency.

Optimal Debt Ratio: A balance of debt and equity that maximizes a company's value while minimizing its cost of capital.

Regulatory Compliance: Adhering to laws, regulations, guidelines, and specifications relevant to the business's processes and operations.

Scenario Planning: A strategic planning method used by organizations to make flexible long-term plans that can take into account possible future scenarios or events.

Solvency: Describes a business's ability to meet its long-term financial obligations by having more assets than liabilities.

Tangible Assets: Physical assets such as machinery, buildings, and land that a business owns and uses in its operations.

Tax Shield: A reduction in taxable income for an individual or corporation achieved through claiming allowable deductions such as interest on debt.

Trade-Off Theory in Finance: A theory that suggests companies manage and balance the benefits and costs of debt financing, considering aspects such as tax shields and financial distress.

10.10 UNDERSTANDING THE CHAPTER

1. Can a business keep taking loans because it provides a tax shield? Is there a problem that may arise if the loan amount because too high?
2. Why should we not use OLS regression when there is multicollinearity in the data?
3. Penalized regression is used to address which of the following issues?
   - **a.** Autocorrelation
   - **b.** Heteroscedasticity
   - **c.** Homoscedasticity
   - **d.** Multicollinearity
   - **e.** Lagged variables
4. Which of the following statements regarding multicollinearity among predictors is *false*?
   - **a.** Variance inflation factor (VIF) values of more than 5 indicate multicollinearity.
   - **b.** Variance inflation factor (VIF) values of less than 5 indicate multicollinearity.
   - **c.** Bar charts cannot test for multicollinearity.
   - **d.** Variance inflation factor (VIF) can test for multicollinearity.
   - **e.** Scatterplots can indicate multicollinearity.
5. Which of the following statements is *true* about filing for Chapter 7 bankruptcy?
   - **a.** The business can be restructured and turned around.
   - **b.** The process is similar to a Chapter 11 filing.
   - **c.** Most businesses do it every year.
   - **d.** The business ceases (stops) to operate.
   - **e.** Chapter 7 is applicable to individuals and not to businesses.
6. Which of the following statements is *true* about filing for Chapter 11 bankruptcy?
   - **a.** The business can be restructured and turned around.
   - **b.** The process is similar to a Chapter 7 filing.
   - **c.** Most businesses do it every year.
   - **d.** The business ceases (stops) to operate.
   - **e.** Chapter 11 is applicable to individuals and not to businesses.
7. Private equity is likely to acquire a business using leveraged buyout. Which of the following statements is *false* about leveraged buyout?
   - **a.** More than 90% of the loan has to be funded via equity.
   - **b.** More than 90% of the loan can be funded via debt.
   - **c.** The assets of the acquired business are used as collateral.
   - **d.** It is considered hostile by the acquired business.
   - **e.** It can result in restructuring the acquired business.

ENDNOTES

1. Tibshirani, R., "Regression Shrinkage and Selection via the LASSO," *Journal of the Royal Statistical Society*: Series B (Methodological) 58, no. 1 (1996): 267–288.
2. Sing T., O. Sander, N. Beerenwinkel, and T. Lengauer, "ROCR: Visualizing Classifier Performance in R," *Bioinformatics* 21, no. 20 (2005): 3940–3941, http://rocr.bioinf.mpi-sb.mpg.de.
3. Friedman, J., T. Hastie, and R. Tibshirani, "Regularization Paths for Generalized Linear Models via Coordinate Descent," *Journal of Statistical Software* 33, no. 1 (2010): 1–22, https://www.jstatsoft.org/v33/i01/.
4. Makowski, D., "The Psycho Package: An Efficient and Publishing-Oriented Workflow for Psychological Science," *Journal of Open Source Software* no. 3, 22 (2018): 470, https://github.com/neuropsychology/psycho.R.
5. Wickham, H., et al., "Welcome to the tidyverse," *Journal of Open Source Software* 4, no. 43 (2019): 1686, https://doi.org/10.21105/joss.01686.
6. Wickham, H., *ggplot2: Elegant Graphics for Data Analysis* (New York: Springer-Verlag, 2016).
7. Fox, J., and S. Weisberg, *An R Companion to Applied Regression*, 3rd ed. (Thousand Oaks, CA: Sage), https://socialsciences.mcmaster.ca/jfox/Books/Companion/.

11 FORENSIC ACCOUNTING USING OUTLIER DETECTION ALGORITHMS

CONTENTS

LEARNING OBJECTIVES

1. Use machine-learning models for accounting
2. Understand forensic accounting
3. Identify outliers for forensic accounting
4. Choose methods for global and local outlier detection

5. Detect local outliers for forensic accounting
6. Use LoOP to identify fraudulent accounts

11.1 MACHINE LEARNING FOR ACCOUNTING

Automation tools are regularly used in accounting. Robotic process automation can perform activities such as copying and pasting data between various applications or reconciling and cross-referencing data between different systems.[1] These tools are used for tracking progress of the annual audit plan, monitoring key risk indicators, populating management report templates, ensuring a balanced scorecard for an internal audit, and evaluating accounting data quality. Please see the glossary in Section 11.8 for some definitions of accounting terms used in this chapter. Recently, this automation also has started incorporating machine-learning tools.[2] Machine-learning algorithms can receive an invoice, match it to a purchase order, determine which expense account to charge, and place it in a pool of documents for payment; a human expert can then review the documents and release them for payment. Machine learning can help with tax-related activities. As tax laws continue to grow more complex and the Internal Revenue Service processes for identifying a taxpayer for an audit become more sophisticated, machine learning may allow tax accountants to better predict deductions that will be disputed by the IRS and identify the regulations that allow for those deductions. Machine-learning algorithms can also help in contract analysis. These algorithms can be used to review documents related to lease accounting and revenue recognition standards as well as other business activities such as mergers and acquisitions. Text analysis is used in accounting to compile large quantities of unstructured data that would be challenging to manually compile and synthesize. For instance, management and annual reports, news releases, company web pages, earning call transcripts, and so on are compiled to gather information about stocks, new products, or even sentiment expressed in financial reports that can affect investor perception.[3]

An important application of the predictive power of analytics is in the area of forensic accounting. Forensic accounting can be considered performing financial detective work. It involves searching through numerous financial records and transactions to uncover any abnormalities that could be indicative of fraudulent activities. Evidence of suspicious transactions may indicate employee fraud and could be used in a court of law. The different activities that can be considered fraudulent in an organizational setting can fall into categories such as financial theft by customers or employees, debt defaults, securities fraud, tax evasion, and money laundering. For the purposes of this chapter, we will use the example of corporate credit card fraud.

11.2 FORENSIC ACCOUNTING

Let's work with the example of Ogenes, a hypothetical health care equipment and service company with more than 1,000 employees. Ogenes has given its employees a corporate credit card that they can use for business-related expenses such as travel and meals with clients. While most of the employees use their cards solely for business expenses, there have been cases where a small number of employees have used their cards for personal expenses. Ogenes's goal is to identify such fraudulent usage before it becomes a big drain on the company's assets. The challenges Ogenes faces in identifying fraudulent usage are similar to the ones faced in identifying activities like vendor fraud, tax fraud, money laundering, and wire transfer fraud. While a vast majority of accounting transactions are legitimate, a small group of transactions are fraudulent. Despite the relatively small number of fraudulent transactions, they cost the global economy over $5 trillion each year.[4] Identifying fraud mainly relies on finding anomalous transactions or entries that do not appear like the majority of other transactions. Such identification falls under the broad umbrella of *forensic accounting*.

Even in the recent past, accountants have had to go over numerous transactions to flag fraudulent activities, resulting in a huge investment of resources. However, as machine-learning algorithms or models have grown more efficient and powerful, forensic accounting has become automated. Machine-learning models can easily be taught to distinguish between regular and fraudulent expenses, and they offer several distinct advantages. First, these methods have increased the efficiency with which fraud can be investigated. The Abnormal Trading and Link Analysis System (ATLAS) of the Securities and Exchange Commission (SEC) can identify insider trading by using trading data and other sources of information to deduce if stock trades have taken place based on prohibited information.[5] Second, these methods help uncover fraud that was almost impossible to find just a few years back. Forensic accountants analyzed 500 million Airbus documents and found evidence of fraud and bribery that led to €3.6 billion (US$3.8 billion) in fines in 2021.[6] Third, machine-learning methods reduce inconsistencies that occur when transactions are flagged and reviewed by different individuals. The Centers for Medicare and Medicaid Services use machine-learning methods to promptly identify fraud within the health insurance system as opposed to less efficient methods that rely on people reporting a fraud they experienced using consumer hotlines or information from whistle-blowers who witnessed a fraud.[7] Fourth, machine-learning methods offer an organization the ability to flag fraud in real time so remedial steps can be taken quickly. Visa has deployed algorithms that can constantly check transactions and flag those that might be fraudulent. Finally, these methods are cost effective and make forensic accounting accessible to smaller organizations.

11.3 MACHINE LEARNING FOR FORENSIC ACCOUNTING

There are two ways to deploy machine-learning models to detect financial fraud. If firms have records of previous examples of fraudulent behavior (i.e., they have *labeled data*), they can use *supervised algorithms* such as support vector machines or deep learning algorithms to flag future fraudulent transactions. However, firms using supervised algorithms face two challenges. First, they deal with sophisticated fraudsters who keep changing their tactics to avoid being flagged. These changing tactics alter the input features given to the model, making prediction difficult. Moreover, changing tactics make the previously obtained labeled data less useful. Second, there is a big imbalance between data points labeled as *fraud* and *not fraud* because a majority of data points are generated from legitimate transactions, with only a small number stemming from fraudulent transactions. Such an imbalance results in many supervised algorithms labeling fraudulent transactions as legitimate. Given these challenges, many firms have to identify fraud using unlabeled data, and the only clue they have for such identification is that fraudulent transactions appear distinct from legitimate transactions. Hence, fraud detection from unlabeled data appears to be like searching for a pearl in the ocean. In such cases, a commonly used method is *unsupervised outlier detection*, which flags those observations (e.g., transactions) that appear anomalous. Before we try to use such a method for forensic accounting, we need to understand what outliers, or anomalous observations, are.

11.4 UNDERSTANDING OUTLIERS

Outliers are defined as observations that stand out so much from other observations as to raise questions that they were generated by a different mechanism.[8] Outliers differ from noise. *Noise* can be generated through a random process and tends to be uninformative. Removal of noise is considered a part of data processing since its presence can affect the data range and distribution as well as model training and eventual prediction. However, identification of outliers can be informative because they provide an insight into natural variation in the underlying process that generated the data. As an example, a fraudulent transaction is not an outcome of a random process. It is an outcome of a process that is different from the one that generates normal transactions. Outlier detection methods can largely be divided into two methods: global and local outlier detection.

11.4.1 Global Outlier Detection Methods

One of the most commonly used methods removes observations in normally distributed data that are more than three standard deviations away from the mean (referred to as the 3SD rule). A robust alternative to this rule is the median absolute deviation.[9] However, these methods are best used on univariate data, when we are considering only one variable. For multivariate data with more than one variable, methods such as Mahalanobis distance are helpful in detecting outliers. Examples of multivariate data include having repeated measurements from the same set of consumers, measuring pollution levels over time, and measuring different variables that affect sales of a product. According to the Mahalanobis distance method, an anomaly represents an observation whose distance from the mean value is greater than some cutoff value. However, Mahalanobis distance assumes that the data are following a normal multivariate distribution (i.e., it depends on the mean, making it nonrobust) and can be used only if outliers are separate and not clustered together. If the data show a cluster of outliers, then the estimation of mean is affected because the cluster of outlying points starts masking as inliers. In order to address some of the limitations of Mahalanobis distance estimation, research has proposed different modifications, including the minimum volume ellipsoid, the MCD,[10] and the FAST-MCD method.[11]

All of these methods are called global outlier detection methods because they consider the complete dataset while making a recommendation about whether a point is an outlier. They assume one global mechanism that generates points in a dataset. Hence, an outlier is a point that appears not to be generated from a global mechanism and appears different from the majority of the points or inliers. However, in reality this may not always hold since outliers can be generated for a variety of reasons. Hence, in this chapter we will focus on local outlier detection methods in detail. Such methods allow for identifying outliers generated for a variety of *local* reasons.

11.4.2 Local Outlier Detection Methods

Local outlier detection methods consider the neighborhood around each point to determine whether a point is an outlier.

11.4.2.1 Local Outlier Factor

One commonly used local outlier detection method is the *local outlier factor (LOF)*. Let's first understand the intuition behind LOF through a simple, everyday example. Imagine a city surrounded by mountains where most people reside in the valley. However, there is one resident who owns a log cabin high in the mountains and lives there. Anyone looking at the homes in this city will say that the log cabin resident is an outlier since everyone else lives far from this resident in the valley. We come to this conclusion by observing that there are very few other houses near this log cabin house, while there are a lot more houses around every other house in the valley. Stated differently, the density of houses around this log cabin is low compared to the density of houses around any house in the valley. LOF works by calculating the relative density of an observation (which we can refer to as a point in the dataset) compared to its neighbors.

The first step when using LOF is to define neighbors. Who are the neighbors of the log cabin house in the mountains? If we use distance to define neighbors, then we will conclude that there are no neighbors because the log cabin is far from all houses in the valley. However, we can define neighborhood by the number of houses closest to the log cabin and assume that its neighborhood is the five houses that are nearest to it. Note, these five houses may be miles away from the log cabin, but compared to all the other houses in the city, they are the closest to it. Now, in order to determine if this log cabin is an outlier, we can calculate the relative density of this log cabin with its five nearest neighbors. That is, we compare the density of houses around this log cabin with the density of houses around each of the five houses that we determined to be the nearest neighbors of the log cabin. Since the five houses are in the valley, the density of houses around them will be much higher than the density of houses around the log cabin. Lower relative density is used as a marker of an outlier in LOF. We next discuss each estimation step.

First, let's describe our log cabin example with some simple details. Assume there are only four houses in the city. Three are in the valley, and the fourth one is the log cabin high in the mountains. We then superimpose a grid pattern on the houses in such a way that each house has its unique coordinates as shown in Figure 11.1. *D* is the log cabin.

FIGURE 11.1 ■ Outlier Example

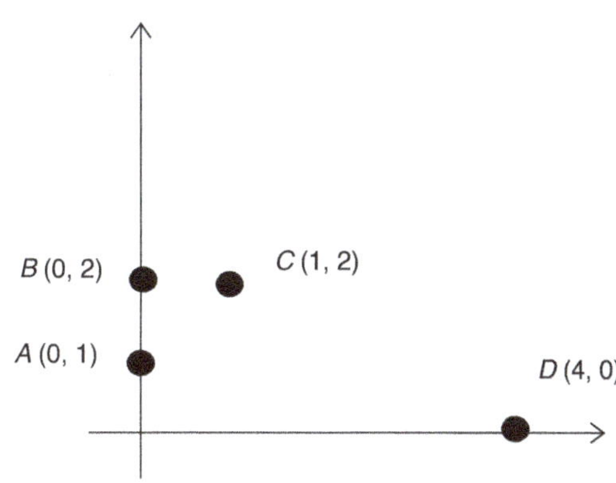

Here, we define K as 2, which means we consider the neighborhood size (K) to be 2. To determine the two nearest neighbors of every house (represented as a point in Figure 11.1), we calculate the distance among all the points. We can use different metrics to measure distance; here, we use Manhattan distance.[12]

	A	*B*	*C*
B	1		
C	2	1	
D	5	6	5

As the interpoint distance matrix shows, the two nearest neighbors of point A are B and C (at distances 1 and 2, respectively), the nearest neighbors of point B are A and C, the neighbors of point C are A and B, and those of point D are A and C.

Figure 11.2 depicts the neighborhoods of A (solid line) and D (dashed line).

FIGURE 11.2 ■ Outlier Example

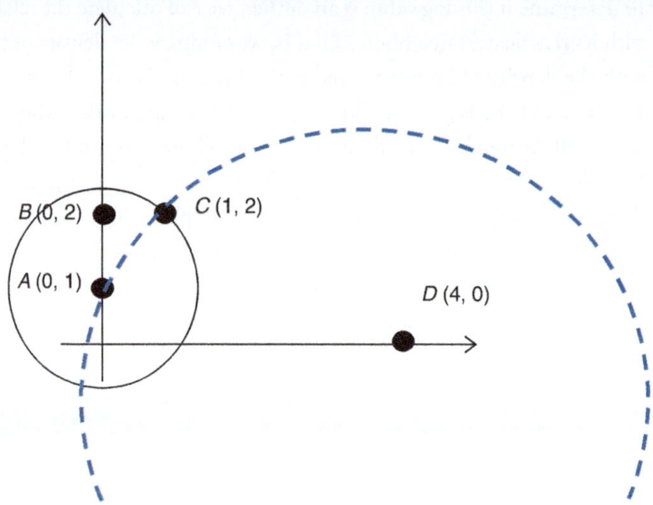

11.4.2.2 Reachability Distance

Our next step is to calculate the *reachability distance* of each point. Intuitively, it is the radius of a point's neighborhood (i.e., the distance of the target point to the farthest point in the neighborhood). Let's take the example of point A (whose neighbors are B and C): The radius defining the neighborhood of A will be the distance of A to the farthest point from A, which is C. The Manhattan distance from A to C is 2. This is the reason we will calculate reachability in A's neighborhood as 2. Even though the actual Manhattan distance between A and B is 1, the reachability is 2, resulting in $(A \rightarrow B) = 2$. Next, when we calculate the reachability of B, we see that the farthest points defining *B*'s neighborhood are both *A* and *C* because both are at a distance of 1 from *B*. Therefore, the radius of *B*'s neighborhood is 1 and we get $(B \rightarrow A) = 1$ and $(B \rightarrow C) = 1$. Similarly, the Manhattan distance of *D* from each of its neighbors *A* and *C* is 5; hence, the radius of its neighborhood is 5, and reachability is 5 for both *A* and *C*, resulting in $(D \rightarrow A) = 5, (D \rightarrow C) = 5$.

The following is the reachability distance of each point to every other point:

$$\begin{aligned} \text{Reachability distance } & (A \rightarrow B) = 2, (A \rightarrow C) = 2, (B \rightarrow A) = 1, (B \rightarrow C) = 1, \\ & (C \rightarrow A) = 2, (C \rightarrow B) = 2, (D \rightarrow A) = 5, (D \rightarrow C) = 5 \end{aligned}$$

11.4.2.3 Local Reachability Density

Having calculated the reachability distance of each point from every other point, we can now determine the density of points around each point. Intuitively, the density around any point will be high if all the neighbors are close by. In other words, density is the inverse of radius (i.e., reachability distance) of one's neighborhood. Therefore, if the reachability distance to all the neighbors is very low (i.e., houses are close to one another), the density will be very high. This density is defined as the local reachability density (LRD) and is estimated using the following formula:

$$\begin{aligned} LRD &= \frac{1}{\frac{\text{sum of reachability distance to all the neighbors}}{\text{number of neighbors}}} \\ &= \frac{\text{number of neighbors}}{\text{sum of reachability distance to all the neighbors}} \end{aligned}$$

Using the reachability distance calculated in the prior subsection, we can calculate LRD for each point. Next we will calculate it for point A, which has *B* and *C* as its neighbors.[13]

$$LRD(A) = \frac{2}{\text{Reachability Distance}(A \rightarrow B) + \text{Reachability Distance}(A \rightarrow C)} = \frac{2}{2+2} = 0.5$$

$$\text{Similarly, } LRD(B) = \frac{2}{1+1} = 1, LRD(C) = \frac{2}{2+2} = 0.5, LRD(D) = \frac{2}{5+5} = 0.20$$

It is not surprising that the density around *D* is the lowest.

11.4.2.4 LOF Calculation

Finally, we calculate the local outlier factor (LOF). It is the average of the ratio of the local reachability density of a point and those of its neighbors. Hence, if we consider point *D*, which has *A* and *C* as its neighbors, then it is the average of the ratio of $\frac{LRD(A)}{LRD(D)}$ and $\frac{LRD(C)}{LRD(D)}$. Since each neighborhood has two points, we divide by 2 to calculate the average. In other words,

$$LOF(D) = \frac{\frac{LRD(A)}{LRD(D)} + \frac{LRD(C)}{LRD(D)}}{2} = \frac{\frac{0.5}{0.2} + \frac{0.5}{0.2}}{2} = 2.5$$

Similarly, *LOF*(*A*) = 1, *LOF*(*B*) = 0.5, and *LOF*(*C*) = 1. Since the LOF of *D* is the highest, *D* can be classified as an outlier.

Let's visually see how the LOF works by using a simple dataset of two input features: *x* and *y*. Plotting the data in Figure 11.3 gives us the following output, in which we can see that there are two big and one small cluster of observations.

FIGURE 11.3 ■ Data Plot

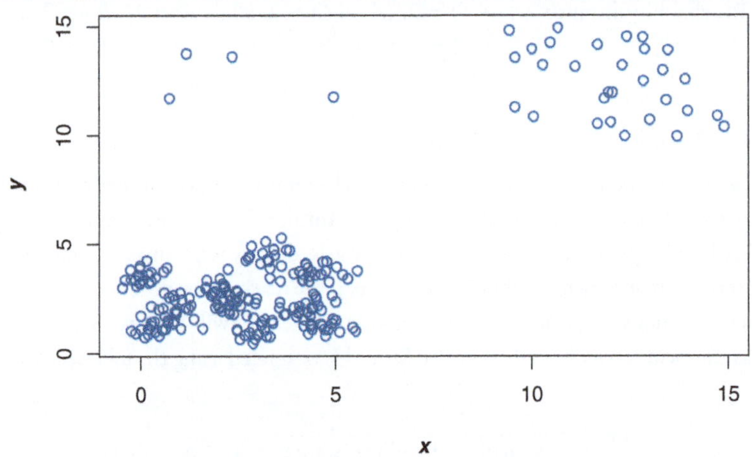

Recall that LOF calculations require the user to specify the size of the neighborhood. In this case, let's provide six neighborhood sizes from 5 to 10. The model will calculate LOF scores for each observation for each neighborhood size. Since we have provided six different neighborhood sizes, it will calculate six different LOF values for each observation of the data.

Now we estimate the median LOF for each observation that currently has six LOF values. Finally, we plot data points and label LOF values greater or equal to 2 in Figure 11.4.

FIGURE 11.4 ■ LOF Values

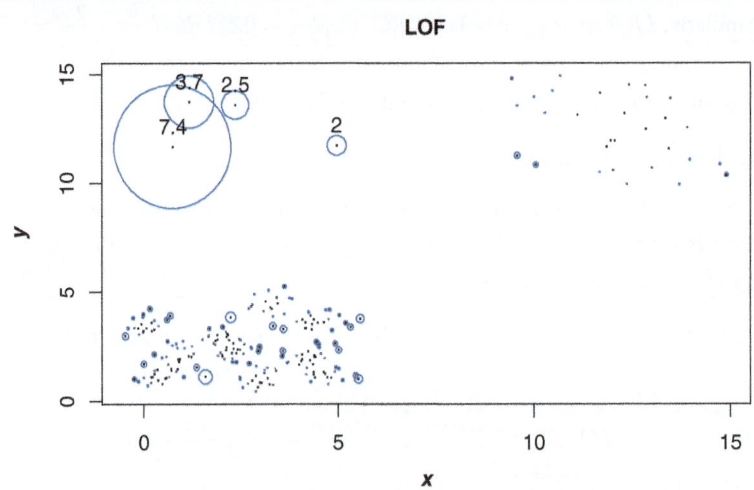

11.4.2.5 Local Outlier Probability

One issue with LOF is that we need to set a cutoff LOF value to identify outliers with more than that cutoff value. Sometimes it is not easy to decide the correct cutoff value of LOF. To address this issue, a modification of LOF called LoOP (local outlier probability), is available. LoOP uses LOF scores to calculate the probability of a point being an outlier. The output, therefore, is not a score but a probability value between 0 and 1. LoOP essentially determines whether an observation lies in a low-density neighborhood (potentially outlier observations) or a high-density neighborhood (regular observations). Then this information is used to calculate the probability of the observation being an outlier. LoOP makes two assumptions: (1) that, geometrically, each point's neighborhood is centered on that point, and (2) that distances of each of the points in the neighborhood to the target point follow approximately a half-Gaussian distribution (this is distinct from assuming all distances in the dataset follow a half-Gaussian distribution).

Hence, LoOP allows us to have the best of both worlds: It doesn't require the data to follow any distribution, but the interobservation distance estimate has nice distributional properties of being a half-Gaussian distribution in a neighborhood, *S*, that is amenable to statistical calculations. This enables calculating the probability of an observation being an outlier.

To the same two-input dataset on which we applied LOF, we apply LoOP and then filter out data points that have more than a 50% probability of being an outlier (see Figure 11.5).

FIGURE 11.5 ■ Local Outlier Probability (LoOP)

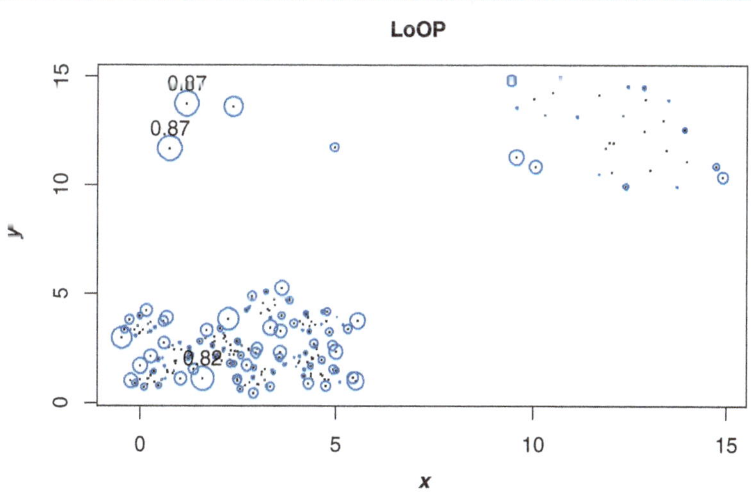

11.5 DETECTING FRAUDULENT TRANSACTIONS USING LOOP

We will use the Ogenes example for understanding how fraudulent transactions can be detected using outlier detection methods. As you recall, Ogenes is a health care equipment and service company with more than 1,000 employees. It has given its employees a corporate credit card to use for business-related expenses. Based on reports, company management has determined that these cards need to be audited because it is believed some employees have been using the corporate card for personal expenses. In order to perform the audit, Ogenes knows that the input features of the fraudulent transactions will appear differently than those of legitimate transactions. Moreover, these transactions are likely to be small in number. Hence, the auditors used the LoOP local outlier detection method. Again, a global outlier detection was not used because the reasons for the fraudulent transactions could be diverse. We will use LoOP to determine which of the transactions were fraudulent. (The data for the Ogenes example are hypothetical.)

Let's assume that the five input features are number of daily transactions on the credit card, average distance from the corporate office and the place where the card was used, average daily amount spent using the card, number of times the card was declined each day, and number of foreign transactions for which the card was used in the last six months. In our case, LoOP is provided with 500 rows of data for the five input features and asked to identify the outliers that Ogenes would consider as potentially fraudulent.

Note that in order to verify how well the model is able to truly detect outliers given these specific input variables for a specific organization, data with labels are typically used so that the output of the model can be compared to the ground truth. In this case, we do the same; we have data with output labels—that is, we have ground truth information for whether a transaction was fraudulent. However, as mentioned earlier, we did not provide this information to LoOP but only provided LoOP with information on the five input features. Using the input features, we ask LoOP to decide which of these 500 observations appear different from the others. Once we have the output from LoOP, we can compare it to our ground truth and examine whether the observations that LoOP determined as different were indeed the fraudulent ones.

In order to compare LoOP output with the ground truth, we first convert LoOP-generated probability values into a binary response of `fraud` and `no fraud`. To convert probabilities into binary class, we set a threshold of 50% probability. If predicted probability is 50% or less, we classify that prediction as `no fraud` (+1). Probabilities above 50% are classified as `fraud` (–1). We then obtain a confusion matrix (see Chapter 9 on logistic regression for more details about the confusion matrix).

As we can see from the confusion matrix, there are eight observations that are misclassified by LoOP. These eight observations were predicted to be not fraudulent by LoOP but were actually fraudulent, which we know from the ground truth. In other words, 492 out of 500 observations were correctly predicted by LoOP. The accuracy of LoOP, therefore, is $\frac{492}{500} = 0.984$ (i.e., 98.4%). Therefore, using LoOP, we can find out with quite a high level of accuracy which of the transactions were fraudulent. An outlier detection method works in this case because the fraudulent transactions are not the norm and appear as outliers compared to the other transactions and, hence, are successfully detected using LoOP.

11.6 BUSINESS INSIGHTS AND CONCLUSION

The main intent of this chapter was to examine how machine-learning models can be used to identify fraudulent transactions. Specifically, in forensic accounting, the task of detecting a few fraudulent transactions among thousands of regular transactions is challenging. Hence, the method commonly used for such a process is outlier detection, in which fraudulent transactions, by the very fact that they are not a regular transaction, start exhibiting features that make them appear different. We discussed several outlier detection methods, ranging from the simple 3SD rule to global and local outlier detection methods such as Mahalanobis distance, LOF, and LoOP. LoOP is a modified version of LOF that does not need to specify a cutoff threshold to determine which observations should be considered outliers. Using LoOP, we understood how to detect fraudulent credit card transactions. Using a confusion matrix, we determined how accurate the outlier method is in detecting fraud. In sum, this chapter discussed how machine-learning methods are being applied to many accounting functions that range beyond routine compiling of transactions to more advanced applications of robotic process automation in audits and identifying tax frauds in forensic accounting.

11.7 IMPLEMENTATION USING R: OUTLIER DETECTION FOR IDENTIFYING FRAUDULENT TRANSACTIONS

LoOP uses the 500 rows of data with the five input features to identify the outliers that Ogenes would consider as potentially fraudulent. Let's understand the R code line by line. The library needed are caret and DDoutlier.[14,15]

`options(scipen = 100)` suppresses scientific `e` notations.[16] Next we import the data. The dataset has labels indicating fraudulent transactions, which helps us verify how well this method is working. However, in the real world there will be no labels attached to the dataset, and since LoOP is an unsupervised method, it does not require any labels. Therefore, in the next line of code (`fraud_data[,1:5]`), we just choose the five features of the dataset. Recall that this method requires a user to specify the neighborhood size, so we are providing 11 different neighborhood size values in `sapply(50:60, function(k) LOOP(fraud_predictors, k))`. Here, `sapply` applies a function (i.e., `LOOP`) to all the values of neighborhood size between `50` and `60`. This code generates 11 values of LoOP, one for each neighborhood size, including the endpoints of 50 and 60. In order to obtain the median values, we use `apply(loop,1,median)`, which provides the median LoOP value for each observation.

```
options(scipen = 999)
library(DDoutlier)
library(caret)


fraud_data <- read.csv(url
            ("http://data.mishra.us/files/chapter_outlier/fraud_dataset.csv"))


fraud_predictors <- fraud_data[,1:5]


loop<- sapply(50:60, function(k) LOOP(fraud_predictors,k))
loop<-apply(loop,1,median)
```

Using the input features, we ask LoOP to decide which of these 500 observations appear different from the remaining observations. We then compare them to our ground truth to see whether the observations that LoOP determined as different were indeed the fraudulent ones.

To convert LoOP-generated probabilities into binary class, we set a threshold of 50% probability. If predicted probability is 50% or less, we classify that prediction as `no fraud (+1)`. Probabilities above 50% are classified as `fraud (-1)`. `loop_binary<-ifelse(loop > 0.5, -1,1)` performs the conversion from probabilities to binary response and stores it in a new variable `loop_binary`. We then convert this new variable into a factor by using `as.factor(loop_binary)`. Finally, using the `confusionMatrix()` function, we create a confusion matrix.

```
loop_binary<-ifelse(loop > 0.5, -1,1)

loop_binary<-as.factor(loop_binary)

library(caret)
cm = confusionMatrix(loop_binary,as.factor(fraud_data$fraud),
                    positive = "1")
cm$table
##                Reference
##       Prediction -1      1
##       -1         42      0
##       1          8       450
```

Out of 500 observations, 492 were correctly predicted by LoOP, while only 8 observations were misclassified by LoOP.

11.8 APPENDIX: GLOSSARY OF ACCOUNTING TERMS

Annual Audit Plan: A comprehensive plan that outlines the scheduled auditing activities for a year to help conduct audits systematically and review key risk areas.

Balanced Scorecard: A performance metric used to identify and strategically improve some internal functions of an organization to improve outcomes.

Contract Analysis: The evaluation of contractual documents to understand, organize, and manage several financial obligations of an organization such as reviewing the payment schedule, identifying financial and liability clauses, evaluating insurance needs, ensuring compliance with current regulatory accounting standards, and so on.

Corporate Credit Card Fraud: This could include the unauthorized use of a company-issued credit card for personal expenses or financial gain.

Debt Defaults: Failure to repay a debt, including the principal or interest, by a borrower at the agreed-upon time.

Financial Theft: The process of illegally taking money or other financial assets from an organization.

Invoice Matching: The process of comparing invoices to purchase orders or delivery receipts to ensure accuracy and consistency in financial transactions and recordkeeping.

Key Risk Indicators: Metrics or measures used to identify and evaluate risks that an organization might face, assisting in monitoring and managing potential threats effectively.

Lease Accounting: Accounting for the various aspects related to leased assets, such as recognizing the assets that are leased, correctly presenting the information per regulations, and disclosing the payment timelines and contingencies related to leases in financial statements.

Money Laundering: The process by which money earned from illegal activities, such as organized crime, embezzlement, corruption, and tax evasion, is made to appear legal.

Revenue Recognition Standards: Guidelines that determine when and how revenue is reported in financial statements, ensuring consistency and accuracy in financial reporting.

Robotic Process Automation (RPA): A type of automation technology that uses bots or other software to perform repetitive tasks, with the aim of improving efficiency and accuracy. These tasks could include data entry and basic administrative tasks.

Securities Fraud: A deceptive practice related to stocks, bonds, or other investments, such as insider trading, spreading fake news, lying about a company's financial health, or misrepresenting information to investors.

Tax-Related Activities: A wide variety of activities encompassed within an organization's accounting operations, such as tax planning that includes developing strategies to minimize tax liabilities as well as future financial planning to estimate future tax liabilities. Tax-related activities could also include calculating payroll taxes, sales taxes, operations taxes, and the like to ensure that the organization's functions are complaint with the relevant tax laws and regulations.

Tax Evasion: An illegal act in which an individual or business intentionally avoids paying their true tax liability. This could involve underreporting income, inflating deductions, hiding money and its interest in offshore accounts, or not filing tax returns altogether.

11.9 UNDERSTANDING THE CHAPTER

1. Can machine-learning models be used for making accounting decisions? Give one example where efficiency increases when such models are used.
2. Are outliers in a dataset always noise? Should outliers always be removed from the dataset before performing any analysis?
3. The local outlier factor (LOF) method relies on which of the following metrics?
   - **a.** Euclidean distance
   - **b.** Mahalanobis distance
   - **c.** Minkowski distance
   - **d.** Manhattan distance

4. The LOF is representative of which of the following?
   a. The inverse of the variance–covariance matrix
   b. The sum of absolute deviations from the mean
   c. The average local reachability density (LRD) of all data points
   d. The LRD of a data point in relation to that of its neighbors

5. If the LRD of a data point is low, then _______.
   a. distance to its neighbors is small
   b. distance to its neighbors is large
   c. the number of neighbors is large
   d. the number of outliers is small

6. What is one assumption of global outlier detection methods?
   a. One single mechanism created the dataset.
   b. The underlying mechanism generates a normal distribution.
   c. The data are independent and identically distributed.
   d. Outliers are always at least three standard deviations away from the sample mean.

7. What is the difference between global outlier detection and local outlier detection?
   a. Global outlier detection assumes a global mechanism created the dataset.
   b. Local outlier detection assumes that the dataset is drawn from a single mechanism.
   c. The detection methods are the same but apply to different business cases.
   d. Local outlier detection cannot work on a global, or macro, dataset.

ENDNOTES

1. PwC, "Robotic Process Automation: A Primer for Internal Audit Professionals," 2018, https://www.pwc.com/sg/en/publications/assets/ra-robotic-process-automation-for-ia.pdf.
2. Haq, Izhar, Michael Abatemarco, and Jeffrey Hoops, "The Development of Machine Learning and Its Implications for Public Accounting," *The CPA Journal* 90, no. 6 (2020): 6–9.
3. Ranta, Mikko, Mika Ylinen, and Marko Järvenpää, "Machine Learning in Management Accounting Research: Literature Review and Pathways for the Future," *European Accounting Review* 32, no. 3 (2023): 607–636.
4. "Fraud Costs the Global Economy Over US$5 Trillion," Crowe, July 12, 2019, https://www.crowe.com/global/news/fraud-costs-the-global-economy-over-us$5-trillion.
5. West, Darrell M., "Using AI and Machine Learning to Reduce Government Fraud," Brookings Institution, September 10, 2021, https://www.brookings.edu/research/using-ai-and-machine-learning-to-reduce-government-fraud/.
6. Dempsey, Michael, "How to Investigate a Firm With 60 Million Documents," BBC, January 19, 2021, https://www.bbc.com/news/business-55306139.
7. West, "Using AI and Machine Learning."
8. Hawkins, Douglas M., *Identification of Outliers*, Vol. 11 (London: Chapman and Hall, 1980).
9. Hampel, Frank R., "The Influence Curve and Its Role in Robust Estimation," *Journal of the American Statistical Association* 69, no. 346 (1974): 383–393.

10. Rousseeuw, Peter J., "Least Median of Squares Regression," *Journal of the American Statistical Association* 79, no. 388 (1984): 871–880.

11. Rousseeuw, Peter J., and Katrien Van Driessen, "A Fast Algorithm for the Minimum Covariance Determinant Estimator," *Technometrics* 41, no. 3 (1999): 212–223.

12. Manhattan distance is $d_{manhattan} = \sum_{i=1}^{n} |x_i - y_i|$

13. Note that the "sum of reachability distance to all the neighbors" is essentially the number of neighbors multiplied by the reachability distance.

14. Kuhn, Max, "caret: Classification and Regression Training," R package version 6.0-94 (March 21, 2023), https://CRAN.R-project.org/package=caret.

15. Jacob H. Madsen (2022). DDoutlier: Distance & Density-Based Outlier Detection in R. R package version 0.1.0. https://cran.r-project.org/web/packages/DDoutlier/DDoutlier.pdf

16. In these **e** notations, 24 becomes `2.4 × 10^1` or `2.4e + 01`.

PART IV

OPERATIONS AND SUPPLY CHAIN ANALYTICS

12 MANAGING DECISION UNCERTAINTY USING RANDOM FORESTS

CONTENTS

LEARNING OBJECTIVES

1. Understand the importance of efficient business decisions, anticipating demand
2. Learn decision-making under uncertainty
3. Apply decision tree models to predict uncertain decisions
4. Review the advantages and limitations of tree models
5. Employ boosted decision trees to predict stocking decisions

12.1 DECISION-MAKING UNDER UNCERTAINTY

Decision-making under uncertainty has been studied as a continuum of decisions that are made when information is missing or is available only in probabilistic form (e.g., the likelihood of success is 80%).[1] Consider the following two scenarios that highlight the inherent uncertainty in business decision-making.

In the first scenario, a major airline, considered a dominant player at one of its hub airports, is faced with a new challenge: the entry of a low-cost, no-frills competitor. It has to decide whether to react to the new entrant (action) or not do anything (inaction). Both decisions carry inherent uncertainties. If it decides to take an action and reduce price, there are several uncertain outcomes. First, will a price reduction deter customers from flocking to the new entrant? Second, will it actually increase market share, or will it erode profits? Third, will the price drop strengthen its brand image, or will it be seen as a sign of weakness? Fourth, actions like price reductions can sometimes lead to price wars, which might hurt the industry as a whole. Alternatively, the airline can maintain the status quo, but this inaction has its own uncertainties. First, how many existing customers might be persuaded away by the competitor's lower prices or novel offerings. Second, staying the course might be perceived by stockholders as either a confident move, showcasing the brand's strength, or indicating an unwillingness to adapt to changing market dynamics. Third, by not adjusting to the changing market dynamics, there's a potential loss of opportunities that the new entrant might exploit. Fourth, will the business be able to recover its position if it realizes too late that a response was necessary?

In the second scenario, an electronics retailer is preparing to stock a new smartphone. Due to supply chain issues from the manufacturer, the retailer learns that they will receive only half of the originally ordered units triggering the following decision dilemma: Should the retailer accept backorders, allowing customers to reserve now and receive the product later when more stock arrives, or should they sell only the available stock and potentially lose sales to competitors? Both decisions have their inherent uncertainties.

First, it is unclear how many customers will prefer immediate purchase compared to those willing to wait for a backordered item. Second, offering backorders might be seen as a service, but extended wait times can negatively affect customer satisfaction, leading to refunds and poor customer reviews. Third, if the timeline for additional shipments from the manufacturer is not clear, it adds to the uncertainty. A short delay may be acceptable to customers, but longer ones can affect sales and customer trust. Fourth, information (or lack of information) about the stock availability at competitor outlets can add to the uncertainty. If competitors also do not have sufficient stock, not offering backorders might result in lost sales.

These scenarios highlight business decisions with inherent uncertainty. Other decisions fraught with uncertainty include, for instance, (1) deciding between offering price discounts to encourage growth or increasing prices to increase profitability, (2) decisions about allocating resources to retain current customers versus recruit new ones, (3) whether to invest in an immediate profitable venture or focus on long-term projects that might yield larger returns later, or (4) projecting the impact of weather and other natural events on the supply chain that can disrupt transportation, delay deliveries, and affect raw material availability.

12.2 FEATURES OF DECISION UNCERTAINTY

Uncertain decisions have several important features that need to be considered.[2] First, what is the value in taking a decision under uncertainty versus gathering more information before proceeding? Let's take the example of a pharmaceutical company that is performing drug trials for a new cancer treatment. It will use randomized controlled trials (RCTs) to control for all factors and find the influence of the focal drug on cancer treatment; this is generally referred to as internal validity. However, the uncertainty that the company has to face is how the drug will fare when patients with different comorbidities, of different races, or with any other characteristics that makes them respond to the drug differently, actually take the drug after it has been introduced in the market; this is generally referred to as external validity. Therefore, the company has to weigh the value of introducing a beneficial drug against the risk associated with such an introduction.

A second feature of uncertain decisions is to determine when and how to respond. Consider the earlier example of a major airline when a low-cost competitor enters the scene. The airline must decide when and by how much to modify its fares and whether to introduce new offers. The decision resembles a balancing act between ensuring profitability and incurring costs from strategy changes. To determine the best course of action, companies often conduct sensitivity analyses. This involves tweaking different decision variables and observing the potential impact on outcomes at different points in time. By doing so, the airline can gauge which factors, when and to what degree, might necessitate a change in their initial decision.

A third feature of uncertain decisions is to determine which options to follow: Should the business stick to conventional options or explore new ones? For instance, in our earlier example when an electronics retailer is confronted with a backorder situation for a popular new smartphone, the conventional approaches are to either sell the available stock or continue accepting backorders. However, given the uncertainties and potential customer dissatisfaction, they might consider a new strategy: offering discounts to those customers willing to backorder and wait for delivery. While this strategy might entail a short-term reduction in profit, it has the potential to increase long-term customer loyalty and mitigate dissatisfaction from extended wait times.

To reduce decision uncertainty, prediction models are used that simulate different potential situations and how these situations will impact different aspects of the business. In this chapter, we will examine how machine-learning algorithms can be used to solve problems in supply chain management, especially when decisions need to be made with uncertain information. One such decision-making under uncertainty is identifying products that will be backordered.

12.3 BACKORDER AND ITS IMPLICATIONS

Beginning in 2020, the microchip industry faced supply chain issues because of the pandemic, labor shortages, and geopolitical unrest. This resulted in many technological products going out of stock. Consumers who placed orders were left waiting, sometimes indefinitely, because the firms were not sure when they would receive the chips to fulfill these orders. The Defense Logistics Agency of the U.S. Department of Defense, which manages the global defense supply chain, faces similar challenges. It routinely takes steps to maximize combat readiness by minimizing backorders.[3]

Backorder can be defined as an order of a product that a firm cannot fill due to the product's unavailability but expects to fill at a future date. Backorders result in disappointed consumers and reduced profitability for firms as backorders can deter consumers from purchasing the product. Recent research has demonstrated that consumers whose products were backordered are far less likely to purchase the product in the future compared to consumers whose products were not backordered.[4] The longer the backorder lasts, the greater the drop in future purchases. Hence, businesses try their level best to avoid the situation of backorders piling up because of its long-term impact on customer satisfaction, ability to retain customers, and firm profitability. One commonly recommended way to avoid backorders is to accurately forecast demand. However, that is easier said than done because several factors outside the influence of the business introduce uncertainties in forecasting, such as changing customer tastes that make demand uncertain, economic upturns and downturns, gross domestic product (GDP), geopolitical conflicts, unrest, or a pandemic. Firms do not want to lose customers or lose their trust by not being able to fulfill an order on time. However, the enormous pressure that firms face to ensure timely delivery of products, especially when the firm itself is reliant on other suppliers for parts, is not trivial. This pressure can result in increased labor and production costs, overstocking to prevent shortages, and high shipment expenses.

Backorders also cause the *bullwhip* effect, which occurs when a small change in demand is overestimated and communicated through the supply chain to retailers, wholesalers, distributors, and eventually manufacturers. However, if the demand is temporary, it dies out, causing an oversupply of some products. We witnessed this during the pandemic when people staying home started remodeling and a huge demand for furniture ensued, resulting in furniture being severely backordered. To make up for the increased demand, firms manufactured more furniture. However, with the easing of the pandemic restrictions, the demand for furniture went down, resulting in an oversupply of furniture. This is a classic example of the bullwhip effect depicted in Figure 12.1.

FIGURE 12.1 ■ Bullwhip Effect

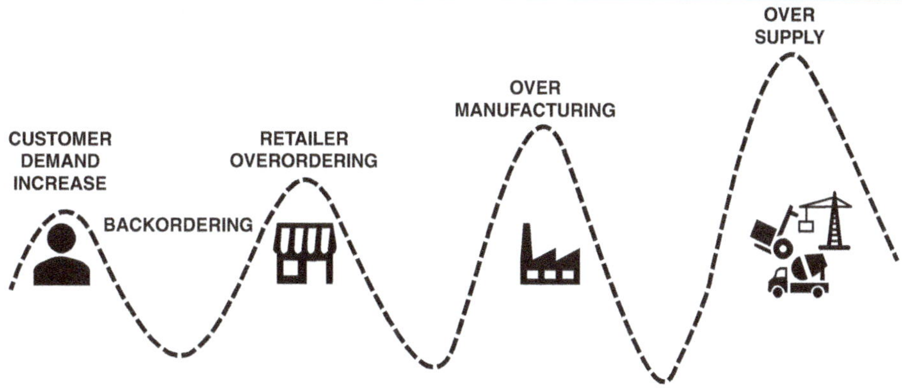

However, we need to keep in mind one important factor when considering backorders. Although estimating which products are likely to be backordered may be one of the most uncertain situations to predict and can cause a high level of disruption for the business and its customers, it is not an issue that businesses face routinely or at predictable intervals. It is possible that a business may not have faced a backorder issue for several years. Hence, the data the business needs to predict backorders may be imbalanced. That is, businesses may not have a very good method to predict why and when they might face a backorder issue. We know that the predictive model is only as good as the data it is trained on. Hence, having imbalanced data can affect the quality of predictions. Machine-learning methods are now routinely used to tackle the problem of backorder forecasting, given their ability to analyze large structured and unstructured datasets that are unbalanced.

We next present a tree-based machine-learning method that has been used to estimate backorders so that strategies can be devised to address this supply chain issue.

12.4 MACHINE-LEARNING OPTIONS TO AID IN DECISION-MAKING UNDER UNCERTAINTY

Machine learning, especially tree-based models, offer businesses a structured way to make decisions under uncertainty. These models segment data based on different conditions, providing insight into complex scenarios. For instance, the airline faced with competition from a low-cost carrier could use decision trees to analyze historical data on passenger preferences, price sensitivities, and other factors to predict potential outcomes. Similarly, the electronics retailer uncertain about how to manage stock for a new smartphone could deploy tree-based models to evaluate previous product launches and understand customer behavior patterns in the face of backorders. Through these models, businesses can simulate various decision pathways, assess probable outcomes, and make more informed choices even in the presence of uncertainty.

12.4.1 Components of a Decision Tree Model

Decision trees are *supervised algorithms* that require labeled data (i.e., data where the relationship between the predictor and the outcome variable is available). Decision trees can be used for both regression tasks and classification depending on whether the outcome variable is continuous or categorical. The term *classification and regression tree* (CART) captures this ability of tree models (we will use the terms *decision tree* and *tree model* interchangeably, but they mean the same thing). For backorder predictions, we will focus on classification trees.

Before we discuss how classification trees make predictions, let's understand the different components of a decision tree as depicted in Figure 12.2.

FIGURE 12.2 ■ Components of a Decision Tree

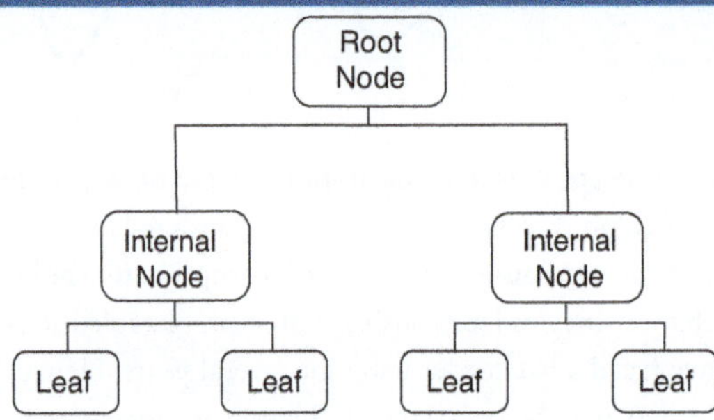

- The *root node* is the first node in a decision tree. This also represents the predictor variable or feature that is split first to divide the entire data into two sets.
- The *terminal node* or *leaf* is the final node of a decision tree that cannot be divided further. These terminal nodes contain the mean value of the outcome variable (if the outcome is a continuous variable) or the majority class (if the outcome is a classification task).
- The *internal/decision node* is a subnode of the tree between the root node and the terminal node. At an internal or decision node, the data are further divided into new internal nodes or into leaf nodes.
- A *branch* represents the connection or relationship between a root node and an internal node, between internal nodes, or between an internal node and a leaf node.
- The *depth* of a tree is the longest distance between the root node and any terminal node (leaf). The tree in Figure 12.2 has a depth of 2.

12.4.2 Classification Trees

Consider a simple illustration of backorder prediction. Assume our dataset has two predictor variables: *forecasted sales* and *transit time for the product to arrive*. Both are categorical variables with two levels: low and high. That is, the forecasted sales for a product can be low or high, and the transit time for the product to arrive from the manufacturer to a retailer can also be low or high. The outcome variable is whether the product was backordered (*yes* or *no*). Our goal is to come up with a simple prediction model that tells us if a product will be backordered based on its forecasted sales and transit time. The data are presented in Table 12.1.

TABLE 12.1 ■ Sample Data for Backorder Prediction

Forecasted sales	*Transit time*	*Backordered*
Low	Low	No
High	Low	Yes
Low	Low	No
High	High	Yes
Low	Low	Yes
High	High	No
High	Low	Yes
Low	High	No
High	High	Yes

The first challenge in building a classification tree is to choose a variable that first splits the root node. Let's consider Figure 12.3. The dark circles represent when the product was backordered, and the light circles represent when it was not backordered. We see that the variable of forecasted sales performs better at classifying whether a product was backordered. In the low-forecast group, three out of the four data points are not backordered, and in the high-forecast group, four out of the five data points are backordered. In an intuitive way, high- and low-forecast groups are able to segregate backordered and not-backordered data points more effectively than high- and low-transit-time groups. But this is just a visual assessment. How can we quantify which variable is a better classifier? Gini impurity provides us with one way to do this. Each predictor variable at each level is 1 – (fraction of *backordered* = *"Yes"* datapoints)^2 – (fraction of *backordered* = *"No"* datapoints)^2. Lower values of Gini impurity are preferred over higher values. Let's understand how to calculate the Gini index for the example we are working with.

FIGURE 12.3 ■ Gini Index Calculation

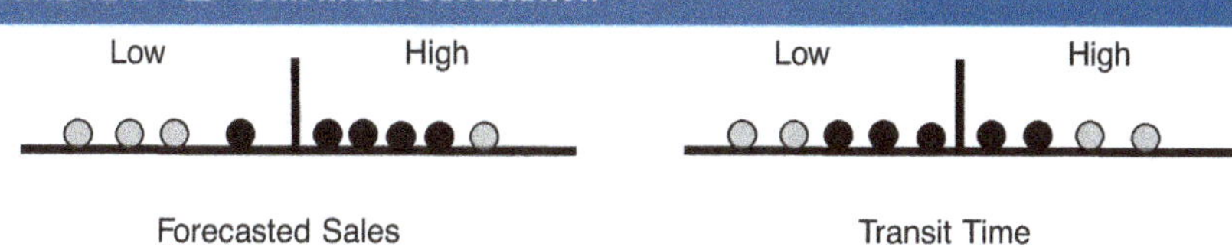

For forecasted sales as shown in Figure 12.3, we have five data points with high-forecast sales and four data points with low-forecast sales. Among the five data points in the high-forecast group, four are for backorders, and one is not. The fraction of items backordered in this group is $\frac{4}{5}$, and the fraction of items not backordered is $\frac{1}{5}$. The Gini impurity for this group is

$1-\left(\frac{4}{5}\right)^2-\left(\frac{1}{5}\right)^2=0.32$. Among the four data points in the low-forecast group, one was backordered, and three were not. The fraction of items backordered in this group is $\frac{1}{4}$, and the fraction of items not backordered is $\frac{3}{4}$. The Gini impurity for this group is $1-\left(\frac{1}{4}\right)^2-\left(\frac{3}{4}\right)^2=0.375$. Now we can calculate Gini weighted impurity for forecasted sales. Since there are nine data points, the weighted Gini impurity for the low-forecast group will be $\frac{5}{9}$, and for the high-forecast group it will be $\frac{4}{9}$. The weighted average will be $\left(\frac{5}{9}\right)0.32+\left(\frac{4}{9}\right)0.375=0.34$.

Similarly, we can calculate weighted Gini impurity for the transit time variable (as depicted in Figure 12.4).

FIGURE 12.4 ■ Gini Impurity for Forecasted Sales and Transit Time

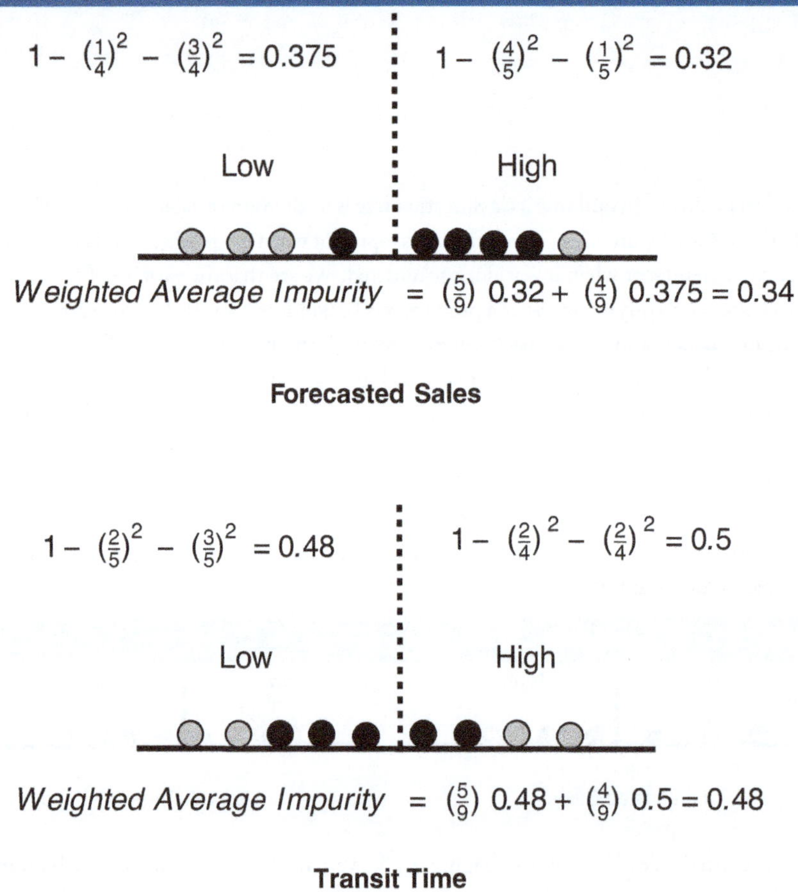

We find that Gini impurity is lower with forecasted sales; hence, it becomes the variable to split the root node. The resulting decision tree will look like Figure 12.5, in which it splits further based on the transit time.

FIGURE 12.5 ■ Decision Tree Splits

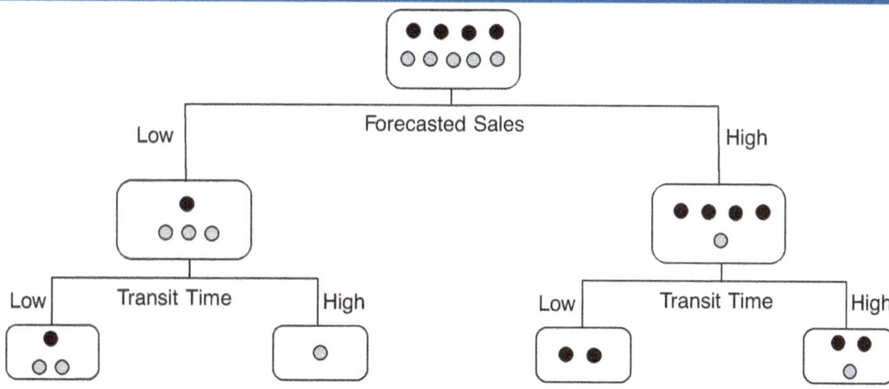

Since we have only two predictor variables, this will not be split further, and the final nodes will be the terminal nodes or leaves. Predictions associated with each leaf will reflect the majority class. As an example, if the majority class in the leftmost leaf is *no* (2) and the minority class is *yes* (1), then the prediction associated with this leaf will be *no*.

12.4.3 Advantages, Disadvantages, and Ways to Improve Classification Trees

Classification trees offer many advantages. First, several types of predictor variables (numeric or categorical in nature) can be included in the analysis, and they don't need to be scaled or standardized. Second, outliers don't influence classification tree predictions; therefore, no outlier removal is necessary before analysis. Third, trees are not affected by the presence of irrelevant predictors. If an irrelevant predictor is included in the analysis, the analysis is not affected even when the user is uncertain which predictors have a significant influence. Classification trees can also handle the presence of correlated predictors (multicollinearity), which is very common in real-world data since many of the predictors that users might identify as being important for the analysis could be correlated with one another. Fourth, interactions among predictor variables are automatically incorporated in the analysis; therefore, there is no need to prespecify interactions, which is necessary in methods such as ordinary least squares (OLS) regression and logistic regression.

However, there are some *disadvantages* of using classification trees. Individual trees do not have as much predictive power as many other methods such as logistic regression or neural nets. Trees are also very sensitive to variations in the training data. In other words, if we divide the training data randomly into two parts and train two different trees, then there is a high likelihood that both trees will fail to make similar predictions.

One way to improve the predictive power of trees and reduce their sensitivity to variations in the training data is to combine the predictions of many trees. The intuition behind combining various trees can be understood through the example of measuring temperature. Imagine we have a thermometer that has some random error. Every time we measure temperature, it gives slightly different readings. One way to obtain a more stable and reliable estimate of temperature is to take several measurements of temperature and then average them. In a similar vein, when we combine predictions of various trees, we reduce variation in their predictions and improve their predictive power. The combination of several trees is known as an ensemble of trees; since an ensemble of trees is a forest, the method that creates this ensemble is called random forest.

12.5 RANDOM FOREST

The first step builds multiple distinct trees by using bootstrap samples of training data. *Bootstrapping* is a process of sampling data points from the original dataset with replacement. Imagine we have 30 balls in a box and each of them has a distinct number written on it. In sampling with replacement, we first randomly pick a ball, write down the number written on the ball, and put it back in the box. We again pick a ball, write down the number, and put it back in the box. We are allowed to randomly pick the same ball more than once. Repeating this process 30 times will give us our first bootstrap sample. For a dataset, bootstrap samples are formed by sampling rows with replacement from the original dataset. Since we are replacing each row, there is a possibility that some rows will be picked up more than once, that our bootstrap sample will have duplicate rows of data, and that some rows from the original dataset will be missing in our bootstrap sample. This is exactly what we want because this will help us build diverse trees. This process of building trees from several bootstrap samples and combining their prediction is called *bagging* (short for *bootstrap aggregation*).

In a regular decision tree, all the predictor variables are considered at each split; however, this leads to a problem. If there is a predictor variable that is very good at predicting the outcome variable, then regardless of how many bootstrap samples we use, there is a very high chance that all the trees will look the same and their predictions will be very correlated. In other words, we will fail to build diverse trees. The second step of random forest, therefore, goes beyond simple bagging. It combines bagging with an idea known as *subspace sampling* (also referred to as *feature bagging*). At each split, it randomly selects a subset of predictor variables that are the only ones considered; then a new subset of predictors is considered at the next split from the remaining predictors. So if there are 20 predictor variables, then 5 are randomly chosen at each split. Their performance on a criterion like Gini impurity is compared, and the best-performing variable splits the data. At the next split, a new random sample of 5 predictors from the remaining set of 19 predictors is chosen. This method ensures that if a strong predictor exists, then it is not always chosen to split the data. This way, we get diverse trees from bootstrap samples.

In the third step of random forest, each tree makes its prediction, and the final prediction is based on the consensus value. The outcome that receives the most votes is the final prediction. As an example, if we build 100 trees for a new product where the outcome is unknown, and out of these 100 trees 65 trees predict that the product will be backordered and 35 predict that the product will not be backordered, then the final prediction of the random forest will be *yes*.

As can be noticed, we have not discussed any method to find the optimum number of predictor variables randomly sampled in the second step. There is no way to estimate the optimum number from the dataset. Therefore, this becomes a hyperparameter that needs to be tuned using cross-validation. Another hyperparameter is the number of trees we want to grow. This also needs to be tuned using cross-validation.

12.6 BACKORDER PREDICTION USING RANDOM FORESTS

Let's assume that a manufacturer of small machines has set up an inventory system to ensure that it can keep track of obtaining machined parts from its suppliers so it can build its machines and deliver them on time to its customers. However, recently, the manufacturer has noticed some backorder issues, leading to dissatisfied customers. To prevent such backorder issues from occurring in the future, the manufacturer uses random forests to build a model for predicting (and hence addressing) backorders. Let's understand the process and perform the analysis ourselves. We will refer to the business as the manufacturer, and the machines it manufactures as products.

12.6.1 Data Import and Selection

The variables in our analysis include the following.[5] The outcome variable indicated whether a product was backordered (*yes* vs. *no*). The random forest was provided with 16 predictor variables such as the current level of inventory; usual and current transit time; sales forecasts for the next 3, 6, and 9 months; sales in the past 3, 6, and 9 months; minimum recommended stock; and machined parts due from the manufacturer's suppliers.

We begin our analysis by importing the data and checking the class of nonnumeric variables. We want to ensure that nonnumeric or categorical variables are recognized as factors in the analysis.

As we discussed earlier, backorder data tend to have a class imbalance, where the number of items that were backordered is proportionately less than the number of items that were not backordered. Let's check this in our data through a simple plot (Figure 12.6).

FIGURE 12.6 ■ Data Imbalance

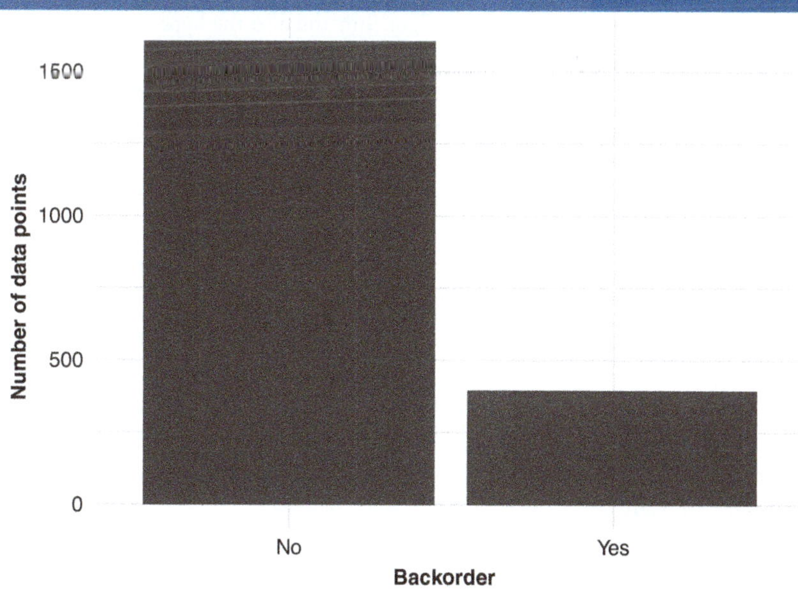

The plot shows that products that were backordered (i.e., when the outcome variable was *yes*) represented approximately $\frac{1}{5}$ of the data. This makes the times the product was not backordered (i.e., when the outcome variable was *no*) a majority level (also referred to as majority class). *Yes* becomes a minority level. It is necessary to use a sampling method that provides an appropriate representation to the minority level. Next we discuss one such sampling method.

12.6.2 Imbalance in the Data

To handle the issue of class imbalance, we use a downsampling method that samples rows from the training data in such a way that the majority level (when the products were not backordered—i.e., when outcome variable = *no*) is sampled less. This increases the proportion of the minority level (when the products were backordered) in model training. We set the train data in such a way that the backorders are at most 1.5 times as many rows as minority levels. If we compare this situation to our base situation when no sampling is applied, we will have majority levels with 4 times as many rows as minority levels.

However, having corrected for the imbalance in the training data so that the model has enough data points from which to learn how backorders are affected by the predictors, we need to ensure that the model is tested on a dataset that captures the real world. The real world has a data imbalance, where backorders are fewer in number; therefore, we need to have test data that reflect this smaller number of backorders compared to all orders so that the efficacy of the model in the real world can be tested. Thus, in the test data, no undersampling is used, and the imbalance is retained.

12.6.3 Hyperparameter Tuning

We formulate the model with backorder as the outcome variable and all other variables as predictors. We then specify the random forest algorithm and also the hyperparameters—such as the number of predictors randomly sampled at each split when a tree is created, the number of trees contained in a random forest, and the minimum number of data points in a node required for the node to be split further (please see the Technical Appendix for a detailed description of hyperparameters). Each hyperparameter is then tuned through a grid search. Since our outcome variable is categorical (*yes* and *no*), we need to ensure that our model type is specified as a classification model.

We use fivefold cross-validation, indicating that there will be five partitions of the training dataset and that the performance of each hyperparameter combination will be assessed using this cross-validation procedure. Moreover, we specify 50 different hyperparameter combinations. For each of the 50 hyperparameter combinations, a model is fit on the four partitions, and its performance is assessed on the fifth partition. The AUC ROC (area under the curve receiver operating characteristics) curve and overall accuracy of the model are computed (please refer to Chapter 9 on logistic regression, which provides a detailed description of interpreting AUC ROC values for a model).

We then pick the best hyperparameter combination.

The analysis reveals that the best hyperparameter combinations are the following: the number of predictors randomly sampled at each split when a tree is created = 5, the number of trees contained in a random forest = 69, and the minimum number of data points in a node that is required for the node to be split further = 31.

12.6.4 Testing the Performance of Our Random Forest Model

We fit the model using the best hyperparameter combination on the entire training set and then validate its performance on the test data. The accuracy and ROC values (Table 12.2), along with the confusion matrix for the test data (Table 12.3), are reported.

12.6.4.1 Accuracy and ROC Values

TABLE 12.2 ■ Accuracy and ROC Values

.metric	.estimator	.estimate	.config
accuracy	binary	0.8223553	Preprocessor1_Model1
roc_auc	binary	0.9076335	Preprocessor1_Model1

TABLE 12.3 ■ Confusion Matrix

	No	Yes
No	329	16
Yes	73	83

The results show that the accuracy is 82.2%, and the AUC is 0.908. Given the imbalance in levels of the outcome variable and the fact that the minority level (when the products were back-ordered) is more important for the prediction task, we need to estimate the sensitivity as well as the specificity of this prediction.

12.6.4.2 Confusion Matrix, Sensitivity, and Specificity

A quick recap from Chapter 9 on logistic regression explains the confusion matrix. Let's work with the following example to understand the process of calculating sensitivity and specificity.

TABLE 12.4 ■ Confusion Matrix

	Truth	
Prediction	No	Yes
No	i	iii
Yes	ii	iv

Given the confusion matrix in Table 12.4, sensitivity and specificity are as follows:

$$Sensitivity = \frac{iv}{iii + iv} \text{ and } Specificity = \frac{i}{i + ii}$$

Intuitively, sensitivity is the true positive rate and represents the ability of our model to correctly classify products that were backordered. Specificity is the true negative rate and represents the ability of our model to correctly classify products that were not backordered. If sensitivity of our model is low, then we will not be able to identify ahead of time products that are likely to be backordered. On the other hand, if specificity is low, then we will end up overordering products that are less likely to be backordered. For our model, sensitivity is $\frac{83}{83+16} = 0.838$, and specificity is $\frac{329}{329+73} = 0.818$.

12.6.4.3 Role of Downsampling

In the preceding analysis, we used *downsampling* to handle the issue of class imbalance. This downsampling method sampled rows from training data in such a way that the majority level (i.e., when the products were not backordered) is sampled less. But let's check how the results would change if we didn't downsample. The results when downsampling is not used are represented in Table 12.5, along with the confusion matrix in Table 12.6.

TABLE 12.5 ■ Results When Downsampling

.metric	.estimator	.estimate	.config
accuracy	binary	0.8602794	Preprocessor1_Model1
roc_auc	binary	0.9038896	Preprocessor1_Model1

TABLE 12.6 ■ Confusion Matrix

	No	Yes
No	393	61
Yes	9	38

We notice that both accuracy and AUC values are high and comparable to the earlier analysis when we did downsampling. However, when we estimate sensitivity and specificity, we observe a very different picture. Without downsampling, sensitivity is $\frac{38}{38+61} = 0.384$, and specificity is $\frac{393}{393+9} = 0.978$. There is a big drop in sensitivity from 0.838 to 0.384 and an increase in specificity from 0.818 to 0.978. This shows that in the absence of downsampling, our model is not able to identify products that will eventually be backordered. Downsampling addresses this weakness, and the cost we pay is a drop in specificity. Downsampling ensures that without compromising on AUC and accuracy values, we can make sensitivity and specificity very comparable. Note that downsampling is one of the many subsampling methods that are available in analysis packages (see www.tidymodels.org/learn/models/sub-sampling/ for other subsampling methods that can be used).

12.7 BUSINESS INSIGHTS AND SUMMARY

In this chapter, we examined backorders, a major supply chain topic that can cause multiple issues such as dissatisfaction, reduced purchase probability, and reduced profitability. In order to predict potential backorder issues, we used random forests to build a predictive model. Random forests belong to the larger set of decision tree models that are sometimes preferred over opaque predictive models because they allow some transparency about model working. They also are preferred since they have the ability to work well with different types of categorical and continuous predictor variables, multicollinear data, and outliers.

The random forest model includes 16 predictor variables to predict whether or not a product is likely to be backordered. Since we relied on a categorical variable (*yes* vs. *no*) as the outcome variable, we use a confusion matrix to examine the accuracy, specificity, and sensitivity of the random forest model. We also learned that products that are likely to be backordered form a smaller proportion of the dataset than those that will not be backordered. We then understood how the downsampling method can be used to address the issue of imbalanced data. In addition, we discussed how we can check for whether the accuracy of the model is changed because of downsampling.

12.8 IMPLEMENTATION USING R: BACKORDER PREDICTION

The outcome variable was whether the product went on backorder or not. The random forest was provided with 16 predictor variables such as the following:

- went_on_backorder = the outcome variable of whether a product was backordered or not and could take the value of *yes* or *no*
- national_inv = indicates the current level of inventory

- lead_time = measures the transit time for the product
- in_transit_qty = indicates how much of the product is currently in transit
- forecast_3_month, forecast_6_month, forecast_9_month = three different predictors capturing the sales forecast for the coming 3, 6, and 9 months
- sales_1_month, sales_3_month, sales_6_month, sales_9_month = four variables indicating sales of the product in the last 1, 3, 6, and 9 months
- min_bank = the minimum amount of product that is recommended to keep in stock
- pieces_past_due = captures whether any parts are overdue from the supplier
- perf_6_month_avg, perf_12_month_avg = two variables representing the product performance in the past 6 and 12 months
- local_bo_qty = captures the amount of orders overdue
- deck_risk, ppap_risk = two different types of risk in delivery represented in a binary form of *yes* and *no*

We first read in the data and the libraries such as `readxl`,[6] `tidymodels`,[7] `dplyr`,[8] `ranger`,[9] and `themis`.[10]

After loading the required packages, we import the data and check the class of nonnumeric variables. We want to ensure that nonnumeric variables such as `deck_risk`, `ppap_risk`, and `went_on_backorder` are categorical variables and will be recognized as `factor` by R.

```
set.seed(12345)
library(readxl)
library(tidymodels)
library(dplyr)
library(ranger)
library(themis)
library(ggplot2)
library(doParallel)

back_order_data <-read.csv(url
    ("http://data.mishra.us/files/chapter_decision_uncertainty/backorder.csv"))

sapply(back_order_data,class)
##   national_inv        lead_time        in_transit_qty  forecast_3_month
##    "integer"          "integer"          "integer"        "integer"
##   forecast_6_month  forecast_9_month   sales_1_month   sales_3_month
```

```
##    "integer"          "integer"          "integer"        "integer"
##   sales_6_month      sales_9_month      min_bank         pieces_past_due
##    "integer"          "integer"          "integer"        "integer"
##   perf_6_month_avg   perf_12_month_avg  local_bo_qty     deck_risk
##    "numeric"          "numeric"          "integer"        "character"
##     ppap_risk went_on_backorder
##    "character"        "character"
```

Since these categorical variables are appearing as characters, we convert them into factors and check again their class assignment.

```
back_order_data <- as.data.frame(unclass(back_order_data),
                                 stringsAsFactors = TRUE)
sapply(back_order_data,class)
## national_inv       lead_time          in_transit_qty   forecast_3_month
##   "integer"          "integer"          "integer"        "integer"
## forecast_6_month   forecast_9_month   sales_1_month    sales_3_month
##   "integer"          "integer"          "integer"        "integer"
## sales_6_month      sales_9_month      min_bank         pieces_past_due
##   "integer"          "integer"          "integer"        "integer"
## perf_6_month_avg   perf_12_month_avg  local_bo_qty     deck_risk
##   "numeric"          "numeric"          "integer"        "factor"
## ppap_risk went_on_backorder
##   "factor"           "factor"
```

As we discussed earlier, backorder data tend to have a class imbalance, where the number of items that were backordered is proportionately less than the number of items that were not backordered. Let's check this in our data through a simple plot, shown in Figure 12.6.

```
ggplot(back_order_data, aes(went_on_backorder))+
  xlab("Backorder")+ylab("Number of data points")+
  geom_bar()+
  theme_minimal()
```

The plot shows that items that were backordered (i.e., when the outcome variable `went_on_backorder = yes`) represented approximately $\frac{1}{5}$ of the data. This makes `went_on_backorder = no` the majority level (also referred to as majority class) and `went_on_backorder = yes` a minority level. It is necessary to use a sampling method that provides appropriate representation to minority level.

As the first step to build a model to predict backorder, we split the data into train and test groups. Let's use 75% data for training and 25% for testing the model.

```
backorder_split <- initial_split(back_order_data, strata = went_on_backorder,
                    prop = 0.75)
backorder_train <- training(backorder_split)
backorder_test <- testing(backorder_split)
```

Next we define the model formulation in `recipe` and indicate that `went_on_backorder` is the outcome variable and all other variables are predictors.

To handle the issue of class imbalance, we use `step_downsample()`. This function samples rows from training data in such a way that the majority level (i.e., `went_on_backorder = ` *no*) is sampled less. This increases the proportion of the minority level (i.e., `went_on_backorder = ` *yes*) in model training. However, it is important to note that such undersampling does not occur in the test data, which ensures that model performance is tested in data that closely represent the real world (i.e., where one class is overrepresented). `under_ratio = 1.5` implies that majority levels will have at most 1.5 times more rows than minority levels. If we compare this situation to our base situation when no sampling is applied, we will have majority level with 4 times as many rows as minority levels.

```
backorder_recipe <- recipe(went_on_backorder ~ ., data = backorder_train)%>%
  step_downsample(went_on_backorder,under_ratio = 1.5)
```

Using `rand_forest()`, we specify the random forest algorithm and also the hyperparameters such as `mtry` (the number of predictors randomly sampled at each split when a tree is created), `trees` (the number of trees contained in a random forest), and `min_n` (the minimum number of data points in a node that is required for the node to be split further). `tune()` specifies that each hyperparameter needs to be tuned though grid search. `set_engine("ranger")` specifies that our computational engine is `ranger`, a fast implementation of random forests. Since our outcome variable is categorical (*yes* vs. *no*), `set_mode("classification")` specifies that our model type is a classification model.

```
model_backorder <- rand_forest(
  mtry = tune(),
  trees = tune(),
  min_n = tune()) %>%
  set_mode("classification") %>%
  set_engine("ranger")

backorder_folds <- vfold_cv(backorder_train, v = 5)
```

Next, we aggregate the recipe and model using `workflow()`. `add_model` adds the `model_backorder` specified in the last step with `backorder_recipe`, which contains information about predictor and outcome variables and dummy coding.

```
backorder_wf <- workflow() %>%
  add_model(model_backorder) %>%
  add_recipe(backorder_recipe)
```

We next specify the cross-validation process using `vfold_cv()`. `V = 5` specifies that there will be five partitions of the training dataset and that each hyperparameter combination's performance will be assessed using this cross-validation procedure. `doParallel::registerDoParallel(cores = 10)` registers that 10 cores will be used for parallel execution of the model. We can change the values of the cores depending on the computational resources available.

`grid = 50` in `tune_grid()` specifies that 50 different hyperparameter combinations should be created. `resamples = backorder_folds` uses cross-validation specified in `vfold_cv()` and helps to avoid overfitting the training data. For each of the 50 combinations of hyperparameters, a model will be fit on the four partitions, and its performance will be assessed on the fifth partition.

```
backorder_folds <- vfold_cv(backorder_train, v = 5)
doParallel::registerDoParallel(cores = 10)
backorder_tune <-
  backorder_wf %>%
  tune_grid(
    resamples = backorder_folds,
    grid = 50
  )
```

We use `select_best("roc_auc")` to pick the best hyperparameter combination.

```
best_model <- backorder_tune %>%
 select_best("roc_auc")

best_model
## # A tibble: 1 × 4
##      mtry trees min_n  .config
##     <int> <int> <int>  <chr>
## 1       5    69     31 Preprocessor1_Model20
```

The analysis reveals that the best hyperparameter combination is `mtry` = 5, `tree` = 69, and `min_n` = 31. Now we will use these hyperparameter values to update the workflow using `finalize_workflow`. `finalize_workflow` adds the best model to the workflow `backorder_wf` created earlier. This gives us the `final_workflow` that captures all the information about the model, hyperparameters, outcome variable, and predictors.

```
final_workflow <-
  backorder_wf %>%
  finalize_workflow(best_model)
```

We fit the model using the best hyperparameter combination on the entire training set and then validate its performance on the test data. `last_fit` helps us accomplish this. `split = backorder_split` specifies that `backorder_split` contains information about the test and train split performed earlier. Using `collect_metrics`, we report the accuracy and ROC AUC values. Finally using `conf_mat()`, we produce a confusion matrix.

```
final_fit <-
  final_workflow %>%
  last_fit(split = backorder_split)

final_fit %>%
  collect_metrics()
## # A tibble: 2 × 4
##     .metric    .estimator   .estimate  .config
##     <chr>      <chr>            <dbl>  <chr>
## 1   accuracy   binary           0.822  Preprocessor1_Model1
## 2   roc_auc    binary           0.908  Preprocessor1_Model1
final_fit %>%
  collect_predictions()%>%
  conf_mat(truth = went_on_backorder, estimate = .pred_class)
```

```
##             Truth
##   Prediction  No  Yes
##           No  329  16
##          Yes   73  83
```

The results show that the accuracy is 82.2% and AUC is 0.908. Given the imbalance in levels of the outcome variable and the fact that the minority level (i.e., `went_on_backorder = ` *yes*) is more important for the prediction task, we estimate sensitivity as well as specificity of this prediction. We use Table 12.4 and the formula for sensitivity and specificity defined earlier for our calculations.

For our model, sensitivity is $\frac{83}{83+16}=0.838$, and specificity is $\frac{329}{329+73}=0.818$.

12.9 UNDERSTANDING THE CHAPTER

1. Given a dataset where instances of backorders are vastly outnumbered by regular orders, hyperparameter tuning in Random Forest, such as the number of trees or minimum data points per node, can be used. How might adjusting these parameters specifically aid or not aid in improving prediction accuracy for the minority class (backorders)?

2. Consider a predictive modeling task involving a Random Forest classifier. Explain the role and significance of employing k-fold cross-validation (CV) in the model evaluation process. How does k-fold CV work, and in what ways does it attempt to provide a robust estimate of the model's performance? Moreover, discuss the trade-offs involved in choosing a specific k value (e.g., $k = 5$ vs. $k = 10$).

3. Decisions that are made with some information missing are called which of the following?
   a. Risky decisions
   b. Decisions under certainty
   c. No decision can be made
   d. Binary decisions

4. From the options provided, which are features of decisions made under uncertainty? (Choose all that apply.)
   a. Weighing the risks of making the decision versus the benefits of the decision
   b. Weighing the risks versus the costs of making the decision
   c. Weighing the benefits of the decision versus profits from the sales
   d. Evaluating existing options versus new ones

5. Which of the following statements is *true* about the bullwhip effect?
   a. It occurs when a small change in demand is overestimated, resulting in oversupply.
   b. It occurs when a small change in supply is underestimated.
   c. It occurs when demand matches supply.
   d. It occurs when inflation causes demand to fall.

6. For decision trees, the metric used to find which variable is a better classifier is which of the following?
   a. Gini impurity
   b. Coefficient of determination
   c. Variance inflation factor (VIF)
   d. Cophenetic correlation coefficient

7. Which of the following statements about bagging is *false*?
   a. Bagging is bootstrap aggregation.
   b. Bagging involves sampling with replacement.
   c. Bagging involves sampling without replacement.
   d. Bagging helps build diverse trees.

8. Which of the following statements about downsampling is *false*?
   a. It addresses the issue of data imbalance.
   b. It allows the model to better learn the features of the minority class.
   c. It severely reduces accuracy of the model.
   d. It slightly decreases specificity but improves sensitivity significantly.

9. Let's assume that we are using a decision tree to find out which predictor variable(s) can better classify the outcome variable: whether or not customers will buy a product. Given the following Gini impurity values for the three predictor variables—Predictor A = 0.55, Predictor B = 0.24, and Predictor C = 0.76—which of the following options would be considered the optimal classifier of the buy/no buy decision?
   a. Predictor A
   b. Predictor B
   c. Predictor C
   d. Both Predictor A and Predictor C

ENDNOTES

1. Heath, Chip, and Amos Tversky, "Preference and Belief: Ambiguity and Competence in Choice Under Uncertainty," *Journal of Risk and Uncertainty* 4, no. 1 (1991): 5–28.
2. Fischhoff, Baruch, and Alex L. Davis, "Communicating Scientific Uncertainty," *Proceedings of the National Academy of Sciences* 111, Suppl. 4 (2014): 13664–13671.
3. IBM Corporation, "Scientific and Technical Report: Backorder Prediction," for Defense Logistics Agency Research and Development (Contract No. SP4701-20-C-0052), submitted February 26, 2021, https://apps.dtic.mil/sti/pdfs/AD1141471.pdf.
4. Bhan, Hyung Sup, and Eric T. Anderson, "Multiyear Impact of Backorder Delays: A Quasi-experimental Approach," *Marketing Science* 22, no. 2 (2022): 314–335.
5. The data for the analysis is a subset of data adopted from Santis et al. (2017). It was made available as a Kaggle competition and is posted at https://github.com/rodrigosantis1/backorder_prediction. Santis, Rodrigo B., Eduardo Pestana de Aguiar, and Leonardo Goliatt, "Predicting Material Backorders in Inventory Management Using Machine Learning," Fourth IEEE Latin American Conference on Computational Intelligence, Arequipa, Peru (2017).
6. Wickham, Hadley, and Jennifer Bryan, "readxl: Read Excel Files," R package version 1.4.3 (July 6, 2023), https://CRAN.R-project.org/package=readxl.
7. Kuhn, Max, et al., "Tidymodels: A Collection of Packages for Modeling and Machine Learning Using tidyverse Principles" (2020), https://www.tidymodels.org.

8. Wickham, Hadley, Romain François, Lionel Henry, and Kirill Müller, "dplyr: A Grammar of Data Manipulation," R package version 1.1.3 (September 3, 2023), https://CRAN.R-project.org/package=dplyr.

9. Wright, Marvin N., and Andreas Ziegler, "ranger: A Fast Implementation of Random Forests for High Dimensional Data in C++ and R," *Journal of Statistical Software* 77, no. 1 (2017): 1–17, https://doi.org/10.18637/jss.v077.i01.

10. Hvitfeldt, Emil, "themis: Extra Recipes Steps for Dealing With Unbalanced Data," R package version 1.0.0 (2022), https://CRAN.R-project.org/package=themis.

13 PREDICTING EMPLOYEE SATISFACTION USING BOOSTED DECISION TREES

CONTENTS

LEARNING OBJECTIVES

1. Describe the importance of employee satisfaction
2. Measure employee satisfaction
3. Predict employee satisfaction with decision tree models
4. Comprehend advantages and limitations of tree models
5. Use boosted decision trees to predict employee satisfaction

13.1 EMPLOYEE SATISFACTION DRIVES CUSTOMER SATISFACTION

Consider the following initiatives that businesses undertake.

- Google offers free lunches, fitness facilities, free haircuts, laundry, and some work-from-home days.
- Before remote working became popular, JetBlue offered reservations staff the ability to work remotely and not have to come in to the office.
- Whole Foods has encouraged the formation of decentralized small teams or work groups that have a large say in who the next team member will be. Members join the team on a trial basis, and the other members of the team determine whether the new member stays or not.[1]

A common theme among these examples is that they are employee-focused initiatives and follow a similar line of thinking as Zappos's ad campaign of "Happy People Making People Happy." Or the statement by Virgin Atlantic's Richard Branson: "Happy staff are proud staff, and proud staff deliver excellent customer service, which drives business success." All these statements attest to the strong belief that ensuring your employees are engaged with the business helps in retaining existing customers as well as gaining repeat customers.[2]

13.1.1 Reasons for Investing in Employee Satisfaction

Employee satisfaction plays a critical role in an organization's success.

1. Satisfied employees lead to satisfied customers. Investing in employee satisfaction, therefore, is a consumer-centric strategy for many organizations, especially those in the service sector, such as health care and hospitality, where there is greater employee–customer interaction.
2. Investing in their satisfaction also helps to attract and retain key employees. Key employees who have stayed with an organization for a long time and are satisfied with the workplace contribute significantly to the success of an organization. Satisfied employees consider the organization initiatives to improve their well-being as a gift that needs to be reciprocated. This relationship building with employees results in higher employee motivation, greater employee effort, and employees' adoption of the organization's goals as their own goals. In other words, employees perceive working for the organization as working for themselves, a relationship that benefits both the organization and the employees.[3]
3. The organization benefits from higher employee satisfaction in diverse ways. For instance, worker motivation improves the organization's financial performance and the quality of output.[4] Firm productivity has been shown to increase because of such initiatives.[5] Some findings have demonstrated that organizations focused on employee

well-being produce better-quality patents and also a greater number of patents—leading to better market valuation and improved future performance.[6]

4. Another important reason why organizations focus on employee satisfaction is to preempt employee dissatisfaction. Firms lose when employees are dissatisfied with their working conditions because it results in lowered commitment to the organization, absenteeism, grievances, and high turnover.[7]

13.1.2 Identifying Factors Affecting Employee Satisfaction

If people were asked to come up with ways to improve employee satisfaction, they might state that compensation is the top consideration. However, research in organizational behavior has demonstrated that employees may be more motivated by factors such as recognition, opportunities for growth, security, and workplace culture.[8] It is important to note that factors resulting in job *dissatisfaction* are not the same as those that result in job *satisfaction*. Dissatisfaction can be caused by low compensation, the presence of bureaucratic rules, an unfair structure in the organization, or even difficult workspaces. However, satisfaction might be driven by factors in the job that improve employee self-esteem and sense of achievement.[9] Therefore, misidentifying a dissatisfaction factor (e.g., compensation) and using it to improve satisfaction may not be optimal since greater compensation can decrease dissatisfaction but might not increase satisfaction.

13.2 MEASURING EMPLOYEE SATISFACTION

One method that many organizations use to measure employee satisfaction and well-being is to annually survey employees. Employees are asked to respond to questions such as whether they would "recommend this organization to others as a great workplace" and whether "their work provides them with a feeling of personal accomplishment (or appears routine)." Organizations also obtain employee satisfaction data from exit interviews when employees decide to leave the firm.

Note that both of these methods provide retrospective satisfaction data. Several incidents might occur between annual surveys that affect an employee's experienced satisfaction. Relying solely on annual surveys makes it difficult for a firm to immediately identify and address a source of dissatisfaction. Satisfaction data obtained during an exit interview arrive too late to avert the employee's departure.

Implementing any proactive intervention (e.g., wage increase, new job responsibility, promotion) to enhance employee satisfaction poses challenges to an organization as it requires real-time assessment of employee satisfaction.[10] One way to obtain a real-time picture of employee satisfaction is using prior data to predict employee satisfaction. In addition, such predictive analysis can assess how interventions such as new job responsibilities and a promotion would affect employee satisfaction. This can help in generating effective interventions.

13.2.1 Measuring Employee Satisfaction Using Machine Learning

Prediction models such as logistic regression, deep neural nets, and decision trees can be used to predict employee satisfaction. For the purposes of this chapter, we will use a boosted tree model for predicting job satisfaction. In Chapter 12, which described random forest decision models, we discussed the basic information needed to understand a decision tree model, including the different components of a tree model and advantages of using decision trees. We also used a random forest tree model to understand backorders in supply chain management. We will build on that information to apply a different tree model in this chapter. Since a boosted tree model can be a black box model, we will also discuss methods to explain such black box models. These methods fall under the category of XAI (explainable AI).

13.2.2 Using a Decision Tree Model for Human Resource Analytics

To understand the application of regression trees to human resources, let's start with a simple example. Consider an organization that has surveyed its employees about how satisfied they are with their job. The company wants to make a simple prediction about how the number of years an employee has worked in the organization (years of experience) affects their job satisfaction. In other words, let's consider a dataset that has *years of experience at the organization* as the predictor variable and *job satisfaction* as the outcome variable. The first step in building a regression tree is to partition years of experience (the predictor) into two groups. Then, for each observation that falls into a specific group, we make predictions about its value, which is simply the average of all the observations in that group. Figure 13.1 is a simple regression tree built on the job satisfaction data.

FIGURE 13.1 ■ Regression Tree

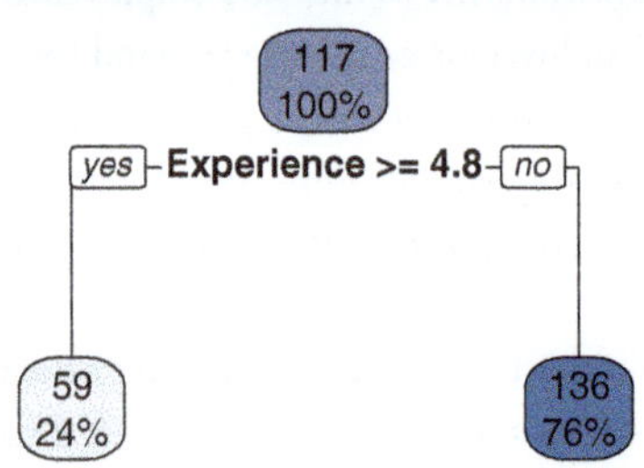

Figure 13.1 shows that in the overall data, the average satisfaction value is 117 (as shown in the *root node* at the top of the figure). The tree uses a cutoff value of 4.8 years to create the first partition. Thus, employees with 4.8 years or more of experience form one group (on the left of the figure), and those with less than 4.8 years of experience form the second group (on the right of the figure). The average satisfaction of employees with more than 4.8 years of experience is 59 (representing 24% of the data), while the average satisfaction of employees with less than 4.8 years of experience is 136 (representing 76% of the data). Since there are numerous cutoff values one can set to partition the data, how does the decision tree arrive at the value of 4.8 years? Intuitively, it considers all possible cutoff values and chooses a cutoff value that creates the most homogeneous groups. Homogeneity is assessed by the *residual sum of squares* (RSS)[11] of each

group. What is the RSS? It is the overall difference between the actual data values and the values predicted by the regression tree in each group. Formally, it can be represented as follows:

$$RSS = \sum_{i \in R_1} (y_i - \bar{y}_{R_1})^2 + \sum_{i \in R_2} (y_i - \bar{y}_{R_2})^2$$

In the preceding equation, y_i is the job satisfaction rating, R_1 and R_2 are two groups created by a specific cutoff value of experience, $\bar{y}_{R_1}$ is the average satisfaction of all the employees assigned to R_1, and $\bar{y}_{R_2}$ is the average satisfaction of all the employees assigned to R_2.

The regression tree estimates the RSS—as in the preceding equation—for each possible value of experience in the dataset and chooses the cutoff value that gives the lowest estimate of the RSS. The partitions created by the regression tree can also be understood by superimposing a decision boundary on a scatterplot.

FIGURE 13.2 ■ Decision Boundary

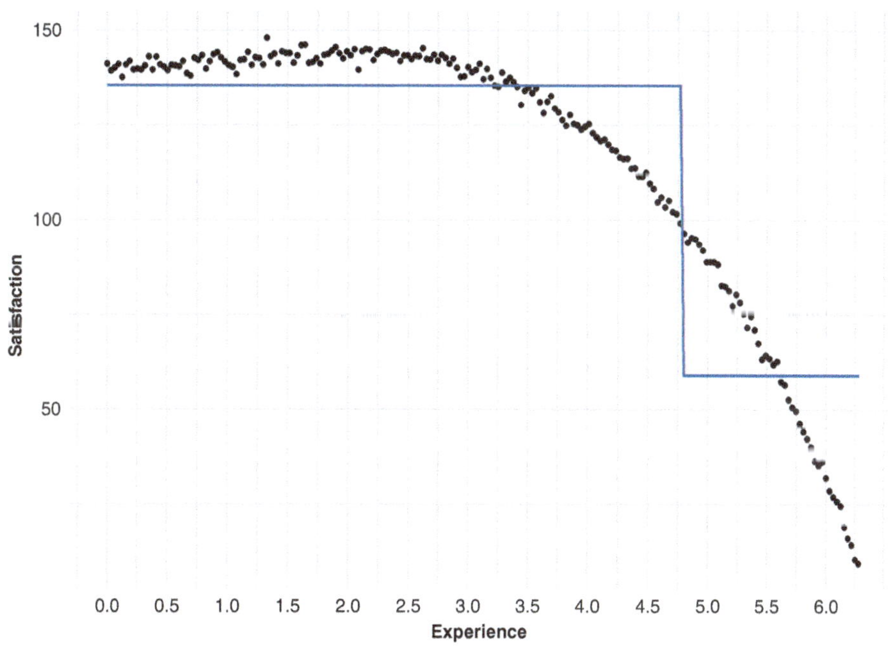

In Figure 13.2, the dark line indicates the average job satisfaction for employees with less than 4.8 years of experience and for employees with 4.8 years or more experience. Since the goal of this regression tree is to learn the relationship between years of experience and job satisfaction and eventually make predictions about employee job satisfaction based on the years of experience working at the company (i.e., make predictions for any employee not part of this dataset), the tree we have used up until now would predict that if an employee's work experience is less than 4.8 years, their satisfaction will be 136, but an employee with more than 4.8 years of experience will have a job satisfaction value of 59.

13.2.3 Tree Depth

The process of using the RSS to find the optimum cutoff value of experience can be repeated. We can split the internal nodes of the decision tree further. Figure 13.3 depicts the regression tree and its corresponding decision boundary.

FIGURE 13.3 ■ Splitting Internal Nodes

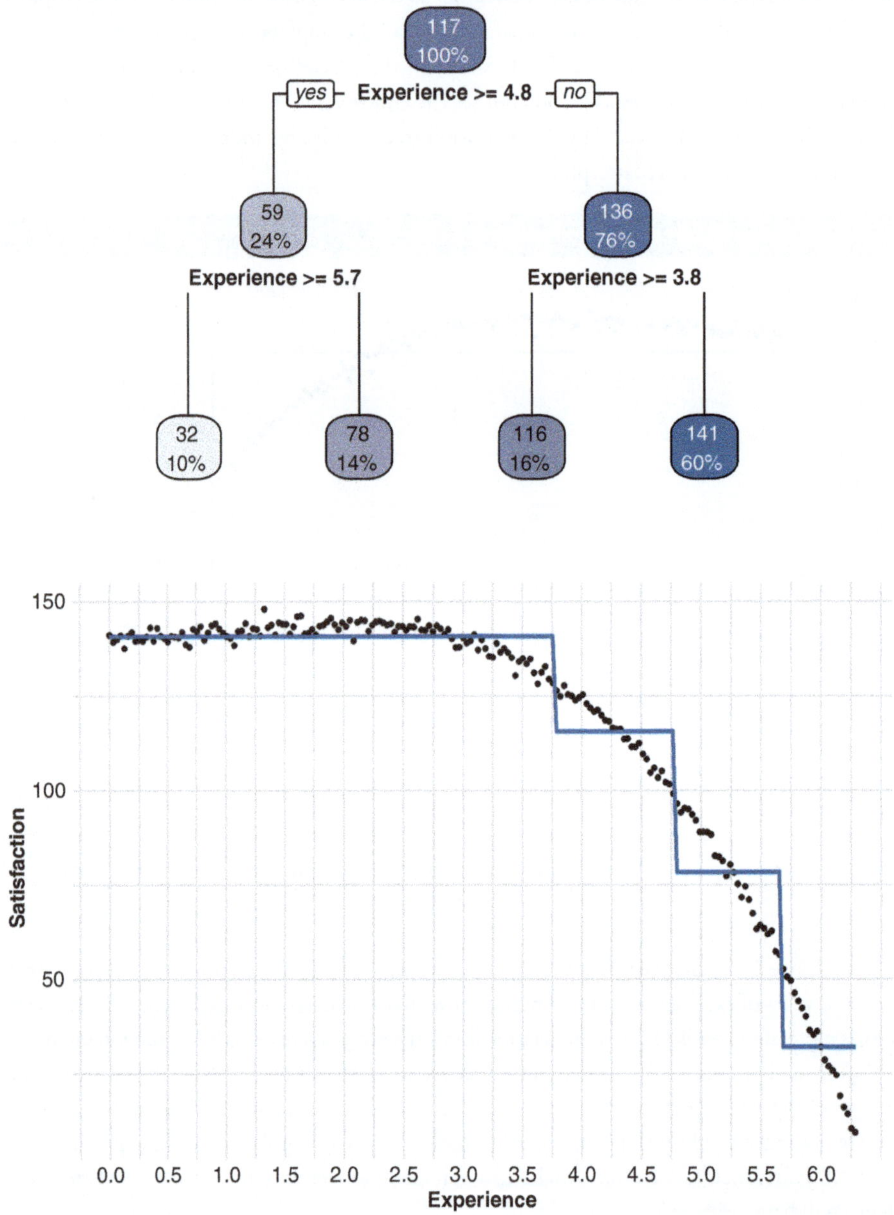

This subdivided tree shows that the group consisting of employees with 4.8 years or more of experience is further divided into two more groups: those with work experience greater than 5.7 years and those with between 4.8 and 5.7 years of experience; the job satisfaction of these groups is 32 and 78, respectively. A similar process of subdivision is repeated for those with less than 4.8 years of experience where they are further dividing into those between 4.7 and 3.8 years and those with less than 3.8 years of experience.

A tree can be divided multiple times, as shown in Figure 13.4, which can lead to a very dense tree ending in multiple leaf nodes.

FIGURE 13.4 ■ A Dense Tree

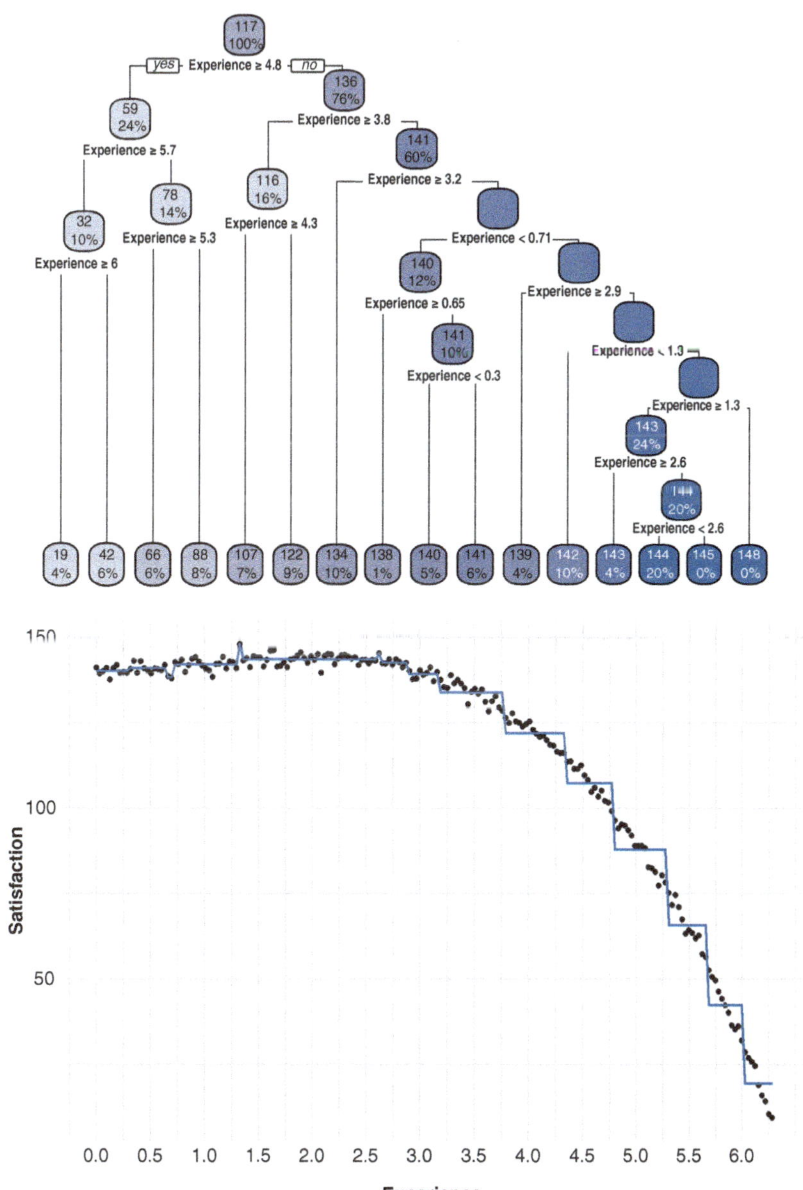

When trees are being subdivided to produce more granular divisions, we need to ask an important question: Is there any harm involved in a very dense tree? The answer is evident in the decision boundary shown in Figure 13.4. While dense trees can explain the training data very well (by helping the model learn the relationship between the input and output variables), they are doing so in *this* dataset. Hence, they suffer from overfitting and will perform poorly in test datasets. So, at what point should we stop splitting the tree further? The answer is to grow the tree as much as possible and then prune it to smaller-sized subtrees. One pruning approach is cost-complexity pruning.

The idea behind cost-complexity pruning is to penalize the RSS of a tree, using the size of the tree. Intuitively, we know that a dense tree with a lot of leaves will explain the training data better than a less dense tree. To avoid overfitting the training data, we need to increase the cost of adding more leaves. Therefore, the goal is to choose a subtree that balances the RSS and the density of the tree. Formally, this can be represented as

$$RSS_\alpha = RSS + \alpha(\text{Number of leaves})$$

where RSS_α is the residual sum of squares after adding the penalty (α) for the size of the tree (number of leaves). Let's understand this equation. If $\alpha = 0$, then $RSS_\alpha = RSS$, which means that if there is no penalty for tree size, then the best tree would be the densest tree. However, if α increases, then RSS_α would also increase for dense trees, which means that the trees with less density will start showing lower RSS_α than dense trees. But how do we choose α? Note that there is no predetermined value of α. It is a hyperparameter that needs to be fine-tuned using cross-validation. Therefore, the process of tree pruning includes the following steps:

1. Grow a large, dense tree.
2. For various values of α, obtain RSS_α and choose the subtree with the lowest RSS_α. This will produce different subtrees for each value of α.
3. Using k-fold cross-validation, make predictions on the left-out kth fold, using the subtrees obtained in Step 2. Estimate the mean squared prediction error.
4. Choose the α and the corresponding subtree that minimizes the mean squared prediction error.

13.2.4 Limitations of Decision Tree Models

Via a pruning process, trees can be designed that do not overfit the data; however, regression trees can still suffer from some other weaknesses. First, they are not usually as accurate as other methods such as generalized linear models and support vector regression. Second, they have difficulty in modeling smooth functions. Finally, the tree structure depends on the data sample; small changes in training data, like the presence of outliers, can result in a very different series of splits.[12] These factors could limit the usage of trees and hamper their predictive performance.

In order to address these limitations and increase the usage of trees, researchers have developed a method of aggregating many poor-performing trees to produce improved predictions. *Gradient boosting* is one such aggregation method that we will discuss next.

13.3 GRADIENT-BOOSTED TREES

Boosting is an iterative process of building a model from simpler models (also known as "weak learners"). To intuitively understand how gradient-boosted tree (GBT) models work, let's imagine a classroom in which students are collaboratively solving a large jigsaw puzzle.

1. First Decision Tree (Student A's Initial Attempt): Think of the first decision tree in GBT as Student A trying to solve a part of a puzzle. This first attempt provides a starting point but has some errors.
2. Identifying Errors (Calculating Missteps): We then measure the errors by comparing the part that has been assembled to the final picture of the puzzle to see which parts have been assembled incorrectly. Analogously, in GBT, the error identification process can be considered as calculating the difference between the outcomes predicted by the model and the actual outcomes. The difference between predicted and actual is called *residuals* (this is very similar to residual calculation for any model from linear regression to neural nets).
3. Correction (Student B Corrections): Next, Student B tries to fix Student A's errors by adjusting some pieces of the puzzle. The same process applied to GBT would involve a second decision tree being built to address the residuals (errors) from the first tree.
4. Iterative Improvement (Student C and Further): More students take turns, each one focusing on correcting the errors that they identify when it is their turn to work on the puzzle. Correspondingly, in GBT, additional trees are built to keep correcting the residuals left by all previous trees.
5. Final Model (Assembled Puzzle): The final assembled puzzle, which is a collective effort of all students, represents the final GBT model, in which each tree has contributed to reducing the errors and arriving at a more accurate solution.

Through this intuitive example we can understand how while individual simple models might not make very accurate predictions, collectively they improve if each model learns from the errors of the previous model. In the case of boosted trees, these simple models are shallow trees (e.g., a node with two leaves). We add these shallow trees one after another, where each new tree tries to correct the residual of the previous tree (i.e., the difference between the observed and the predicted value). Figure 13.5 formally describes the boosting process in a stepwise manner.

FIGURE 13.5 ■ The Boosting Process

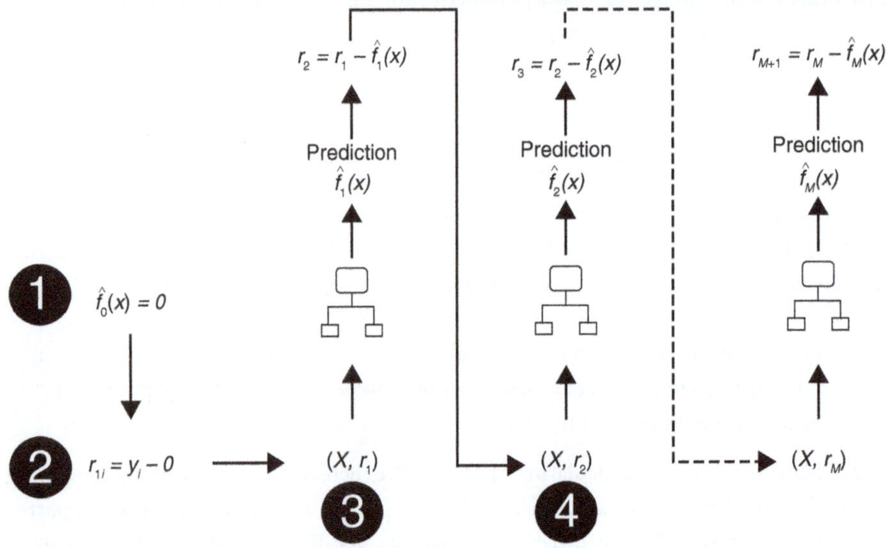

Let's understand how boosting works with the employee satisfaction data.

- Step 1: Let's set the first prediction for the entire dataset as zero: $\widehat{f_0}(x) = 0$. If we think that setting the prediction value to zero is a bad prediction, that is right. At this stage, we know nothing about a good prediction. Hence, we start with $\widehat{f_0}(x) = 0$.
- Step 2: We then calculate the difference between the actual employee satisfaction value (y_i) and the value predicted by the tree: $\widehat{f_0}(x)$. The difference is called the residual (r_1). Since we set our first prediction as $\widehat{f_0}(x) = 0$, the residual will be $r_1 = y_i - \widehat{f_0}(x)$.
- Step 3: Using years of experience as the predictor (X) and the residual (r_1) as the outcome, we can now fit a shallow regression tree $\widehat{f_1}$. This gives us a new model: $r_1 = \widehat{f_1}(x)$ or $y_i - \widehat{f_0}(x) = \widehat{f_1}(x)$. We again estimate the residual: $r_2 = r_1 - \widehat{f_1}(x)$.
- Step 4: In this step, we repeat the process described in Step 3, using experience as the predictor (X) and the residual (r_2) as the outcome. This gives us the new model $r_2 = \widehat{f_2}(x)$ or $y_i - \widehat{f_0}(x) - \widehat{f_1}(x) = \widehat{f_2}(x)$. Here, $\widehat{f_2}(x)$ is the second tree. The residual in this case is estimated to be $r_3 = r_2 - \widehat{f_2}(x)$.
- We continue the process of adding trees to explain the residual for a total of M times. That is, we add M shallow trees in a sequential manner, such that each subsequent tree is constructed to explain the residual from the previous tree.
- The final boosted model will be the sum of all the trees we have sequentially fit.

$$\widehat{f}(x) = \sum_{j=1}^{M} \widehat{f_j}(x)$$

Why do we call this an additive model? It is easy to see that at Step 4, the model is $y_i - \widehat{f_0}(x) - \widehat{f_1}(x) = \widehat{f_2}(x)$ or $y_i = \widehat{f_0}(x) + \widehat{f_1}(x) + \widehat{f_2}(x)$. Therefore, by adding M trees the final additive model is $\hat{f}(x) = \sum_{j=1}^{M} \hat{f}_j(x)$.

This process is known as GBT because in each training step, a shallow tree is built, and its predictions are compared to the true values in the dataset (i.e., the ground truth). The difference between the predicted and true values (i.e., the residual) represents the error in our model's prediction. If we use a squared loss function, $L = \left(y - \hat{f}\right)^2$, then the residual is actually the gradient of this loss function with respect to f: $\left[\frac{\partial L(y, f)}{\partial f}\right]_{f=\hat{f}} = -2\left(y - \hat{f}\right)$. Since shallow trees are fit on residuals, the process we are following resembles gradient descent over functions, where each shallow tree represents a new function trying to explain the residuals. This gradient descent process is similar to the one we utilized when reducing the error in predictions of a neural net, for instance, while predicting prices (Chapter 6) or customer churn (Chapter 8).

13.3.1 Choosing and Tuning Hyperparameters

While there are many hyperparameters in GBTs, in this chapter, we will focus on three important ones. Hyperparameter values can be adjusted by the user to improve predictions—unlike parameter values that get tuned by the model itself and are not controlled by the user (please see the Technical Appendix for a detailed description of hyperparameters).

The first significant hyperparameter is the *learning rate*. In regression trees, we build a model by sequentially adding trees to previous trees. However, if we allow each tree to be added to the prior set of trees as it is, we will end up with a final model that could overfit our data. One solution is to slow down the learning process from the training data by shrinking the contribution of each shallow tree. In our earlier puzzle-building example, it is similar to telling each student to make smaller, more cautious corrections to avoid disturbing what has already been correctly assembled. The learning rate (also called the shrinkage factor), λ, controls the contribution of each shallow tree. It is kept substantially lower than 1. This increases learning time, but the resulting additive model is more stable and accurate. Formally, after adding M trees, the final additive model will be $\hat{f}(x) = \lambda \sum_{j=1}^{M} \hat{f}_j(x)$.

Reducing the learning rate can reduce the chances of overfitting the training data, but it requires that more shallow trees are added to the model. While adding more trees can potentially improve model performance, it can increase computational cost. Therefore, the second significant hyperparameter is the *number of trees*. By keeping this number moderate, we can balance between overfitting and computational cost.

The third significant hyperparameter is *tree depth*—in other words, how deep each subsequent tree needs to be. Shallower trees are computationally efficient but end up requiring more trees to achieve good predictive accuracy. However, if we keep adding deep trees, we will increase the chance of overfitting. Therefore, this is another hyperparameter that the user can tune to avoid overfitting while also ensuring good predictive accuracy.

Optimal values of these three hyperparameters are determined by cross-validation. We will discuss this further when we implement boosted regression trees on a dataset.

13.4 USING BOOSTED DECISION TREES TO UNDERSTAND WHAT IMPACTS JOB SATISFACTION

Let's use the example we discussed earlier of trying to find out which factors affect job satisfaction of employees. For this, we work with a dataset that is a subset of the IBM employee attrition dataset—a fictional dataset created by IBM data scientists.[13]

In our analysis, we use several input features related to the employee, such as the number of years worked at this organization, years in the current role, years since the employee received a promotion, and years working with the current manager or supervisor. The output variable is in the form of a single variable: the level of job satisfaction reported by employees captured on a 1 to 4 rating scale, with 1 indicating low satisfaction and 4 indicating high satisfaction.

As before, when we build a prediction model, we first split the data into train and test groups. Such a split helps train the tree model to understand the relationship between, for instance, years of experience and job satisfaction and then to predict job satisfaction on new data points in the test dataset. Let's use 80% data for training and 20% for testing the model.

13.4.1 Hyperparameter Tuning

The decision tree model that we will use for our analysis is the GBT model implemented via the XGBoost package. We can tune a few hyperparameters. Note that hyperparameter values can be specified in the model, allowing users the flexibility to change values in such a way that the best model fit can be achieved. Therefore, when we say *tuning* the hyperparameter, we mean trying out different values of the hyperparameter to find one that results in the best model performance. However, remember that to avoid subjectivity, increase efficiency, and prevent an overfit model, it is best practice to use a grid search process that algorithmically tries to find the optimal hyperparameter value. The hyperparameters that we can tune in this case are `trees` (number of trees contained in the ensemble), `tree_depth` (the maximum depth of the tree), and `learn_rate` (learning rate). In this analysis, we are tuning just three hyperparameters, although `XGBoost` offers the flexibility to tune many more hyperparameters.

We perform grid search and specify that we want four levels of each of the three hyperparameters. This results in $4^3 = 64$ combinations of the three hyperparameters. In order to find out which of the 64 possible combinations of hyperparameters is optimum, we use cross-validation.[14] We specify a fivefold cross-validation, such that there will be five partitions of the training dataset. One of the 64 boosted decision tree hyperparameter combinations will be fit on the four partitions, and its performance will be assessed on the fifth partition. Such a cross-validation procedure helps reduce overfitting.

Up to this point, we have specified the predictors, the outcome variable, hyperparameters and their levels, and the cross-validation procedure. We can now go ahead and run the model and ask it to provide predictions. Once the model has been run, we can evaluate how well the model has performed using metrics such as the root mean square error (RMSE). The RMSE is calculated for each of the 64 possible hyperparameter combinations.

We then ask the model to provide us with the hyperparameter combination that has the lowest RMSE value.

TABLE 13.1 ■ Hyperparameter Combination

trees	tree_depth	learn_rate	.config
667	1	0.1	Preprocessor1_Model14

The analysis, shown in Table 13.1, reveals that the best hyperparameter combination is trees = 667, tree depth = 1, and learning rate = 0.1.

We fit the model using the best hyperparameter combination on the entire training set and then validate its performance on the test data. The model outputs the RMSE and R-squared values for the test data, shown in Table 13.2, indicating how well the model performed on the test data after the best hyperparameter values were used to train the model.

TABLE 13.2 ■ Performance on Test Data

.metric	.estimator	.estimate	.config
rmse	standard	0.9494875	Preprocessor1_Model1
rsq	standard	0.3249158	Preprocessor1_Model1

13.4.2 Explaining the Gradient-Boosted Tree Results

As discussed in Chapter 9 on explainable models, the user makes the decision to choose an opaque model that gives good predictions but does not explain why it reached such predictions versus one that answers *why* such a prediction was reached. If the user is only interested in a prediction, then an opaque model should be fine. However, if a user wants to know the *why* underlying the answer (e.g., an organization wants to know why employees working in a specific department experience higher job satisfaction, or an employee wants to know why they did not receive an annual salary raise), this requires the use of a transparent or explainable model. We can think of linear regression as being a transparent model, while neural nets are opaque because the latter do not let the user know how each of the inputs affects the outcome variable. GBTs fall in the middle because they provide some explanation for the results.

Let's understand the results of the boosted decision tree model visually by plotting which variables played an important role. This visual depiction also allows us to understand how explainable the model is (see Figure 13.6).

FIGURE 13.6 ■ Boosted Tree Feature Importance Plot

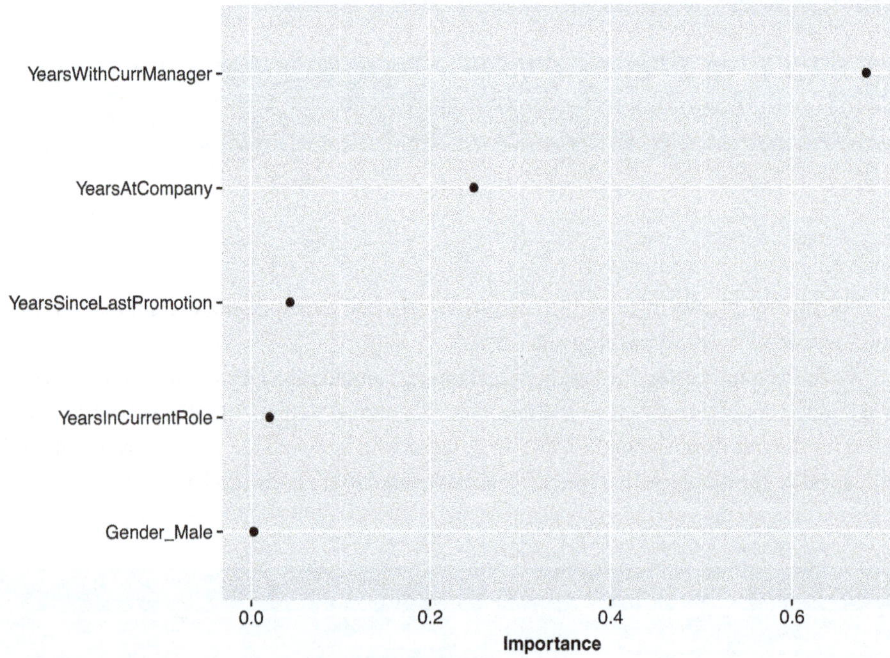

We can see that `YearsAtCompany`, `YearsWithCurrManager`, and `YearsInCurrentRole` are the three most important predictors. If we want to examine how these predictors influenced the outcome variable (job satisfaction), we can plot their partial dependence graphs.

In situations when we are trying to obtain accurate predictions, we tend to use opaque models, as we did in this case. However, when we want to have the ability to look inside the model, one option is to use partial dependence plots (PDP). They help explain the nature of the relationship between a predictor and the outcome variable. We can consider one or at most two variables (if one of them is categorical) to be the predictors of interest and examine their influence on the outcome variable by marginalizing the influence of the other variables.

Let's understand with an example. Assuming we want to examine the influence of `YearsAtCompany` on the outcome of job satisfaction, we might pick about 100 observations to create the PDP. The PDP works by holding the values of all other predictor variables constant at their average or median values, and then varying only the value of the predictor variable of interest (`YearsAtCompany` in this case) across its range. Thus, if `YearsAtCompany` ranges from 1 to 20 years, then for each of the values from 1 to 20, the model's prediction for job satisfaction will be computed while keeping the values of the other predictors constant. A plot can then be drawn showing the average predicted job satisfaction across the range of `YearsAtCompany`, illustrating how job satisfaction is influenced by `YearsAtCompany` while averaging out the effects of the other variables. This resulting plot is the PDP. The same procedure can be performed for any predictor whose influence on the outcome we want to see. Hence, what appears in the plot is the partial influence, as we are just seeing the influence of the predictor of interest while controlling for the other variables.

We create two profiles, one with predictor `YearsAtCompany` and the other with predictor `YearsWithCurrManager` (Figures 13.7 and 13.8). We can also add groups to examine if there is any difference by gender.

FIGURE 13.7 ■ Partial Dependence Profile With "Years at Company"

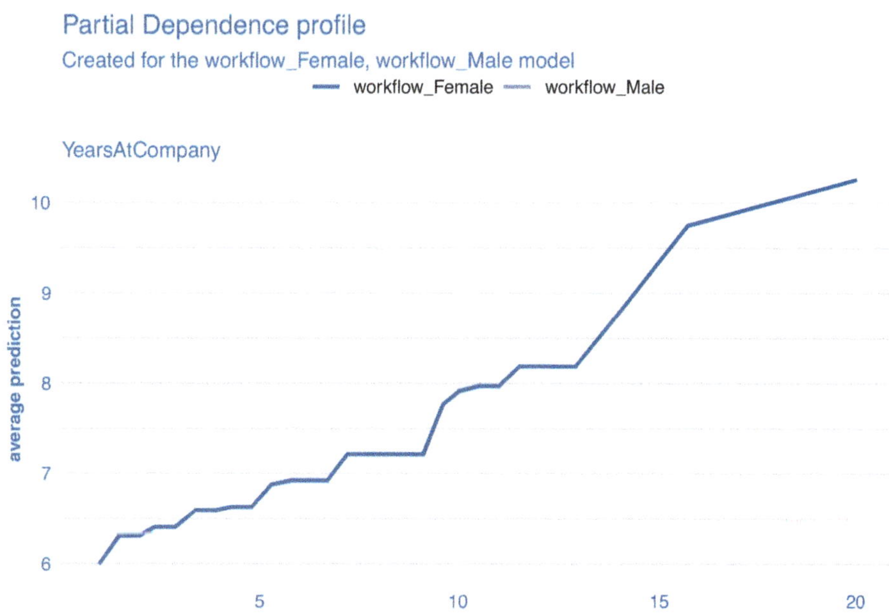

FIGURE 13.8 ■ Partial Dependence Profile With "Years With Current Manager"

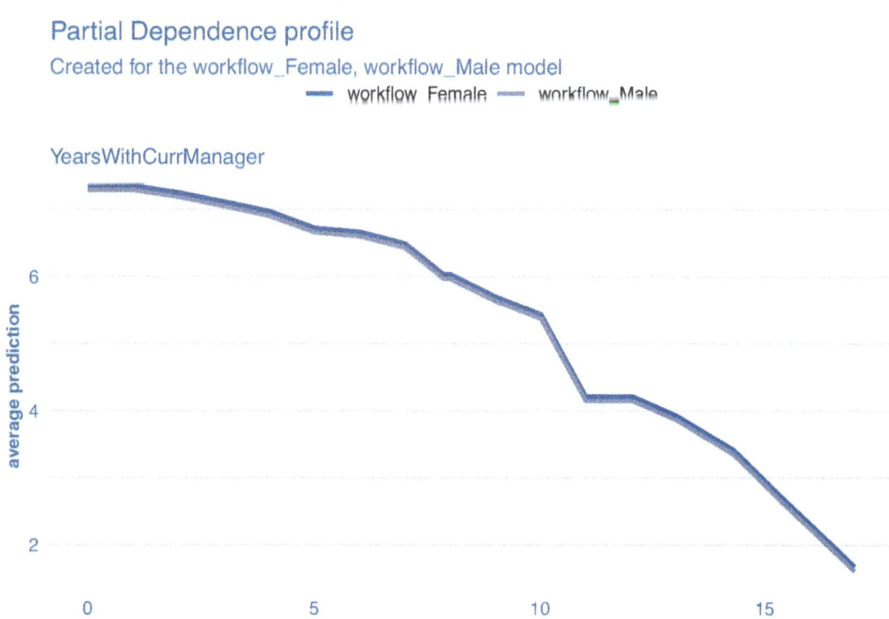

The results indicate that men and women experience job satisfaction similarly. More years working at the company lead to more job satisfaction, but working longer with the same manager leads to less satisfaction.

13.5 BUSINESS INSIGHTS AND SUMMARY

In sum, in this chapter we learned how to use boosted decision trees to analyze employee satisfaction data. These models are black box models, but using one of the XAI methods, PDP, allowed us to gather some insights into how different predictor variables affect satisfaction, making it more explainable. Since many of the human resource prediction tasks are related to understanding human perception and decision-making processes, it has been argued that analytics, especially machine-learning methods that tend to be opaque, are not best suited for such tasks. However, with the increase in the different types of information that need to be compiled for analysis, it is not surprising to see analytic models being used as a decision aid in human resource functions. Models are now used to predict a variety of human resource functions such as predicting what features of an employee best fit a certain job, who would or would not be classified as a good employee, which benefits or incentives are rated as important by employees, and what factors positively or negatively affect employee turnover. Another instance of machine-learning methods in human resources is the use of natural language processing to go over a vast number of résumés to compile information that can assist organizations in their hiring decisions. Advancements in XAI methods to explain opaque models are making it more feasible to deploy machine-learning models in human resource management.

13.6 IMPLEMENTATION USING R: EMPLOYEE SATISFACTION

We first import the data that are based on an organizational survey and include the following input variables: `YearsAtCompany`, `YearsInCurrentRole`, `YearSinceLastPromotion`, and `YearsWithCurrManager`. `JobSatisfaction`, as rated by the employees on a scale of 1 (*low satisfaction*) to 4 (*high satisfaction*), serves as the outcome variable. We use the following libraries: `dplyr`,[15] `tidymodels`,[16] `xgboost`,[17] `vip`,[18] and `DALEXtra`.[19]

We split the data into train and test groups; **`prop = 0.8`** specifies that 80% of the data will be used for training and 20% will be kept as a test dataset.

```
library(tidymodels)
library(xgboost)

employees <-read.csv(url
("http://data.mishra.us/files/chapter_employee_satisfaction/satisfaction_data.csv"))

set.seed(123)
employee_testtrn <- initial_split(employees, prop = 0.8,
                            strata = JobSatisfaction)
```

```
employee_train    <- training(employee_testtrn)
employee_test     <- testing(employee_testtrn)
```

Next, we define the model formulation JobSatisfaction ~ ., which shows that JobSatisfaction is the outcome variable and all other variables are predictors. Among the four predictors, one variable, Gender, is a factor variable with values Male or Female, which in their text form are not amenable to analysis; step_dummy converts Gender to a numeric binary form. A new variable is created, Gender_Male, with values 1 and 0 such that 0 means Female and 1 means Male. prep(training = employee_train) applies a preprocessing step of creating a dummy variable for the training data: employee_train.

```
rec_employee <- recipe(JobSatisfaction ~ ., employee_train) %>%
       step_dummy(Gender)%>%
       prep(training = employee_train)
```

Until now, we have not specified the type of model we will be using, which we do in the next line of code. boost_tree() defines the boosted decision tree model and specifies hyperparameters such as trees (number of trees contained in the ensemble), tree_depth (the maximum depth of the tree), and learn_rate (learning rate). tune() specifies that each hyperparameter needs to be tuned though grid search. set_engine("xgboost") specifies that our computational engine is XGBoost. set_mode("regression") specifies that our model type is regression. If the outcome variable were a categorical variable such as *stayed* versus *left the organization*, we would have used set_mode("classification"). It is important to note that in this analysis, we are tuning just three hyperparameters, but XGBoost offers the flexibility to tune many more hyperparameters.[20]

```
model_employee <- boost_tree(
            trees = tune(),
            tree_depth = tune(),
            learn_rate = tune()) %>%
  set_engine("xgboost", verbosity = 0) %>%
  set_mode("regression")
```

In order to tune the three hyperparameters, the next step is using grid search. grid_regular is helpful in creating various combinations of the three hyperparameters. levels = 4 indicates that we want to create four levels of each hyperparameter. This will generate four values each for trees, tree_depth, and learn_rate. In other words, $4^3 = 64$ combinations of these three hyperparameters will be created. We can check this by typing hyper_grid in the R console. In order to find out which combination of hyperparameters out of the 64 is optimum, we use cross-validation, which vfold_cv helps us achieve. v = 5 specifies that there will be five partitions of the training dataset. Boosted decision trees with one of the 64 hyperparameter combinations will be fit on the four partitions, and its performance will be assessed on the fifth partition. Such a cross-validation procedure helps reduce overfitting.

```
hyper_grid <- grid_regular(
                          trees(),
                          tree_depth(),
                          learn_rate(),
                          levels = 4)

employee_folds <- vfold_cv(employee_train, v = 5)
```

Let's assess what we have achieved so far:

1. A `recipe` that specifies the outcome variable and predictors, as well as the preprocessing that needs to be performed (in this case dummy coding)
2. A specified analysis method and computational engine (`XGBoost`), along with hyperparameters that we need to fine-tune
3. A grid of hyperparameters and a cross-validation procedure

Now we can aggregate all this information to fit the model and use it for prediction, which `workflow()` helps us accomplish. `add_model` adds the `model_employee` specified earlier with `rec_employee`, which contains information about predictor and outcome variables and preprocessing.

```
employee_wf <- workflow() %>%
  add_model(model_employee) %>%
  add_recipe(rec_employee)
```

We can now compute the performance metric RMSE (root mean squared error) of our model for each of the 64 possible hyperparameter combinations. Since `XGBoost` uses parallelization, `doParallel:: registerDoParallel(cores = 10)` registers that 10 cores will be used for parallel execution of the model. The values of the cores can be changed depending upon the computational resources available.

```
doParallel::registerDoParallel(cores = 10)

set.seed(1234)
employee_tune <-
  employee_wf %>%
```

```
  tune_grid(
    resamples = employee_folds,
    grid = hyper_grid,
    metrics = metric_set(rmse)
  )
```

We use select_best("rmse") to pick the best hyperparameter combination.

```
best_model <- employee_tune %>%
  select_best("rmse")
best_model
```

```
## # A tibble: 1 × 4
##   trees tree_depth learn_rate .config
##   <int> <int>      <dbl>      <chr>
## 1  667      1        0.1      Preprocessor1_Model14
```

The analysis reveals that the best hyperparameter combination is trees = 667, tree depth = 1, and learning rate = 0.1. With these hyperparameter values, we can now update the workflow using finalize_workflow, which adds the best model to the workflow employee_wf created earlier. This gives us the final_workflow that captures all the information about the model, hyperparameters, outcome variable, and predictors.

```
final_workflow <-
  employee_wf %>%
  finalize_workflow(best_model)
```

We fit the model using the best hyperparameter combination on the entire training set and then validate its performance on the test data. last_fit helps us accomplish this. split = employee_testtrn specifies that employee_testtrn contains information about the test and train split performed earlier. Using collect_metrics, we report rmse and rsq (*R*-squared) values.

```
final_fit <-
  final_workflow %>%
  last_fit(split = employee_testtrn)

final_fit %>%
  collect_metrics()
```

```
##  # A tibble: 2 × 4
##     .metric .estimator .estimate .config
##     <chr>   <chr>          <dbl>  <chr>
##  1  rmse    standard       0.949  Preprocessor1_Model1
##  2  rsq     standard       0.325  Preprocessor1_Model1
```

Let's understand the results of the model visually by plotting which variables played an important role.

```
library(vip)
final_workflow %>%
  fit(data = employee_train) %>%
  pull_workflow_fit() %>%
  vip(geom = "point")
```

We can see that `YearsAtCompany`, `YearsWithCurrManager`, and `YearsInCurrentRole` were the three most important predictors. If we want to examine how these predictors influenced the outcome variable (job satisfaction), we can plot partial dependence graphs.

`explain_tidymodels` creates a representation of our best-fit model. Using this representation, we create a partial dependence profile that explores our best-fit-model response as a function of selected predictor variables. We create two profiles, one with predictor `YearsAtCompany` and the other with predictor `YearsWithCurrManager`. We also add `groups = "Gender"` to see if there is any difference of gender.

```
library(DALEXtra)
model_fitted <- final_workflow %>%
 fit(data = employee_train)
explainer_rf <- explain_tidymodels(model_fitted,
                           data = employee_train[,-6],
                           y = employee_train$JobSatisfaction,
                           type = "pdp",verbose = FALSE)

pdp_yrscomp <- model_profile(explainer_rf,
                           variables = "YearsAtCompany",
                           groups = "Gender", N=NULL)
pdp_yrsmanager <- model_profile(explainer_rf,
                           variables = "YearsWithCurrManager",
                           groups = "Gender",N=NULL)

plot(pdp)_yrsmanager)
plot(pdp_yrscomp)
```

The results, shown in Figure 13.6, indicate that men and women experience job satisfaction similarly. More years working at the company lead to more job satisfaction (as depicted in Figure 13.7), but working longer with the same manager leads to less satisfaction (shown in Figure 13.8).

13.7 UNDERSTANDING THE CHAPTER

1. You are asked to optimize a gradient-boosted tree (GBT) model to predict employee job satisfaction based on various features such as years of experience, department, and workload. You decide to tune three crucial hyperparameters: learning rate, number of trees, and tree depth.
   a. Explain the role of the learning rate in GBTs and how it impacts the model's performance. How would you decide on an appropriate learning rate for your model?
   b. Discuss the significance of the number of trees in a GBT model. How does increasing the number of trees affect the model's predictive accuracy and generalization? What considerations should be taken into account to choose an optimal number of trees?
   c. Describe the effect of tree depth on the model's ability to capture complex relationships in the data. What are the trade-offs associated with setting a shallow or deep tree depth, and how would you determine an optimal tree depth for your model?
2. In boosted decision trees, what is the purpose of boosting?
   a. To increase the complexity of individual trees
   b. To improve the predictive performance of the model
   c. To reduce the number of input features
   d. To decrease the computational time of the model
3. What is the main advantage of using boosted decision trees over a single decision tree?
   a. They are easier to interpret.
   b. They have a lower risk of overfitting.
   c. They have better predictive performance.
   d. They require fewer input features.
4. Which technique is commonly used to prevent overfitting in boosted decision trees?
   a. Early stopping
   b. Feature selection
   c. Pruning
   d. Regularization
5. What is the main disadvantage of boosted decision trees compared to a single decision tree?
   a. They require more input features.
   b. They are less interpretable.
   c. They have a higher risk of overfitting.
   d. They have lower predictive performance.

6. In boosted decision trees, how are additional trees added to the model?

- **a.** By increasing the depth of the existing trees.
- **b.** By fitting new trees to the residuals of the previous trees.
- **c.** By randomly selecting a subset of input features.
- **d.** By combining multiple trees through voting.

7. How can the results of boosted decision trees be used for employee satisfaction prediction in practical applications?

- **a.** To identify areas for improvement in employee satisfaction
- **b.** To predict employee turnover rates
- **c.** To match employees to suitable job roles
- **d.** To inform salary negotiations

8. Which of the following best describes the concept of boosting in the context of decision trees?

- **a.** Combining multiple weak models to create a single strong model
- **b.** Increasing the depth of a single decision tree for better accuracy
- **c.** Reducing the size of the dataset to simplify the model
- **d.** Replacing missing values in the dataset with estimated values

9. Why are partial dependence plots used in conjunction with boosted decision trees?

- **a.** To visualize the impact of individual features on the model's prediction
- **b.** To increase the accuracy of the boosted decision trees
- **c.** To reduce the computational complexity of the model
- **d.** To identify clusters within the data

ENDNOTES

1. Erickson, Tamara J., and Lynda Gratton, "What It Means to Work Here," *Harvard Business Review* 85, no. 3 (2007): https://hbr.org/2007/03/what-it-means-to-work-here.
2. Hyken, Shep, "How Happy Employees Make Happy Customers," *Forbes*, May 27, 2017, https://www.forbes.com/sites/shephyken/2017/05/27/how-happy-employees-make-happy-customers/?sh=79c8bc565c35.
3. Organ, Dennis W., "A Reappraisal and Reinterpretation of the Satisfaction-Causes-Performance Hypothesis," *Academy of Management Review* 2, no. 1 (1977): 46–53.
4. Bryson, Alex, John Forth, and Lucy Stokes, "Does Employees' Subjective Well-Being Affect Workplace Performance?" *Human Relations* 70, no. 8 (2017): 1017–1037; McNeese-Smith, Donna, "Increasing Employee Productivity, Job Satisfaction, and Organizational Commitment," *Journal of Healthcare Management* 41, no. 2 (1996): 160.
5. Oswald, Andrew J., Eugenio Proto, and Daniel Sgroi, "Happiness and Productivity," *Journal of Labor Economics* 33, no. 4 (2015): 789–822.
6. Chen, Chen, Yangyang Chen, Po-Hsuan Hsu, and Edward J. Podolski, "Be Nice to Your Innovators: Employee Treatment and Corporate Innovation Performance," *Journal of Corporate Finance* 39 (2016): 78–98.
7. McNeese-Smith, "Increasing Employee Productivity."

8. Erickson and Gratton, "What It Means to Work Here."

9. Ibid.

10. Haltom, Brooks, and David Allen, "Better Ways to Predict Who's Going to Quit," *Harvard Business Review*, August 16, 2019, https://hbr.org/2019/08/better-ways-to-predict-whos-going-to-quit.

11. RSS is also known as the sum of squared residuals (SSR) or the sum of squared estimate of errors (SSE).

12. Hastie, Trevor, Robert Tibshirani, and Jerome H. Friedman, *The Elements of Statistical Learning: Data Mining, Inference, and Prediction*, Vol. 2 (New York: Springer, 2009).

13. It was made available as a Kaggle competition and is posted at www.kaggle.com/datasets/pavansubhasht/ibm-hr-analytics-attrition-dataset.

14. As you may recall, cross-validation is the process of partitioning the training dataset into subsets, such that the model is trained on some of these subsets (training folds) and validated on the remaining subset (validation fold). This process helps to evaluate which hyperparameter values yield the best predictions. Specifically, the model learns from the training folds and makes predictions on the validation fold, without having access to the actual outcome values of the validation fold. This cycle is repeated so that each fold serves as the validation fold at least once, allowing a thorough assessment of the model's performance across different portions of the data. It's important to note that the data used in cross-validation are distinct from the 20% data set aside as the test or validation set. These 20% test data are utilized to evaluate the model's performance on new data points it has never seen before, after the optimal hyperparameters have been determined through cross-validation on the remaining 80% training data.

15. Wickham, Hadley, Romain François, Lionel Henry, and Kirill Müller, "dplyr: A Grammar of Data Manipulation," R package version 1.1.3 (September 3, 2023), https://CRAN.R-project.org/package=dplyr.

16. Kuhn, Max, et al., "Tidymodels: A Collection of Packages for Modeling and Machine Learning Using tidyverse Principles" (2020), https://www.tidymodels.org.

17. Chen, Tianqi, et al., "xgboost: Extreme Gradient Boosting," R package version 1.7.5.1 (March 30, 2023), https://CRAN.R-project.org/package=xgboost.

18. Greenwell, Brandon M., and Bradley C. Boehmke, "Variable Importance Plots—An Introduction to the VIP Package," *The R Journal* 12, no. 1 (2020): 343–366, https://doi.org/10.32614/RJ-2020-013.

19. Maksymiuk, Szymon, Alicja Gosiewska, and Przemyslaw Biecek, "Landscape of R Packages for eXplainable Artificial Intelligence," *arXiv* 6–7, 11, 15, last revised March 26, 2021, https://arxiv.org/abs/2009.13248.

20. See online documentation to learn more about which other hyperparameters can be tuned: https://xgboost.readthedocs.io/en/latest/parameter.html.

14 NEW PRODUCT DEVELOPMENT WITH A/B TESTING

CONTENTS

LEARNING OBJECTIVES

1. Introduce new products in the marketplace
2. Recall the steps in the new product development process
3. Support new product development with machine learning
4. Use A/B testing for new product development
5. Introduce a digital product

14.1 INNOVATIONS IN THE MARKETPLACE

Chase introduced its new credit card, the Chase Sapphire Reserve, in 2016, which offered users 100,000 sign-up bonus points for the first year and led to Chase exceeding its annual sales target in the first few weeks. The enthusiasm with which millennials adopted the card because of the free points was a key factor in its success. However, Chase needed to see beyond the first year of product introduction to assess how the card would do in the next years after the promotional offer expired and annual fees kicked in. Despite high annual fees of $550, it is considered the best travel card around because of the perks it offers—including airport lounge access and application fee credit for Global Entry and TSA PreCheck.[1] This is one example of a product launch that was designed and launched well, and the right strategies are helping Chase sustain its success.

Nintendo released the Switch in 2017, which sold 2.74 million units in the first month. Its design allowed for handheld and console gaming that appealed to a broad user base. The launch titles, such as *The Legend of Zelda: Breath of the Wild*, captured people's attention. The Switch was priced competitively, and its features such as local multiplayer gaming and portability helped it perform successfully in the marketplace.

The concept of a product has evolved in the digital age. Technological advances in artificial intelligence, cloud computing, 3D printing, and wireless sensor networks have now made it possible to build products that do not have a physical presence but that live entirely on the web, such as health monitoring apps on smartphones and facial recognition apps for fraud detection; even in automobiles much of the driving is controlled by algorithms, such as with self-driving technology. Netflix is a good example of how algorithmic power has been harnessed for new product offerings. Netflix began algorithmic recommendation as early as 2010. Gradually algorithms helped it decide which movies to show, how to display them on screens, and which pictures should be used to advertise them. Today the company's algorithms are not just used for providing recommendations to users; user interactions with the Netflix platform inform the company, for example, what content to develop next and what type of show is likely to garner the most viewership. As early as 2013, Netflix was using predictive analytics to determine what type of new content needed to be included in its show *House of Cards* to ensure a specific size of viewership.

14.2 NEW PRODUCT DEVELOPMENT STAGES

How can we define a new product? Is it something entirely new that customers have never seen before, such as the microwave oven that was introduced as a substitute for the conventional gas/electric range? Or is it a product that is merely an extension of an existing product, or a newer model with enhanced features, such as a new version of the iPhone that has more memory or functionality than an earlier version? New products get categorized broadly as breakthrough or incremental depending on whether they completely disrupt the existing marketplace or offer newer benefits to consumers. Breakthrough innovations are relatively rare, accounting for less than 10% of all products that get introduced in the marketplace. Many product launches are merely extensions of existing products or me-too products with barely any innovation that are introduced at a lower cost. Moreover, the failure rate for new products is quite high. Many ideas never culminate in a viable product. Even among those new products that do get developed, more than 50% are not profitable. Before we see a product in the marketplace—be it a biotechnology, pharmaceutical, automotive, or digital product—it has gone through a long process of being designed and introduced. What are the steps in new product development? They commonly are the following, with many of these steps being iterative. Next, we will go through the steps in the new product development (NPD) process (see Figure 14.1) in the context of creating an entertaining game with various levels of difficulty.

FIGURE 14.1 ■ New Product Development Process

14.2.1 Idea Generation

The first step of any project is idea generation (this is Step 1 in Figure 14.1). This can be a structured process in some businesses where regular brainstorming involves discussing what consumers need and what type of (as well as whether) new products can be developed. For instance, in some industries, new models or brand extensions are an outcome of such a structured process. Alternatively, new product ideas can emerge as a by-product or even accidentally while working on other projects. In the context of game development, this step could involve generating ideas for a puzzle-adventure game in which players travel different worlds where each world represents a unique level of difficulty. Such a game can be developed in the realm of fantasy, science fiction, or history.

14.2.2 Idea Screening

The second step involves the rigorous evaluation of product ideas with each idea undergoing a comprehensive assessment to determine its viability, innovation, and market appeal.

- *Viability:* This considers whether the idea is technically feasible and economically sustainable, ensuring that the product can be developed as well as marketed successfully.
- *Innovation:* An important criterion is to determine the product idea's uniqueness or substantial improvement over existing products. It ensures that the product features are indeed novel to the market.
- *Market Appeal:* The idea is evaluated for its potential attractiveness to the intended target segment, determining whether it meets customer needs and preferences effectively.

The aim of this step is to filter and retain only those ideas that show potential for success.

For game development, after careful consideration, the idea of a multilevel, puzzle-adventure game rooted in medieval history was chosen for its engaging concept and scalability.

14.2.3 Concept Development and Testing

In this step, the ideas start to take shape. We can think of it like a sketch turning into a detailed blueprint. The designers start defining the product's features, how the product functions, and what makes it unique. It is possible that more than one version of the product is built to find the best-performing one. This could involve the shape, size, or weight of a physical product or the seamless connectivity of a digital product. At this step the designers may use surveys or focus groups to test the product with potential users. Consumers' feedback is helpful in tweaking the product, making sure it is something people will find valuable.

For the puzzle-adventure game, detailed features such as the game rules, objectives, and varying levels of difficulty are established at this step, ensuring that the game is well structured, engaging, immersive, and challenging. To ensure that the developed concept aligns with user expectations and preferences, testing can also be conducted with users in this step.

14.2.4 Business Analysis

The aim of this step is to figure out the business or market viability of the developed concepts. Different types of comprehensive business analysis such as cost estimation, sales projections, and profitability analysis are conducted to assess the potential business impact and commercial success of the new product.

For game development, this step will involve analyzing the costs associated with developing the game, the product price, and estimating potential revenues based on market research.

14.2.5 Product Development and Design

In this step, the developed concepts are further developed into tangible products. The product design is finalized, incorporating all the necessary features and functionalities, ensuring it's user-friendly and aesthetically appealing. Prototypes or samples are developed, getting the product ready for market introduction.

This step for our game development example would involve probably programming the game mechanics, designing unique worlds for each difficulty level, and ensuring that the user interface is intuitive and engaging.

14.2.6 Test Marketing

Before the product is launched in the market, it is tested in select markets to obtain user reactions to both design and cost. We can think of this to be a dress rehearsal before the main performance, in which a select audience is invited to provide their review of the performance. This allows for any last-minute adjustments or improvements. The arrow pointing back from Step 6 to Step 5 in Figure 14.1 indicates the possibility of such feedback. Any necessary corrections can be made at this stage based on test market results.

Step 6 for game launch could include the game being soft-launched in select markets or platforms to gather user feedback, analyze gameplay data, and make any needed improvements.

14.2.7 Commercialization

After adjustments or improvements are included in the product following the test marketing step, the product is officially launched in the market. In this step, several marketing strategies are deployed, aiming for a successful launch and a wide market adoption.

When the game is launched in the market, it is likely to involve launching the fully optimized puzzle-adventure game globally, implementing a comprehensive marketing strategy to maximize visibility and downloads.

14.2.8 Evaluation and Control

The new product development process does not conclude after the product launch. The business will closely monitor the product's market performance. This step involves evaluating the product's success against the company's expectations regarding sales as well as customer reviews.

It could also include assessment of how well the product performs in comparison to any other competitor that was introduced in the market.

For the game, its performance is continuously monitored postlaunch, and updates are made to improve the game, fix bugs, and keep the content fresh and engaging based on user feedback and evolving gaming trends.

14.3 THE IMPORTANCE OF TESTING AND MARKET RESEARCH

As we just learned through the different processes of ideating, designing, and launching a new product, the role of continuously getting feedback from potential users is very important since the process can include many uncertainties. This includes how consumers and competitors will react; if any external factors in the economic or social environment will change before, during, or immediately after the launch; what the price of the product should be; through which channel the product should be launched; and how the product should be promoted. Even before launching a new product in the market, the manager needs to weigh the cost of designing the new product: Will the design be financially viable? How long will it take to move from design, to production, to launch stage? What does the company have to give up to invest in this new product? In order to answer these questions and reduce some of the uncertainty, companies sometimes conduct surveys to find out which features of the product or launch environment result in greater acceptance by consumers.

14.3.1 For Design Evaluation

Whether the product is digital or physical, it is important to incorporate user experience and feedback into the product during the design stage. A commonly used method to gather user feedback is through A/B testing to find out which product design will attract the most interest. For instance, for digital products like apps that people view online, click rate is used to determine interest (and eventual purchase). As we discussed in Chapter 7, a multi-armed-bandit-based algorithm is now being deployed by large firms to determine quickly which combination of product features will result in the highest interest and purchase.

14.3.2 For Engaging Customers in an Omnichannel World

When the product is ready for launch, algorithms again are used to determine the best way to engage customers in today's omnichannel world. This has both benefits and shortcomings. Traditionally, people gained product information through one channel such as television or in- store behavior. Today, however, people can be reached through multiple interconnected channels, which makes the task challenging because businesses need to find the optimal channels as well as to customize the message depending on the channel. Hence, a one-message/one-channel policy may not be successful.

14.3.3 For Incorporating Feedback and Customer Experience

Just as user feedback is gathered during the design stage, once the new product is launched it again becomes essential to find out how customers are reacting to it. In the design stage, the feedback is probably gathered from a smaller sample of people, while in the postlaunch stage, a larger set of customers can be reached to find out what they like (or don't like) about the product. This feedback now happens on an ongoing basis, building a continuous chain from users to designers and back.

14.4 THE INTRICACIES OF A/B TESTING

As we discussed in Chapter 7 on advertising, there are several steps that need to be followed to develop a sound A/B test. This includes ensuring that the experimental design is causal (an A/B test is really another name for causal experimentation) and not correlational. For this, we need to ensure that we are keeping all features of the A/B test constant and only varying the feature(s) whose influence we want to examine. Second, we need to create groups (also called conditions or treatments) that vary different levels of the feature that we want to examine. Finally, we should be careful that participants are *randomly assigned* to the various groups and that there is no issue of self-selection. What exactly is self-selection? Self-selection occurs if participants are allowed to choose which group (or treatment) they want to be part of. For instance, if we design an A/B test for video games to find out which color of the visual interface is more immersive (e.g., blue vs. green) and let participants choose to play using their choice of color, then the experimental design is not randomized because we are allowing participants to *self-select* their experimental group based on color preference.

14.5 USING A/B TESTING TO TEST GAMING PROTOTYPES

For this chapter let's use the example of a video game company. GameV has been working on a new game idea that its designers believe will be more immersive and engaging than other games that GameV currently has developed. However, before they launch the game, GameV designers have generated several prototypes of the game so they can launch the version that is likely to retain the most players. They know from previous data in the gaming industry that every point of engagement in the game results in players who will return. For instance, many players don't return after the first session because of glitchy install or because of game features that are less than immersive. Therefore, GameV wants to use A/B testing to assess specific features. The game lets players earn an extra life by performing some tasks. GameV has determined three levels of difficulty: 25, 35, and 45. They want to find out which level of difficulty results in greater engagement. It is possible that if players have earned a life by performing a difficult task, it could result in their feeling more engaged. Alternatively, it is possible that earning a life with a more difficult task results in players giving up. Hence, GameV wants to find out which difficulty level engages more players in this game environment. One can think of the three levels of difficulty as low, medium, and high.

GameV believes that a good outcome metric to figure out the success of the prototype is the time players spend playing. Since the game is a prototype, players have never played it before, and the time they spend playing the game will help GameV determine which of the prototypes results in greatest engagement and immersion. The outcome variable (unlike in Chapter 7) is continuous in nature. Therefore, we will use an *F* test to find out which level of difficulty results in highest immersiveness.

14.5.1 Experimental Design

GameV has developed the three prototypes in such a way that each prototype is designed with one of the three levels of difficulty. Each prototype offers unique game features that correspond to its specific difficulty level, providing players with a variety of experiences. In the experimental design, the level of difficulty is the only factor that varies across the three prototypes, with specific levels set at 25, 35, and 45. Every other feature of the game stays the same; only the features associated with the level of difficulty are different. Moreover, during A/B testing, a player who plays prototype-25 will not be playing prototype-35 or prototype-45. That is, one player will see and play only one game prototype. Such a design is called a *one-factor, between-participants design*. GameV followed the usual steps to run its A/B test:

1. It recruited 1,200 video game players who agreed to test the game in return for free games from GameV. Hence, the sample for the A/B test is 1,200.
2. It randomly assigned about 400 players to each of the three groups: prototype-25, prototype-35, and prototype-45.
3. Players played the game for 10 rounds, during which they were presented with the difficulty level specific to their group. They could continue to play after 10 rounds for another 2 rounds, or they could quit and leave.
4. Time played was recorded for each participant and served as a measure (also called a proxy) for immersiveness and engagement with the game.
5. The null hypothesis would be that changing the difficulty level would not influence the immersiveness, resulting in no difference in the time spent playing among players in the three groups.

14.5.2 Analyzing the Data and Presenting the Results

Before we determine what analysis needs to be run, we first should examine the nature of the data. If the data are *normally distributed*, then we can go ahead and use parametric tests such as an *F* test or *t* test. However, if the data are not normally distributed, this failure of the normality assumption might require the use of nonparametric tests like the Mann-Whitney.

14.5.3 *F* Test

The *F* test, also called the *F* statistic, is used to describe tests that use the *F* distribution to determine whether a factor has a *significant* influence on the outcome variable. When we use an *F* test for A/B testing, we want to examine whether the intervention we have used in each of the groups results in different values of the outcome. In our A/B test, we want to examine whether the three levels of difficulty result in different levels of immersion as measured through time spent playing the game prototype. The null hypothesis states that there is no difference in time spent playing across the three levels of difficulty. We can reject the null hypothesis only if there is a difference in playing time. When we use an F test, we are comparing the groups to test whether there are variances among the groups. Hence, an F test is frequently used for analysis of variance (ANOVA) testing, which is a common test for causal experimentation.

The F test can be performed if the data follow an F distribution and the group data are independent. In A/B testing, group data are obtained independently because the intervention for one group is different from the intervention for the other groups. Note, when we use an F test for correlational analysis, the assumption is that the predictors have an independent influence on the outcome variable. For our example, we have three levels of one factor—that is, three independent groups with no interaction (we will discuss interactions later). Hence, our A/B test design will examine the main effect, which is the effect of each of the groups on the outcome.

The three main effects for prototype-25, prototype-35, and prototype-45 constitute the model equation.

$$SS_M = SS_{25} + SS_{35} + SS_{45}$$

The *sum of squares* (SS_M) captures how much variance is explained by each of the factors. For instance, SS_{25} indicates how much variation in the immersiveness experienced by players is captured by a difficulty level of 25. Here, we have only one factor but with three levels. However, along with SS we need something called *degrees of freedom* (df) to calculate the F test.

$$df_M = k - 1 \text{ where } k = \text{number of experimental groups (here } k = 3)$$

14.5.4 Testing Statistical Difference

Imagine we ran the A/B test and obtained data for each of the three conditions. Assume that mean (average) time spent with prototype-35 is higher than the averages of time spent with prototype-25 and prototype-45. How can we quantify that prototype-35 is indeed more immersive? The only way we can answer this is by testing if the averages are statistically different. The testing process begins with the hypothesis that there is no difference in the averages across conditions; this serves as the null hypothesis. It implies that all prototypes are equally immersive. Now our goal is to test this hypothesis. A one-way ANOVA makes it possible to simultaneously compare the averages of more than two conditions and determine if they are statistically different. ANOVA is a generalization of the t test that compares the means of two conditions.

Traditional ANOVA (also known as the ANOVA F test) makes the following assumptions.

Independence: The observations should be independent of each other. This implies that participants providing responses in each condition are unique and that no participant is included in more than one condition. The assumption of independence is related to the design of the study. If participants are randomly assigned to only one of the conditions and do not influence or get influenced by other participants, then this assumption is met.

Homogeneity of Variance: This assumption requires that variance (spread of values around the average) among groups should be similar. In our case, the variance of the outcome variable, time spent on the app, should be similar in each of the conditions.

Normal Distribution: The population of all the respondents (players) from which the sample was drawn is normally distributed. In the context of GameV's A/B test, this assumption implies that the time spent by all the users (*note:* all users, not only those in our sample) of the game follows a bell-shaped distribution. Some users will spend a lot of time and some less time, but the majority of users' time will spread around the average.

The use of an ANOVA is not recommended if the independence assumption is violated, although sometimes an ANOVA is used despite violation of the normality assumption since an ANOVA can still perform reasonably well if a large sample size is used. However, the assumption of homogeneity of variance tends to be frequently violated in many real-world datasets. In fact, assuming unequal variances might be a more realistic approach when working with real-world datasets.[2] Therefore, assuming unequal variance, it is advisable to use Welch's ANOVA as it does not assume homogeneity of variance.

The output of Welch's ANOVA will provide an estimate of p value. Let's understand what p value means. It is the probability of observing the obtained results if the null hypothesis was actually true. In the context of our A/B test, it is the probability of wrongly concluding that the group means are not the same (i.e., rejecting the null hypothesis) when they are actually the same (i.e., the null hypothesis is true). We want to reduce the probability of such wrong conclusions; thus, smaller p values are preferred. The convention is to set the threshold p value at 0.05; if the estimated p value is less than 0.05, then we can conclude that the averages are statistically different.

If the results of Welch's ANOVA show that the averages across all conditions are not the same, then the next step is to ask the following questions: Which conditions are different, and how do they differ? Post hoc pairwise comparisons help us answer these questions. Given the frequent violation of the homogeneity of variance assumption, it is advisable to use the Games-Howell method for pairwise comparison, which allows unequal variance in pairwise comparisons.

We will follow these steps closely in the next sections when we analyze the A/B test for GameV.

14.6 USING THE A/B TEST IN NEW PRODUCT DEVELOPMENT

We first import data and create a boxplot. The data are hypothetical and created for the purposes of this chapter.

TABLE 14.1 ■ Summary Statistics

condition	count	mean	min	sd
Prototype_25	195	46.52970	11.174987	15.06432
Prototype_35	175	51.23371	9.062043	16.61373
Prototype_45	185	47.41703	18.099590	10.65673

FIGURE 14.2 ■ A Boxplot of Time Spent With Different Prototypes

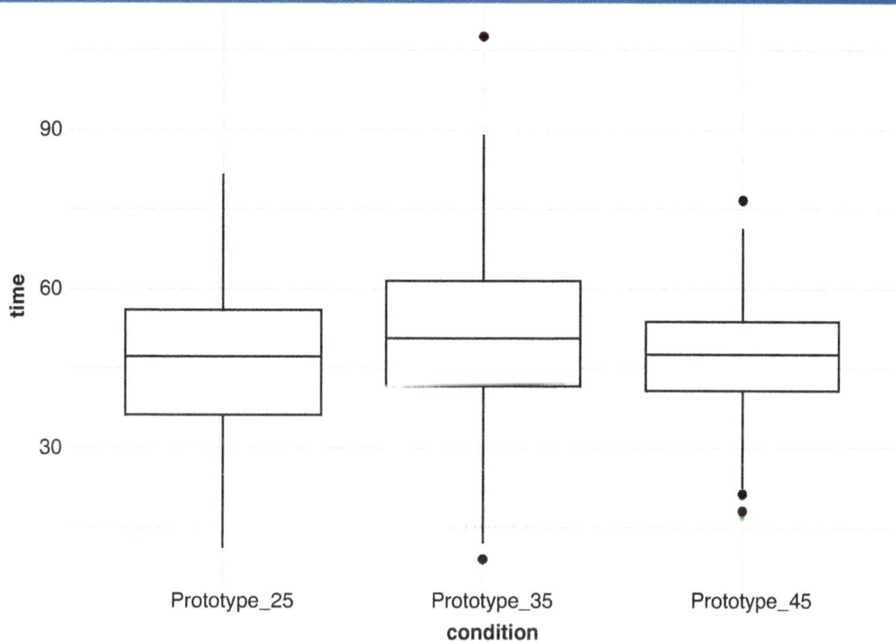

We see from Table 14.1 and Figure 14.2 that the average time players spent with prototype-35 is higher than with either prototype-25 or prototype-45. Having obtained this result, we need to determine if the average time spent is statistically different across conditions.

The first step is to test if our data satisfies the normality assumption by performing the Shapiro–Wilk normality test.

TABLE 14.2 ■ Testing for Normality Assumption

condition	variable	statistic	*p*
Prototype_25	time	0.9922398	0.3874756
Prototype_35	time	0.9895805	0.2286476
Prototype_45	time	0.9913752	0.3363401

Across all the conditions, we see that the p value is more than 0.05 (see Table 14.2). This shows that our data do not violate the assumption of normality.

The second step tests the homogeneity of variance assumption. We use Levene's test for homogeneity of variance across groups. The null hypothesis of this test states that variances in the three groups are the same (i.e., they are not significantly different).

TABLE 14.3 ■ Levene's Test

df1	df2	statistic	p
2	552	14.29075	9e-07

The obtained p value is less than 0.05, so the null hypothesis is rejected (see Table 14.3). We can conclude that our data do not meet the assumption of homogeneity of variance. As we discussed earlier, the ideal method when the assumption of homogeneity of variance is violated is *Welch's* ANOVA. We implement it next.

TABLE 14.4 ■ Welch's ANOVA

.y.	n	statistic	DFn	DFd	p	method
time	555	4.51	2	350.8273	0.012	Welch ANOVA

The p value of Welch's ANOVA is less than 0.05 (see Table 14.4). This shows that the means across the three conditions are not the same. In order to find out how they differ across conditions, we use the Games-Howell test. It compares means across all possible combinations of conditions and tests if the differences between conditions are statistically significant or not.

TABLE 14.5 ■ Games-Howell Test

.y.	group1	group2	estimate	conf.low	conf.high	p.adj	p.adj. signif
time	Prototype_25	Prototype_35	4.7040084	0.8073325	8.6006842	0.013	*
time	Prototype_25	Prototype_45	0.8873367	-2.2508397	4.0255130	0.784	ns
time	Prototype_35	Prototype_45	-3.8166717	-7.3036038	-0.3297396	0.028	*

The results show that prototype-35 players spent statistically more time with the game than both prototype-25 and prototype-45 players (see Table 14.5).

14.6.1 Insights Derived From the A/B Test

Given the finding that prototype-35 results in greater immersiveness than prototype-25 and prototype-45, the insights we can draw are quite informative. The results indicate that for lower levels of difficulty (prototype-25), players do not find the game immersive. However, as the difficulty level increases to prototype-35, immersiveness increases. At this point, GameV might have wrongfully concluded that increasing difficulty will always increase immersiveness since players feel a greater sense of achievement when they win more difficult games. Hence, including prototype-45 was informative since it indicated that its increased level of difficulty resulted in lowered immersiveness. The results clearly indicate that as difficulty increases, immersiveness increases initially, peaks at a certain level, and then starts to decrease. In other words, the results seem to follow an inverted-*U* shape. Therefore, GameV can now identify what level of difficulty should be retained to obtain the maximum immersiveness.

The A/B test we ran had one factor with multiple levels and no interactions. Interaction occurs when an experimental design has two factors (or independent variables) and we want to find the combined (or interactive) influence of the two factors on the outcome variable. Of course, there can be more than two factors; in that case, we would be examining the interactive influence of three or four factors on the outcome. However, the more factors we include in an experimental design, the larger and more complicated the design becomes, requiring that each factor's interactive influence be examined on the outcome variable. For instance, if we had an experimental design with three factors and each of them had two levels, then the model equation would include three main effects, three two-factor interactions, and one three-factor interaction, indicating that the experimental design should include $2 * 2 * 2 = 8$ groups. Assuming a sample size of 50 participants per group, we would need a sample of 400 participants.

14.7 IMPLEMENTATION USING R: THE A/B TEST

First, we import the data and the libraries `rstatix`,[3] `dplyr`,[4] and `ggplot2`.[5] We then summarize the data by creating a boxplot as shown in Figure 14.2.

```
library(rstatix)
library(dplyr)

data_game <-
  read.csv(url("http://data.mishra.us/files/chapter_NPD/data_game.csv"))


data_game %>%
  group_by(condition) %>%
  summarise(
```

```
    count = n(),
    mean = mean(time),
    min = min(time),
    sd = sd (time)
  )
```

```
## #   A tibble: 3 × 5
##     condition     count   mean    min     sd
##     <chr>         <int>  <dbl>  <dbl>  <dbl>
## 1   Prototype_25    195   46.5   11.2   15.1
## 2   Prototype_35    175   51.2   9.06   16.6
## 3   Prototype_45    185   47.4   18.1   10.7
```

```
library(ggplot2)
p <- ggplot(data_game, aes(condition,time))
p + geom_boxplot()+theme_minimal()
```

The average time spent with prototype-35 is higher than that with both prototype-25 and prototype-45. Next, we determine if average time spent is statistically different across the three groups.

We perform the Shapiro–Wilk normality test to test for the normality assumption.

```
data_game %>%
  group_by(condition) %>%
  shapiro_test(time)
```

```
## #   A tibble: 3 × 4
##     condition     variable statistic      p
##     <chr>         <chr>        <dbl>  <dbl>
## 1   Prototype_25  time         0.992  0.387
## 2   Prototype_35  time         0.990  0.229
## 3   Prototype_45  time         0.991  0.336
```

Across all conditions, we see that the p value is more than 0.05. This shows that our data do not violate the assumption of normality.

We next use Levene's test for homogeneity of variance across groups. The null hypothesis of this test states that the variances across the three groups is similar.

```
levene_test(time ~ condition,data = data_game)
```

```
## #   A tibble: 1 × 4
##       df1    df2 statistic              p
##     <int>  <int>     <dbl>          <dbl>
## 1       2    552      14.3    0.000000889
```

The obtained p value is less than 0.05; hence, we conclude that our data do not meet the assumption of homogeneity of variance. We implement Welch's ANOVA next.

```
welch_anova_test(time ~ condition, data=data_game)
```

```
## # A tibble:     1 × 7
##     .y.          n  statistic      DFn     DFd      p method
## *  <chr>     <int>      <dbl>    <dbl>   <dbl>  <dbl> <chr>
## 1  time       555        4.51        2    351.  0.012 Welch ANOVA
```

The p value of Welch's ANOVA is less than 0.05. This shows that the means across the three conditions are not the same. In order to find out how they differ across conditions, we use the Games-Howell test.

```
games_howell_test(time ~ condition,data=data_game)
```

```
## # A     tibble: 3 × 8
##    .y.   group1       group2       estimate conf.low conf.high p.adj p.adj.signif
## * <chr> <chr>        <chr>        <dbl>    <dbl>    <dbl>     <dbl> <chr>
## 1 time Prototype_25 Prototype_35  4.70      0.807    8.60     0.013 *
## 2 time Prototype_25 Prototype_45  0.887    -2.25     4.03     0.784 ns
## 3 time Prototype_35 Prototype_45 -3.82     -7.30    -0.330    0.028 *
```

The results show that with prototype-35 players spent statistically more time than with either prototype-25 or prototype-45.

14.8 UNDERSTANDING THE CHAPTER

1. What is the difference between causal testing and correlational testing? Is A/B testing causal or correlational?
2. What is the difference between a null hypothesis and an alternate hypothesis in an A/B test?

3. What is the primary purpose of an A/B test?

a. To compare two different advertisement designs
b. To determine the effectiveness of an intervention between groups
c. To test the effectiveness of a new medication
d. To find correlations between variables

4. Which statistical test would you use to compare the means of three or more groups?

a. *t* test
b. *F* test
c. chi-square test
d. Pearson correlation

5. What is the null hypothesis in an A/B test?

a. There is a significant difference between the groups.
b. There is no significant difference between the groups.
c. The intervention causes the observed difference.
d. The observed difference is due to chance.

6. What is the main advantage of using Welch's ANOVA over the standard *F* test (ANOVA)?

a. It is more powerful when the variances are equal.
b. It is less sensitive to unequal variances.
c. It has a higher Type I error rate.
d. It requires fewer assumptions.

7. When should you use a post hoc test after an *F* test (ANOVA)?

a. When the null hypothesis is rejected
b. When the null hypothesis is not rejected
c. Always after an *F* test
d. Only when the sample sizes are unequal

8. In which situation would you choose to use Welch's ANOVA over the standard *F* test?

a. When the data are normally distributed
b. When the variances within each group are equal
c. When the variances within each group are unequal
d. When the groups are dependent

ENDNOTES

1. Saks-Frankel, Robin, and Kelly-Ann Franklin, "Chase Sapphire Reserve Card Review 2023," *Forbes Advisor*, August 31, 2023, https://www.forbes.com/advisor/credit-cards/reviews/chase-sapphire-reserve/.

2. Delacre, Marie, Daniël Lakens, and Christophe Leys, "Why Psychologists Should by Default Use Welch's *t*-Test Instead of Student's *t*-Test," *International Review of Social Psychology* 30, no. 1 (2017).

3. Kassambara, Alboukadel, "rstatix: Pipe-Friendly Framework for Basic Statistical Tests," R package version 0.7.2 (February 1, 2023), https://CRAN.R-project.org/package=rstatix.

4. Wickham, Hadley, Romain François, Lionel Henry, and Kirill Müller, "dplyr: A Grammar of Data Manipulation," R package version 1.1.3 (September 3, 2023), https://CRAN.R-project.org/package=dplyr.

5. Wickham, Hadley, *ggplot2:Elegant Graphics for Data Analysis* (New York: Springer-Verlag, 2016).

PART

V

BUSINESS ETHICS AND ANALYTICS

15 FAIRNESS IN BUSINESS ANALYTICS

CONTENTS

LEARNING OBJECTIVES

1. Appreciate the importance of artificial intelligence algorithms
2. Define fairness metrics
3. Consider the causes behind algorithmic fairness
4. Mitigate algorithmic bias
5. Debias algorithms using preprocess, in-process, and postprocess steps

15.1 INTRODUCTION

In this chapter we move beyond examining the applications of analytic methods to different business domains to understand how these methods can be (and are being) used to better society. Artificial intelligence (AI) algorithms are increasingly influencing every facet of life. They are major influencers of such decisions as which brands to buy, books to read, clothes to wear, foods to eat, and places to visit; their influence extends even to job offerings and potential life partners.[1] Algorithms can now detect boredom, confusion, delight, engagement, and frustration among K–12 students. Knowledge of how a student is feeling helps these algorithms adjust the pace and content of learning by offering encouragement, altering materials to better suit the student, and redirecting the student to a different task when they become disengaged.[2] Which news and social media posts we get to see are now influenced by algorithms.[3] Algorithms also are short-listing suitable candidates from among those applying for a job.[4] They help predict a defendant's risk of committing another misdemeanor or felony—data that the courts are using in sentencing decisions.[5] Actions such as filling out a small-claims court filing, disputing a fine, or contesting a nondisclosure agreement, which were once in the realm of human lawyers, are now being influenced by algorithms that are automating these tasks or working as decision aids.[6] Skin cancer, the most common malignancy in humans, can now be detected by algorithms with a level of competence comparable to that of dermatologists.[7]

The presence of algorithms in minor to major life decisions is now a reality that humans live with. At its core, the use of algorithms aims to improve human life and provide people with a variety of benefits. However, since algorithms influence so many aspects of decision-making, the people whose lives are affected need to feel confident that algorithmic decisions are fair and inclusive. If algorithmic decisions are unfair, then they have the ability to harm people. Unfortunately, examinations across some domains show that sometimes algorithmic output can be unfair. The following are some examples:

1. The profiles of online platform users identified as male were much more likely to be shown advertisements for high-paying executive jobs than those the platform had identified as female, even when their résumés were otherwise equivalent in terms of experience and skills.[8]

2. Search engines amplify negative stereotypes by showing arrest-record advertisements in response to queries regarding names predominantly given to African American babies, but not for other names.[9]

3. Algorithms that determine who gets access to high-risk health care management such as organ donation programs routinely let healthier racial-majority-group patients into the programs ahead of racial-minority-group patients who are actually less healthy and more in need of the program.[10]

4. Recruiting algorithms penalize résumés that contain the word *women's* in the text and downgrade the résumés of women who attended women's colleges, resulting in preference given to men.[11]

5. Algorithms behind commercially available facial recognition software systems fail to recognize darker-skinned complexions.[12]

It would be wasteful not to harness the power of algorithms, but it would be much more beneficial if algorithms could learn to reach fair decisions.

15.2 WHAT ARE THE CAUSES BEHIND ALGORITHMIC UNFAIRNESS?

To understand algorithmic unfairness, the first step is to understand the sources through which algorithms learn biases. Biases in algorithms can enter through different ways. These include historical biases, algorithmic objective, overrepresentation or underrepresentation in data, and biases caused by "proxy" attributes.

15.2.1 Historical Biases

In their simplest form, AI algorithms are simple mathematical rules that are devoid of any understanding of race, gender, or any other characteristic. Their main purpose is to optimize the criteria assigned to them. Consider a lender's algorithm that is designed to minimize the potential for loan default. Learning from past data, it will create profiles of good and bad borrowers to ensure that only loan applications of those who show the least probability of default are approved. For such an algorithm, race and gender are just numerical values that help it identify the least risky borrowers. Labels with high versus low risk are provided to algorithms by humans. These labels are in the form of historical data that humans generated when they approved loans. Thus, unfairness in algorithms sometimes comes from human biases inherent in prior data.

Historical human biases are shaped by pervasive and often deeply embedded prejudices against certain groups, which can lead to the reproduction and amplification of these prejudices in computer models. Any algorithm trained on such data will mimic the prior biases. If historical biases are factored into the algorithm, it will make the same kinds of wrong judgments that people do. If a recruitment algorithm is trained on the data derived from the résumés submitted to the business over several years, which were predominantly from one group, the algorithm will learn to identify that group as ideal applicants.

15.2.2 Algorithmic Objective

The outcome that an algorithm is trying to optimize can also lead to unintended consequences.[13] Assume that an algorithm is deployed on a video-sharing platform. The objective of this algorithm is to optimize the number of clicks on an advertisement shown along with the videos. This algorithm will display all types of engaging content that it predicts will make a user watch more videos and click on advertisements. To maximize clicks, the algorithm will keep people fixated on the screen for extended periods of time, causing them to miss out on other important activities. In such instances, more click-throughs (i.e., profit maximization) are at odds with human goals.

Another example could be a traffic-assistance app designed to find the shortest and quickest path to a destination. In order to achieve this goal, it could send drivers through neighborhood streets that are not designed for heavy traffic,[14] thereby increasing pollution and safety risk in such neighborhoods.

15.2.3 Overrepresentation or Underrepresentation in Data

If the data used to train the algorithm are more representative of some groups of people than others, the predictions from the model may also be systematically worse for underrepresented groups. In the facial recognition example mentioned previously, the algorithm made recognition errors related to darker-skinned faces because this group was underrepresented in the training data. That is, the algorithm presumably was relying on certain facial features such as the distance between the eyes, the shape of the eyebrows, and variations in facial skin shades as a way to recognize faces. However, the facial features that were more representative in the training data were not as diverse and, therefore, were less reliable about distinguishing between complexions, leading to several misidentifications.

Data sampling affects bias because the way the data are distributed for two groups can be very different. This occurs because the explanatory variables (e.g., income, education, zip code, and financial standing) map onto the outcome (e.g., loan approved vs. not approved) differently. Moreover, the representation of some groups in the training data is likely to be less because of their lower proportion in the population. When such distributional difference and undersampling meet, the algorithm by default will follow the distribution of the group represented most often in order to reduce errors, causing biases in the algorithm's predictions.

15.2.4 Biases Caused by "Proxy" Attributes

Sometimes algorithms have access to nonsensitive attributes that serve as a proxy for sensitive attributes such as age, race, or gender. The information from these proxy attributes maps onto the sensitive attributes, and even though the algorithm is not provided with information directly about the sensitive attribute, it still can learn and use it in its outcome. We can understand this through one example of technical skills used during recruiting. Technical skills can act as a proxy variable for age because younger applicants may have updated skills compared to older workers. In this case, the algorithm will indirectly infer that those with updated technical skills are younger than those with less updated technical skills. Therefore, even without being provided with the age of the applicants directly, the algorithm can infer age through technical skills.

Now that we are aware of what might be causing algorithms to reach unfair decisions, the important next step is to find ways through which such unfairness can be mitigated in the algorithms' predictions. Mitigation of algorithmic unfairness can occur in two ways: technical and cultural. We discuss each of these two options in the following sections.

15.3 MITIGATING UNFAIRNESS

The first step in mitigating unfairness is to define what exactly is fair versus unfair. Here we discuss a few definitions of fairness that have been proposed, which diverse organizations can use as metrics to help evaluate whether the algorithms are reaching fair decisions.

15.3.1 Defining Fairness

Since fairness has been used differently in different contexts, it is important to have a few standard and agreed-upon metrics to determine fairness of algorithmic output. On a global level, the aim is for the algorithm to reach decisions that are not discriminatory to any group of people defined by characteristics that include age, race, gender, and country. However, when judging whether an algorithm's decision is fair, we need to have clearly defined metrics that can measure and quantify the level of unfairness (if any) in the algorithm's output.

The following discussion focuses on the most commonly applied of the proposed algorithmic fairness metrics.[15] A confusion matrix can help explain how the different fairness metrics can be calculated. For the confusion matrix we use the example of loan approvals.

15.3.1.1 Confusion Matrix

Consider a lending firm that has data on its past borrowers that include borrowers' credit history, requested credit amount, employment, and gender. It also has data on who among this set of borrowers defaulted on their loans. The lender trains an algorithm on these prior data that—given information about credit history, requested credit amount, employment, and gender—predicts if a borrower will default on the loan. The lender wants to assess if the algorithm's predictions are biased against women (let's refer to women as the unprivileged group and men as the privileged group).

Predictions made by an algorithm are depicted in the 2 x 2 confusion matrix as shown in Figure 15.1. Rows represent the ground truth: how many people actually did not default (*p*) and did default (*n*) on the loan. Columns represent the number of people that the model predicted would not default (*p'*) and would default on the loan (*n'*). Each of the four cells represents the number of times predictions matched or mismatched with the ground truth. For instance, True Positive represents the number of times when the ground truth (*p*) and the prediction (*p'*) matched. On the other hand, False Positive shows the number of times when the ground truth was *n* but the prediction was *p'*.

FIGURE 15.1 ■ Confusion Matrix

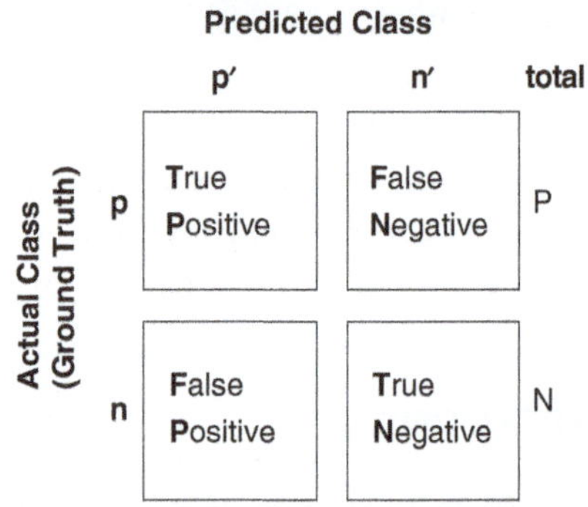

Figure 15.2 shows confusion matrices for men and women. We will use these matrices to understand the various fairness metrics: statistical parity difference, disparate impact, equal opportunity difference, and average odds difference.

FIGURE 15.2 ■ Confusion Matrix for Men and Women

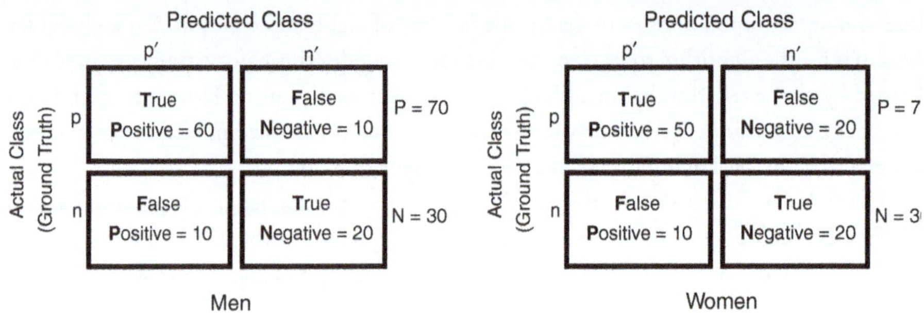

Statistical Parity Difference. According to this metric, an algorithm is unbiased if it classifies the same proportion of individuals from privileged and unprivileged groups as positive. In the loan example, an unbiased algorithm would classify the same proportion of men and women as good borrowers (i.e., those who would not default on the loan). Therefore, the difference between the proportion of an unprivileged group (women) classified as good borrowers and the proportion of a privileged group (men) classified as good borrowers would be zero. Examining the confusion matrices for men and women allows us to calculate their proportions. The proportion of men classified as good borrowers is $\frac{70}{100} = 0.70$, and the proportion of women classified as good borrowers is $\frac{60}{100} = 0.60$. The statistical parity difference, therefore, is $0.60 - 0.70 = -0.10$ or 10%, which means the algorithm is biased against women.

Disparate Impact. In this case, the proportion of individuals in the unprivileged group who received a favorable prediction is compared to the proportion of individuals in the privileged group who received a favorable prediction. The calculation involves the proportion of the unprivileged group that received the positive outcome divided by the proportion of the privileged group that received the positive outcome. In the loan example, this would be $\frac{60/100}{70/100} = 0.85$ or 85%. The ideal value of this metric is 1.0 or 100%, but according to the disparate impact precept the positive prediction for any unprivileged group should be at least 80% of the rate for the privileged group, indicating that values below 0.8 suggest potential discrimination against the unprivileged group.

Equal Opportunity Difference. This metric requires true positive rates to be similar for the privileged and unprivileged groups. Since the true positive rate is the ratio of true positives to the total number of actual positives for a group, this metric is calculated by taking the difference in true positive rates between the unprivileged and the privileged groups. The ideal value is zero. In the loan example, since the true positive rate for women is $\frac{50}{50+20} = 0.71$ and the true positive rate for men is $\frac{60}{60+10} = 0.86$, the equal opportunity difference is $0.71 - 0.86 = -0.15$ or 15%.

Average Odds Difference. This metric captures the difference in the average false positive rate and true positive rate between unprivileged and privileged groups. The false positive rate (FPR) is calculated as false positives divided by the total number of actual negatives; thus, in the loan example it is $\frac{10}{30} = 0.33$ for men and $\frac{10}{30} = 0.33$ for women. The true positive rate (TPR) is calculated as true positives divided by the total number of actual positives; in the loan example, it is $\frac{60}{70} = 0.86$ for men and $\frac{50}{70} = 0.71$ for women. Therefore, the average odds difference is $\frac{0.71+0.33}{2} - \frac{0.86+0.33}{2} = -0.07$. The ideal value is zero. A value of < 0 implies a higher benefit for the privileged group, and a value of > 0 implies a higher benefit for the unprivileged group.

It is important to note that there are many metrics available to measure fairness. This brings up the question of which metric is ideal. The short answer is that no one metric is likely to fit all situations. In the long term, a seemingly ideal metric can lead to unintended consequences. For instance, a bank that is attempting to provide equal access to loans for both privileged and unprivileged groups would use equality of opportunity as a metric. This metric suggests that the true positive rates between the groups should be the same. The bank, therefore, would want to lend to the members of both groups at an equal rate. However, unprivileged group members are likely to have a lower credit score than privileged group members, so the bank would have to lower the credit score threshold for the unprivileged group. A study showed that in this scenario, easier access to loans would have unintended consequences for the unprivileged group.[16] If such a lowering of thresholds increased the number of defaults within that group, it would lower their aggregate credit scores over time. Ideally, several metrics that are chosen by the subject-matter experts and key organizational decision-makers should be used. Like the earlier lending example, it is important to consider not only the immediate consequences of optimizing on a fairness metric but also the long-term effects of using such a metric to design fair algorithms.

In addition, some general rules can be used to short-list potential fairness metrics.[17] If a positive prediction made by the algorithm leads to punishment (e.g., predicting whom to fire in an organization facing financial constraints), there is a significant risk of inflicting harm on people, so the focus should be on reducing false positives. Thus, metrics that are based on a false positive rate should be used in these scenarios. If a positive prediction of an algorithm confers reward (e.g., predicting who should receive a loan or a job offer), the goal is to reduce false negatives. That is, we want to ensure that people who are deserving receive the rewarding outcome. Therefore, metrics that focus on false negatives should be used.

15.3.2 How to Mitigate Unfairness: Technical Solutions

The first step in trying to address unfairness or to debias an algorithm is to know how the algorithm is arriving at biased decisions that are harmful for some protected groups. Accordingly, it is important to learn the sources from which an algorithm might learn bias. Let's work with the example of an organization that wants to avoid gender, racial, or any other bias in its hiring process. It would need to be cognizant of where bias can enter into the algorithm and what it can do to prevent algorithmic learning bias. Let's go over some sources of bias that have been documented in past work and discuss suggested technical steps that can be used to train the algorithm to reach fair decisions. Research has suggested that some of these technical corrections can occur at the data collection, data analysis, and result-dissemination stages.[18]

15.3.2.1 Training Data: Diverse and Representative Sampling

Several findings have demonstrated that one of the main sources of bias arises from the training data that an algorithm uses to learn. These training data could be based on historical data or human decisions that can contain several societal biases. For instance, women have been underrepresented and underpaid in several jobs, despite having the same skill sets as their male counterparts. Therefore, the bias in this case would enter through the past data on which the algorithm has been trained.

If the organization wants to create a fair algorithm, it is important to make sure that the training data are not biased. Some simple precautions can be taken to reduce bias in the training data during the data collection process, including the following:

1. Before organizations embark on data collection, they need to first frame the questions that they will be using for data collection. These questions will determine the type of variables to be used in the training data and in the subsequent predictions. For a hiring decision, organizations may need to ask not who is best for the job given past data, which can bring in gender and racial biases, but rather what skill set is necessary to succeed in order to be agnostic about the gender and race of the person.

2. The data collection process can again be divided into different parts to reduce the likelihood that algorithms will learn bias from the data. The data collected can be primary data: for example, trying to find out through a survey what might be the most suitable set of skills for a specific position. In this case, the survey questions should be

well thought out so that questions about skills a specific group may possess and another group may be deficient in are not inadvertently given more weight. As we discussed earlier, technical skills should not become a proxy for age. If the data collected are secondary, then the data source plays an important role: for example, whether data are mined from different publicly available sources or are just based on past data specific to the organization. In either case, caution should be exercised to ensure that certain groups are not over- versus underrepresented. For instance, computational jobs tend to have a higher representation of men; if the algorithm learns this, it will be converted to a rule that will be applied in future hiring, and the bias against women will become pronounced.

3. Some organizations cite the fact that they do not include protected attributes from their dataset (e.g., gender, race, income, or age) in their training dataset. However, they need to be aware that such *fairness-by-unawareness* steps carry no assurance that the algorithm cannot infer protected attributes, which it can from correlated attributes! And since these correlated features stay in the training dataset, they can cause equal or even more bias in the final output. For instance, in loan approval decisions, financial institutions might not provide race information in the training data and, therefore, expect that since the algorithm did not see the race information it cannot be biased. However, the training data might still have information about neighborhoods that are associated with socioeconomic information and might be race specific. These proxy features would allow the algorithm to infer race even when this information was not directly provided to the algorithm. In such a case, it is important to first check whether algorithmic decisions are biased. And if they are biased, then organizations can use the preprocess or in-process technical debiasing steps to debias the algorithms to ensure that the protected attributes are not being used, even implicitly, in the output.

4. An important step in the data collection process is to make sure that the data sample is as representative and diverse as possible because bias can enter through underrepresentation as well as missing data. Because undersampling of certain groups is a common source of bias in the training dataset, a diverse and balanced sample of income, race, gender, and other demographic variables should be provided to the algorithm so biases resulting from undersampling are avoided. The algorithm will not learn to underrepresent women if it has seen equal samples of both men and women with the same skill set. This sampling adjustment can be done for any group that has been underrepresented in the organization or in the industry.

15.3.2.2 Technical Steps to Debiasing

Technical debiasing solutions can be applied during the preprocess, in-process, or postprocess steps of data analysis.[19]

Preprocess Steps to Debiasing. Correcting processes can be added to the training datasets so that the algorithm doesn't learn to automatically discriminate against a specific group.

Methods such as relabeling or reweighing the data for some groups can update the labels so that their associated learning becomes balanced across different groups. For instance, women's data can be relabeled or their salary information can be reweighed in a manner that reflects the current rather than historical norms, allowing the algorithm to adjust this forward. Reweighing the training data requires adding a different weight to both women's and men's observations. It gives a higher weight to those observations that can increase equity (e.g., women receiving a higher-than-average salary) and a lower weight to observations that reduce equity (e.g., men's salaries being higher than the norm). Reweighing observations occurs before the actual analysis and, hence, is a preprocess step. It does not change actual values of the observations but merely changes the weight received in the analysis to increase fair outcomes.

Different and appropriately weighed thresholds or classifiers can be selected for each group to prevent historical biases from being carried forward.[20] We discuss the use of reweighing as a preprocessing step in Section 15.4 of this chapter. However, one needs to be cautious about the use of such methods because other aspects of algorithmic efficiency or accuracy could be affected. The accuracy of an algorithm is based on how well the algorithm's predictions match the ground truth (the outcome) available in the test dataset. The more accurate an algorithm's predictions are in such out-of-sample datasets (usually the test data), the better it is considered. Organizations pick those algorithms that are more accurate because their outcome positively affects their profitability. However, when algorithms are debiased by reweighing features or relabeling, their ability to predict will be affected adversely. Organizations should be aware of the accuracy–equity trade-off so that they can determine how much unfairness they are willing to accept for the sake of accuracy, and vice versa.

In-Process Steps to Debiasing. Debiasing can occur even when the algorithm is performing the actual analysis. Such in-process debiasing can be done after preprocess debiasing has been conducted or even as a stand-alone process. The outcome can then be checked for whether it has become fairer after the in-process adjustment. A common way to conduct in-process debiasing is to use a tuning parameter or fairness constraints in the model, such that both accuracy and fairness metrics are maximized.[21]

One such in-process tool is adversarial debiasing, which we will discuss in detail and also use in section 15.4. For this, we need to describe adversarial learning briefly. Adversarial learning generally has two deep learning networks—a generator and a discriminator; hence, a commonly used adversarial learning algorithm is known as GAN (generative adversarial learning). The generator simulates outputs based on the training data, and the discriminator determines whether the output is real—good enough to belong to the sample under study (e.g., a product review)—or fake—it doesn't look like a product review. The generator updates learning from the discriminator's decision to eventually produce outputs that the discriminator labels as real.

Given this ability, adversarial learning algorithms are commonly used in various activities ranging from text generation to product design to image classification. Though the generative process can be accurate, it has been shown to be unfair in its output. For instance, a face- modification algorithm was shown to be racist: When it was asked to make faces appear more attractive, it made the skin tone of the generated faces lighter, indicating that it has learned a rule that lighter skin tones are more attractive than darker skin tones.[22]

Adversarial learning can be used as an in-process tool in the following way: Instead of using one discriminator to figure out whether the generator is providing a fake or real output, a second discriminator can be used to determine whether the generator is providing a fair or unfair output.[23] The discriminator can be developed to optimize any of the fairness metrics, such as equal odds, equal opportunity, or demographic parity. The generator tries to predict the output using the input variables and provides an output. The fairness discriminator, working as an adversary, tries to infer the protected group's label (e.g., race, gender, age) from the generator's output. If in the first run the discriminator is able to infer the protected feature from the output, this information is fed back to the generator, which again updates it in such a way that the protected attribute cannot be inferred. This process goes on until the discriminator is not able to infer the protected feature. The assumption is that if the discriminator is not able to infer the protected feature from the output of the generator, this indicates that the generator is not using any of these protected attributes (or even inferring them from proxy variables) in its output.

Postprocess Steps to Debiasing. Postprocessing steps to debias the algorithm are taken after the algorithm has provided its output. At this point, if the algorithm's output is unfair to certain groups, then the output of some of these unfair decisions can be changed. For instance, if the loan is not approved for an individual who may belong to an underprivileged group but who has the same financial scores as a privileged group member, then the output label can be changed from "not approved" to "approved."

15.3.2.3 Decision Explainability

AI systems commonly use opaque models that do not provide any explanation for their predictions. Opaque models such as deep learning algorithms and support vector machines base their computations in higher dimensional space using complex mathematical forms. Which input variables are used and in what form they are used may not be available to the end user. With such an opaque approach, it would be difficult to understand the source of any bias. This approach is more of an issue in decisions that are made autonomously by algorithms. For instance, in loan approval decisions, it is possible that the algorithm will appear biased because certain groups are underrepresented in its training data. However, an opaque model hinders our ability to discern which predictor variables have more or less influence on the final loan approvals.

Consequently, one approach is to employ methods that offer greater transparency or that provide some rationale behind their predictions. Some methods that provide such clarity include linear, logistic, LASSO, and ridge regressions. These techniques provide insights on the influence of the predictor variables on the outcome variable. For instance, in the context of loan approvals, they can explain how higher credit scores increase probability of loan approval. While still not as transparent as the aforementioned methods, methods such as boosted decision trees provide a moderate level of insight. As we discussed in Chapter 13, boosted trees give us some insight of which predictors played an important role in the prediction process. Moreover, it is also possible to interpret the outputs of more opaque models by using processes such as partial dependency plots, which we also discussed in Chapter 13. These plots can help us understand the marginal effect of one or two predictor variables on the outcome variable across a range of values, even if the model's framework remains complex and less interpretable.

We next describe ways in which developing fair algorithms requires creating a culture of fairness in the organization.

15.3.3 How to Mitigate Unfairness: Creating a Culture of Fairness in the Organization

Along with technical solutions to creating fair algorithms, cultural changes in the organization are equally important for developing fair algorithms. However, it is worth acknowledging the challenges related to fairness faced by people in the organization who are designing and using the algorithms.[24] Organizations may not realize how their algorithms might be treating some groups unfairly or whether the bias is entering in during the data collection or model tuning stage. At times they may be working with an ensemble of algorithms, and it becomes difficult for them to clearly identify the source of the bias or ways to debias in their specific organizational context. We next discuss a few ways in which employees can be helped to develop and design fair algorithms at an organizational level.

15.3.3.1 Process to Collect Representative Data

Given that the task of data collection or compilation might be conducted by one team while the work of algorithm development is assigned to another team, it is important that the aims of both teams be clearly communicated. The algorithm developers should be able to communicate to the data collectors what type of data they will need, including well-represented samples, large samples, the type of variables to be included, and the data source. Some research has shown that the lack of communication among teams working in silos can result in bias being present in the training data because the data collectors are not aware of what the algorithm could learn from the data, and the algorithm developers are not aware whether fair data samples were obtained. Moreover, it is important for all teams at the data collection, algorithm development, and algorithm deployment stages to work toward the same goals. Let's assume that the organization wants to increase engagement with its product among a certain customer group. This goal should then be communicated to the data collection team so it can survey this group of customers. In addition, this goal should be available to the marketing team so it can introduce strategies to increase engagement among that group of customers. Such communication about groups of customers that the organization wants to engage in its aim to be inclusive would help the data collection team understand what questions to include (or not include) in its data collection efforts.

15.3.3.2 Accountability

The question of accountability has taken on a new role with the introduction of AI systems that can autonomously make decisions. Who is responsible for the repercussions of the AI system's decisions? Is it the designer, the senior management, or no one? Moreover, having an AI system make and deliver decisions somehow gives a sense of psychological distancing from these decisions, allowing management and employees to feel that they are not directly responsible. Such decision-distancing can lead to many harmful outcomes for humans at the receiving end of the decision. Therefore, it is important that just as humans are held accountable for their personal decisions, accountability for algorithmic business decisions should be distributed across senior management, frontline users of AI-backed programs, software engineers, those who collect and prepare data, and others involved in AI design and training. One suggestion to make certain of fair outcomes is to have a human in the loop. This concept ensures that although the algorithm is being used to improve the efficiency with which decisions are made (e.g., by compiling vast amounts of data), ultimately there is human oversight to confirm that biased decisions are not being made unchecked. Having a human in the loop to provide oversight helps in several ways: Humans don't have to process large bits of information, the algorithmic decision is implemented uniformly in different domains within an organization, there is consistency in how the organization responds to fairness initiatives, and humans trained to spot biases and make fair decisions are ultimately responsible for these decisions (e.g., for protected groups). Another option is to have an external agency audit algorithms so that organizational aims for profitability do not clash with equitable decisions for everyone.

15.3.3.3 Be Proactive

If the organization's aim is to ensure fair outcomes so that no one group of people receives treatment that is too favorable or too unfavorable, it is necessary that these goals be proactively pursued at all levels. Instead of waiting for customers to complain that they have been discriminated against, it helps if the organization steps up proactively to ensure that algorithms are not learning any negative associations with any group of customers. Similarly, organizations should not just develop an algorithm and deploy it without testing for how fair its decisions are. An algorithm that becomes public and then is discovered to be biased will result in negative media publicity that the organization will find difficult to live down.

15.3.3.4 Fairness Framework and Employee Training

Many employees would benefit from a cohesive effort to deploy fair algorithms, beginning with a clear framework that includes fairness metrics appropriate for their organization. As explained earlier, different metrics have the ability to capture different types of fairness; hence, it is necessary to know which fairness metrics are most applicable to one's organization. This might lie in the domain of senior management, which has a more global overview. The framework should also specify the type of inclusivity that the organization is hoping to achieve, which customer or client groups need to be represented and engaged, what algorithmic checks need to be conducted, and how frequently and what type of data need to be collected to ensure that the organization's fairness goals are being achieved. Employees can also be provided with proper training so they become familiar with the way in which fair algorithms can be developed.

15.3.3.5 Recognizing Biases Among Humans in the Decision Loop

Another source of bias could be humans who are in the different stages of the algorithm developmental loop. For instance, a lot of training data available to organizations may not have labels. The task of labeling is usually done by human experts or human crowd workers. Such human-produced labels can be checked to ensure that they are not affected by human biases, which can be held implicitly (i.e., without the awareness of the individuals who hold them). Several options are possible to ensure that human bias of the labelers does not affect the labeling task. Labelers can be trained beforehand to be aware of such bias and thus prevent it from affecting the task. The same information with different labels can be presented to them to check whether there may be bias in their decisions.[25] For example, the same audio content provided by a male or female voice or with different accents can be presented to the labelers with a request that they score the content. Ideally, the score should be the same as it was previously because the content of the audio is the same; just the source has been changed. Differences in scores would indicate that irrelevant factors have affected the scores of the labelers, potentially introducing bias in the training data.

15.3.3.6 Reward Fairness Efforts

A cohesive message can resonate across the organization if employees are not only encouraged but rewarded for their efforts to develop fair algorithms. One option is that employees be rewarded through bonuses or awards if they are able to improve the fairness of algorithms. Along with the aim of developing accurate and efficient algorithms, organizations should give importance to developing fair algorithms. As mentioned earlier, accuracy and fairness may not pan out at the same time because there is an inherent trade-off between achieving both simultaneously.

15.3.3.7 Build a Diverse Workforce

A diverse workforce highlights an organization's commitment to fair outcomes. Diversity and inclusivity in the workplace make these features prominent in different decisions and strategies so biases and their downstream effects can be addressed directly and appropriately. Having inputs from a diverse workforce at different stages of algorithmic development makes it easier to visualize the harms of a biased algorithm and the benefits of a fair algorithm.[26]

15.4 IMPLEMENTATION USING PYTHON: DEBIASING AN ALGORITHM

For implementation, we will use the AI Fairness 360 (`aif360`) library.[27] The code is in Python because `aif360` relies on TensorFlow, which is well integrated in the Python environment. The code can be run on Google Colab (short for Colaboratory), which is a free, cloud-based platform. To install `aif360` in Google Colab, run the following as the first line of code.

```
!pip install aif360 # Run it once per session; rerun if the runtime is reset.
```

In the following lines of code, we import entire libraries like pandas, numpy, and tensorflow and give them aliases such as pd, np, and tf for ease of reference in the code. We also import specific classes such as Reweighing, AdversarialDebiasing, and BinaryLabelDatasetMetric from different modules of the library aif360. We also import train_test_split and LogisticRegression from the sklearn.model_selection module. Finally, tf.compat.v1.disable_eager_execution() is a setting for TensorFlow. It changes how TensorFlow performs calculations. Specifically, it turns off a mode called "eager execution," which needs to be done to work with certain techniques like adversarial debiasing.

```
# Import necessary libraries
import pandas as pd
import numpy as np
import tensorflow as tf
from aif360.datasets import BinaryLabelDataset
from aif360.algorithms.preprocessing import Reweighing
from aif360.algorithms.inprocessing import AdversarialDebiasing
from aif360.metrics import BinaryLabelDatasetMetric
from sklearn.model_selection import train_test_split
from sklearn.linear_model import LogisticRegression
from sklearn.metrics import confusion_matrix, accuracy_score

# Disabling eager execution to handle the adversarial debiasing model
tf.compat.v1.disable_eager_execution()
```

Next, we import the dataset. The data are a subset of the German credit data.[28] The data we use for the purposes of this chapter include 400 observations and 5 features (independent variables) of the applicants: gender (Man = 1, Woman = 0)—note that we use the gender class as reported in the dataset); employment (Employed = 1, Unemployed = 0); number of dependents; age; and credit amount requested. The outcome variable is response and has two possible values of whether the applicant was considered creditworthy: 1 = creditworthy and 0 = not creditworthy.

After importing the data, we split the dataset into a train (75%) and test dataset (25%) using train_test_split function. The test_size=0.25 argument specifies that a quarter of the data is reserved for testing.

```
# Load the dataset
url = "http://data.mishra.us/files/chapter_fairness/credit.csv"
```

```
german_credit = pd.read_csv(url)

# Split the dataset
train, test = train_test_split(german_credit, test_size=0.20,
random_state=1234)
```

Next, we assess the level of bias that exists in this train and test dataset. This provides a baseline measure of bias and helps us assess if any debiasing mechanisms that are applied are effective in reducing the bias. In order to obtain a baseline measure of bias, we convert both the test and train dataset to the `aif360` format. The class `BinaryLabelDataset` creates an AIF-compatible dataset. The protected attribute is `gender`. Men belong to the privileged group, and women belong to the unprivileged group.

```
# Define privileged and unprivileged groups
privileged_groups = [{'gender': 1}]
unprivileged_groups = [{'gender': 0}]

# Convert the datasets into an AIF-compatible dataset
dataset_train = BinaryLabelDataset(df=train, label_names=['response'],
protected_attribute_names=['gender'])
dataset_test = BinaryLabelDataset(df=test, label_names=['response'],
protected_attribute_names=['gender'])
```

The next lines of the code assess the level of disparity in the dataset. Metrics like disparate impact and statistical parity difference are calculated and printed to gauge the initial level of bias present in the dataset.

```
# Calculate the disparate impact and statistical parity difference


metric_train = BinaryLabelDatasetMetric(dataset_train, unprivileged_
groups=unprivileged_groups, privileged_groups=privileged_groups)
metric_test = BinaryLabelDatasetMetric(dataset_test, unprivileged_
groups=unprivileged_groups, privileged_groups=privileged_groups)

print("Train Disparate Impact:", metric_train.disparate_impact())
print("Train Statistical Parity Difference:", metric_train.
statistical_parity_difference())
print("Test Disparate Impact:", metric_test.disparate_impact())
print("Test Statistical Parity Difference:", metric_test.
statistical_parity_difference())

Train Disparate Impact: 0.8354430379746836
```

```
Train Statistical Parity Difference: -0.11818181818181817
Test Disparate Impact: 0.5778947368421052
Test Statistical Parity Difference: -0.34598792062122524
```

Both the test and train datasets show some bias against women (the unprivileged group). We will first implement a preprocess algorithm: reweighing.

15.4.1 Preprocess Algorithm: Reweighing

As discussed in the section on technical solutions to debiasing, reweighing changes the weight given to the data points of privileged and underprivileged groups to increase fairness. In order to perform reweighing, the model initially creates an instance `rw` of the **`Reweighing`** class, assigning it to the specified privileged and unprivileged group. Then, it fits this instance to the training dataset with the `rw.fit(dataset_train)` method, which allows the algorithm to learn the necessary parameters to adjust the weights of the dataset instances. Finally, the `rw.transform(dataset_train)` method is applied, producing a new version of the dataset (`dataset_train_transformed`) where the instances are reweighed to mitigate biases in the defined privileged and unprivileged groups. We then calculate and print disparate impact and statistical parity difference after reweighing.

```
# Apply reweighing
rw = Reweighing(unprivileged_groups=unprivileged_groups,
privileged_groups=privileged_groups)
rw.fit(dataset_train)
dataset_train_transformed = rw.transform(dataset_train)

# Calculate the disparate impact and statistical parity difference after
reweighing
metric_train_transformed = BinaryLabelDatasetMetric(dataset_train_transformed,
unprivileged_groups=unprivileged_groups, privileged_groups=privileged_groups)

print("After Reweighing: Train Disparate Impact:", metric_train_transformed.
disparate_impact())
print("After Reweighing: Train Statistical Parity Difference:", metric_train_
transformed.statistical_parity_difference())

After Reweighing: Train Disparate Impact: 1.0000000000000002
After Reweighing: Train Statistical Parity Difference: 2.220446049250313e-16
```

As these metrics show, reweighing reduced bias against women. Without reweighing, the disparate impact in train data was 0.83, and the statistical parity difference was -0.11. After reweighing, the disparate impact is 1, and the statistical parity difference is close to 0. If we use the reweighed (or fairness-updated) data to train any model, the level of bias should drop when predictions are made with the test data also. We try to accomplish that next.

The next lines of code prepare the dataset for training the model. It extracts the features, labels, and instance weights from the transformed dataset (dataset_train_transformed). Each component (features, labels, and weights) is assigned to a separate variable (X_train, y_train, weights) to be used in the training process. X_train are features (or predictor variables) in the training data, and y_train is the outcome variable.

```
# Prepare the reweighed dataset for model training

X_train = dataset_train_transformed.features
y_train = dataset_train_transformed.labels.ravel()
weights = dataset_train_transformed.instance_weights
```

Subsequently, a logistic regression model is fitted using the reweighed dataset. In the fitting process, the weights assigned to each row of the training data are also incorporated in the logistic regression model (sample_weight=weights). Hence, this weighed logistic regression model helps in making predictions that take into account the reweighed instances to minimize bias.

```
# Train a logistic regression model using the reweighed dataset

model = LogisticRegression()
model.fit(X_train, y_train, sample_weight=weights)
```

The model then proceeds to make predictions on the test dataset. It drops the response column from the test dataset and uses the remaining features to make predictions. These predictions are then added back to the test dataset in a new column called 'binary_prediction'.

```
# Make predictions on the test dataset

X_test = test.drop(columns=['response'])
y_pred = model.predict(X_test)

# Add the predictions back to the test dataset
test['binary_prediction'] = y_pred
```

After obtaining predictions, the code recalibrates the test dataset into an aif360 format with the new predictions. This conversion is essential for calculating fairness metrics. The fairness of these predictions is then evaluated using the BinaryLabelDatasetMetric function. This step helps us evaluate whether the reweighing process has indeed been effective in mitigating biases within the dataset.

```
# Calculate fairness metrics on the predictions
dataset_test_modified = BinaryLabelDataset(df=test, label_names=['binary_pre-
diction'], protected_attribute_names=['gender'])
metric_test = BinaryLabelDatasetMetric(dataset_test_modified, unprivileged_
groups=unprivileged_groups, privileged_groups=privileged_groups)

print("Test Disparate Impact :", metric_test.disparate_impact())
print("Test Statistical Parity Difference:", metric_test.
statistical_parity_difference())

Test Disparate Impact: 1.0166666666666666
Test Statistical Parity Difference: 0.016393442622950838
```

Compared to the earlier baseline estimates of disparate impact (0.57) and statistical parity difference (–0.34) on test data, we observe that after training a logistic regression model on the reweighed train data, the disparate impact is now close to 1 and statistical parity difference is 0.01.

So far, we have not estimated how bias mitigation might have affected model accuracy. As we discussed earlier, bias mitigation sometimes adversely affects model accuracy. The next lines of code estimate model accuracy when bias mitigation was performed versus when it was not (i.e., baseline accuracy). To estimate model accuracy without bias mitigation, we simply omit the `sample_weight=weights`—that is, we do not consider the weights estimated in the reweighing step while fitting the model.

```
# Without Reweighing
model_unweighted = LogisticRegression()
model_unweighted.fit(X_train, y_train) # Train without using the weights

# Make predictions on the test dataset
y_pred_unweighted = model_unweighted.predict(X_test)

# Calculating confusion matrix and accuracy for unweighted model
conf_matrix_unweighted = confusion_matrix(test['response'], y_pred_unweighted)
accuracy_unweighted = accuracy_score(test['response'], y_pred_unweighted)
```

Since we already have a model trained with reweighing and predictions, we next calculate the confusion matrix and accuracy for the weighted model. Finally, we compare model accuracy with and without reweighing.

```
# With Reweighing

conf_matrix_weighted = confusion_matrix(test['response'], y_pred)
```

```
accuracy_weighted = accuracy_score(test['response'], y_pred)

# Print the accuracies with and without reweighing
print(f"Accuracy (no reweighing): {accuracy_unweighted}")
print(f"Accuracy (after reweighing): {accuracy_weighted}")

Accuracy (no reweighing): 0.725
Accuracy (after reweighing): 0.725
```

While bias mitigation sometimes reduces accuracy, we see that in this instance after reweighing, accuracy does not drop.

15.4.2 In-Process Algorithm: Adversarial Debiasing

Adversarial debiasing can be used as an in-process debiasing tool—as described in the technical solutions section—to help develop fair algorithms. The adversarial algorithm has two neural nets: a generator and a discriminator. The work of the generator is to generate accurate as well as fair predictions. The discriminator, playing the role of the adversary, tries to infer the label of the protected group (e.g., race, gender, income, or age). The adversarial process continues until the discriminator is unable to infer the label of the protected group from the output of the generator. At this point, it is assumed that the generator's output is fairer than previously since it is not using the protected group's label to provide its output.

Using `tf.compat.v1.reset_default_graph()`,we first reset the current TensorFlow graph to ensure that there are no leftover variables or operations from previous runs that might interfere with the current execution. TensorFlow uses sessions to execute parts of the graph. We create a session using `tf.compat.v1.Session()`.

```
# Reset TensorFlow graph
tf.compat.v1.reset_default_graph()

# Create a session

sess = tf.compat.v1.Session()
```

We utilize the `AdversarialDebiasing` class from the `aif360` library. `privileged_groups` and `unprivileged_groups` define which groups are considered privileged and unprivileged, respectively. `scope_name` sets a name for the TensorFlow scope, which is a mechanism to group and organize related variables and operations. `debias=True` enables the debiasing adversarial component. `sess` is the TensorFlow session we created earlier for model training.

Subsequently, we train the adversarial debiasing model using the training dataset.

```
# Apply adversarial debiasing

adv_debias = AdversarialDebiasing(privileged_groups=privileged_groups,
                                  unprivileged_groups=unprivileged_groups,
                                  scope_name='adv_debias', debias=True,
                                  sess=sess)

adv_debias.fit(dataset_train)
```

We then make predictions on the test dataset using the trained adversarial debiasing model and calculate fairness metrics based on the model's predictions. Finally, we print the calculated fairness metrics.

```
# Get predictions from the adversarial debiasing model
dataset_test_pred = adv_debias.predict(dataset_test)

# Calculate fairness metrics on the adversarial debiasing predictions
metric_test = BinaryLabelDatasetMetric(dataset_test_pred, unprivileged_
groups=unprivileged_groups, privileged_groups=privileged_groups)

print("Test Disparate Impact after adversarial debiasing:", metric_test.
disparate_impact())
print("Test Statistical Parity Difference after adversarial debiasing:", met-
ric_test.statistical_parity_difference())

Test Disparate Impact after adversarial debiasing: 1.0
Test Statistical Parity Difference after adversarial debiasing: 0.0
```

Compared to the earlier baseline estimates of disparate impact (0.63) and statistical parity difference (–0.30) on test data, we observe that adversarial debiasing improved both disparate impact (1) and statistical parity difference (0).

15.5 UNDERSTANDING THE CHAPTER

1. Describe how historical bias can affect algorithmic decisions.
2. Is it possible that algorithms used in business decisions can provide a biased output? Explain, giving one example.
3. Which of the following metrics is *not* used to measure fairness?
   a. Disparate impact

   b. Equal opportunity difference
   c. Statistical parity difference
   d. Algorithmic complexity

4. Which of the following methods can be used to address algorithmic fairness?
   a. Reweighing
   b. Adversarial debiasing
   c. Both a and b
   d. None of the above

5. Which of the following is a critical step in creating a culture of fairness in an organization?
   a. Hiring diverse employees
   b. Implementing fair algorithms
   c. Regularly auditing algorithms for fairness
   d. All of the above

6. What kind of data representation can contribute to algorithmic unfairness?
   a. Overrepresentation of certain groups
   b. Underrepresentation of certain groups
   c. Both overrepresentation and underrepresentation
   d. None of the above

7. Which of the following is the primary goal of adversarial debiasing?
   a. To increase algorithmic complexity
   b. To minimize the influence of sensitive attributes on the algorithm's decision-making
   c. To maximize the accuracy of the algorithm
   d. None of the above

8. What is a "proxy" attribute?
   a. An attribute that is directly related to the target variable
   b. An attribute that is unrelated to the target variable
   c. An attribute that indirectly represents the sensitive attribute
   d. None of the above

9. Why is measuring fairness important?
   a. To ensure a diverse workforce
   b. To maintain transparency in organizations
   c. To identify and mitigate potential biases in algorithms
   d. All of the above

10. Which of the following is *not* a method to deploy algorithmic fairness?
   a. Reweighing
   b. Adversarial debiasing
   c. Overfitting
   d. None of the above

11. What does the disparate impact metric measure?
  a. The difference in positive outcomes between two groups
  b. The overall accuracy of the algorithm
  c. The difference in negative outcomes between two groups
  d. None of the above

12. What is the goal of reweighing in addressing algorithmic fairness?
  a. To change the weights of each data point to minimize bias
  b. To increase the overall accuracy of the algorithm
  c. Both a and b
  d. None of the above

13. What does the equal opportunity difference metric measure?
  a. The difference in true positive rates between two groups
  b. The difference in false positive rates between two groups
  c. Both a and b
  d. None of the above

14. Which of the following is the primary objective of statistical parity difference?
  a. To measure the difference in overall accuracy between two groups
  b. To measure the difference in the proportion of positive outcomes between two groups
  c. Both a and b
  d. None of the above

15 Which of the following is the primary challenge in addressing algorithmic fairness?
  a. Ensuring diversity in the workforce
  b. Balancing fairness and algorithmic performance
  c. Regularly auditing algorithms for fairness
  d. All of the above

ENDNOTES

1. Schrage, Michael, "Big Data's Dangerous New Era of Discrimination," *Harvard Business Review*, January 29, 2014.
2. Bosch, Nigel, Sidney K. D'Mello, Ryan S. Baker, Jaclyn Ocumpaugh, Valerie Shute, Matthew Ventura, Lubin Wang, and Weinan Zhao, "Detecting Student Emotions in Computer-Enabled Classrooms," in *Proceedings of the Twenty-Fifth International Joint Conferences on Artificial Intelligence* 16 (2016): 4125–4129.
3. Bucher, Taina, "The Algorithmic Imaginary: Exploring the Ordinary Effects of Facebook Algorithms," *Information, Communication & Society* 20, no. 1 (2017): 30–44.
4. Van Esch, Patrick, J. Stewart Black, and Joseph Ferolie, "Marketing AI Recruitment: The Next Phase in Job Application and Selection," *Computers in Human Behavior* 90 (2019): 215–222.

5. Dressel, Julia, and Hany Farid, "The Accuracy, Fairness, and Limits of Predicting Recidivism," *Science Advances* 4, no. 1 (2018): eaao5580.

6. Fitch, Asa, "Would You Trust a Lawyer Bot With Your Legal Needs?" *The Wall Street Journal*, August 10, 2020, https://www.wsj.com/articles/would-you-trust-a-lawyer-bot-with-your-legal-needs-11597068042.

7. Esteva, Andre, Brett Kuprel, Roberto A. Novoa, Justin Ko, Susan M. Swetter, Helen M. Blau, and Sebastian Thrun, "Dermatologist-Level Classification of Skin Cancer With Deep Neural Networks," *Nature* 542, no. 7639 (2017): 115–118.

8. Datta, Amit, Michael Carl Tschantz, and Anupam Datta, "Automated Experiments on Ad Privacy Settings: A Tale of Opacity, Choice, and Discrimination," *Proceedings on Privacy Enhancing Technologies* 2015, no. 1 (2015): 92–112.

9. Noble, Safiya Umoja, *Algorithms of Oppression: How Search Engines Reinforce Racism* (NYU Press, 2018).

10. Obermeyer, Ziad, Brian Powers, Christine Vogeli, and Sendhil Mullainathan, "Dissecting Racial Bias in an Algorithm Used to Manage the Health of Populations," *Science* 366, no. 6464 (2019): 447–453.

11. Hamilton, Isobel Asher, "Why It's Totally Unsurprising That Amazon's Recruitment AI Was Biased Against Women," *Business Insider*, October 13, 2018; Vincent, James, "Amazon Reportedly Scraps Internal AI Recruiting Tool That Was Biased Against Women," *The Verge*, October 10, 2018.

12. Hardesty, Larry, "Study Finds Gender and Skin-Type Bias in Commercial Artificial-Intelligence Systems," *MIT News*, February 11, 2018, https://News.mit.edu/2018/Study-Finds-Gender-Skin-Type-Bias-Artificial-Intelligence-Systems-0212.

13. Overdorf, Rebekah, Bogdan Kulynych, Ero Balsa, Carmela Troncoso, and Seda Gürses, "Questioning the Assumptions Behind Fairness Solutions," 2018, *arXiv Preprint arXiv:1811.11293*.

14. Lopez, Steve, "On One of LA's Steepest Streets, an App-Driven Frenzy of Spinouts, Confusion and Crashes." *Los Angeles Times*, April 4, 2018, https://www.latimes.com/Local/California/La-Me-Lopez-Echo-Park-Traffic-20180404-Story.html.

15. Barocas, Solon, Moritz Hardt, and Arvind Narayanan, "Fairness in Machine Learning," *NIPS Tutorial* 1 (2017); Garg, Pratyush, John Villasenor, and Virginia Foggo, "Fairness Metrics: A Comparative Analysis," in *IEEE International Conference on Big Data* (Institute of Electrical and Electronics Engineers, 2020), 3662–3666.

16. Liu, Lydia T., Sarah Dean, Esther Rolf, Max Simchowitz, and Moritz Hardt, "Delayed Impact of Fair Machine Learning," 2018, *arXiv Preprint arXiv:1803.04383*.

17. Foster, Ian, Rayid Ghani, Ron S. Jarmin, Frauke Kreuter, and Julia Lane, *Big Data and Social Science: A Practical Guide to Methods and Tools* (CRC Press, 2016).

18. Friedler, Sorelle A., Carlos Scheidegger, Suresh Venkatasubramanian, Sonam Choudhary, Evan P. Hamilton, and Derek Roth, "A Comparative Study of Fairness-Enhancing Interventions in Machine Learning," in *Proceedings of the Conference on Fairness, Accountability, and Transparency* (Association for Computing Machinery, 2019), 329–338; Pessach, Dana, and Erez Shmueli, "Algorithmic Fairness," 2020, *arXiv Preprint arXiv:2001.09784*.

19. Pessach, Dana, and Erez Shmueli, "Algorithmic Fairness," 2020, *arXiv Preprint arXiv:2001.09784*.

20. Chouldechova, Alexandra, "Fair Prediction With Disparate Impact: A Study of Bias in Recidivism Prediction Instruments," *Big Data* 5, no. 2 (2017): 153–163; Menon, Aditya Krishna, and

Robert C. Williamson, "The Cost of Fairness in Binary Classification," in *Conference on Fairness, Accountability and Transparency* (Association for Computing Machinery, 2018), 107–118.

21. Kamishima, Toshihiro, Shotaro Akaho, Hideki Asoh, and Jun Sakuma, "Fairness-Aware Classifier With Prejudice Remover Regularizer," in *Joint European Conference on Machine Learning and Knowledge Discovery in Databases* (Springer, 2012), 35–50.

22. Plaugic, Lizzie, "FaceApp's Creator Apologizes for the App's Skin-Lightening 'Hot' Filter," *The Verge*, April 25, 2017.

23. Xu, Depeng, Shuhan Yuan, Lu Zhang, and Xintao Wu, "Fairgan: Fairness-Aware Generative Adversarial Networks," in *IEEE International Conference on Big Data* (Institute of Electrical and Electronics Engineers, 2018), 570–575; Zhang, Brian Hu, Blake Lemoine, and Margaret Mitchell, "Mitigating Unwanted Biases With Adversarial Learning," in *Proceedings of the 2018 AAAI/ACM Conference on AI, Ethics, and Society* (Association for the Advancement of Artificial Intelligence and Association for Computing Machinery, 2018), 335–340.

24. Holstein, Kenneth, Jennifer Wortman Vaughan, Hal Daumé III, Miro Dudik, and Hanna Wallach, "Improving Fairness in Machine Learning Systems: What Do Industry Practitioners Need?," in *Proceedings of the 2019 Chi Conference on Human Factors in Computing Systems* (Association for Computing Machinery, 2019), 1–16.

25. Malouff, John M., and Einar B. Thorsteinsson, "Bias in Grading: A Meta-Analysis of Experimental Research Findings." *Australian Journal of Education* 60, no. 3 (2016): 245–256.

26. Lee, Nicol Turner, Paul Resnick, and Genie Barton, "Algorithmic Bias Detection and Mitigation: Best Practices and Policies to Reduce Consumer Harms," Center for Technology Innovation, Brookings Institution, 2019, https://www.brookings.edu/research/algorithmic-bias-detection-and-mitigation-best-practices-and-policies-to-reduce-consumer-harms/.

27. Bellamy, Rachel K. E., Kuntal Dey, Michael Hind, Samuel C. Hoffman, Stephanie Houde, Kalapriya Kannan, Pranay Lohia, et al., "AI Fairness 360: An Extensible Toolkit for Detecting, Understanding, and Mitigating Unwanted Algorithmic Bias," *arXiv preprint arXiv:1810.01943* (2018).

28. Hofmann, Hans, *Statlog* (German Credit Data), UCI Machine Learning Repository (1994), https://doi.org/10.24432/C5NC77.

TECHNICAL APPENDIX

CONTENTS

1. ALGORITHMS

Traditionally, an *algorithm* is a step-by-step procedure or a set of instructions for performing a specific task or solving a particular problem. Machine learning has introduced new algorithms that learn data representations and rules from human-provided data and output, enabling autonomous learning. Machine-learning algorithms can now learn rules and apply them to new situations, outperforming previous analytic methods that require explicit programming for each data instance. These algorithms can learn representations from data, enabling decision-making without human input by leveraging numerous combinations of previously processed features. For example, convolutional neural networks can accurately identify dogs versus cats in new images after processing numerous training images. Recent machine-learning algorithms can also process unstructured data such as text, sound, image, and video, which was previously challenging.

2. BIAS–VARIANCE TRADE-OFF

A model can have three types of generalization errors: irreducible error, bias, and variance.

The *irreducible error* arises from the inherent noise in the dataset that cannot be reduced but can sometimes be addressed through better data collection, cleaning, or preprocessing. *Bias* measures how much our model's predictions deviate from the true value. This often results from incorrect assumptions, such as assuming a linear relationship when the true relationship is more complex. *Variance* occurs when the model is excessively sensitive to small variations in the training data. A high-variance model ends up overfitting the training data by capturing the noise within the training. Such a model performs poorly on new and unseen data. Variance is further exacerbated if some samples have outliers or more noise than others.

Bias variance can also be understood in terms of model complexity. To reduce bias, people might add more predictor variables to the model, hoping to better capture the true relationship in the population. However, doing so may cause the model to overfit training data and fit poorly with other sample datasets, increasing variance. Conversely, reducing model complexity can decrease variance in predictions across samples but may result in higher bias because the model cannot capture the true relationship.

This phenomenon is called the *bias–variance trade-off* because reducing bias often in-creases variance, and vice versa.

3. CONSTRAINED OPTIMIZATION

Optimization is the process of mathematically finding the best-possible value of a variable (e.g., the outcome variable in a regression) among many possible variables. When such a process is performed under certain constraints or conditions, it is called *constrained optimization*. For instance, if we aim to maximize customers' satisfaction given their budgetary constraints, we are trying to find the maximum satisfaction that a customer can attain within a budget. And firms seeking to minimize their costs are constrained by the fact that they have to manufacture and fulfill orders. Therefore, optimization can mean we are trying to maximize or minimize a function, usually referred to as $y = f(x)$ and known as the objective function. Note that when we are minimizing $f(x)$, we also tend to call it the loss function, error function, or cost function.

In order to find the minimum or maximum of a function, we calculate its first derivative, $\frac{dy}{dx}$, which is essentially the slope of $f(x)$ at x. It specifies how to change the input x by a small amount to bring out a corresponding change in the output $f(x)$. This derivative is also known as the gradient descent when we are trying to find the minimum of the function through an iterative process. This is important for understanding neural nets and, hence, any deep learning algorithms (see the discussion of gradient descent later in this appendix).

For instance, in penalized regression, we use constrained optimization when we constrain the sum of the β coefficients' values to less than a specific value. This constraint of the sum needing to be less than a specific value helps to shrink the β values to zero (LASSO) or near zero (ridge). Similarly, support vector regression uses constrained optimization when the model tries to reduce cost.

4. CORRELATION VERSUS CAUSATION

Regression analysis helps us understand how different predictors influence the outcome variable. We can use this information to predict future values of the outcome variable. For example, we can use past data on advertising expenditure and sales to analyze how advertising expenditure affects sales. However, we cannot assume that there is a causal link between the two variables. We can only infer that they are related. In contrast, when we conduct a causal experiment (also known as a study or A/B testing), it allows us to test whether changes in the predictor variable cause changes in the outcome variable. For instance, we can test whether the type of message framing in an advertisement (e.g., "Protect your skin from harmful UV rays with our new sunscreen" vs. "Don't risk skin damage from the sun. Use our new sunscreen") causes changes in the sales of the advertised product. We test whether the predictor (message framing) actually causes the outcome (change in sales) and, if so, to what extent.

5. FUNCTIONS, MODELS, AND DISTRIBUTIONS

A *function* explains the relationship between an input or inputs and an output. It is generally represented as $y = f(x)$, where the output y is some form of x: for instance, $y = 5x$ or $y = mx + c$, which is the equation of a line segment. Functions can be representations of simple mathematical models that describe the relationship between the input and the output variables. Sometimes a function is just considered a rule that describes the relationship between one input and one output; for example, $f(x)$ is the function that is reliant on the input x (e.g., $f(x) = 4x$).

On the other hand, a *model* is a description of a system, which could be the combination of several different functions coming together to explain a system. A model could represent a physical system such as Einstein's famous model $E = mc^2$, or it could represent an economic system such as the inverse proportionality between demand and price: $demand \propto \frac{1}{price}$. A model is used not just to understand the relationship between the input and output variables (i.e., for inference); it is also important for predicting the output, given new values of the input variables (i.e., for prediction). For instance, a regression model can be used to explain the relationship between the input and output variables, and it can also be used for prediction.

Probability distributions are used by data scientists to figure out relationships or patterns between input and output variables, given the data. Invariably, when we work with samples of data, we have to predict the relationship between input and output variables—from predicting coin flips or dice throws to real-world examples such as predicting which customers will stay loyal versus which customers will drop out. In such predictions, given the nature of the outcome variable—such as whether it is discrete (e.g., the number of customers) or continuous (e.g., the price of a product)—assumptions can be made that the data follows a specific probability distribution. Such assumptions are made for models where there are many variables that could affect the outcome about which we have little or no information (i.e., there are many unknowns). Probability distribution can be understood using an analogy in which a box randomly dispenses balls. The mechanism dictating the number of balls dispensed at each instance is unknown. In such a case, if the balls represent discrete, non-negative counts, we might assume a Poisson distribution to model this process. Examples of probability distributions include normal, Bernoulli, Poisson, multivariate, exponential, Dirichlet, and gamma.

6. GRADIENT DESCENT

Gradient descent is an optimization technique used to minimize the error in a model's predictions. In the context of neural networks, gradient descent is used to minimize the error (represented by the loss function), which quantifies how well the neural net's predictions compare with the actual data or ground truth. It can be understood as a process of finding the lowest point of a complex function, much like trying to reach the bottom of a steep hill in the dark by taking small, careful steps. Since the loss function can be complex and unknown, we use gradient descent to iteratively minimize the error through a process called backpropagation, which helps us update the weights of the network.

To find the minimum loss function, the model takes small steps in updating the weights by learning from its prediction error. Calculus is used in gradient descent for computing the gradient or slope of the loss function. This gradient guides the model to adjust its weights, helping in finding the minimum error (i.e., it helps fine-tune the model's weights, leading to optimized performance).

7. LOSS FUNCTION

A *loss function*, also known as a cost function or objective function, is a way to measure how bad a model's predictions are. It estimates the difference between the predicted output of a model and the actual output. In order to make accurate predictions, the goal of machine-learning methods is to minimize the loss function. One of the simplest examples of a loss function is the mean squared error (MSE) used in linear regression.

$$MSE = \frac{1}{n}\sum_{i=1}^{n}(y_i - \hat{y}_i)^2$$
$$= \frac{1}{n}\sum_{i=1}^{n}(y_i - \underbrace{(a_0 + a_1x_1 + \ldots + a_px_p)}_{\hat{y}_i})^2$$

y_i is the true value of the outcome variable for the ith data point.

$\hat{y}_i$ is the model's predicted value of the outcome variable for the ith data point.

$a_0, a_1, \ldots a_p$ are the regression coefficients.

$x_1, x_2, \ldots x_p$ are the input variables.

n is the number of data points.

By minimizing the loss function, the model (linear regression in this example) can come up with optimum values of regression coefficients $a_0, a_1, \ldots a_p$.

8. OVERFITTING

An overfit model is good at making predictions with the training data, but it lacks the ability to make accurate predictions with data that it has not seen before (e.g., test data that the model has not been trained on). *Overfitting* occurs when a model learns "noise" or irrelevant information in the training dataset. This leads to the inability of a model to generalize its learning to new data sets. Overfitting happens when (a) the model is complex or (b) the training data are of insufficient size, allowing the model to memorize every (unique) aspect of *this* training dataset, which may not be present in other data samples. Along with using less complex models and more training data, overfitting can be reduced by using methods such as cross-validation and regularized regression.

9. PARAMETER VERSUS HYPERPARAMETER

Parameters are essential because they help us make predictions about the unknown outcome variable, using both input variables and model parameters. To estimate these parameters, we use known values of predictors and outcome variables from our sample data. For example, in a regression model, we estimate the β coefficients based on the data. Other examples of parameters include the weights in a neural network, word frequencies in text analysis, and support vectors in a support vector machine model. Estimating these parameters typically involves using some optimization algorithm to search for the best values, given the data sample we have available.

On the other hand, *hyperparameters* are usually not estimated from the data; instead, we must choose initial values for these hyperparameters based on intuition, expertise, or heuristics, and then tune them to improve model fit, or prediction. Therefore, hyperparameter values are determined by the user. Examples of hyperparameters include the number of layers in a deep neural net, the number of trees in a random forest, and the number of clusters in a clustering algorithm. We often tune hyperparameters using techniques like grid search or random search.

10. REGULARIZATION

Regularization is a technique used to prevent overfitting in machine-learning models by discouraging overly complex models (e.g., models that have too many predictor or input variables). The main goal of regularization is to prevent the model from fitting noise in the dataset; less noise leads to better model generalization to new data. Regularization achieves better model fit by adding a penalty term to the model's loss function, which discourages large changes to the model's parameters. This helps prevent the model from overfitting on the training data.

There are two common types of regularization techniques: L1 regularization and L2 regularization. L1 regularization (e.g., used in LASSO regression) adds an absolute value penalty term to the loss function. L2 regularization (e.g., used in ridge regression) adds a squared value penalty term to the loss function. Both techniques help to create simpler models that generalize better to new data.

11. RESAMPLING METHODS

The primary goal of any predictive model is to learn the relationship between the input and outcome variables and make accurate predictions on new, unseen data samples. To achieve this, we typically divide our dataset into two parts: a training set and a test (or validation, or hold-out) set. The training set is used to train the algorithm, while the test set is used to evaluate its performance on new data. Ideally, we want to have a large training set to allow the algorithm to learn better, but we also need a sizable test set to assess its out-of-sample accuracy.

A common issue that arises during this process is overfitting, in which the algorithm learns to predict exceptionally well on the training data but poorly on other, unseen datasets. To balance the need for large training and test sets while mitigating the risk of overfitting, we employ resampling methods such as *k*-fold cross-validation and bootstrapping.

Resampling methods involve splitting the dataset into multiple training and test sets, allowing the model to be trained and evaluated on different subsets of the data. This approach helps us better understand the model's performance on unseen data and provides a more accurate estimate of its generalization capabilities.

11.1 Cross-Validation

In *cross-validation*, a resampling method, we randomly split the dataset into *k* equal partitions. For example, we can divide the data into 12 parts and arrange them into 3 groups, each containing 4 parts. In a threefold cross-validation, we would use one part from each group as the test set and train the model on the remaining two groups.

A popular variation of cross-validation is the leave-one-out cross-validation (LOOCV). In LOOCV, if we partition the data into *k* parts, in any iteration, we can use *k* - 1 sets for training the algorithm; the *k*th set serves as the test set, making it a *k-fold cross-validation*. Using the same example of data portioned into 12 parts, we would leave out one part as the test set and train the model on the remaining 11 parts. In this case, we would perform a twelvefold cross-validation, training the model 12 times, each time using a different part as the test set.

To further improve the evaluation, we can perform repeated *k*-fold cross-validation. In this approach, we repeat the process of splitting the data into 12 parts and performing cross-validation using each of the 12 parts as test data multiple times. This repetition ensures that even single data points can end up in any one of the 12 parts, providing a more robust evaluation of the model's performance.

11.2 Bootstrapping

Bootstrapping is a resampling method that allows us to sample, with replacement, from the same dataset. This means that even if a data point is selected in one sample, it can be chosen again in another sample. To perform bootstrapping, we need two parameters: the sample size and the number of times bootstrapping should be repeated. Often the sample size is the same as the original dataset; however, if the dataset is very large, a smaller sample size may be used for computational efficiency.

The appropriate number of repetitions, sometimes even in the thousands, depends on when meaningful sample statistics, such as the mean and standard deviation, can be calculated. One advantage of bootstrapping is that it allows us to compute confidence intervals around these statistics.

In the bootstrap process, some data points may be selected multiple times, while others might not be selected at all. The data points that are not chosen are used as out-of-bag samples, which essentially serve as the test set for making predictions. Some people prefer bootstrapping over cross-validation because bootstrap errors are considered to have less uncertainty than those in *k*-fold cross-validation.

12. SAMPLE VERSUS POPULATION

When analyzing a variable in a dataset, we can use either the entire data *population* or a *sample* drawn from it. For example, if we want to examine how income level impacts purchase behavior among all customers who purchased a soda brand last year, analyzing the income level of every customer in the population would involve analyzing the entire data population. However, if we randomly select 1,000 customers from the population, then we are analyzing a sample. Typically, we use a sample rather than the entire population because it is less computationally expensive. However, using a sample can lead to less accurate out-of-sample predictions if the sample is not truly representative of the population. To avoid this issue, the sample should be randomly drawn and be as representative of the population as possible. When variables are measured in a sample, they are called sample *statistics*, while variables representing the population are called *population parameters*. The difference between a sample statistic and the true, unknown population parameter is called the *sampling error*.

13. STANDARDIZATION AND NORMALIZATION

We standardize data to make interpretation easier, especially when dealing with variables that have different scales. For example, if we have two predictor variables—amount spent, represented in millions of dollars, and unemployment rate, ranging from 1% to 15%—comparing the influence of these variables can be difficult because of their different scales. Standardizing the data puts both variables on the same scale, making analysis and inference more straightforward. To standardize data, we calculate the mean and standard deviation of each variable. Then, for each value in the dataset, we subtract the mean and divide the result by the standard deviation. This process rescales the data to have a mean of 0 and a standard deviation of 1. This allows us to describe each data point in terms of how many standard deviations away from the mean it is.

Normalization scales the data into a specific range, for instance, between 0 and 1 or -1 and 1. It is useful when the features of the data have different units or different distributions. By bounding the values into a specific range, normalization helps models to interpret the features consistently. Standardization is different from normalization. Standardization reshapes the data to have a mean of 0 and a standard deviation of 1, while normalization rescales the data to a range between 0 and 1. Both methods can be applied irrespective of whether the data follows a normal distribution.

14. SUPERVISED VERSUS UNSUPERVISED ALGORITHMS

In analytics, particularly in machine learning, algorithmic learning can be categorized as supervised or unsupervised. The availability of labels in the dataset and the problem we're trying to solve will determine which type of algorithm we can use.

14.1 Supervised Algorithms

Supervised algorithms are used when the dataset contains labels for both predictor and outcome variables. The label for the outcome variable is also known as the ground truth. For example, if we want to determine which customers are profitable, we must have data that indicate which features or behaviors make them profitable. For instance, are frequent buyers more profitable, or are heavy users more profitable? If our data allow us to identify frequent buyers and heavy users, as well as their profitability score as the outcome, then we have labeled data (or we know the ground truth). In supervised learning, the algorithm is trained using labeled data and aims to learn a function that best approximates the relationship between the predictor and the outcome. Supervised algorithms are useful for predicting outcomes and measuring prediction accuracy, feature association, and significance testing. Some examples of supervised learning algorithms include linear regression, logistic regression, Bayesian analysis, support vector machines, artificial neural networks, and random forests.

14.2 Unsupervised Algorithms

In some cases, data are unlabeled, meaning that we don't have prior knowledge about how the predictor variables are associated with the outcome variable. Assume that we want to find out which customers are likely to refer other customers to a new business. However, we don't have any information or labels about whether a customer has referred the store to another person. Instead, we have various features for each customer—such as the products they purchase, how much they spend, and their zip code. Since we lack an outcome label (i.e., whether a customer is likely to refer someone or not), we cannot directly associate the predictor values (the customer features) with the outcome variable (referral behavior). This means we are working with unlabeled data. With these unlabeled data, we cannot train a supervised learning algorithm to predict referral behavior. *Unsupervised algorithms* are used for such unlabeled data and help infer the natural structure of the data without the aid of existing labels.

In unsupervised learning, the data structure, rather than existing knowledge (or labels), informs the researcher about observations. These models can sometimes be more useful than supervised ones because they learn from the data structure itself rather than relying on user-provided labels.

Without data labels, it's more challenging to compare model performances. The most common tasks of unsupervised learning are exploratory analysis and dimensionality reduction, which involve using visualization methods or clustering to examine the data and gather insights. Since there are no prior examples (labels), unsupervised learning can be more challenging as there may be multiple possible solutions. Some examples of unsupervised learning algorithms include clustering, principal component analysis, representational learning, and density estimation.

Despite the challenges inherent in unsupervised learning, these algorithms are some of the most widely used tools in machine learning because a vast majority of available data (e.g., text, audio, and images) is unlabeled. The abundance of unlabeled data encourages the usage of unsupervised learning methods.

15. TYPES OF DATA: CATEGORICAL, NUMERIC, AND PANEL

There are mainly two data types: categorical and numeric. If we add a longitudinal or temporal component, then we get time-series or panel data. The analysis methods used for categorical, numeric, and panel data are different.

Categorical data, also called nominal data, represent categories such as sports (football, basketball, tennis) or letters (A, B, C) that cannot be meaningfully converted into a numeric form, although one can assign these categories numeric values. In other words, these categories have no inherent order or ranking. For instance, *basketball* is just a label we are providing to a category. In any analysis, if we are dummy coding and assigning the following codes such as basketball = 0 and tennis = 1, it doesn't mean that tennis is 1 unit more than basketball. Hence, the dummy code doesn't have any numeric meaning; it is just used to make the analysis easier. For example, in a regression analysis, such dummy coding allows us to run a single regression model for all categories rather than run separate models for each category.

Numeric data are also sometimes referred to as quantitative data and can be exactly quantified using numbers. For instance, age is a good example of numeric data because the difference between any two consecutive ages (34 and 35, for example, or 67 and 68) will always be 1 year. Numeric data can be counted (discrete data) or measured (continuous data). Discrete data can be counted, such as the aisles in a store, the population of a country, or even the grains of sand in a desert (they are infinitely countable; i.e., if one wanted to, one could count them). Continuous data, on the other hand, cannot be counted, but they can be measured (e.g., the quantity of water that we drink can be measured in liters but can't exactly be counted).

Within continuous data there are subdivisions known as interval data and ratio data. The difference between interval and ratio data is that many types of mathematical operations (addition, multiplication, subtraction, and division) are possible with ratio data because they have a true zero, but only addition and subtraction are possible with interval data, which do not have a true zero. For instance, temperatures measured in Celsius or Fahrenheit are interval data because they do not have a condition of no temperature (true zero), but weight measurements in pounds or kilograms are ratio data.

Panel data are a common data form in business, combining both cross-sectional (data measured at one given point in time) and time-series (data measured over time) features. An example of business panel data is customers' purchase behavior for a specific brand measured over a time period, such as weeks, months, or years. Panel data allow firms to consider factors related to the product (e.g., advertisement, price, or online/offline location) or characteristics of the customer (e.g., demographics or personality) that could affect sales. In this case, the panel data would be at the individual level because the purchase behavior is examined for each customer. This data can be aggregated into groups to analyze how different customer segments behave. Monitoring stock prices over time is another example of panel data. Panel data are generally analyzed using versions of regression, such as fixed effects and random effects models.

INDEX